REBUILDING CIVILIZATION ON THE BIBLE

~

PROCLAIMING THE TRUTH ON 24 CONTROVERSIAL ISSUES

See the
Advance Reviews and Endorsements
in the back of the book
on pp. 324-329.

REBUILDING CIVILIZATION ON THE BIBLE

PROCLAIMING THE TRUTH ON 24 CONTROVERSIAL ISSUES

Dr. Jay Grimstead
FOUNDER-DIRECTOR
COALITION ON REVIVAL

Dr. Eugene Calvin Clingman
EXECUTIVE ADMINISTRATOR
INTERNATIONAL CHURCH COUNCIL PROJECT

Nordskog
Publishing inc.

REBUILDING CIVILIZATION ON THE BIBLE
Proclaiming the Truth on 24 Controversial Issues

Jay Grimstead and Eugene Calvin Clingman

International Standard Book Number: 978-0-9882976-8-5

Library of Congress Control Number: 2014937474

Editor and Design: Desta Garrett

Copy Editor: Mary Malcolm

Nordskog Publishing, Inc.
2716 Sailor Avenue, Ventura, California 93001, USA
1-805-642-2070 • 1-805-276-5129

www.NordskogPublishing.com

MEMBER

CHRISTIAN SMALL
PUBLISHERS ASSOCIATION

A Personal Word from the Author

Dear Reader,

First I want to share four very positive Bible verses which God has recently put on my heart regarding His plans for His people. For 50 years during daily jogging time I meditate on Bible verses on little cards God-inspired during my daily *quiet time*, or sometimes I memorize new verses. I felt that God was nudging me to include these four verses in this book.

God told Jeremiah (6:27), *"I have made you an assayer and a tester among my people,"* and God told me to apply that verse to myself years ago. The 24 theological documents in this book and the Christian survey tools in the Appendix exist as "plumb lines" and tests by which the Body of Christ may measure and assay herself to see if she is Biblical or un-Biblical.

In Isaiah 58:12, God tells us that *"Those from among you will REBUILD the ancient ruins, you will RAISE UP THE AGE OLD foundations, and you will be called the REPAIRER of the breach, the RESTORER of the streets* [paths] *in which to dwell"* (EMPHASIS ADDED). God has told many leaders called to help ignite a revival and reformation to apply that verse to us and to all His sons and servants who are called and burdened by the Church's big need for revival and reformation. These 24 documents can help re-establish the Church on God's ancient, eternal FOUNDATIONS.

Hebrews 13:20-21 says, *"Now the God of peace…equip you in every good thing to do His will, working in us that which is pleasing in His sight."* For those of us who sincerely and deeply feel our great inadequacy to serve Him well, the good news is that He, by His Holy Spirit, personally "equips" us for doing His will, and He works "in us that which is pleasing in His sight!"

In Romans 11:4-5, Paul reminds us that one of the greatest Old Testament prophets, Elijah, thought he was the only one standing true for Jehovah out of all Israel. And thousands of leaders who try to mobilize God's people for Godly, Biblical action around the globe often wonder "where are God's warriors at this crisis point in history?" The Holy Spirit inspired Paul to remind us that God told Elijah, *"I have kept for Myself 7000 men who have not bowed the knee to Baal."* Paul applies that statement of God from about 850 BC to the first century; and I claim we twenty-first century Christians have a similar right to apply to our situation Romans 11:5, where God said, *"In the same way then, there has also come to be at the present time a remnant according to God's gracious choice!"* This greatly encourages my old warrior's heart that God has already picked and is preparing an army of His sons, servants, and soldiers for these times, and we just need to somehow identify each other in every city, county, state, and nation, and prepare to advance Christ's Kingdom, however God tells us to mobilize His people.

Jay

Church's Theological Timeline from the Cover

"Contend earnestly for the faith which was once for all delivered to the saints" is Jude's admonition to the Church, *"For certain men have crept in unnoticed...who turn the grace of our God into lewdness and deny the only Lord God and our Lord Jesus Christ."* (Jude 1:3-4, NKJV) It was false teachings threatening to corrupt the Church with heresy that forced church leaders to join together in councils, where they codified the orthodox teaching of the Bible in creeds received by the mainline church as faithful distillations of Scriptural truth and as a bulwark against future corruption. We depicted the following prominent ones:

Apostles' Creed 3ʳᵈ to 4ᵗʰ Century

The Holy Scriptures are the lifeblood of the church. Having received through them the faith once for all delivered, the infant church distilled the teaching into what has come to be called the Apostles' Creed. Possibly as early as the middle of second century AD, at least portions of the Apostle's Creed were used by the Church. This creed has since then been an anchor to both saint and assembly.

The Nicene Creed, AD 325, AD 381

Also known as the Nicene-Constantinopolitan Creed, the Nicene Creed was originally drafted in AD 325 at the Council of Nicea and was later appended in AD 381 at the Council of Constantinople. The primary issue in 325 was the Arian heresy. Arias contended, as do Jehovah's Witnesses today, that Jesus Christ was not God, not a person of the Trinity, but created by the Father out of nothing in similar manner as the rest of the created creatures, though Christ was the first. In AD 325, Christ's nature as fully God and not created was determined to be the orthodox faith. In 381, at the Council of Constantinople, three significant accomplishments were gained: First, the reaffirmation of the Nicene orthodoxy after 50 years of political and theological struggle against the Arians. Second, a clarification of the nature of Christ as being both 100% God and at the same time 100% man. Thirdly, an extension of the creed in which the Holy Spirit was acknowledged as the Third Person of the uncreated, consubstantial, and coeternal Trinity — Father, Son, and Holy Spirit — and clarified as eternally proceeding from both the Father and the Son.

Council of Chalcedon, AD 451

This council both ratified the Nicene Creed and drafted the Chalcedonian Definition, giving further clarification of the dual nature of Christ as both God and man in one Person, "Two Natures unconfusedly, unchangeably, indivisibly, inseparably"; not a mixing of the two natures but union of the two in Christ.

For centuries these councils and creeds held the Church to orthodox Christianity. However corruptions in teaching and leadership eventually brought the once glorious apostolic church and faith to a reproachful condition in which the poor were oppressed in many ways, not least of which was the selling of indulgences to enlarge the coffers of Rome.

Martin Luther's 95 Theses

Protestants mark the beginning of the Reformation as 1517. In that year the learned monk Martin Luther was stirred by God to speak against the inequities of the Pope and church leaders, particularly in regard to indulgences. He posted his Ninety-Five Theses on the door of the Wittenberg castle church, arguing that there must be true repentance for salvation, that salvation involved unrestrained turning to God by the sinner, not merely a desire to escape judgment, and that indulgences could not force God to forgive sins. He also denied the Pope's power over purgatory, stated that believers always have forgiveness of sins without indulgences, and condemned the Church's emphasis on money and its neglect of compassionate pastoral care for souls. The Reformation called for "Scripture alone!"

Chicago Statement on Biblical Inerrancy, 1978

Dr. Jay Grimstead was led by God to form the International Council on Biblical Inerrancy (ICBI) and serve as the Executive Director the first 20 months. In October, 1978, during Reformation Week, the ICBI theologians created the Chicago Statement on Biblical Inerrancy. History acknowledges its creedal standing. It is set forth as an accepted standard in systematic theologies such as Robert L. Raymond's *A New Systematic Theology of the Christian Faith* (1998, p. 70), and is quoted in its entirety in Wayne Grudem's *Systematic Theology* (1994). Every year each member of the Evangelical Theological Society (ETS) must sign a statement declaring faith in the Bible as God's inerrant Word. At its annual convention in 2001, ETS adopted the Chicago Statement on Biblical Inerrancy as the definition of inerrancy to which their members must subscribe.

The International Church Council, 2017 (& 2019 & 2021)

The Church is once again at a time of crisis! Though the global Church is far more fragmented and disunited than it was in AD 325, and though we do not presume to speak with "Papal power" or any special divine authority, we are proposing and calling for an International Church Council. As Christian leaders who care deeply for both the Biblicalness of what is taught today in the name of Christianity, and for the unity of Christ's Body for which Christ Himself calls, we sense that it is time for the global Body of Christ to discuss these 24 controversial issues in each nation and then come together in a global Church council in 2017 to settle these issues and form a "united, Biblical-theological standard of doctrine" accepted by a vast number of Christian leaders and their followers in most of the nations which participate in this Council. To this end with fervent prayer and heartfelt concern, the authors present this book to the Body of Christ. *May His Kingdom come and His will be done on earth as it is in heaven!*

—**Dr. Eugene Calvin Clingman**, ICCP

Help spread the word and engage your friends!

Additional copies of this book are available from Nordskog Publishing: www.NordskogPublishing.com; Jerry Nordskog <Jerry@NordskogPublishing.com>, phone: 805-642-2070 or fax: 805-642-1862.

Quantity discounts available.

COR-ICCP Contact Information:

E-mail to **COR-ICCP@goldrush.com** for inquiries, requests or to contact COR, ICCP, or the authors; and for the various information and participation forms offered in this book, such as:

- Declaration of Biblical Truth information and sign up form, and Minor Reservations form;
- National Councils on Theology "Membership Requirements" and "Application";
- Inquiries for scheduling a public Dialogue and Debate Forum;
- Copy of the Commitment Sheets participants signed before attending the first National Conference (p. 34); and
- To purchase at cost Dr. Jay's chapter by chapter study notes to four books by Dr. Francis Schaeffer.

For printable copies of the 24 Documents included in this book and additional appendices to two of them, go to the ICCP Website at: **www.ChurchCouncil.org**, and select "Documents" on the top menu bar, then select "Official Documents."

For printable copies of "A Manifesto for the Christian Church" or the 17 Worldview Documents, go to the COR Website at: **www.Reformation.net**, and look in right side column. See also www.solemnassembly.net.

An additional Website of interest is www.reform500.org.

Mailing Address: Coalition on Revival (COR)
P.O. Box 1139
Murphys, CA 95247

FOREWORD

A BOOK FOR
ALL CHRISTIANS

You hold in your hands a valuable resource for every serious Christian, an enjoyable source of inspiration and personal study, and for our leaders, solid material for teaching and preaching. But more significantly, this book is presented to the global Body of Christ by the Coalition on Revival's (COR) network of theologians, pastors, and Christian leaders as an essential corrective for the Church and a weapon targeting 24 areas of false doctrine which to a large degree have been absorbed by the Church to her great detriment. COR invites Christian leaders to participate in the International Church Council scheduled for Reformation Week 2017 in Wittenberg, Germany during the 500th Anniversary of Martin Luther nailing his 95 Theses to the castle church door, with followup Councils in 2019 and 2021.

The goal of COR's International Church Council Project (ICCP) is:

> "To establish for the twenty-first century a united, Biblical-theological standard of doctrine for the global Body of Christ which is consistent with the mainstream theology of the first 20 centuries."

It is our firm conviction that the 24 theological documents in this book represent well, however imperfectly, the Bible's perspective on all 24 issues, and also represent what the mainstream Church of the past 20 centuries believed and taught. We are convinced that to whatever degree sincere Christians have been tainted and misled by modern liberal and neo-orthodox relativistic theologians and teachers (whose teachings these documents target), to that degree those Christians and their churches, schools, and organizations are on a dangerous path that leads inevitably to the deterioration of the Church, the damaging of their own lives and families, and the self-destruction of their society. It is this relativistic, liberal, false theology which has greatly weakened and compromised the Church and helped lead her to be the ineffective, superficial, marginalized entity she largely is today, her influence being but a flicker of her once bright witness and influence in all areas of Western culture.

These 24 documents do not represent ALL that the Church should believe, but rather 24 battle lines on which the enemy is currently attacking the Church. Much of the evangelical church is not aware of the spiritual war on these fronts and has unknowingly allowed the enemy within the gates. Our theologians have labored and prayed for over three decades in creating these documents, and now these prayers and labors are coming to a head with the presentation of them to the global Body of Christ. At the same time we extend an invitation to the global Church to participate in the global International Church Councils previously mentioned.[1]

The authors are convinced that the western church as well as many nations will undergo a major Revival and Reformation within the coming decades, and probably within the lifetime of many of us. We want our readers to know we are optimistic about what our great God will cause to happen in the future of the world. We believe a large number of nations will see Biblical Christianity eventually flourish as the populations of those nations come to recognize that ONLY the principles of the Bible work in the real world of life and living for any area of life, including law, government, economics, education, media, arts, science, family, helping the hurting, etc. and that ANTI-BIBLICAL PRINCIPLES DO NOT WORK FOR ANY SOCIETY ANYWHERE AT ANYTIME as history has proven again and again. We are encouraged by the essential doctrinal unity that already exists within the global Church (see "Document 3: The 42 Articles on the Essentials of a Christian Worldview"). We have great hope and confidence that our Lord's High Priestly Prayer "that they may be one" (John 17:11) as Jesus and the Father are one, will come about, not by compromise of Biblical truth, but by applying these three essential actions: The Church must contend for the faith once for all delivered to the saints; The Church must actually live in obedience to the Bible in all areas of life rather than simply teach the Bible's truth accurately as if that were her whole task; and the Church must operate in Biblical love, unity, and commitment to ALL the other members of Christ's Body, and somehow learn to tolerate ("forbear") some of the "weird ways" other Christians and churches attempt to obey King Jesus and live by His Biblical principles.

May our wonderful God bless, guide, and mobilize all who read this book to love Him more passionately and to live more wholeheartedly in obedience to His inerrant written Word, the Bible.   Amen!

Dr. Jay Grimstead
Founder-Director
Coalition on Revival and
International Church Council Project

---

1 All 24 of the COR documents are in this book and also available as printable downloads from the International Church Council Project Website at www.ChurchCouncil.org. For more information, direct inquiries to: COR-ICCP@goldrush.com.

TABLE OF CONTENTS

INTRODUCTION
TO THE
THEOLOGICAL DOCUMENTS
OF THE
COALITION ON REVIVAL (COR)

by Dr. Jay Grimstead
FOUNDER-DIRECTOR

During the thirty-seven years between 1977 and 2014,[2] the Lord called me to birth and carry forward three theological movements to define and defend the traditional doctrines of Christian orthodoxy by creating modern, creed-like, position statements through the cooperative work of a consortium of evangelical theologians working together by consensus. The theologians, writers, and Christian leaders involved believed that each movement was raised up by God to theologically "stand in the gap" for such a time as this regarding each issue they clarified.

These movements within the Body of Christ, occurring especially in North America, were connected historically, spiritually, and theologically, even though ICBI and COR were not connected organizationally or legally.

The evidence is clear that each successive movement flowed naturally and logically out of the "womb" of the previous movement, and all of them developed out of the burden for reformation and theological honesty from within my heart which I trust was influenced by the Holy Spirit. The birth of each of these three movements is explained in more detail later in this book.

THE DETERIORATION OF THE AMERICAN AND WESTERN CHURCH IN THE PAST 180 YEARS

It is our conviction that beginning around 1830, the Christian churches and their pastors and leaders in America and the western world have been deteriorating incrementally in the areas of theology and personal obedience to Christ and the Bible.

I see four historical stages of this deterioration of the American Church and Culture.

---

2 For a 37-year history of the participants and development of the 24 Documents to be presented and debated at the International Church Councils starting in 2017, see Appendix P, pp. 297–308.

A. From 1800 to 1885:

From approximately 1800 to 1885, the sincere, Bible-believing Body of Christ in America (without any intentional effort on their part) foolishly and incrementally turned from a "God-centered" religion to a "man-centered" religion, as it turned away from the old Calvinistic Puritan and the Pilgrim Christianity which had made America outstandingly Christian, just, free, powerful, and prosperous.

This was a movement away from a Biblical understanding of "The Gospel of the Kingdom of God" permeating and influencing all areas of society, to a movement of "The Gospel of Personal Salvation" focused on personally getting to heaven and on getting excited about end-time prophecy and the secret "rapture" of the Church. It was a move away from being "salt and light" with a Biblical permeation of the fields of Law, Government, Economics, Education, Science, the Arts, and Media as these areas of life were carelessly and irresponsibly left to non-Christian leadership. This anti-Biblical retreat to inside the four walls of the church was enhanced by the invention of Dispensationalism in 1825, and fostered later by the Scofield Bible notes. And in 1830, Horace Mann launched the first American public school system. Also, in 1885, Oliver Wendell Holmes, Jr., who later became associate Justice of the Supreme Court, radically changed American Law and the courts by eliminating "Blackstone's Commentaries on Law" (a very Biblical perspective on Law based on the Pentateuch) as America's chief textbook for law schools and moved the U.S. into a focus on "case law" and on relativity in law and in the courts. Holmes was a major influence toward moving America from a Christian base to a humanistic base.

This period reflects the influence on the American Church by Immanuel Kant's philosophical dichotomy viewpoint that was followed by virtually all non-Christian philosophers. Kant's viewpoint states that there can be no logical or verbal connection between the physical, visible world of history and science and the spiritual, invisible world of "religion" since both worlds exist in (what we might refer to as) impenetrable, air-tight compartments. (The "post-modern" thinking of today is grounded in Kant's dichotomy. See a full explanation in Appendix K, pp. 258-260.)

Also, the Church was affected by the fact that, in 1805, the Calvinists who controlled Harvard University, America's premier school, were ousted and Harvard came under the control of the Unitarians who reject the Bible's inspiration, miracles, and the deity and resurrection of Christ.

B. From 1885 to 1935:

Then during the fifty-year period of 1885 to 1935, the major denominations of America (Baptist, Presbyterian, Congregational, Lutheran, Methodist, Episcopal, etc.) increasingly accepted the anti-Biblical teachings of what is called "old liberalism" which rejects the Bible's view of Christ, the resurrection, the Bible, miracles, God's sovereignty, etc., and rejected the historic orthodox teachings of the Church's first 1800 years. During the early 1900s and the '20s and early '30s, the Bible-believers within those denominations (called "the fundamentalists") were in a theological and ecclesiastical struggle with the liberals (called "the modernists"), and by 1935, the liberals had won and were in charge of the seminaries, the publications, and the headquarters of those major denominations. Our conservative side lost that major battle. Thus, humanism and relativism took over most of the major denominations at that time.

C. From 1935 to 1964:

By the 1940s, most of the Bible-believing leadership, pastors, and teachers had left those now liberal denominations and started their own more conservative denominations, seminaries, colleges, mission agencies, and parachurch organizations. In reaction to the liberal take-over of churches, some new denominations and seminaries were started such as the Orthodox Presbyterian Church (OPC) and the Presbyterian Church of America (PCA), Westminster Seminary among Presbyterians; and among Baptists, the General Association of Independent Baptist Churches and the Conservative Baptist Association of America; Fuller Seminary; The Foursquare Church; and The Lutheran Hour serving the greater Body of Christ since the 1930s. Also, not so much as a reaction to liberalism but out of a positive burden to create new, more effective tools for evangelism, communication, etc., new organizations were birthed such as Youth for Christ, Young Life, Youth With a Mission (YWAM), The Navigators, Campus Crusade for Christ, the National Association of Evangelicals (NAE), *Christianity Today,* the Billy Graham Evangelistic Association, etc. These conservative new denominations, independent churches, schools, mission groups, and publishing houses eventually flowed naturally into the movement then called "evangelicalism" as differentiated from the old "fundamentalists" of the 1920s and 1930s who were more confrontational and less irenic. Even some of these mentioned above have turned or begun to turn liberal in recent years. Up until the late 1960s and 1970s, most groups and leaders who referred to themselves as "evangelicals" still believed in the basic orthodox teachings of the historic Church and in the inerrancy and full inspiration of the Bible.

D. From 1964 to the Present:

Even though a large percentage of American adults had given up on Biblical Christianity as their personal worldview from the 1880s through the 1950s, still since Christianity and its principles were deeply ingrained in the culture, most non-Christians still accepted Christianity's morals so that the culture in the U.S. operated in what Francis Schaeffer called "the memory" of Christianity, and society looked and operated in general as if it were truly Christian.

But the slow, incremental deterioration of the generations from 1830 on came to a crisis point in 1964, with the occurrence of "The Free Speech Movement" on the Berkeley University campus, along with the hippy thing and the drug thing and the radical, socialistic efforts of the Students for a Democratic Society (SDS) under Saul Alinsky, and other immoral and anti-Biblical radicals.

Thus at that moment of U.S. History, "the Christian cultural dam" broke and most of America's Christian culture, beliefs, and approach to life were washed away with the flood of moral relativism, philosophical chaos, and violent socialism, and we are now living in the relativity and chaos of the breaking of that "Christian cultural dam."

This deterioration of Christianity in America was thus greatly accelerated in the 1960s. The historical "Christian consensus" on morals which had prevailed there since the *Mayflower* landed in 1620, was, as a cultural "partial Christian memory," still operating in American society up through the 1950s, wherein most citizens including non-Christians still believed that adultery, homosexuality, abortion, and pornography, etc. were unhealthy evils for society, and those evils were still illegal in most states. Also, the majority of people believed in a Creator God, and most families had both a mom and a dad and lived more or less responsibly before other humans. Most cities and private homes were *safe*.

The cultural flood waters poured out relentlessly and America experienced a massive social, moral, and political revolution that has swept most of that previous "Christian consensus" away almost completely, so that now Biblical Christianity is a distinct minority viewpoint, and Christianity is systematically under attack and persecution by the mainstream establishment. Such an open, aggressive attack on Christian principles (plus open disdain for the principles of the Founding Fathers) by our nation's establishment as we now witness daily was unknown and unthinkable as late as the 1950s. And the Church's basic problem during all these years of deterioration has been that, generally, she has allowed herself to be transformed step by step into the image of the world, rather than successfully transforming the world from Satan's domain and influence to Christ's Kingdom and His principles as Christ commanded us to do in His Great Commission and His Lord's Prayer.

INERRANCY OF THE BIBLE AS THE WATERSHED IN THE CHURCH'S DETERIORATION

The history of the Church the past 100 years has demonstrated that, when a pastor, writer, or theologian gives up the view that the Bible is fully God-inspired and inerrant in all it says, then a long list of other Christian doctrines and positions begin to unravel and fall over like a set of falling dominos. He then proceeds (almost inevitably) to accept more and more liberal, anti-Biblical positions, because he has no logical "system of brakes" to stop him from going too far in his descent into relativism. Based upon his own now liberal assumptions, there is no logical point at which he can tell himself, "I have gone too far in my slide downhill towards total relativism." Where he does stop in his downward slide can only be a matter of his own personal, subjective preference and feelings about the matter.

Thus, one who wants to reject only the inerrancy of the Bible but keep all the other Christian doctrines intact has no way of logically stopping himself from soon denying the resurrection of Christ or the very existence of God and eternity. This is so because he has moved from being guided by the *objective* Word of God to being guided by his own *subjective* and arbitrary decisions about the Bible.

It is easy to demonstrate that most of the 24 false teachings we are opposing in this book were promoted and defended by a theologian or liberal leader who had already in the past given up belief in the inerrancy and total Divine inspiration of the Bible. There is close to a "one-to-one ratio" regarding this connection between a rejection of Biblical inerrancy and belief in the liberal falsehoods that attack Biblical, orthodox Christianity.

Dr. Francis Schaeffer, in his last book, *The Great Evangelical Disaster* (Crossway Books, 1984), deals with this essential doctrine of the inerrancy of the Bible and shows how large sections of the general evangelical world have rejected this basic doctrine of inerrancy taught in the Bible itself. We strongly recommend that every Christian leader, pastor, and teacher read Dr. Schaeffer's book and learn its contents to prepare them for what we face. We are sad to offer our estimate that as much as half or more of all evangelicals in North America have given up on believing in Biblical inerrancy, either by a deliberate decision or a process like "osmosis" or "catching the measles" from leaders they respect who do not believe the Bible is both inspired and inerrant.

The history of the Church for the past 100 years demonstrates that when a pastor, writer, or theologian gives up on the view that the Bible is fully inspired and inerrant, a whole list of Christian doctrines and positions begin to unravel. Without inerrancy, there is no objective, logical point at which to stop the descent into relativism. Christ's bodily resurrection is up for grabs just as much as the six-day creation.

THREE THEOLOGICAL MOVEMENTS
A. International Council on Biblical Inerrancy (ICBI)
In 1977, I called leading, world-respected theologians and Christian leaders (like Dr. Francis Schaeffer, Dr. R. C. Sproul, Dr. Norman Geisler, Dr. J. I. Packer, Dr. D. James Kennedy, and Dr. Bill Bright, with fifty other such Christian leaders) to form a "theological army" to defend the inerrancy of the Bible and create a new, historic statement for the Church on that topic as well as produce several books defending Biblical inerrancy. I served

as the Executive Director for the first two years of the ICBI's existence.

God powerfully blessed that effort and it appears to have reversed the dangerous trend at that moment of history in which large segments of evangelical Christianity were sliding downhill quickly into a relativistic view of the Bible governed by the assumptions of old liberalism and neo-orthodoxy.[3] The ICBI's "Chicago Statement on Biblical Inerrancy" has made its way into books on systematic theology and has now taken its place in such books alongside such Church history documents as: The Apostles' Creed, The Nicene Creed, The Thirty-Nine Articles, The Westminster Confession of Faith, and The New Hampshire Baptist Confession. As per my suggestion to the ICBI Board our first year, we gave ICBI a ten-year life span, and at the end of 1987, ICBI shut down and turned all its many boxes of records, pictures, and correspondence, etc. over to the Archives of the Dallas Theological Seminary Library where ICBI research may take place.

B. The Coalition on Revival (COR)

In 1984, 1985, and 1986, in Denver, Dallas, and Washington, D.C. respectively, a COR team of approximately 300 theologians, writers, and experienced Christian leaders from the major spheres of society met in seventeen committees at those three Worldview Conferences to create seventeen worldview documents. Each document was to explain how the Bible applies to one of those seventeen spheres of life and ministry such as: law, government, economics, the media, medicine, science, the family, evangelism, discipleship, helping the hurting, etc.[4] The Steering Committee of the Coalition on Revival was composed of over 100 Christian leaders — pastors, writers, and heads of Christian organzations. Appendix C shows this list as it was in 1986.

In 1988, just two years after COR had completed the 17 Worldview Documents and held its culmination conference and National Solemn Assembly at the Lincoln Memorial in Washington, D.C. on July 4, 1986, the Church in America was bombarded with a series of false teachings and some outright heresy from schools and organizations within evangelicalism. Soon controversies arose within evangelical circles over various issues such as: The Kingdom of God, The Omniscience of God, The Atonement, The Eternal Fate of Unbelievers, Socialism, Feminism, Homosexuality, and Abortion on Demand. Our COR team of theologians began discussing these matters and writing papers to counteract these falsehoods one by one. By 1991, there were many of these false teachings (and even outright heresy) being promoted right from within evangelical schools, denominations, and organizations.

---

3 *Neo-orthodoxy*, a new kind of "existential liberalism" from Karl Barth in 1919, holding to Kant's radical dichotomy, is explained more fully in Appendiices K and L, pp. 258–264 and defined in the Glossary.

4 All 17 of these Worldview Documents are available and downloadable at our COR Website at www. Reformation.net. They will also be available in a subsequent COR book, Vol. II, to be published soon.

C. The International Church Council Project (ICCP)

It soon became painfully obvious that, to deal adequately with this "avalanche" of false teachings from within previously Bible-believing groups, a global Church council somewhat after the model of the Nicene Council of AD 325 would need to be held to properly address these multiple doctrinal issues. We realized also that there needed to be formed, in most of the civilized countries of the world, a "National Council on Theology" composed of representatives of many of each nation's denominations, Christian schools, organizations, and mission agencies with a broad range of denominational perspectives represented on each National Council and then gathered into the International Church Councils.

We have been quietly and systematically working towards that goal and, in the process, have created a dba for COR with the name, the "International Church Council Project" (ICCP), which is now slowly coming into operation. So the ICCP is a division of COR and operates under COR's 501(c)(3) status and under COR's board of directors.

National Councils: In similar fashion the rest of the 24 documents were developed over the years with the view of having them evaluated and affirmed by trans-denominational "National Councils on Theology," which we expect to gather from possibly 80 or more targeted countries. As these 24 topics are being discussed, affirmed, and then defended against opponents in public dialogue and debate forums, we believe they can act as catalysts and rallying points in those countries to separate truth from error by drawing a clear line in the sand that declares what the Bible and 2000 years of the Church's history teach on each topic.

International Church Council in 2017: The official delegates from each country are to come together in Wittenberg, Germany during Reformation Week in late October of 2017 for our International Church Council, which will coincide with the 500th anniversary of Martin Luther's nailing of his 95 theses to the Wittenberg castle church door. The tasks of these delegates will be to: First, formally affirm and endorse all 24 Documents. Second, decide which *minor wording changes* are to be dealt with at the 2019 Zurich Council which were offered by National Councils members who signed the Declaration with minor reservations. Third, discuss how the global Church should respond to the *areas of major concern* which were offered in the lists of concerns presented by October 2016 by each National Council on Theology.[5] Not too many years after that point it is our hope that our ICCP Mission Statement will be accomplished which states:

---

5 For more information about signing the Declaration or submitting minor reservations or lists of concerns in advance of the global councils, see Appendix E, pp. 239–240, or email to COR-ICCP@goldrush.com

"To establish for the twenty-first century a united, Biblical-theological standard of doctrine for the global Body of Christ, which standard is consistent with the mainstream theology of the first 20 centuries."

A significant milestone in the life of COR's International Church Council Project was in 2003, when we had completed twenty of the twenty-four documents. August 6 thru 9 of that year, the ICCP called for qualifying theologians to gather at Knox Theological Seminary in Fort Lauderdale, Florida for the Western Hemisphere Consultation on Theology. The delegates discussed each document thoroughly and then signed "A Declaration of Biblical Truth," affirming their agreement with the twenty topic documents. The statement those delegates signed reads:

"We declare that the 20 documents of Affirmations and Denials of the Coalition on Revival represent well, however imperfectly, what the Bible teaches on those 20 topics and also reflect what the mainstream Body of Christ has generally believed over the past 2000 years.

"We urge all Christians who believe in the inerrancy of the Bible to study these 20 documents, and then join with us in signing this Declaration of Biblical Truth and in promoting and teaching these Biblical principles to all who will listen.

"We further declare that to the degree the Scriptural principles reflected in these Affirmations and Denials are neglected, rejected, or opposed by any individual Christians, churches, schools, or organizations, to that degree will those people unwittingly lead the Church into further deterioration, confusion, self-destruction, and irrelevance and render her less capable of being God's salt and light to a lost and sinful world."

The delegates of that same consultation also created and signed "A Statement on Homosexuality," which appears on p. 260 with Document 18 on Homosexuality later in this book. Currently there are 24 topics and documents.

In the following pages we offer a brief explanation of each of the COR documents, how they came to be written, and why it is important for the evangelical Body of Christ to hold the Biblical view on each of these issues, which view we believe we present both in the introduction and in the official document on each topic. We also will examine the dire consequences we think any church, organization or group of Christians may expect if they disregard the Biblical teaching about each of these issues. May our great God give you understanding and clarity as you look over these issues we present to the Body of Christ, and may this book serve to help you become more informed on these matters and more committed to the truth by confronting the errors being taught by many misguided evangelical pastors, teachers, writers, and theologians.

AN INVITATION TO INTERACT WITH THIS MOVEMENT

Liberal and neo-orthodox teachers and teaching have compromised much of the Church to such a degree that she has lost her ability to significantly influence the society in which God has set her to be salt and light. Compromises in the 24 areas COR addresses, if not remedied, will continue to weaken the Church and render her yet more ineffective as she slides away from the truth of God's Word. Therefore, the Coalition on Revival's International Church Council Project is calling for a global Church council.

Between now and 2017 Christian leaders are invited to participate as members of a "National Council on Theology" (NCT) for their nation to discuss and officially affirm these 24 Documents, sign the Declaration of Biblical Truth, and defend any of the documents in public dialogue and debate forums against those who oppose them from within their own nation and who may be willing to enter into such a public debate of worldviews. The members of any NCT are to serve as official representatives of their own denomination, seminary/college, Christian organization, or mission agency, etc., so that each Council has a broad spectrum represented both theologically and denominationally. For NCT eligibility and application, email your request to: COR-ICCP@goldrush.com.

Part of our confidence that it will be possible for global denominations and organizations to unite around a new, commonly held "Biblical-theological standard of doctrine" is because we have already seen amazing theological unity emerge among leaders of vastly different denominations and theologies (but all of whom believe in the Bible's inerrancy and full inspiration), who have all been happy to sign COR's "42 Articles on the Essentials of the Christian Worldview." (This is Document 3 on pp. 33–42 in this book. In the introduction to that Topic, you will find the history of how these "42 Articles" were developed.)

Whether a pastor, head of a Christian organization, or college or seminary professor or administrator, we urge those leaders within evangelical circles who stand strongly opposed to the Biblical principles in any of these 24 theological documents to challenge our team to a public, taped and/or televised Dialogue Forum wherein their team of theologians may dialogue with members of our team to hear each other's reasoning as to which position is more Biblical, more logical, and more consistent with the realities of history and science. We will meet in any state of the U.S. at any time both our schedules can be coordinated. If interested in setting up a Dialogue Forum, contact ICCP by email to: COR-ICCP@goldrush.com.

We are simply and honestly seeking to obey the God of the Bible in creating these 24 documents, in holding these International Church Councils, in writing this book and, with many others, in calling for revival and reformation of the Bible-believing Church. It is in our hearts to work with all Christians who carry this same burden for the Church's reformation and her theological "Biblicalness."

We believe God is calling many of us leaders, imperfect as we are and failing as we may be, to step up into a higher level of service to Him and to the Church and to rise to the level of many of those great Christian heroes who have gone before us. Whether we like it or not, or want it or not, God is calling many in leadership in these days to become heroes like those godly, older brothers mentioned in Hebrews 11, and like a long list of Church history examples we could also assemble which might include heroes such as: Peter, James, John, Paul, Athanasius, Augustine, Wycliffe, Hus, Luther, Zwingli, Tyndale, Calvin, Knox, Bradford, Rutherford, Whitefield, Wesley, Edwards, Blackstone, John Adams, Henry, N. Webster, Carey, Livingstone, Spurgeon, Kuyper, Warfield, Machen, and many others down to Francis Schaeffer and R. J. Rushdoony in the last half of the twentieth century.[6]

We encourage you to read this book with an open heart. As you do, you may find that a price is required of you: "If anyone wishes to come after Me, let him deny himself, and take up his cross daily and follow Me" (Luke 9:23). As per the title of this book, we must say that, *"No civilization is going to be rebuilt upon the principles of the inerrant Bible unless and until meaningful percentages of the Christians in that civilization are wholeheartedly living in obedience to the Bible, and are mobilizing their churches and organizations to get the Bible's principles and the God of the Bible honored and obeyed within the various structures and institutions of that society."*

We also want you to know that if you connect with this movement, you are connecting with Christians who are convinced that Jesus, the Co-Creator and Sustainer of the universe, wins more and more of the unbelieving world to His side before He returns in glory to usher in the last judgment and the new heaven and new earth. Our calling and yours in the meantime is as Jesus taught us: To pray and to labor that His Kingdom come and His will be done on earth as it is in heaven, according to His own counsel and will to whatever degree He ordains before Jesus comes again, without our having to agree in advance just how much of this planet will or will not be operating under the Biblical principles of King Jesus when He does return.

---

6 Regarding these last two Christian thought-leaders, I wish to encourage the next two generations of Christian leaders to read as many books by R. J. Rushdoony and Francis Schaeffer as you can. For Dr. Rushdoony, I recommend his classic three-volume work, *Institutes of Biblical Law.* For Dr. Schaeffer, I recommend four of his 22 books, four which I think are critical and foundational for God-called "world-changers" to bring Reformation to a sleepy, blinded, Body of Christ in the Western world: *How Should We Then Live, A Christian Manifesto, The Great Evangelical Disaster,* and *Escape from Reason.* To purchase at cost a copy of my study questions on all chapters of any of these four books, please contact Dr. Jay at COR-ICCP@goldrush.com.

The Theological DOCUMENTS

of the

Coalition on Revival and Its International Church Council Project

TOPIC 1

Biblical Inerrancy

INTRODUCTORY COMMENTS

by Dr. Jay Grimstead

The Bible is our only objective, absolute, written connection between the invisible world and this visible, physical world of time and space. Without the Bible, mankind has no answers to the basic life questions man must answer, nor can he have any certainty that anything is real or meaningful including his own body and his own thoughts. Thanks to God's love and desire to communicate absolute truth to mankind, we have a Book in human language wherein every word and sentence is inspired by God through the men whom God selected to do the writing as His co-authors. God not only inspired every word and every book in the Bible, He also worked so that the inspired authors wrote an accurate picture of theology, history, the physical world, and the invisible world, and this to such an extent we can claim the Bible is "inerrant." The Bible, thus co-authored, is the "written Word of God," written 100 percent by God and at the same time, 100 percent by man. As Christ is the "living Word of God," 100 percent God and at the same time 100 percent man, so the Bible is 100 percent by God, while also 100 percent by man under the inspiration of the Holy Spirit. This is what the mainstream, historic Church has believed for the past two millennia. Skepticism about the Bible's inerrancy and total inspiration by God has only come onto the scene of history as a major controversy since the late 1700s and early 1800s, and only has been a concern for the Body of Christ in America since the early 1900s.

The Bible is the absolute standard by which Christians are to measure all other books, philosophies, thoughts, statements, laws, histories, and what the world calls science, because it is God's Word, God's thoughts. Therefore, if a Christian leader or follower builds his theology, life, or ministry on a Bible he believes is part true and part false (not totally inspired and not inerrant), that Christian will be living, ministering, and standing solidly upon mud and wet sand unsupported by God's, absolute, inerrant, written Word. We therefore strongly proclaim that it is incumbent upon every serious, evangelical Christian to make sure they have the view of the Bible that was held by Moses, Isaiah, Jesus, Paul, and the major Church history heroes down through the ages. That view is that the Bible we have is fully inspired by God and is therefore authoritative and inerrant in the original manuscripts. (For the record, our ICBI scholars who created the "Chicago Statement on Biblical Inerrancy," and our COR theologians and apologists are in agreement with the majority of conservative Bible scholars that the inerrancy of the Bible applies to the original manuscripts of the Old and New Testaments, so that all copies and translations are also the inerrant Word of God to the degree those copies and translations represent the original manuscripts.)

By 1977, many evangelical seminaries, colleges, churches, denominations, mission agencies, and publishing houses were absorbing a less-than-Biblical, neo-orthodox view of the Bible from liberals who were ensconced within evangelical circles. Thus they were departing step by step from the basic, historic doctrines of Christianity while all along thinking it was alright to do so. Because we live in a fallen world of fallen men wherein the devil, though defeated and dethroned, is still running around with great freedom, every excellent church or organization God raises up at any point in history will have a tendency to deteriorate and "float downstream with the current," unless a constant watch is maintained by "watchmen on the wall" to guard from this tendency. Thus by 1977, a major "reformation" was needed in the area of reinstating the Bible to its proper place with the honor due to it as the fully inspired, authoritative, inerrant Book from God which it is.

My explanation of how the ICBI was formed to lead the evangelical world back into a full, informed, and wholehearted belief in the inerrancy of the Bible is explained in the introduction to this book and in Appendix P. As I mention in the Introduction, God led me to call together a virtual "army" of theologians and Christian leaders in 1977 as a formal, united team to take a stand for the historical inerrancy view of the Bible and to identify the 17 different falsehoods about the Bible which were being taught at that moment in many evangelical seminaries and Christian colleges.

Once we had the basic plan set and the team of some 53 world-respected theologians and Christian leaders united in this purpose, we assigned 14 white papers to be written by this team. Within these 14 white papers each of the 17 major issues about the Bible were addressed so the falsehoods being taught could be exposed and so the true history and true Biblical principles could be clarified. Some of the chapter headings dealing with the key issues involved were: "Christ's View of Scripture" and "The Apostles' View of Scripture," "Higher Criticism," "The Inerrancy of the Autographa," "The Adequacy of Human Language," and "The View of Scripture Held by the Church." We sent that set of papers (the mailing packets weighed about two pounds each) to each of the 270 Christian leaders who were personally invited to the Summit Meeting in October of 1978, and asked them to try to look them all over before arriving at the Summit.

This set of 14 scholarly white papers was edited by Dr. Norm Geisler and has been available since shortly after that Summit Meeting with the title *Inerrancy*, published by Zondervan in 1980 (see also footnote 9, p. 18 for e-book including Sproul's commentary). As far as we know the liberals within and without evangelicalism have never attempted to answer these 515 pages which totally refute the liberal's partial and unsatisfactory view of the Bible. For those who can handle the heavy theology, this book, *Inerrancy* is a "theological atom bomb" that demolishes all liberal foolishness which attempts to undermine the Bible.

We had realized in the fall of 1977 that we would also need to create a book to explain the various facets of this theological battle for the Bible to laymen and to the average pastor who may not be oriented toward heavy, scholarly pursuits. A perfect opportunity for us to speak to the major falsehoods of neo-orthodoxy in layman's language came to us when Dr. Jack Rogers of Fuller Seminary was the contributing editor of the book *Biblical Authority* by seven evangelicals in 1977, which was a failed attempt to claim that the old view of the inerrancy of the Bible is scientifically outdated and unscholarly, and that the new neo-orthodox, more flexible way to look at truth was superior. That editor attempted to prove that the Bible can still have authority for our lives and our ministries even if it is not all true and inerrant. Our ICBI team happily and energetically took up this challenge, right there at that September 1977 meeting, and assigned themselves chapters of our first ICBI book which was to answer Roger's *Biblical Authority* chapter for chapter, and offer the Biblical and the traditional historical Christian truth side by side with Dr. Roger's false, un-Biblical positions. Our team did write such a book and it was published and ready to give to each of the 270 participants of our Summit Meeting on the Bible's Inerrancy that following October in 1978. The title of our ICBI book was *The Foundation of Biblical Authority*, edited by Dr. James Montgomery Boice, published by Zondervan in 1978.[7]

This four-day summit conference was held at the Hyatt Regency Hotel at the

---

7 This book is out-of-print but still available at Amazon.com. COR hopes to get it reprinted, as it is an excellent book to introduce thinking laymen and pastors to this whole battle for the Bible, and to offer them great ammunition for defending our faith. Dr. Francis Schaeffer wrote the foreword to the book. The six chapters were also written by modern evangelical heroes such as: Dr. R. C. Sproul, who is probably the most respected American theologian in the world today; Dr. John Gerstner, who had an encyclopedic mind and was Dr. Sproul's professor and mentor; Dr. J. I. Packer, who is probably the most respected British theologian in the world; Dr. Gleason Archer, who taught 27 different languages and kept fluent in 15 of those languages by having his personal, daily quiet time with God in a different language every three weeks; Dr. James Boice, Chairman of the ICBI board and pastor of Tenth Presbyterian in Philadelphia; and Dr. Kenneth Kantzer, Dean of Trinity Evangelical Divinity School and Editor of *Christianity Today*.

O'Hare Airport outside of Chicago during Reformation Week.[8] Our theologians spoke at plenary sessions to the 270 Christian leaders who were there from all over the world, and discussions were held on each of the issues at stake. Each of the attendees could participate in about three of the 14 different discussions going on based on the 14 white papers our scholars had written.

A NEW CHAPTER IN EVANGELICAL HISTORY

Based on those 14 white papers and the fruits of the daily discussions, our theologians late into the night, every night, were crafting what came to be our historic statement on the inerrancy of the Bible, "the 19 articles of 'The Chicago Statement on Biblical Inerrancy'." We believe God used that Summit Meeting, those books, that new global momentum, and the 19 articles on inerrancy to create a new chapter of history in the Christian world, which re-established the Bible as our absolute, inerrant, and only foundation for our faith, for our ministry, and for any solid philosophy of life that operates according to the flow lines of the universe as God created it.

The results were dramatic and astounding. Right up to that very weekend, many liberal-oriented professors, writers, and leaders within evangelical circles were putting down the inerrancy of the Bible as if those who believed in it were unscientific, medieval, backward bumpkins, and some evangelical liberals claimed that no reputable scholar except Dr. Francis Schaeffer and Dr. Harold Lindsell still believed in the Bible's inerrancy. At that point these inerrancy gainsayers went into the closet and we hardly heard a peep from them for a full two years.

As a young reformer who had just recently entered the field of theological battle and had, with fear and trembling, initiated the ICBI inerrancy movement and called those leading theologians into being an "army," I did not have the confidence I needed to take the ICBI into the next step beyond a bold declaration worldwide that the Bible was indeed inerrant and that here were the Biblical, theological, and historical reasons why that was so. I said then:

> "The next step that needs to be taken by this august team of world-respected Christian leaders is to take this battle right up to the door step of those seminaries, colleges, and denominations which had gone soft on the Bible's inspiration, challenge them to public debate on the various theological points where they claimed the Bible is not inerrant, and hold seminars in every major city to teach the historic

---

8 Reformation Week celebrates Luther nailing his 95 Theses to the Wittenberg castle church door in 1517 on the day we call Halloween, which is the evening before "All Saints Day," November 1, in the Catholic Church.

inerrancy view and train up an entire generation of warrior reformers to continue this battle into the future."

When I presented this plan as the next step to leading men on the Executive Committee, they told me that these 1970s are not a time for "confrontation" but of gentle persuasion and being politically cool and not to confront, so my suggestion for a confrontational approach at that point was rejected. Had I known then some 30 plus years ago what I know now of the vast deterioration of the general evangelical world today, and the great damage the invasion of "post-modern relativism" has done to all those circles of Christianity which did not firmly believe in the inerrancy of the Bible, I would have been emboldened, "come hell or high-water," to find some way to bring this appropriate confrontation to the doorstep of those liberal institutions sitting within evangelicalism. I think that if I had had the courage to take those needed, confrontational steps, perhaps the evangelical church in America today might have not slipped so far downhill theologically and philosophically. I believe it was "fear of man" in my young reformer's heart that allowed me to be silenced organizationally at that point, and fear of renowned theologians who were my superiors theologically but who were, in retrospect, misguided by their own commitment to a "non-confrontational" approach in the battles for truth.

DOCUMENT 1

The Chicago Statement on Biblical Inerrancy

PREFACE

The authority of Scripture is a key issue for the Christian Church in this and every age. Those who profess faith in Jesus Christ as Lord and Savior are called to show the reality of their discipleship by humbly and faithfully obeying God's written Word. To stray from Scripture in faith or conduct is disloyalty to our Master. Recognition of the total truth and trustworthiness of Holy Scripture is essential to a full grasp and adequate confession of its authority.

The following Statement affirms this inerrancy of Scripture afresh, making clear our understanding of it and warning against its denial. We are persuaded that to deny it is to set aside the witness of Jesus Christ and of the Holy Spirit and to refuse that submission to the claims of God's own Word which marks true Christian faith. We see it as our timely duty to make this affirmation in the face of current lapses from the truth of inerrancy among our fellow Christians and misunderstanding of this doctrine in the world at large.

This Statement consists of three parts: a Summary Statement, Articles of Affirmation and Denial, and an accompanying "Exposition" which is not included here.[9] It had been prepared in the course of a three-day consultation in Chicago. Those who signed the Summary Statement and the Articles wish to affirm their own conviction as to the inerrancy of Scripture and to encourage and challenge one another and all Christians to growing appreciation and understanding of this doctrine. We acknowledge the limitations of a document prepared in a brief, intensive conference and do not propose that this Statement be given creedal weight. Yet we rejoice in the deepening of our own convictions

---

9 Available as an e-book for $2 at www.BastionBooks.com: *Explaining Biblical Inerrancy: Official Commentary on the ICBI Statements.* This 85-page PDF e-book contains the articles of affirmation and denial from the Chicago Statement on Biblical Inerrancy (1978) with expository commentary by Dr. R. C. Sproul, and the articles of affirmation and denial from the Chicago Statement on Biblical Hermeneutics (1982) with expository commentary by Norman L. Geisler.

through our discussions together, and we pray that the Statement we signed may be used to the glory of our God toward a new reformation of the Church in its faith, life, and mission.

We offer this Statement in a spirit, not of contention, but of humility and love, which we purpose by God's grace to maintain in any future dialogue arising out of what we have said. We gladly acknowledge that many who deny the inerrancy of Scripture do not display the consequences of this denial in the rest of their belief and behavior, and we are conscious that we who confess this doctrine often deny it in life by failing to bring our thoughts and deeds, our traditions and habits, into true subjection to the divine Word.

We invite response to this Statement from any who see reason to amend its affirmations about Scripture by the light of Scripture itself, under whose infallible authority we stand as we speak. We claim no personal infallibility for the witness we bear, and for any help which enables us to strengthen this testimony to God's Word, we shall be grateful.

A SHORT STATEMENT

1. God, who is Himself Truth and speaks truth only, has inspired Holy Scripture in order thereby to reveal Himself to lost mankind through Jesus Christ as Creator and Lord, Redeemer and Judge. Holy Scripture is God's witness to Himself.

2. Holy Scripture, being God's own Word, written by men prepared and superintended by His Spirit, is of infallible divine authority in all matters upon which it touches: it is to be believed, as God's instruction, in all that it affirms; obeyed, as God's command, in all that it requires; embraced, as God's pledge, in all that it promises.

3. The Holy Spirit, Scripture's divine Author, both authenticates it to us by His inward witness and opens our minds to understand its meaning.

4. Being wholly and verbally God-given, Scripture is without error or fault in all its teaching, no less in what it states about God's acts in creation, about the events of world history, and about its own literary origins under God, than in its witness to God's saving grace in individual lives.

5. The authority of Scripture is inescapably impaired if this total divine inerrancy is in any way limited or disregarded, or made relative to a view of truth contrary to the Bible's own; and such lapses bring serious loss to both the individual and the Church.

ARTICLES OF AFFIRMATION AND DENIAL

ARTICLE I

We affirm that the Holy Scriptures are to be received as the authoritative Word of God.

We deny that the Scriptures receive their authority from the Church, tradition, or any other human source.

ARTICLE II

We affirm that the Scriptures are the supreme written norm by which God binds the conscience, and that the authority of the Church is subordinate to that of Scripture.

We deny that Church creeds, councils, or declarations have authority greater than or equal to the authority of the Bible.

ARTICLE III

We affirm that the written Word in its entirety is revelation given by God.

We deny that the Bible is merely a witness to revelation, or only becomes revelation in encounter, or depends on the responses of men for its validity.

ARTICLE IV

We affirm that God who made mankind in His image has used language as a means of revelation.

We deny that human language is so limited by our creatureliness that it is rendered inadequate as a vehicle for divine revelation.

We further deny that the corruption of human culture and language through sin has thwarted God's work of inspiration.

ARTICLE V

We affirm that God's revelation in the Holy Scriptures was progressive.

We deny that later revelation, which may fulfill earlier revelation, ever corrects or contradicts it.

We further deny that any normative revelation has been given since the completion of the New Testament writings.

ARTICLE VI

We affirm that the whole of Scripture and all its parts, down to the very words of the original, were given by divine inspiration.

We deny that the inspiration of Scripture can rightly be affirmed of the whole without the parts, or of some parts but not the whole.

ARTICLE VII

We affirm that inspiration was the work in which God by His Spirit, through human writers, gave us His Word. The origin of Scripture is divine. The mode of divine inspiration remains largely a mystery to us.

We *deny* that inspiration can be reduced to human insight, or to heightened states of consciousness of any kind.

ARTICLE VIII

We *affirm* that God in His Work of inspiration utilized the distinctive personalities and literary styles of the writers whom He had chosen and prepared.

We *deny* that God, in causing these writers to use the very words that He chose, overrode their personalities.

ARTICLE IX

We *affirm* that inspiration, though not conferring omniscience, guaranteed true and trustworthy utterance on all matters of which the Biblical authors were moved to speak and write.

We *deny* that the finitude or fallenness of these writers, by necessity or otherwise, introduced distortion or falsehood into God's Word.

ARTICLE X

We *affirm* that inspiration, strictly speaking, applies only to the autographic text of Scripture, which in the providence of God can be ascertained from available manuscripts with great accuracy.

We *further affirm* that copies and translations of Scripture are the Word of God to the extent that they faithfully represent the original.

We *deny* that any essential element of the Christian faith is affected by the absence of the autographs.

We *further deny* that this absence renders the assertion of Biblical inerrancy invalid or irrelevant.

ARTICLE XI

We *affirm* that Scripture, having been given by divine inspiration, is infallible, so that, far from misleading us, it is true and reliable in all the matters it addresses.

We *deny* that it is possible for the Bible to be at the same time infallible and errant in its assertions. Infallibility and inerrancy may be distinguished, but not separated.

ARTICLE XII

We *affirm* that Scripture in its entirety is inerrant, being free from falsehood, fraud, or deceit.

We *deny* that Biblical infallibility and inerrancy are limited to spiritual, religious, or redemptive themes, exclusive of assertions in the fields of history and science.

We further deny that scientific hypotheses about earth history may properly be used to overturn the teaching of Scripture on creation and the flood.

ARTICLE XIII

We affirm the propriety of using inerrancy as a theological term with reference to the complete truthfulness of Scripture.

We deny that it is proper to evaluate Scripture according to standards of truth and error that are alien to its usage or purpose.

We further deny that inerrancy is negated by Biblical phenomena such as a lack of modern technical precision, irregularities of grammar or spelling, observational descriptions of nature, the reporting of falsehoods, the use of hyperbole and round numbers, the topical arrangement of material, variant selections of material in parallel accounts, or the use of free citations.

ARTICLE XIV

We affirm the unity and internal consistency of Scripture.

We deny that alleged errors and discrepancies that have not yet been resolved vitiate the truth claims of the Bible.

ARTICLE XV

We affirm that the doctrine of inerrancy is grounded in the teaching of the Bible about inspiration.

We deny that Jesus' teaching about Scripture may be dismissed by appeals to accommodation or to any natural limitation of His humanity.

ARTICLE XVI

We affirm that the doctrine of inerrancy has been integral to the Church's faith throughout its history.

We deny that inerrancy is a doctrine invented by Scholastic Protestantism, or is a reactionary position postulated in response to negative higher criticism.

ARTICLE XVII

We affirm that the Holy Spirit bears witness to the Scriptures, assuring believers of the truthfulness of God's written Word.

We deny that this witness of the Holy Spirit operates in isolation from or against Scripture.

ARTICLE XVIII

We affirm that the text of Scripture is to be interpreted by grammatico-historical exegesis, taking account of its literary forms and devices, and that Scripture is to interpret Scripture.

We deny the legitimacy of any treatment of the text or quest for sources lying behind it that leads to relativizing, dehistoricizing, or discounting its teaching, or rejecting its claims to authorship.

ARTICLE XIX

We affirm that a confession of the full authority, infallibility, and inerrancy of Scripture is vital to a sound understanding of the whole of the Christian faith.

We further affirm that such confession should lead to increasing conformity to the image of Christ.

We deny that such confession is necessary for salvation.

We further deny, however, that inerrancy can be rejected without grave consequences, both to the individual and to the Church.

TOPIC 2
Bible Hermeneutics

INTRODUCTORY COMMENTS

by Dr. Jay Grimstead

As soon as we had created the "ICBI Chicago Statement on Biblical Inerrancy" in 1978, Dr. Norman Geisler and I both realized at our Summit Meeting (and we convinced the other board members) that some liberals within evangelicalism, who did not seem to have the same honesty and integrity in theological matters as we had, would begin claiming falsely that they believed in the Bible's inerrancy (because now it was the "politically correct' thing to claim) and begin to say that they just wanted the right to be able to "interpret" the inerrant Bible the way they felt it should be interpreted. This would be their means of getting around the clear teaching of Scripture on certain points they did not like and then continue on their pathway towards more and more relativity regarding the Bible.

So Norm and I suggested to our Executive Committee and other scholars at the Summit Meeting that within a year or two we needed to call another conference and create another document stating the affirmations and denials for true Biblical hermeneutics. We did just that and the team met again near Chicago in the spring of 1982 and hammered out "The Chicago Statement on Biblical Hermeneutics." This document on Hermeneutics is important for today because these basic principles appear to be almost unknown by many serious Bible teachers who seem to allow their imagination to impose itself upon the Biblical text to make the Bible say what it does not really say. Within evangelicalism there seems to be a great "over-tolerance" for allowing any Bible teacher to have the Bible teach almost anything he wants it to teach.

Though these four hermeneutic principles immediately following are not officially included in the ICBI statement on hermeneutics, they are compatible with the thought and flow of the ICBI hermeneutic statement. These are general principles to which most conservative Christian exegetes and pastors would agree and by which they already operate. We include them here for the personal help they may be to any Christian reading this who has not had a class on exegesis or hermeneutics (the science of interpreting any piece of literature, sacred or secular). I learned these principles from Dr. E. J. Carnell at Fuller Seminary in the 1950s.

1. The New Testament interprets the Old Testament (without contradicting the Old Testament).

2. The Epistles interpret the Gospels (as a more complete revelation of Jesus' life and teaching).

3. The systematic passages interpret the incidental passages. (Any single verse anywhere needs to be interpreted within the context of whatever systematic, more full explanation is given regarding the point being made in a single, stand-alone verse).

4. The literal passages interpret the symbolic passages. (We look to the literal passages to tell us what the symbolic passages mean rather than vice versa. However, a symbolic passage may enrich and further develop a literal passage, but may not contradict it or overpower it.)

DOCUMENT 2

The Chicago Statement on Biblical Hermeneutics

ARTICLES OF AFFIRMATION AND DENIAL

ARTICLE I

We affirm that the normative authority of Holy Scripture is the authority of God Himself, and is attested by Jesus Christ, the Lord of the Church.

We deny the legitimacy of separating the authority of Christ from the authority of Scripture, or of opposing the one to the other.

ARTICLE II

We affirm that as Christ is God and Man in one Person, so Scripture is indivisible, God's Word in human language.

We deny that the humble, human form of Scripture entails errancy any more than the humanity of Christ, even in His humiliation, entails sin.

ARTICLE III

We affirm that the Person and work of Jesus Christ are the central focus of the entire Bible.

We deny that any method of interpretation which rejects or obscures the Christ-centeredness of Scripture is correct.

ARTICLE IV

We affirm that the Holy Spirit who inspired Scripture acts through it today to work faith in its message.

We deny that the Holy Spirit ever teaches to anyone anything which is contrary to the teaching of Scripture.

ARTICLE V

We affirm that the Holy Spirit enables believers to appropriate and apply Scripture to their lives.

We deny that the natural man is able to discern spiritually the Biblical message apart from the Holy Spirit.

ARTICLE VI

We affirm that the Bible expresses God's truth in propositional statements, and we declare that Biblical truth is both objective and absolute.

We further affirm that a statement is true if it represents matters as they actually are, but is an error if it misrepresents the facts.

We deny that, while Scripture is able to make us wise unto salvation, Biblical truth should be defined in terms of this function.

We further deny that error should be defined as that which willfully deceives.

ARTICLE VII

We affirm that the meaning expressed in each Biblical text is single, definite, and fixed.

We deny that the recognition of this single meaning eliminates the variety of its application.

ARTICLE VIII

We affirm that the Bible contains teachings and mandates which apply to all cultural and situational contexts and other mandates which the Bible itself shows apply only to particular situations.

We deny that the distinction between the universal and particular mandates of Scripture can be determined by cultural and situational factors.

We further deny that universal mandates may ever be treated as culturally or situationally relative.

ARTICLE IX

We affirm that the term hermeneutics, which historically signified the rules of exegesis, may properly be extended to cover all that is involved in the process of perceiving what the Biblical revelation means and how it bears on our lives.

We deny that the message of Scripture derives from, or is dictated by, the interpreter's understanding. Thus *we deny* that the "horizons" of the Biblical writer and the interpreter may rightly "fuse" in such a way that what the text communicates to the interpreter is not ultimately controlled by the expressed meaning of the Scripture.

ARTICLE X

We affirm that Scripture communicates God's truth to us verbally through a wide variety of literary forms.

We deny that any of the limits of human language render Scripture inadequate to convey God's message.

ARTICLE XI

We affirm that translations of the text of Scripture can communicate knowledge of God across all temporal and cultural boundaries.

We deny that the meaning of Biblical texts is so tied to the culture out of which they came that understanding of the same meaning in other cultures is impossible.

ARTICLE XII

We affirm that in the task of translating the Bible and teaching it in the context of each culture, only those functional equivalents which are faithful to the content of Biblical teaching should be employed.

We deny the legitimacy of methods which either are insensitive to the demands of cross-cultural communication or distort Biblical meaning in the process.

ARTICLE XIII

We affirm that awareness of the literary categories, formal and stylistic, of the various parts of Scripture is essential for proper exegesis, and hence we value genre criticism as one of the many disciplines of Biblical study.

We deny that generic categories which negate historicity may rightly by imposed on Biblical narratives which present themselves as factual.

ARTICLE XIV

We affirm that the Biblical record of events, discourses, and sayings, though presented in a variety of appropriate literary forms, corresponds to historical fact.

We deny that any event, discourse, or saying reported in Scripture was invented by the Biblical writers or by the traditions they incorporated.

ARTICLE XV

We affirm the necessity of interpreting the Bible according to its literal, or normal, sense. The literal sense is the grammatical-historical sense, that is, the meaning which the writer expressed. Interpretation according to the literal sense will take account of all figures of speech and literary forms found in the text.

We deny the legitimacy of any approach to Scripture that attributes to it meaning which the literal sense does not support.

ARTICLE XVI

We affirm that legitimate critical techniques should be used in determining the canonical text and its meaning.

We deny the legitimacy of allowing any method of Biblical criticism to question the truth or integrity of the writer's expressed meaning, or of any other Scriptural teaching.

ARTICLE XVII

We affirm the unity, harmony, and consistency of Scripture and declare that it is its own best interpreter.

We deny that Scripture may be interpreted in such a way as to suggest that one passage corrects or militates against another.

We deny that later writers of Scripture misinterpreted earlier passages of Scripture when quoting from or referring to them.

ARTICLE XVIII

We affirm that the Bible's own interpretation of itself is always correct, never deviating from, but rather elucidating, the single meaning of the inspired text. The single meaning of a prophet's words includes, but is not restricted to, the understanding of those words by the prophet and necessarily involves the intention of God evidenced in the fulfillment of those words.

We deny that the writers of Scripture always understood the full implications of their own words.

ARTICLE XIX

We affirm that any pre-understandings which the interpreter brings to Scripture should be in harmony with Scriptural teaching and subject to correction by it.

We deny that Scripture should be required to fit alien pre-understandings, inconsistent with itself, such as naturalism, evolutionism, scientism, secular humanism, and relativism.

ARTICLE XX

We affirm that since God is the author of all truth, all truths, Biblical and extra-Biblical, are consistent and cohere, and that the Bible speaks truth when it touches on matters pertaining to nature, history, or anything else.

We further affirm that in some cases extra-Biblical data have value for clarifying what Scripture teaches and for prompting correction of faulty interpretations.

We deny that extra-Biblical views ever disprove the teaching of Scripture or hold priority over it.

ARTICLE XXI

We affirm the harmony of special with general revelation and therefore of Biblical teaching with the facts of nature.

We deny that any genuine scientific facts are inconsistent with the true meaning of any passage of Scripture.

ARTICLE XXII

We affirm that Genesis 1-11 is factual, as is the rest of the book.

We deny that the teachings of Genesis 1-11 are mythical and that scientific hypotheses about earth history or the origin of humanity may be invoked to overthrow what Scripture teaches about creation.

ARTICLE XXIII

We affirm the clarity of Scripture and specifically of its message about salvation from sin.

We deny that all passages of Scripture are equally clear or have equal bearing on the message of redemption.

ARTICLE XXIV

We affirm that a person is not dependent for understanding of Scripture on the expertise of Biblical scholars.

We deny that a person should ignore the fruits of the technical study of Scripture by Biblical scholars.

ARTICLE XXV

We affirm that the only type of preaching which sufficiently conveys the divine revelation and its proper application to life is that which faithfully expounds the text of Scripture as the Word of God.

We deny that the preacher has any message from God apart from the text of Scripture.

TOPIC 3

The 42 Articles on the Essentials of a Christian World View

INTRODUCTORY COMMENTS

by Dr. Jay Grimstead

"The 42 Articles on the Essentials of a Christian World View" is a trans-denominational statement of faith which covers the essential theological and philosophical points of the Bible's view of: God, the Universe and Man, Truth and Values, Authority and Salvation, Government and History. It was created by theologians associated with the organization called the Coalition on Revival (COR) which I founded in 1984.

What our theologians felt was needed at this point in the Church's history was a "generic statement of faith" which all Bible-believers in all denominations could probably wholeheartedly sign, but which was structured for answering the basic philosophical questions about life being discussed among leaders in all fields of life, rather than being structured according to the traditional theological categories of God, Man, Salvation, the Church, and the Future. Nonetheless these basic theological categories are included in the 42 Articles on the Essentials of a Christian World View.

Throughout the process of creating and editing this document, our focus was on what we were convinced were the foundational basics of Christian theology and philosophy that separate Biblical Christians from "liberal Christians" and all other religious and philosophical positions. *Thus, we intentionally left unstated those denominational distinctives which separate one denomination from another* such as teachings on: the sacraments, eschatology, church government, modes of worship, charismatic gifts of 1 Corinthians 12, and matters of Christian freedom differences such as issues about smoking, dancing, etc.

The historical occasion for the creation of "The 42 Articles" was our forma-tion of the Coalition on Revival which has as its stated purpose, "to rebuild civilization upon the principles of the Bible," which is essentially the title of this book. There were 113 national and regional Christian leaders who composed the Steering Committee members whom I had gathered together to be a united team from a vast breadth of denominational and theological perspectives whom we expected to work together peacefully and productively. This Steering Committee was composed of Calvinists and Arminians, Charismatics and Anti-Charismatics, High Church and Low Church, pastors and theologians, and those who worshipped with rigid, dignified ceremony, and those who "worked up a sweat" in noisy, unstructured, exuberant, praise to God. Four months before our first "experimental" National Conference, our Executive Committee realized we would, at this first conference, be creating for ourselves a "theological hurricane and earthquake" if we did not have a unifying "Statement of Faith" which they could all enthusiastically sign before they even showed up at the first national meeting. Also, all conference participants had to sign six pages of "Commitment Sheets" before they were admitted to this "Continental Congress on the Christian World View," which sheets covered their written commitment to: orthodox theology, their view of Bible inerrancy, Christian maturity, Christ's Lordship, the unity of the Church, and a "Non-Quarreling Policy" during this conference. (We have never seen such theological and character demands put on participants of any other conference ever.) Those "Commitment Sheets" can be received by e-mail request addressed to COR-ICCP@goldrush.com.

That was the motivation that drove me to call some of our theologians together the week of Good Friday 1984, in Dallas, Texas, to lock ourselves into a "cloister" for three days and hammer out the first draft of these 42 Articles. I honestly believe God's Spirit clearly led and anointed our efforts those three days, for what came out of that working session (which at the time was only 39 Articles) was a first draft that we were happily shocked to find was a combination of comprehensiveness, conciseness, and deep Biblicalness. What we did in this intense theological working-session, so to speak, was to take a "helicopter ride" over the past 2000 years of the Church's theological history, gather up all the major points from every denomination and segment of the Church, then pour it all into a huge beaker and boil it all down into a fine, white powder which became these "42 Articles on the Essentials of the Christian Worldview." There were three primary theologians working on creating these 42 Articles. I was among them and confess that I was by far the junior theologian among the three; the other two theologians requested that their names not be mentioned.

Though our primary objective was to state the basic points of theology the Bible gives us, we also attempted to state in the same document what the mainstream, orthodox teachings of the Church have been over the past 2000 years. After we spent another year with our whole COR Steering Committee editing and affirming the points in these 42 Articles and adding three new articles, we sent a finalized copy to every conservative denomination, mission agency, and Christian organization for which we could locate an address and asked their headquarters to please tell us if these 42 Articles represented the theology their group believed and taught.

We were not surprised but were very pleased to hear that every denomination, mission agency, and Christian organization which took the trouble to write back to us told us this was "right on" with where they stood theologically and were very pleased such a generic theological document had been created. And a number of Christian organizations and churches which had been considered "non-creedal," (and therefore had no official statement of faith other than the Bible itself), asked our permission to utilize these 42 Articles as a Statement of Faith for their own church or organization. And in the intervening years since the mid 1980s, many Christian leaders within various churches, denominations, schools, and mission agencies from all around the world have also said this document clearly and powerfully represents what their group believes and teaches.

Thus, I believe that 30 years ago God supernaturally helped our theological team to create a document which, at this point in history, can serve as an effective tool to unite the Body of Christ in any country of the world around a Biblical theology that crosses most denominational and theological boundary lines, and thus help us advance towards a Biblical, united, global theology for the Body of Christ for the twenty-first century.

In these 42 Articles on the Christian Worldview, we believe we already have in our hands an "early stage version" of what could possibly become "A Global Statement of Faith," which the great majority of conservative denominations, associations, churches, missions, Christian schools, and organizations could whole-heartedly sign if those people believed in the full inspiration and inerrancy of the Bible and in basic orthodox theology.

This real possibility and hope is what gives us the optimism that our efforts will be successful at accomplishing COR's Mission Statement for this Church Council which attempts "To establish for the twenty-first century a united, Biblical-theological standard of doctrine for the global Body of Christ which is consistent with the mainstream theology of the first twenty centuries."

DOCUMENT 3

The 42 Articles on the Essentials of a Christian World View

COPYRIGHT 1984, THE COALITION ON REVIVAL

ARTICLES OF AFFIRMATION AND DENIAL

The Nature of God

ARTICLE I

We affirm that there is only one living God who is infinite in being and perfection, a most pure spirit, invisible, and absolutely distinct from His creation.

We deny any and all views of God that negate or deviate from the traditional Judeo-Christian concept of God, including atheism, deism, finite-godism, panentheism (process God), polytheism, and pantheism.

ARTICLE II

We affirm that God is both transcendent over and immanent in His creation.

We deny that in His being God is totally *Other*[10] or that He is identified with His creation.

ARTICLE III

We affirm that from time to time God supernaturally intervenes in the course of natural or human events to accomplish His redemptive purposes.

We deny any naturalistic view which rejects either a supernatural God or His miraculous intervention in nature or history.

ARTICLE IV

We affirm that God is a personal, infinite, eternal, self-existent, unchangeable, indivisible, omnipotent, omniscient, omnipresent, spiritual being Who is the creator and sustainer of the universe.

---

10 *"Other"* comes from Karl Barth's writing where he refers to God as "Totally Other" and so different from us that we cannot get to him by normal logic or language (which is a restatement of Kant's dichotomy).

We deny that God is impersonal, finite, temporal, changeable, divisible, material, or is limited in His power, knowledge, or presence in the universe.

ARTICLE V

We affirm that God is absolutely holy, just, good, true, loving, and merciful in His being and all His activities.

We deny that God is any less than absolutely and totally perfect in all of His attributes.

ARTICLE VI

We affirm that this one God exists eternally in three distinct Persons (Father, Son, and Holy Spirit), each of whom shares equally in all the divine attributes.

We deny that God is more than one Being (as in Tri-theism) or that He is less than three eternal Persons (as in strict monotheism, Arianism, or modalism).

The Nature of the Universe

ARTICLE VII

We affirm that the entire universe, including all finite beings, was created by God out of nothing (*ex nihilo*).

We deny that the universe is not created or that it was created out of God (*ex deo*) or out of pre-existing material (*ex materia*).

ARTICLE VIII

We affirm that the space/time universe is finite, temporal, and real.

We deny that the space/time universe is infinite, eternal, or illusory.

ARTICLE IX

We affirm that the entire universe is absolutely distinct from and utterly dependent upon its Creator-God.

We deny that the universe is in any way to be identified with God or that it exists independently of God.

ARTICLE X

We affirm that man (male and female) was specially created by God.

We deny that man evolved from or is genetically derived from the lower forms of life.

ARTICLE XI

We affirm that man was created in the image and likeness of God, and consequently is endowed by God with immeasurable dignity and worth.

We deny any view that tends to demean or diminish the God-given freedom, dignity, and value of man or reduce him to the status of a mere animal.

ARTICLE XII

We affirm that man as a rational and moral being is ultimately responsible and accountable to God.

We deny that man's moral actions are determined genetically or environmentally, or that his responsibility is limited to himself or society.

ARTICLE XIII

We affirm that because of man's rebellion against God, both he and his environment exist in a corrupted state and stand under the condemnation of God.

We deny that either man or the world in their present corrupted state may be perfected by natural or human agencies alone.

ARTICLE XIV

We affirm that man, from the moment of conception, is a creature who has individual conscious existence eternally beyond physical death.

We deny that man is a merely mortal creature whose individual conscious existence terminates at physical death, or that man's unborn offspring are less than human.

The Nature of Truth

ARTICLE XV

We affirm that God is the ultimate author of all truth.

We deny that man can be the ultimate author and determiner of truth.

ARTICLE XVI

We affirm that truth is objective, absolute, and ultimately non-contradictory.

We deny any view that reduces truth to a purely relative, subjective, experiential, or a paradoxical status.

ARTICLE XVII

We affirm truth to be that which corresponds to and accurately describes and explains reality.

We deny any view that conceives of reality as mere subjective experience, existential encounter, mere coherence, dialectical process, or that conceives of reality in any other relativistic manner.

ARTICLE XVIII

We affirm that insofar as God has revealed truth, whether in general or special revelation, it is knowable by man even though it is neither exhaustive nor comprehensive.

We deny that the limitations of man's knowledge of God's truth leave him incapable of knowing, communicating, or using that truth.

ARTICLE XIX

We affirm that all truth disclosed in God's special revelation, the 66 books of the Bible, is propositional.

We deny that the human language of the Bible is an inadequate vehicle for communicating God's truth to man.

The Nature of True Values

ARTICLE XX

We affirm that God is the source of all right and just values and that they reflect His moral character.

We deny that true values are ultimately derived from man or any other finite source.

ARTICLE XXI

We affirm that the basis of all true values is objective and absolute.

We deny that the basis of all true values is merely subjective, relative, or cultural.

ARTICLE XXII

We affirm that true values are determined by God and merely discovered by man.

We deny that it is legitimate for man to create his own true values on either the personal or societal level.

ARTICLE XXIII

We affirm the true values revealed by God place a prescriptive obligation on man by which he must order his life.

We deny that true values are merely descriptive of human behavior or that man is not obliged to live by them.

ARTICLE XXIV

We affirm that the only perfect, comprehensive, and complete expression of God's values is to be found in the Bible.

We deny that those who are unaware of the Bible are thereby excused from moral obligations revealed by God in the hearts of men.

The Nature of Authority

ARTICLE XXV

We affirm that the ultimate source of authority is God.

We deny that man has the authority to create his own moral standards.

ARTICLE XXVI

We affirm that God has expressed His authority to His creatures in general revelation and most clearly and fully in special revelation.

We deny that human society, culture, or consensus is a legitimate basis for man's moral conduct.

ARTICLE XXVII

We affirm that God in his general revelation, through the works of creation and the consciences of men, has revealed His eternal power and deity with His moral law in the hearts of all men, even though they in their corrupted state suppress this truth in unrighteousness.

We deny that man is either an amoral creature or that he is inherently good or naturally perfectible.

ARTICLE XXVIII

We affirm that God's normative, special revelation is expressed in and limited to His authoritative, inerrant, written Word, the Bible, which is the final bar of appeal in all matters of faith and life and stands in judgment over all reason, revelation, and experience.

We deny that God has left man without any normative special revelation or that there is any other or additional normative special revelation from God.

ARTICLE XXIX

We affirm that the laws of man must be based upon the laws of God.

We deny that the laws of man have any inherent authority of their own or that their ultimate authority is rightly derived from or created by man.

The Nature of Salvation

ARTICLE XXX

We affirm that God alone is the source of man's salvation.

We deny that man can initiate or attain his own salvation.

ARTICLE XXXI

We affirm that Jesus Christ, the God-Man, by virtue of His perfect life, His substitutionary, atoning death, and His bodily resurrection, is the only Mediator between a Holy God and sinful man.

We deny that man can achieve salvation by means of secular education, social programs, political action, genetic engineering, psychology, or self-realization, or by any other means.

ARTICLE XXXII

We affirm that Jesus Christ in His Incarnation is wholly God and wholly man, two natures in one person, without confusion, without change, without division, without separation.

We deny that the two natures of Jesus Christ can be confused, changed, or divided, or that the one Divine Person can be separated from either nature.

ARTICLE XXXIII

We affirm that God's gift of salvation is supernaturally applied to those who believe by the gracious working of God the Holy Spirit.

We deny that in the matter of his salvation, man is left to his own resources or that he can merit this salvation by his own works.

ARTICLE XXXIV

We affirm that salvation is from the presence, power, and penalty of sin and to joyful obedience and service to God in His present and future kingdom.

We deny that salvation applies only to the eternal destinies of man.

The Nature of Human Government

ARTICLE XXXV

We affirm that the institution of human government has been ordained by God.

We deny that any form of government (or ruler) has authority from any source other than God or that God approves governments indiscriminately.

ARTICLE XXXVI

We affirm that God has established a multiplicity of human governments such as individual, familial, ecclesiastical, and civil.

We deny that any form of human government (or ruler) has valid authority from any source but God or that any human government has either absolute or complete jurisdiction over all other governments.

ARTICLE XXXVII

We affirm that it is the duty of all citizens to obey God ordained authority.

We deny that any citizen is obliged to obey any government when it transgresses its God-given mandate or requires him to disobey God's Laws.

ARTICLE XXXVIII

We affirm that it is always the obligation of believers to participate in promoting good government.

We deny that a Christian can fully discharge his duty to God apart from social, cultural, and political action aimed at influencing society for God and for human good.

The Nature (and Purpose) of Government

ARTICLE XXXIX

We affirm that the Sovereign God is providentially directing the course of human history and that the saving purposes of God in Christ are accomplished within the same history.

We deny any philosophy which espouses a naturalistic, chaotic, cyclical, dialectical, two-leveled, or any other view that neglects or negates the directive activity of God in history.

ARTICLE XL

We affirm that the purpose and meaning of history is to bring praise and glory to God and abundant life to His children.

We deny any view which rejects meaning or purpose in history or which has man, nature, or anything other than God enshrined as its ultimate object.

ARTICLE XLI

We affirm that although man may be the primary focus and subject of history, God is its ultimate author and finisher.

We deny any view in which man is elevated to the level of architect, director, or determiner of the course of historical events.

ARTICLE XLII

We affirm that the consummation of history is the final triumph of God over all death and evil and their consequences, and its ultimate goal is the manifestation of the glory of God.

We deny any view which embraces reincarnation, universalism, the ultimate overpowering of good by evil, the annihilation of man, or the elimination of a place of eternal punishment and separation from God.

TOPIC 4

The 25 Articles on the Kingdom of God

INTRODUCTORY COMMENTS

by Dr. Jay Grimstead

In 1988, during my own personal journey towards a full, Biblical understanding of the Great Commission and the Church's role in bringing the Kingdom of God to earth to a measurable degree ("Thy will be done, on earth as it is in heaven" Matt. 6:10),[11] it became apparent that COR needed to make a full, theological statement about the Kingdom of God in the way the ICBI team had made a full, theological statement about the inspiration of the Bible.

I gathered together a team of theologians to create such a document in Washington, D.C. (at the Shoreham Hotel) in January of 1989. We locked ourselves into a cluster of seminar rooms for three days to take on the task of creating a theological document that offers a brief but full statement and definition of The Kingdom of God. During 1988, I had written a preliminary set of 12 statements to explain the Kingdom of God which we used as a starting point. We divided our committee into four sub-committees with three or four theologians each so we could deal with each of the preliminary points, edit it, expand it, make it better, and turn it into an "article." Then each committee would turn in our edited version to the two seminary students with computers who served as our secretaries to keep typing into the computer and printing out each new draft of each article we were creating. Periodically we would present drafts of each article to the whole group for comments and thus we progressed through the three days. As we discussed the Biblical view of the Kingdom of God, it soon became obvious that we were going to need 25 Articles to say all that needed to be said in a creed-like statement about this topic.

We decided to build the Articles of this document into creed-like statements of affirmations and denials about each point just as our committee for the

---

11 For an interesting new book on the Kingdom of God, see *Thy Will Be Done: When All Nations Call God Blessed* by Ronald W. Kirk. Ventura, CA: Nordskog Publishing, 2013; go to www. nordskogpublishing.com.

ICBI had done in the 1970s and just as our COR team had done with the Worldview Documents in the 1980s. This forced us to use as concise, strong, and dignified wording and structure as we could create. And regarding the need for a statement to be structured in both affirmations and denials, we agreed with what Dr. Francis Schaeffer told our ICBI committee in the 1970s, that, "In today's world of language confusion and chaos, one cannot be certain that people have understood what you mean, unless you also tell them what you do not mean."

We found ourselves amazed and extremely grateful for the final product which evolved under our hands those days in D.C. We sensed that God had very definitely led us to create a document superior to what we had hoped for. We were very pleased! As far as we knew, there was not another creedal statement that was so comprehensive and concise explaining the Kingdom of God anywhere in the world.

We later sent this Kingdom of God document to many other theologians and scholars for their critique and input but there were no substantive changes suggested from orthodox theologians with one exception. The theologians from the seminaries and Bible schools committed to dispensationalism and to a "pietistic" view of Christianity (wherein they believe the Gospel is only to affect individuals, families, and churches, but not intentionally and systematically make changes in society in the areas of law, government, business, education, the arts and media, and science) differed deeply with a number of our 25 affirmations and denials. So I created a three-day dialogue and debate forum for the following January in 1990, wherein six of our committee who had created this document would meet again in Washington, D.C. at a hotel with six theologians from the schools which were oriented towards a dispensational hermeneutic. We did meet the following year and had a very lively but cordial dialogue and debate with the brothers who disagreed with certain points in this document. What was surprising to me was that after the two-and-one-half days of dialogue and debate, the brothers from the schools oriented toward dispensationalism wished to meet again the following year for a second session of dialogue and debate; so we set up another meeting for the following year and met again, this time with a few new dispensational brothers. It is my somewhat objective opinion that our "pro" side clearly won the debate on each of the points we discussed. But there was a very interesting development that happened the last afternoon of this second dialogue and debate forum.

As we proceeded, it became obvious to several of us that there were far more points of agreement between these two "pro" and "con" sides than anyone expected. I believe this growing unity of position and growing honest friendships came about primarily because, within our knowledge of recent ecclesiastical and theological history up until this time, there had never been a serious, scholarly dialogue and debate forum between the "Covenant Theologians" and the "Dispensational Theologians," since each had simply stayed in their own corners and exchanged theological disputations across the battlefront between their camps without ever actually setting up a face-to-face interchange of ideas.

So during the last few hours together, I asked each of the dispensational-oriented theologians to work over all 25 Articles on the Kingdom of God and put each article in one of three categories:

A. Those Articles where there is already substantial agreement without any word changes;

B. Those Articles where there probably never will be any serious agreement between both sides because there is such deep, foundational disagreement on that point;

C. Those articles which are close enough for substantial agreement that, with minor word changes on the part of our covenant theologians, there could be substantial agreement by the dispensational theologians.

We then worked over and discussed those articles in category C and found minor word changes wherein the covenant theologians were willing to make a minor compromise without harming the basic point being made. When we finally added up the articles where we had come to substantial agreement through discussion from category C, and added those to category A (where there was already agreement), we found we had identified 17 of the 25 articles of affirmation and denial wherein both sides had substantial agreement!!! This amazed us. One of the theological and sociological realities we discovered during this whole procedure is that, within traditional dispensational circles, there are many thoughtful theologians who now refer to themselves as "Progressive Dispensationalists." Such theologians have come a long way towards a traditional Covenental and Reformed theology and have rejected several of the basic "tenets" of the old "Scofield Bible" notes but still hold to their basic dispensationalism and still operate within those parameters. We left this last dialogue meeting parting as good, new friends with most of the men, and both sides claimed that they were impressed that scholars of such caliber existed on the opposite side of the debate. It is my opinion that the creation of the 25 articles on the Kingdom of God and the debates between scholars who took the opposite sides of these issues were both historic events.

DOCUMENT 4

The Kingdom of God: a Summary of the Biblical and Historical View

ARTICLES OF AFFIRMATION AND DENIAL

God's Eternal Sovereign Reign

ARTICLE I

We *affirm* that the Triune God has reigned sovereignly as King of the universe throughout all time, both before and since the incarnation, and will continue to reign eternally.

We *deny* that the reign of Jesus Christ, the God-man, beginning in the first century, suspends the providential reign of Father, Son, and Holy Spirit.

Exod. 15:18; Pss. 96:10; 99:1; 146:10; Prov. 8:15; 9:6-7; Isa. 24:21, 23; 40:12-17; John 19:11; Acts 4:27-28; 17:30; 1 Cor. 15:25; Col. 1:16-19; Heb. 1:13-14; Rev. 1:5; 11:15; 17-18; 15:3-4; 19:6; 22:3-5

Definition of the Kingdom of God

ARTICLE II

We *affirm* that the term Kingdom of God has several applications and may denote (a) the universal rule of Christ over all things, both redeemed and non-redeemed; (b) the special, saving rule of Christ over His people; (c) the life, wisdom, holiness, power, and authority that Christ grants to His people; or (d) the permeating influence of the Word and Spirit in the world.

We *deny* (a) that the term Kingdom of God refers only to the providential rule of the Triune God, and (b) that Christ's rule and realm are limited to the Church.

Gal. 5:21-25; Eph. 1:20-23; 2:4-9; Phil. 2:9-11; 1 John 2:8, 15-17; 3:8; 4:4; 5:4-5; Rev. 1:5; 5:8-13; 19:11-16; 20-21; 22:3-5

Purpose and Fall of Man

ARTICLE III

We affirm (a) that God purposed from the beginning to share His rule over the earth with man; (b) that God created man in His own image and endowed man with faculties for ruling the earth; (c) that God, in the Creation Mandate, commissioned man to rule the earth and granted him delegated authority to fulfill this commission; and (d) that man, by God's design, was made to be the highest created being in the universe because he is the only creature that bears God's image.

We deny (a) that man's fall into sin eradicates the image of God in man; (b) that the fall eliminates or reduces man's responsibility or mandate for exercising dominion under God over the earth; and (c) that all mankind, the righteous or the wicked, ever ceased to be responsible to live under the rule of God in grateful obedience to Him as Lord and King in every area of life.

> Gen. 1:27-30; Deut. 4:5-8; Ps. 8:4-8; Rom. 1:18-25; 2:6-12; Phil. 2:9-11; Heb. 1:13-14; 2:6-8; Rev. 1:5

Inauguration of the Kingdom of God

ARTICLE IV

We affirm (a) that the New Testament phase of the Kingdom of God was inaugurated in fact and history at Jesus' first coming to earth, and (b) that it now operates in reality and power among men in this present age.

We deny that the Church must await the second coming of Christ for the Kingdom of God to be inaugurated on earth in time-space reality and in power.

> Isa. 9:6-7; 52:13-15; 53:1-12; Jer. 31:31-34; Dan. 2:32-35; 43-44; Mic. 5:2; Zech. 9:9; Matt. 2:2-6; 3:1-3; 4:17, 23; 6:9-10; 10:7; 12:28; 16:18-19; 21:4-5; 22:42-45; 28:18; Mark 1:14-15; Luke 8:1; 23:3; John 18:36-37; Rom. 16:20; Eph. 1:19-23; 2:6; Heb. 1:3; 8:10-13; Rev. 1:5

Consummation of the Kingdom

ARTICLE V

We affirm that the Kingdom of God will increase until it is consummated when Jesus delivers it to the Father and that, at the present time, this Kingdom is both already present and not yet consummated.

We deny that the Kingdom of God will be either consummated or realized totally, comprehensively, or perfectly on earth before the return of Jesus.

> Isa. 2:2-4; 9:6-7; Dan. 2:32-35; Matt. 24:14; 25:24-31; Luke 22:29-30; 1 Cor. 2:9; 15:23-28, 51-55; Rom. 8:21-25

The Kingdom Touches all Spheres of Life

ARTICLE VI

We affirm (a) that the Bible reveals God's intentions for the growth of His Kingdom in all nations of the earth during this present age through the proclamation and obedient application of His stated will in Scripture, and (b) that His intention includes the increasing manifestation of His rule over individuals, voluntary associations, families, the church, the state, and all spheres of human activity, some of which are law, government, economics, business, occupations, education, sports, medicine, science, technology, arts, and media.

We deny that God's rulership is limited to transforming only the private lives of individuals to His will.

Isa. 2:2-4; Dan. 2:32-35; Pss. 2:1-10; 96:1, 7, 9-13; John 1:1-4; Acts 4:10-12; 17:30; Rom. 1:19-20; 2:6-10; 1 Cor. 10:31; Phil. 2:9-11; Col. 3:17, 22-24

Man's Dominion over the Earth Restored

ARTICLE VII

We affirm that Christ alone, as representative man and last Adam, by His life, death, resurrection, and ascension to the throne at the right hand of the Father, accomplished redemption, the defeat of Satan, and the beginning of the restoration of man's godly dominion over the earth as God's vice-regent.

We deny that the restoration of man's God-ordained dominion (a) lies outside the scope of Christ's redeeming work as mediator on the Cross, or (b) awaits the physical presence of the returned Christ for its inauguration and expansion.

Gen. 1:26-28; 2:19-20; 3:15; Pss. 2:6-8; 8:6; 72:1-2, 8; 110:1-2; 132:11; Isa. 9:6-7; 11:1; 16:5; 42:1; 45:23; Jer. 23:5; 27:5-6; 33:14-17; Dan. 7:13-14, 18, 22, 27; Zech. 9:9-10; Matt. 16:18-19; 28:18-20; Luke 1:31-33; 9:1-2; 10:18-19; John 5:27; 12:31; Acts 1:6-8; 2:32-35; 4:25-26; 5:31; 7:55-56; Rom. 5:14-15, 17; 6:9-11; 8:16-22; 16:20; 1 Cor. 15:20-28; Gal. 4:4-7; Eph. 1:17-23; 2:5-6; Phil. 2:9-11; Col. 1:13-20; Heb. 1:2-4, 8, 13; 2:5-9, 14; 10:12-13; 1 Pet. 3:22; 4:11; Jude 1:25; Rev. 1:5-6; 5:9-10; 11:15; 12:5; 19:15-16; 20:6

Satan's Defeat and Christ's Rulership

ARTICLE VIII

We affirm that Jesus Christ rules sovereignly over the kings of the earth not only as eternal God but also as the sole mediator between God and men, and that He lawfully defeated Satan *de jure* by His victorious life, death, resurrection, and ascension.

We deny that Satan is the ruler of this world in any sense that undermines the recognition of the rightful rule of Christ over the earth during this present age.

Pss. 2:1-6; 110:1-2; Matt. 4:10; 10:1; 12:24-29; 16:18-19; Luke 10:17-19; John 12:31; 14:30; 16:11; Acts 2:34; 4:25-26; 13:9-11; Rom. 16:20; 1 Cor. 15:24-26; 2 Cor. 10:3-5; Eph. 6:11-13; Phil. 2:9-11; Col. 1:13; Heb. 1:13; 1 John 4:4; 5:4-5; Rev. 19:15; 19-21; 20:1-3, 10

All Authority Given to Christ

ARTICLE IX

We affirm (a) that Jesus, the Son of David and Son of God, was given all authority in heaven and on earth by God the Father; (b) that after His ascension He sat down on the throne at the right hand of God; (c) that from this position of absolute authority in the universe He is bringing all things into submission under His feet, exercising His authority ever more widely and fully on earth as the Gospel spreads and people are converted to Him; and (d) that His exercise of that authority will become more fully manifest after His second coming.

We deny that Christ will ever be given any more power or authority over the earth than He was given at His first coming.

Ps. 2:1-6; Isa. 9:6-7; Dan. 2:32-35; Matt. 28:18-20; Acts 4:10-12; 4:25-26; 17:30; 1 Cor. 15:25-28; Eph. 1:19-22; 2:6; Phil. 2:9-11; Heb. 1:2-5; Rev. 1:5; 5:5-12; 19:11-21

Every Knee Should Bow to Christ Now

ARTICLE X

We affirm (a) that now, even before Christ's second coming, every knee in every nation on earth should bow and every tongue confess that Jesus Christ is Lord of this universe and rightful Ruler of all lives, and (b) that only those who, trusting in His grace alone for forgiveness of sins, repent of their sinful rebellion and submit to Christ as Lord are justified and stand accepted at the bar of God's judgment.

We deny that anyone, Jew or Gentile, believer or unbeliever, private person or public official, is exempt from the moral and juridical obligation before God to submit to Christ's lordship over every aspect of his life in thought, word, and deed.

Ps. 2:1-6; Dan. 2:32-35; Matt. 4:17, 23; 28:18-20; Acts 4:10-12; 17:30; Rom. 3:23-24; 5:8; 8:1-4; Phil. 2:9-11; Rev. 1:5

Submission to the Lordship of Christ Is Essential to Salvation

ARTICLE XI

We affirm that, because the King demands obedience from His subjects and children, (a) repentance is necessary for citizenship in the Kingdom of God, and (b) genuine repentance is evidenced by deliberate and continuing choice to submit obediently to the lordship of Christ.

We deny (a) that anyone can rightly claim Christ as Savior who does not submit to Him as Lord; (b) that Christ will save anyone who refuses to submit in grateful obedience to Him as Lord and King; (c) that this view embraces the idea of salvation by works; and (d) that Christians ever become sinless or outgrow the need for repentance in this life.

> Matt. 4:17-23; 7:21-27; John 14:21, 23; 15:5-6, 10; Rom. 6:1-2, 12-14; 8:13-14; Gal. 6:7-8; Eph. 4:20-24; 5:3-6; Col. 3:1-7; Heb. 10:26-29; James 1:22; 2:17-26; 3:11-17; 2 Pet. 2:20-22; 1 John 2:3-4, 9-11; 2:3-4, 3:10, 17-18

The Church and the Kingdom

ARTICLE XII

We affirm (a) that the Church, which is Christ's Body and Bride, consists of the redeemed and is manifested in the community of believers; (b) that Christ's Kingdom authority is not limited to His Church but extends over all areas of life; and (c) that the Church is the focal point of Christ's Kingdom work here on earth.

We deny (a) that the Church is to be equated with any denomination; (b) that Christ's authority is limited to His Church or any group of believers; and (c) that any institution other than the Church is God's primary instrument for the spread of the Gospel and the extension of Christ's Kingdom.

> Pss. 110:1-3; 118:22-23; Isa. 28:16; 45:23; 60:3, 11-15; 61:3-6; Dan. 7:14, 18, 22, 27; Matt. 16:18-19; 18:18-20; 21:41-44; 28:18-20; Luke 9:2; John 17:18-22; Acts 1:6-8; 20:25-28; 28:28; Rom. 8:16-19; 1 Cor. 6:2; Eph. 1:18-23; Phil. 2:9-11; Col. 1:13-18; Heb. 2:6-9; 8:8-13; 12:22-24; 12:28; 1 Pet. 2:6-9; Rev. 1:6; 2:26; 5:9-10; 20:6; 21:2-7, 23-27

The Great Commission

ARTICLE XIII

We affirm that the Church has an absolute responsibility to obey the Great Commission, and the task of the Church is: (a) to herald Christ as King over all the earth and Judge of all mankind, who now commands all men everywhere to repent; (b) to proclaim the good news of salvation by grace through faith in the atoning blood of Christ; (c) to make disciples of all nations, baptizing them in the name of the Father, and of the Son, and of the Holy Spirit, and teaching them to obey all of God's commands in the Bible that apply to us today.

We deny (a) that the Church can disregard the Great Commission and still walk in godly obedience; (b) that the Great Commission is restricted solely to proclaiming the good news of salvation without the accompanying call to repentance and faithful obedience; (c) that the deliverance believers enjoy from the condemnation of the moral Law exempts them from the obligation to obey it; and (d) that obedience to the Law is a means of salvation.

> Matt. 4:17-23; 10:1, 7-8; 28:18-20; Luke 4:17-20; Acts 1:8; Rom. 6:12-16; Gal. 3:1-5, 23-28

The Lord's Prayer

ARTICLE XIV

We affirm (a) that the intention of the Great Commission is essentially the same as the intention of the second and third petitions of the Lord's Prayer and the Creation Mandate, namely, that the Father's will should be done on earth as it is in heaven, and (b) that these instructions from God call believers to participate by both prayer and action in the expansion of His Kingdom on earth as it is in heaven to whatever extent that is possible before Christ's second coming.

We deny (a) that anyone can pray the Lord's Prayer with sincerity and understanding without desiring that increasing numbers of individuals, private groups, and civil states should grow in obedience to the will of God the Father, and (b) that Christians need to agree in advance to what extent Christ's Kingdom will be operational on earth prior to His second coming before they can work together humbly and productively.

> Gen. 1:27-29; Matt. 6:9-15; 24:36; 28:18-20; Luke 11:1-4; Acts 1:7

The Kingdom and the Holy Spirit

ARTICLE XV

We affirm that the Kingdom of God, however guaranteed in the promises of the Father and embodied in the person of Christ, can never gain entrance or come to full realization in the fabric of human life apart from the agency of the Holy Spirit, who is indispensable to insure Kingdom entrance, to seal Kingdom membership, to implement Kingdom obedience, to build Kingdom character, to furnish Kingdom gifts, to empower to Kingdom outreach, to produce Kingdom growth, and secure Kingdom victory.

We deny that character strength, personal charisma, skillful management, creative imagination, evident talents, financial strength, political action, or educational prowess by themselves can build or advance the Kingdom of God.

> Ps. 104:29-30; Isa. 30:1; 59:19-21; 61:1-3; Ezek. 36:25-27; Joel 2:28-29; Zech. 4:6; Matt. 3:11; 12:28; 28:19; Luke 11:13; 12:12; John 3:5-6; 6:63; 14:26; 15:26; 16:13; Acts 1:5, 8; 2:4, 16-18; 2:33; 4:31; 9:31; Rom. 8:4-17, 26-27; 14:17; 1 Cor. 2:4, 14; 3:16; 6:9-11; 12:4-13; 2 Cor. 1:22; 3:3-11, 17-18; 10:3-5; Gal. 3:3; 5:16-25; Eph. 1:13; 4:30; 6:12-18; Phil. 3:3; 1 Thess. 1:5; Titus 3:5; Heb. 2:4; 2 Pet. 1:21; 1 John 3:24; Jude 1:19

The Church Responsible for Advancing the Kingdom

ARTICLE XVI

We affirm that God holds the Body of Christ responsible for advancing His Kingdom on earth, to whatever extent God has ordained, by applying His Biblical principles through service in all spheres of human activity in all nations, prior to our Lord's glorious return.

We deny (a) that any belief regarding the timing of Christ's second coming, the sequence of events leading up to it, and the possible extent of the Kingdom's growth prior to Christ's return releases anyone from such responsibility; (b) that seeking to apply Biblical principles to the stewardship of all earthly creation detracts from the believer's heavenly hope; and (c) that one can properly lead without an attitude of humble servanthood.

> Deut. 4:5-8; Matt. 10:1, 7-8; 16:18-19; 18:1-4; 21:25-28; 28:18-20; Acts 1:8; John 15:5-8; 17:13-21

The Kingdom of God and Heaven
ARTICLE XVII

We affirm (a) that our primary citizenship is in heaven, though we are citizens of earthly nations as well; (b) that heaven is our true home and treasure; (c) that the Bible teaches us to be heavenly-minded and that only heavenly-minded men and women are useful for God on earth; (d) that we are seated in the heavenly places to rule in and with Christ; (e) that heaven is the pattern for earth; and (f) that we are to live in eager expectation of our being with the Lord in heaven and of Christ's second coming in glory, when heaven shall come down to earth in fullness.

We deny (a) that our heavenly citizenship reduces our responsibilities in society, and (b) that our expectation of heaven and of Christ's coming gives us permission to neglect our duties in this world.

> Ps. 27:4; Matt. 6:19-21, 33; Luke 12:31-34; 20:25; Rom. 8:18-25; 13:1-7; 1 Cor. 13:12; 2 Cor. 4:16-18; 5:1-9; Eph. 2:6-7; Phil. 3:20-21; 1 Thess. 4:13-18; 1 Tim. 4:8; 6:13-19; Titus 2:11-13; Heb. 12:22-23, 28; 13:14; 1 Pet. 2:11-17; 2 Pet. 3:13-15; 1 John 3:2-3; Rev. 21:1-5; 21:10-27; 22:1-5

The Bible Is the Plumb Line for All Nations
ARTICLE XVIII

We affirm that the Kingdom task of making disciples of all nations requires us to hold forth the Bible as God's standard and plumb line by which to measure the justice, morality, and practice of all human endeavors in all jurisdictions: individual, voluntary association, family, church, and civil government.

We deny (a) that the Bible and its view of reality bind only those who voluntarily claim them as their own and are irrelevant to those who reject them, and (b) that unwillingness relieves anyone of the duty to believe and obey the Bible.

> Pss. 1:1-3; 2:1-6; 99:1; 96:9-10; 148:7-12; Isa. 9:6-7; Obad. 1:15; Jon. 3:2-6; Mic. 1:2; Nah. 1:13; Matt. 2:1-2; 5:18-19; 28:18-20; Acts 1:8; 17:30; Phil. 2:9-11; Rev. 1:5

Cause and Effect of Kingdom Principles

ARTICLE XIX

We affirm (a) that when people — individuals or societies, Christian or non-Christian — generally follow, consciously or unconsciously, the moral, economic, and practical commands of the Bible, they tend to reap earthly blessings as a result, and (b) that when people generally fail to follow the moral, economic, and practical commands of the Bible, they tend to reap earthly judgments as a result.

We deny (a) that God will forever allow people to sow the wind without reaping the whirlwind, and (b) that obedience guarantees the believer whatever he claims from God.

> Num. 21:5-8; Deut. 4:2-9; 6:10-19; 28:1-20; Josh. 1:8; Judg. 2:1-12, 14-17; Neh. 9:26-30; Ps. 106:10-15; Prov. 1:5-9,16-19; 3:13-18; 4:4; 11:9-11; Jer. 7:5-15, 23; Matt. 5:18-19; 10:32-33; Rom. 2:6-11; 2 Cor. 9:6; Gal. 6:7-8; 2 Tim. 3:8-9

Suffering as Part of Kingdom Living

ARTICLE XX

We affirm that suffering and persecution are a normal part of the Christian life by which the believer participates with Christ in His sufferings, in selfless service for the advance of the Kingdom.

We deny (a) that suffering is always a sign of God's judgment or displeasure with sin, and (b) that suffering adds to the work of Christ in redemption.

> Matt. 5:10-12; 10:16-25; 16:21-25; Luke 9:23-24; John 21:18-19; Acts 7:52-58; 16:25; 8:1; 2 Cor. 12:10; Gal. 5:11; 2 Tim. 3:11-12

Continuity between the Testaments

ARTICLE XXI

We affirm that there is continuity between the personal and social moral principles of the Old and New Testaments.

We deny that the moral principles of the New Testament are different from the moral principles of the Old Testament, whether individual or social.

> Gen. 15:5-11 (Rom. 4:3); Exod. 11:3-8 (John 1:29; Luke 22:14-20; Rev. 5:4-10); Ps. 2:1-6 (Acts 4:25-26); Ps. 110:1 (Acts 2:34-35); Ps. 118:22; Dan. 2:32-35 (Matt. 21:4, 2; Acts 2:11; 1 Pet. 2:7); Isa. 6:1-4 (Rev. 4:2-8); Jer. 31:31-34 (Heb. 8:8-10); Joel 2:28-32 (Acts 2:17-18). See also Matt. 5:18-19; Luke 16:17; Heb. 1:1-2; 12:26-28

The Kingdom in the Old Testament

ARTICLE XXII

We affirm (a) that the Old Testament Kingdom of Israel was brought about and shaped by the acts of God in history; (b) that this Kingdom was to be based on the principles and laws given by God, but the people fell far short of the ideal and righteous Kingdom that those laws prescribed; and (c) that the development of the Davidic Kingdom was God's way to prepare His people for the coming Messianic Kingdom.

We deny (a) that the Old Testament Kingdom of Israel is to be understood only through naturalistic and nationalistic principles and had nothing to do with God's eternal principles and laws, and (b) that anyone could properly understand or anticipate the Messianic Kingdom apart from Old Testament history and the Davidic Kingdom.

> Deut. 4:5-9; 1 Sam. 8:3-7; 1 Chron. 29:11; Ps. 2:1-12 (Acts 4:25); Ps. 6:8 (Matt. 7:23); Ps. 16:8-11 (Acts 2:25); Ps. 110:1-4 (Acts 2:35); Dan. 2:32-35, 44; Mic. 2:12-13; 4:1-4; 5:2-5, 15; 7:14-17; Hab. 2:13, 14; Zeph. 3:8-20; Hag. 2:6-9, 21-23; Zech. 2:10-13; 3:8-9; 9:9; 14:6-11; Mal. 3:1-3; 4:1-6; Jer. 31:31; Isa. 40:3 (Matt. 3:3); Matt. 5:19; 6:10; Acts 1:6; Rom. 9:25-29; 10:19-21; Col. 1:12-20

Church and State
ARTICLE XXIII

We affirm (a) that the Biblically proper relationship between civil government and ecclesiastical government in any nation consists in each freely conducting its affairs in obedience to God's laws in creation and the Bible, without usurping the other's lawful jurisdiction; (b) that civil government is to enforce on all people laws of civil justice revealed in creation and restated in Scripture, with the physical sword, while ecclesiastical government is to enforce on the church redemption laws of personal and social morality revealed in Scripture, with the spiritual sword; (c) that the state must maintain religious liberty for its citizens without attempting to define correct religious doctrine; and (d) that religious liberty does not grant anyone the right to harm other people physically in their persons, liberty, or property.

We deny (a) that the church ought to rule over the state; (b) that the state ought to rule over the church; (c) that separation of church and state means separation of state and religiously motivated activity; (d) that it is even possible to separate religious motivation from activity in any sphere; and (e) that the church may properly use the coercion of the physical sword.

> Deut. 4:5-8; Pss. 2:1-12; 96:9-13; 110:1-4; Dan. 2:32-35; Matt. 22:17-21; John 18:36-37; Rom. 13:1-7; Heb. 5:5-10; Rev. 1:5

The Kingdom Transcends All National Entities
ARTICLE XXIV

We affirm that the Kingdom of God transcends all national, political, and ethnic boundaries, uniting all believers in its King, Jesus Christ.

We deny that the Kingdom of God can be identified or equated with any geographical, national, political, or ethnic entity.

> Luke 13:27-30; John 12:32; Rom. 4:9-13; Gal. 3:7-9, 26-29; Eph. 2:11-22; Rev. 5:9-13; 21:24

Historic Orthodoxy Supports These Affirmations
ARTICLE XXV

We affirm (a) that the Kingdom of God is a central teaching of the New Testament and cannot be neglected without loss to the Church and the Church's influence upon society; (b) that millennial issues flow from the understanding of the Kingdom of God rather than vice versa; (c) that it is more important strategically for the Church to engage in building the Kingdom of God on earth than for it to resolve its disagreements about the millennium; and (d) that the foregoing affirmations and denials are consistent with the mainstream of historic orthodox Christianity.

We deny (a) that orthodox Christianity has ever adopted a universally accepted position regarding eschatology or regarding the fulfillment of the Kingdom of God, and (b) that Christians should make views such as Premillennialism, Amillennialism, or Postmillennialism a test of orthodoxy.

> NOTE: There are no Scripture references for Article 25 since it concerns a historical period subsequent to the writing of Scriptures.

TOPIC 5

The Omniscience of God

INTRODUCTORY COMMENTS

by Dr. Jay Grimstead

Each of the twenty-four International Church Council Project topics is essential to a sound understanding of historic Christianity, yet some have larger, more far-reaching implications than others. "The Omniscience of God and Human Freedom" is one of those. Dr. Wayne Grudem in His *Systematic Theology*[12] mentions that the quality of knowing everything is called *omniscience* and historic theology has claimed that God knows all things that are actual as well as all things that are possible, so God is always fully aware of everything. There have been seasons in the history of the Church when this topic has been hotly debated. Today a battle is quietly being fought on this topic among a percentage of evangelical theologians.

Christ's Church through the ages (the historic Body of Christ) has believed that God is omniscient, that is, that he knows all — past, present, and future. Among the orthodox (those who believe the simple fundamentals of Christianity), this all-knowing has meant that there is nothing that can be known or will be known that God does not already know. Christians have historically believed God knows the end from the beginning in all details in every area of life, in all places at all times.

Though in theological debate, God's omniscience and foreknowledge can be separated from God's predestation of all things and all historical events, yet as life works out in reality for us humans, God's omniscience and foreknowledge come out to be essentially the same as His predestation of all things. Those two attributes cannot really be separated, though they are distinct attributes from each other and can be discussed separately. Theologians who seek to diminish God's omniscience or His complete predestation in order to make God appear more loving and just than the Bible describes Him to be, do God a disservice by misrepresenting Him and create serious damage to the Body of Christ in trying to help God be more "loving" than He is.

---

12 *Systematic Theology*, Wayne Grudem, Grand Rapids, MI: Zondervan, 1994, 190–191.

There are a few Biblical and theological questions we have which will probably never be answered to our complete, logical satisfaction, which we may describe as "mysteries" whose answers and complete understanding God has reserved for Himself alone, choosing not to share such answers with us humans this side of heaven. Among such "mysteries" are the Trinity, the incarnation, the problem of evil, and God's omniscience and predestination as it relates to man's free will and responsibility. It is our wisdom to be content to remain in the dark at those few points where God has chosen not to give us an answer that appears totally logical to us. Heresy has occurred often within the Church *when men refuse to be bound by the knowledge limits of creature-hood*, and keep insisting on creating an answer where God has chosen to not give us an answer. For example, early heretics who could not accept the possibility of God incarnating Himself into a human being, either wished to make Jesus less than fully God (the Arians, etc.), or wished to make Him less than fully human (the Docetists), both of which are heretical errors that needed to be condemned.

In matters where Scripture claims that two seemingly opposite things are true at the same time without giving us a very satisfying explanation (such as Jesus being 100 percent God and 100 percent man, or God's complete omniscience and predestination on one side and man's free will and personal responsibility on the other), God expects us to accept both of His statements as true and just live with the tension and dissatisfaction of not having a completely satisfying explanation of how both can be true at the same time. Biblical Christianity has only a small handful of such seeming paradoxes. Though Christianity has a few "unanswered questions," it still is far more logical, consistent, philosophically satisfying, and full of the answers to life's larger questions than any other religion or philosophy on the planet. Anti-Christian philosophies and religions have far more "unanswered questions" than does Christianity, and usually have far more huge, gaping holes in their perspective on life than Christianity.

In November of 2001, the main emphasis of the Evangelical Theological Society's (ETS) annual conference (involving theologians who believe in the inerrancy of the Bible) focused on this new form of denying God's omniscience. This new form has been dubbed "the openness of God" after a book by the same name, written by several of its outspoken proponents: Clark H. Pinnock, Richard Rice, and John Sanders. This view teaches that God cannot know beforehand the free-will choices of the people He has created and therefore cannot know the future until it actually comes to pass. It was at that ETS meeting with that debate raging that their executive committee called for a vote to include in the ETS very short statement of faith "that what they mean by the inerrancy of the Bible is defined by the ICBI Chicago Statement on Inerrancy." That vote passed, so it was easier for the traditional, orthodox theologians to win that debate on God's omniscience when it was clearly defined what the ETS members meant by "the inerrancy of the Bible." I know from past experience that some key proponents of this "openness of God" heresy within the ETS had given up on the ICBI definition of the Bible's inerrancy back in the 1970s. Again, this ETS debate shows the foundational importance of having a clear and complete view of the Bible's inerrancy, and shows how the Bible's inerrancy is a basic guardrail and bulwark to keep any Bible student from "driving over the cliff into relativism."

We believe God has given us an inerrant Bible (Document 1 from the ICBI). When we come to any subject, especially the subject of God Himself, we search out what God says about Himself in His Word, the Bible. God is a God who sometimes hides Himself (Isaiah 45:15), and we cannot know Him clearly and accurately unless He chooses to disclose Himself to us which He has done mainly in the Bible, though not exhaustively. Though God gave us a vast amount of information which we need to responsibly carry on life, theology, and ministry, etc., He has chosen not to tell us everything He knows or everything we would like to know. Mankind as a creature needs to rest peacefully in this fact.

The Church through the centuries has believed in the omniscience of God, and though this is not a final proof, it is very significant, for through the centuries godly men from all different perspectives have searched the Scriptures and have continued to come to the same conclusion since the incarnation of Christ. If the "openness of God" professors feel that the teaching of these godly men and theologians through 20 centuries is in error, they should have compelling Scriptural proof for their view. We are convinced they have no such compelling Scriptural proof. In fact, the belief in "openness" undermines the foundation of our inerrant Bible, for if God cannot know the future until His free-will creatures make their choices, how can the predictive prophecy of the Bible be more than very good "guesses" or a prediction of possibilities? If predictive prophecy is only a possibility, it is also possible it will not come to pass. We would then conclude the Bible does indeed contain, or at the very least potentially contains, errors.

What does the Scripture say about God's knowledge? Isaiah 46:9, 10 — "...I am God, and there is no other; I am God, and there is no one like Me, declaring the end from the beginning and from ancient times things which have not been done, saying, 'My purpose will be established, and I will accomplish all My good pleasure.'" An undeniable example of predictive prophecy fulfilled through the free-will actions of men is the crucifixion (Psalm 22; Isaiah 53) in which many specific actions were prophesied including the piercing of Christ's hands and feet, the jeering of those who looked upon His sufferings, death among the wicked (the two thieves on crosses next to Him), the parting of His garments, and gambling for His outer tunic, His burial with the rich (in the tomb of Joseph of Arimathea), etc. Couple this with the fact that the Bible says these actions of men were foreordained in the plan and purpose of God (Acts 2:23; 4:28).

The denial of God's omniscience leaves us with a God who cannot really be trusted, for such a God is ever learning and adjusting to new circumstances coming about through the actions of men. A non-omniscient God could not give trustworthy guidance to His people, for He Himself would not know the future; He would only be able to make educated guesses about the future. However, the primary reason anyone should believe in God's omniscience is that the Bible makes this clear. Historic Christianity of the past 2000 years as well as ancient Judaism believed that God is omniscient, knowing all that *is*—past, present, and future. We believe from the Scripture that God knows the end from the beginning, and there is nothing that He needs to learn, or will learn, for all that is, is in Him and from Him.

DOCUMENT 5

Concerning the Omniscience and Unchangeableness of God and Concerning Human Freedom and Dignity

COPYRIGHT 1988, THE COALITION ON REVIVAL

ARTICLES OF AFFIRMATION AND DENIAL

ARTICLE I

We affirm that God knows all things and that His understanding is infinite.[a]

We deny that God ever changes in His essence[b] and that His infinite knowledge ever increases.[c]

   a. Job 37:16; Ps. 139:1-2; 1 John 3:20; 1 Cor. 2:10-11; Matt. 10:29-30; Heb. 4:13
   b. Ps. 102:25-27; Mal. 3:6; James 1:17
   c. Isa. 40:28; 46:9-11; Pss. 139:4, 16; 147:5

ARTICLE II

We affirm that God's knowledge comprehends all space and all time — past, present, and future.[a]

We deny that the present non-existence of future things and events entails their being unknowable to God, who "calls the things that are not as if they were."[b]

   a. 2 Chron. 16:9; 1 Sam. 10:2-9; Job 28:24; Isa. 46:9-10; Matt. 10:29-30; 1 John 3:20; Rev. 20:13
   b. Rom. 4:17; Prov. 16:33; Isa. 46:9-10; 42:8-9

ARTICLE III

We affirm that God's knowledge is perfect and that His knowledge of the future is as certain as His knowledge of the past.[a]

We deny that God's knowledge admits of either mistake or correction.[b]

   a. 1 Sam. 10:2-9; Job 37:16; Ps. 139:16; 1 John 3:20
   b. 1 Sam. 2:3; 1 Chron. 28:9; Job 28:24; 37:16; Pss. 119:168; 147:4-5; Isa. 40:27-28; Matt. 10:29-30; John 21:17; Rom. 11:34-36; Heb. 4:13; James 1:17; 1 John 1:5; 3:20

ARTICLE IV

We affirm that God knows things present as present, things past as past, and things future as future.[a]

We deny that God's knowledge of temporal relations compromises the certitude of His knowledge of the future.[b]

  a. Deut. 2:7; 2 Chron. 16:9; Job 28:24; Pss. 33:13; 94:9; 119:168; 139:1-4; Isa. 44:7-8, 25-28; 46:9-11; Jer. 2:2-3; Acts 2:23; Rom. 4:17; Rev. 20:13
  b. 1 Sam. 10:2-9; 23:10-13; 2 Kings 13:19; Job 37:16; Ps. 139:16; 147:4-5; Isa. 40:27-28; 42:8-9; 44:25-28; 46:9-11; 48:18; Jer. 38:17-20; Matt. 11:21,23; John 21:17: Acts 2:23; Rom. 4:17

ARTICLE V

We affirm that God's knowledge of the future specifically includes the future choices of all free agents including Himself.[a]

We deny that the freedom of agents in choosing entails either the prior uncertainty or the prior unknowability of their choices.[b]

  a. 1 Sam. 10:2-9; 23:10-13; Job 37:16; Pss. 139:1-4; 147:4-5; Isa. 44:7-8; 44:25-28; Jer. 38:17-20; Matt. 11:21, 23; Acts 2:23
  b. Same as for the Affirmation.

ARTICLE VI

We affirm that the freedom of moral agents entails that their choices are their own, not forced on them by anything external to themselves.[a]

We deny that the freedom of moral agents is founded on the complete liberty of the will from any restrictions inherent in the agents' own moral character or intellectual apprehension.[b]

  a. Jer. 19:5; Hosea 5:3; 6:4; 8:11-13; Matt. 23:13; Eph. 4:17-19; Rev. 20:13 with Isa. 30:18
  b. Gen. 6:5; 8:21; Acts 26:18; Eph. 2:1-3; 4:17-19, 22; 2 Tim. 2:26

ARTICLE VII

We affirm that the moral character of free agents defines the moral content of their choices and that moral choices reveal moral character.[a]

We deny that the will of moral agents either is free from determination by their moral character or defines their moral character.[b]

  a. Ps. 14:1-3; Jer. 13:23; Matt. 15:19; Rom. 1:28-32
  b. Ps. 58:3; Jer. 13:23

ARTICLE VIII

We affirm that God's moral character is infinitely, eternally, and immutably holy, righteous, and good, ensuring that His choices will always be holy, righteous, and good.[a]

We deny that God's moral character is defined by His continuing choices.[b]

  a. Gen. 18:25; Deut. 32:4; Pss. 19:8; 100:5; 106:1; 119:68; 145:9; Isa. 45:19; Mal. 3:6; Matt. 7:11; Acts 14:17; Rom. 8:28, 32; 2 Cor. 7:1; Heb. 12:10; James 1:17; 1 Pet. 1:16
  b. Deut. 32:4; Mal. 3:6

Article IX

We affirm that God created man in His own image,[a] imparting to him, in man's original state, His communicable attributes of knowledge[b] and righteousness.[c]

[NOTE: A Denial was not drafted.]

    a. Gen. 1:27; 9:6; Col. 1:15
    b. Gen. 1:28-30; 2:16, 24; 2 Cor. 3:18; Col. 3:10
    c. Eccles. 7:29; Hosea 6:7; Rom. 8:29; 1 John 3:2

Article X

We affirm that the sin of Adam brought moral guilt and corruption on the whole human race, so that all natural descendants of Adam are born both guilty before the judgment of God[a] and with their wills enslaved to the sin in their own characters, so that all men freely but necessarily sin.[b]

We deny that the effect of Adam's sin is limited to imparting the mere potential for sin and guilt to his descendants, to shaping an environment that occasions or tempts to sin.[c]

    a. Pss. 51:5; 58:3; Jer. 17:9; Rom. 5:12-21; 7:18; Eph. 2:3; 4:18; Titus 1:15
    b. Gen. 6:5; 8:21; Acts 26:18; Eph. 2:1-3; 2 Tim. 2:26
    c. Pss. 51:5; 58:3; Jer. 17:9; Rom. 5:12-21; 7:18; Eph. 2:3; 4:18; Titus 1:15

Article XI

We affirm that just as every man inherits from Adam the image of God, the cultural mandate, and the dignity and rights inherent in being human, so also every man inherits from Adam the guilt and corruption of sin.[a]

[NOTE: A Denial was not drafted.]

    a. Pss. 51:5; 58:3; Jer. 17:9; Rom. 5:12-21; 7:18; Eph. 2:3; 4:18; Titus 1:15

Article XII

We affirm that the faulty definition of free agency as the "power of contrary choice," as some define it, lies at the root of the contemporary movement among some professing Christians to deny the historic, orthodox doctrines of: (1) God's infinite, eternal, and unchangeable knowledge and moral perfection; (2) man's inherent guilt and corruption because of original sin; (3) the substitutionary, satisfactory atonement and redemption wrought in and by the death of Christ; (4) justification as the forensic imputation of the righteousness of Christ to guilty sinners on the grounds of faith; and (5) salvation as the work of God rather than of man.

We deny: (1) that all who believe in the aforementioned faulty definition of free agency as the "power of contrary choice" recognize any or all of these logical implications of the theory; (2) that the fact many adherents to this faulty definition of free agency fail to recognize these implications either justifies a complacent attitude toward the theory or reduces the danger inherent in the theory; and (3) that this faulty definition of free agency is ultimately compatible with the central, orthodox doctrines cited in the Affirmation to Article XII above.

ARTICLE XIII

We affirm that the views of God, man, sin, the atonement, and salvation implied by the theory of free agency as the "power of contrary choice" are un-Biblical, to the extreme of denying Christianity.[a]

We deny that the god of this theory is the God of the Bible. It is instead an idol constructed in the image of fallen and rebellious man.

We further deny that the humanity described in this theory is the humanity described in Scripture, that the atonement portrayed in this theory is the Atonement portrayed in the Bible, and that the gospel outlined in this theory is the true Gospel of the Bible.[b]

   a. Refer to the Affirmations and Denials in Articles I through XI.
   b. Refer to the Affirmations and Denials in Articles I through XI.

TOPIC 6

The Pelagian Controversy

INTRODUCTORY COMMENTS

by Dr. Eugene Calvin Clingman

C an a person come to God on his own, without the special intervention of the Gracious Holy Spirit? Can one live perfectly according to the laws of God without the change of heart brought about by the new birth? Is it possible for a man to be justified before God apart from the sacrifice of Christ? Pelagius said "YES" to these questions; Augustine said "No!" Are all of Adam's descendants (the entire human race) born with sin resident in their nature? Do Adam's descendants die physically because of Adam's sin? To these questions Pelagius answers, "No!" and Augustine, "YES." Pelagianism challenges our understanding of sin and redemption and, in fact, whether or not we need a savior, and stands in sharp contrast to the Gospel in the Bible.

Pelagius lived in the fourth century after Christ. He was a teacher of morality and the Bible, and taught that the sin of Adam affected his descendants only in this way—that by eating the fruit of the Tree of the Knowledge of Good and Evil, Adam set a bad example. According to Pelagius, Adam's posterity sin, not because sin is in them from birth, but because they follow Adam's bad example which they see displayed in the evils of the society into which they are born. According to Pelagius, Adam's descendants have the ability to choose either to follow Adam's bad example, or to do what Adam did not do, which is to perform perfect, unspotted obedience to God and thus win favor with God and obtain eternal life. In this way, according to Pelagius, men are able to present to God a righteousness of their own based in obedience to God's law. Augustine, a contemporary of Pelagius, withstood him in his writings and lectures. The fourth century Church as well as the reformational Church (Protestantism) accepted Augustine's teaching and rejected Pelagius as a heretic. The historic, "mainline" Church (Body of Christ) has recognized Augustine's teachings as the Biblical position on sin and man's ability. Sadly, in our day Pelagianism is one of the more devastating and subtle ways that many in the modern Church have slipped away from (or never arrived at) Biblical teaching. Some evangelical churches that espouse an orthodox statement of faith nevertheless appear to be Pelagian in philosophy and practice.

What then are some doctrinal implications of Pelagianism? First, Pelagianism negates what the Bible says about the Fall of Man by teaching that Adam lost nothing for the human race except the opportunity to provide a good example to his descendants. However, the Bible teaches that Adam's race inherited both Adam's fallen nature (Genesis 5:3; Psalm 58:3; Ephesians 2:3), and fallen position (death, condemnation, and separation from God—Romans 5:12-21; Genesis 6:5; 8:12; Psalm 51:5). Secondly, Pelagianism implies that man has ability which the Bible teaches he does not have, namely that man has the ability, apart from a renewed heart, to attain to a perfect righteousness and so merit eternal life. However, the Bible teaches that man is spiritually dead without inherent righteousness (Isaiah 64:6; Jeremiah 13:23; Romans 3:10-18; Ephesians 2:1-3). Since the Fall, man needs a heart change initiated by God in order to fully obey God's laws (John 3:1-10; Galatians 3:21; Ephesians 2:4-10; Jeremiah 31:31-34). Thirdly, if Pelagius was correct that Adam did not leave us with inherited sin but only with a bad example, then we do not need a savior, but only a good example. Jesus then would be only Example, not Savior (Galatians 2:21; 3:21-22; Matthew 1:21; Psalm 130:8). Fourthly, Pelagius' teaching that man can, of himself, be righteous by obedience to God's law, flatly contradicts the teaching of the Bible (Philippians 3:9; Romans 3:19-20; 10:3, 4).

Can you *make* yourself right before God by keeping the Law? Can you *keep* yourself right before God by keeping the Law? If so, the Bible says you don't need Christ (Luke 5:32), and Christ died for nothing (Galatians 2:21). Paul claimed he was blameless when it came to the righteousness of the law (Philippians 3:6), yet called himself the sinner "foremost of all" (1 Timothy 1:15). Paul kept the outward law (that which Pelagius claimed constitutes righteousness), yet Paul knew himself to be a sinner in desperate need of justification and the righteousness of God which comes through faith in Jesus Christ. Paul's is the experience of a genuine Christian. Pelagius' teachings do not conform to either the teachings of the Bible or to the experience of those who know themselves to be genuinely forgiven and saved from sin.

What implications does Pelagianism have for life in the modern church? Pelagianism leads people to trust in themselves rather than in Christ who is the believer's only righteousness (2 Corinthians 5:21; 1 Corinthians 1:30, 31; Philippians 3:9). Think with me! What happens when one supposes himself innately (apart from Christ) righteous? Motives and actions, which might otherwise be questioned, are assumed to be good. Self-justification and self-righteousness rule the heart, which in turn feeds a growing conformity to the world since human nature is so inclined and the heart assumes its own inclinations and actions are good. This in turn leads to an increasing spirit of "having a form of godliness while denying the power thereof" (2 Timothy 3:5), and slides the Church more and more into the state of the Laodiceans who considered themselves rich, lacking nothing, yet were "wretched and miserable, poor, blind, and naked" (Revelation 3:17,18). Pelagianism sucks passion for the Savior out of the life-blood of the Church; it weans the Church away from her Husband and makes her vulnerable to a flirtatious relationship with worldly standards and philosophies and spirits.

The Biblical (and Augustinian) position regarding the nature of man and his ability is: 1) Adam was created good; yet with the possibility of sinning. Adam had free-will to choose good or evil. 2) Fallen Adam and all his descendants apart from Christ, have no possibility of doing untainted-good (true righteousness). Fallen man retains free-will, but his will, which dictates his actions, is controlled by his fallen nature. 3) Redeemed man in Christ has the possibility of not sinning, but because redemption is not complete he struggles with the sinful flesh and its inclination toward sin. The saints have a renewed nature and yet struggle with the old nature, their free-will can choose either sin or righteousness until their physical death. 4) Man fully redeemed in Heaven no longer has the possibility of sinning, but only of doing righteousness. His will is completely sanctified and made like Christ.

The historic orthodox theologians of the past 2000 years have had general agreement on stating these phases of mankind's ability to sin or not sin using these Latin words from Augustine: "*Posse*" = ability;… "*Peccare*" = sin;… "*Non*" = not.[a-d] Some theologians offer this structure in terms of three phases and other theologians structure this statement in four phases, which we use here.

a. Before the Fall Adam was "*posse peccare*"; able to sin.

b. After the Fall Mankind was "*non posse non peccare*"; not able not to sin.

c. After regeneration a human is "*posse peccare* and *posse non peccare*"; able to sin and able not to sin (to a certain degree with the help of His new nature and the Holy Spirit, but will not be totally sinless until heaven.)

d. In heaven, redeemed mankind will be "*non posse peccare*," not able to sin.

DOCUMENT 6
Concerning the Pelagian Controversy

ARTICLES OF AFFIRMATION AND DENIAL

ARTICLE I

We affirm that, in its original state, all of God's creation was intrinsically good and therefore without reproach.[a]

We deny that any part of God's creation was made immutably and indestructibly good.[b]

    a. Gen. 1:31; Eccles. 7:29
    b. Gen. 2:17; Matt. 19:8; Rom. 5:12; 8:20-21

ARTICLE II

We affirm that man was created good, in the image of God, with a free will that was inclined to the good by virtue of his nature, but with the possibility of sinning (posse peccare).[a]

We deny that the chief excellencies of fallen man are his reason and free will, and that the will is an absolute and indefectible freedom of choice which, from moment to moment, determines itself[b] and is unimpaired by previous choices.[c]

We deny that sin is merely the choice of what is contrary to reason,[d] and that fallen, unredeemed man can at any time avoid choosing sin.[e]

We further deny that man's will, though truly an endowment from God, is at any time independent from God.[f]

    a. Gen. 1:31; 2:16-17; Eccles. 7:29; Hosea 6:7
    b. Gen. 8:21; Ps. 58:3; Jer. 13:23; 2 Tim. 2:26
    c. Prov. 5:21-23; Jer. 13:23; Matt. 7:17-18; Eph. 4:18-19
    d. Hosea 6:7; 1 John. 3:4
    e. (See b. and c. above.); Jer. 17:9
    f. Gen. 2:7; Acts 17:25, 28

ARTICLE III

We affirm that since man in his totality was originally good, his created emotions, impulses, and interests, in their original state, were also good.[a]

We deny that the desires of the flesh, following the Fall, are still without reproach and intrinsically good.[b]

We deny the proposition that desires toward evil are sinful only when they are excessive or implemented.[c]

    a. Gen. 1:31; Eccles. 7:29
    b. Rom. 7:18, 27; 8:3
    c. Exod. 20:17; Matt. 5:27-28; Rom. 7:7-11

ARTICLE IV

We affirm that Adam sinned in total freedom[a] and that his descendents continue to do likewise without any alien/intrusive external or internal compulsion or constraint.[b]

We affirm that in both cases, both physical death and spiritual death are consequences of sin.[c]

We further affirm that both physical death and spiritual death are acquired through original sin and mankind's solidaric relationship with it.[d]

We deny that only physical death, and not spiritual death, is a consequence of sin.[e]

We further deny the proposition that spiritual death is acquired by each man through his own actual sins.[f]

    a. Gen. 2:16-17; Hosea 6:7
    b. Rom. 1:18-32; 2:1; 3:19; Eph. 5:19
    c. Gen. 2:16-17; Rom. 5:12-19; 1 Cor. 15:21
    d. (See c. above.)
    e. Rom. 5:12-19; Rev. 2:11; 21:18
    f. Rom. 5:12-19; 1 Cor. 15:22

ARTICLE V

We affirm that every man at his conception is spiritually dead, that is, rebellious, guilty, and polluted before God by virtue of his participation in and co-responsibility for Adam's sin[a] and that the three components of man's spiritual death explain the need for regeneration, justification, and sanctification.[b]

We affirm that natural man continues to have a will of his own, but since it is determined by his rebellious, guilty, and polluted nature, it is now inclined to all evil and unable to do what is good (non *posse* non *peccare*).[c] Because it is thus utterly unwilling and unable to choose what is good, man's will should be considered both freely surrendered to sin (and thus captive) and fully responsible for sin (and thus accountable).[d]

We deny that every man at his conception is morally "sound," that is, in the same condition as Adam was before he sinned, endowed inalienably by divine grace with natural holiness consisting of reason and free will, and that these are sufficient to enable man to lead a sinless life.

We equally deny that every man at his conception is merely morally "sick," involuntarily polluted by Adam's guilt, and therefore with a lowered responsibility for sin.

  a. Ps. 58:3; Rom. 5:12-19
  b. John 3:3; Rom. 3:21-26; 1 Cor. 6:9-11
  c. Gen. 8:21; Ps. 58:3; Eph. 2:1-3; 2 Tim. 2:26
  d. Jer. 14:10; 2:25; 44:21-23; Hosea 6:7 (See also c. above.)

ARTICLE VI

We affirm that the notions of participation in and co-responsibility for original sin are neither unthinkable nor blasphemous.

We affirm that the idea of all men sinning in Adam makes perfect sense whether all men were actually "in" Adam at the time of his sin or Adam was the federal representative of all men when he sinned.[a]

We further affirm that original sin consisting of rebellion, guilt, and pollution is transmitted through natural generation.[b]

We deny that the idea of man's solidaric relationship with Adam's sin is unthinkable and blasphemous.[c]

We deny that the universal presence of rebellion, guilt, and pollution at conception is inconsistent with the idea of sin as an exercise of free will and implies that God's creation was radically evil.[d]

We deny that God either unjustly regards men before they committed actual sins as sinners[e] or that God is responsible for creating evil natures.[f]

We further deny that the difference between Adam and his descendants is merely a matter of environment; namely that sin in the latter may be explained solely in the fact they are born into a society where evil customs and bad habits prevail.[g]

  a. Rom. 5:12
  b. Gen. 5:3; Pss. 51:5; 58:3; John 3:6
  c. Rom. 5:12
  d. Pss. 51:5; 58:3; Eccles. 7:29; Hosea 6:7
  e. Gen. 18:25; Deut. 32:4
  f. Eccles. 7:29
  g. Gen. 8:21; Pss. 51:5; 58:3

ARTICLE VII

We affirm that Divine Grace is an inner transforming and enabling power that regenerates the nature of man and transforms him from man-centered and corrupt to God-centered and holiness-centered.[a]

We affirm that the redeemed human will reflects this transformation and therefore desires not only forgiveness but also obedience and, encouraged by justifying grace and strengthened by sanctifying grace, is now able not to sin (*posse* non peccare).[b]

Yet we deny the perfectibility of man in this world due to the continuing presence of indwelling sin until the moment of death.[c]

We deny that the term Divine Grace refers to man's natural constitution by virtue of which even some heathen have been perfect men, or that Divine Grace refers only to the law of God by which, to aid man's reason darkened by sin, He reveals what man ought to do, or that the grace of Christ is essentially enlightenment and teaching working through Christ's example through the assurance of forgiveness and the doctrines of the Church.[d]

We deny that grace is merely an external facility that the will may utilize if it chooses to do so, solely a "potential" for leading men into the Kingdom of God, and (sinless) perfection rather than an inward power that exerts an enabling influence upon the will, a principle that inspires righteousness.[e]

   a. Jer. 31:33; Ezek. 36:26; Eph. 4:17-24
   b. Ps. 119:24; Ezek. 26:25-29; Rom. 6:12-22; 1 John 2:29
   c. Rom. 8:29; 1 John 3:2
   d. John 3:5-12; 8:42-25; 10:24-27; Rom. 3:10-18; 7:18-25; 2 Tim. 3:5; 1 John 1:8
   e. Eph. 2:4-10; 1 Pet. 1:3; 1 John 3:9; 4:7; 5:1,4,18

ARTICLE VIII

We affirm that in the state of glory, both human nature and the human will attain perfection, meaning that sin is forever out of bounds and that man will not and cannot sin (non *posse peccare*).[a]

We deny that before the state of glory either human nature, human will, or human action can attain a state of perfection.

We thus, again, deny the perfectibility of man in this world.[b]

   a. Ps. 130:8; Matt. 25:46; Rom. 8:29; 1 Cor. 15:51-57; Gal. 5:5; 1 John 3:2
   b. Phil. 3:20-21; Gal. 5:5; 1 John 1:8

TOPIC 7

The Judicial and Substitutionary Nature of Salvation

INTRODUCTORY COMMENTS

by Dr. Eugene Calvin Clingman

This set of Affirmations and Denials was written primarily by the late Dr. Greg Bahnsen. With very few editorial changes by our committee, it remains essentially as Dr. Bahnsen wrote it.

How amazing that we should need to defend the very foundations of the Gospel from those who call themselves evangelical! Yes, there are those who call themselves Christians, yet deny the Cross of Christ. They teach a gospel different from that taught by the Bible; for from the first pages to the last, the Bible teaches salvation by judicial substitutionary sacrifice! When God clothed fallen Adam and his wife with coats of skins in the book of Genesis, we assume blood was shed in the process, and there we see substitutionary salvation. When we see the Lamb, "standing as if slain," in the last pages of the Bible, we are reminded that the whole message is one of judicial and substitutionary salvation (Revelation 5:12). And the intervening chapters of the Bible are full of descriptions of sin offerings, of peace offerings, of atonement, priesthood, tabernacle, and of blood. Blood, countless barrels of blood! For what? It was substitutionary blood and it was the only hope held out to the race of fallen men. Yet sadly, there are those who still insist the Bible does not teach that Christ's death was for judicial and substitutionary purposes. Jesus' death, they say, means something else.

The historic orthodox Christian belief through the centuries has been that salvation in Christ is both "judicial" and "substitutionary," because the holiness of God requires judgment for sin. Without judicial and substitutionary salvation and man's repentance, sinners will be judged by God for their sin and rebellion, and cast into the Lake of Fire. The Gospel, the Good News, is that God saves guilty sinners, sinners who have violated God's Law, and thus are judicially condemned in the court of God's holiness, where they are held accountable for their guilty deeds. Guilty sinners have no ability to abrogate their guilt, nor pay the debt for their crimes against God and fellow humans. Therefore they must suffer the penalty of their sin, which penalty is the second death, the lake of fire (Psalm 49:7-9; Romans 1:32; 3:23; Revelation 20:14,15). But wait! There is salvation in Jesus! Jesus has paid the price by taking upon Himself the judicial sentence of the sinner's condemnation, becoming his substitute under the wrath of God, and submitting Himself to the death God Himself inflicted on the Cross (Isaiah 53:6,10). In that process of substitution, Christ's perfect righteousness is imputed to sinners, that is, legally, forensically, and actually (in the "heavenly book-keeping"), Christ's righteousness is transferred over to the sinner's "account." Now all who call upon Him while recognizing that their only hope of salvation is in Him, receive the removal of their guilt and condemnation in exchange for the righteousness which is Christ's. As it is written, God "made Him (Jesus) who knew no sin to be sin on our behalf, that we might become the righteousness of God in Him (Jesus)" (2 Corinthians 5:21).

So simple a child can understand it, and though this is indeed the message of the Bible, cover to cover, yet amazingly, there are those who are determined to resist the revelation of God's saving grace, for they exchange the Gospel of our Lord Jesus for a non-judicial, non-substitutionary, non-forensic gospel. This exchange takes several forms.

One of those forms is the "moral influence" theory first advocated by Peter Abelard (1079–1142). This theory says Christ did not die as a payment for sins, but rather that, in the Cross, God showed how much He loved human beings by identifying with their sufferings and, in the process, gave us a model of extreme self-sacrifice which we should follow. In his landmark book, *Christianity and Liberalism*, ardent liberal opponent, Dr. J. Gresham Machen, shows that if the "moral influence" theory is true, then the only thing that makes the Cross of Christ significant is the significance we give it — "The uniqueness of this particular example [of Christ's death], then, can be found only in the fact that Christian sentiment, gathering around it, has made it a convenient symbol for all self-sacrifice; it puts in concrete form what would otherwise have to be expressed in colder, general terms."

Another non-Atonement theory called "the example theory" was promoted by the Socinians, the followers of Faustus Socinus (1539–1604). This theory also denies that God's justice requires payment for sin for it claims that Christ's death simply gives us an example of how we should trust and obey God perfectly, even if that trust and obedience leads to a terrible death.

There are other variations and combinations of these theories, but they all deny the judicial and substitutionary nature of salvation, and in so doing throw away the central truth of the Bible and the sinner's only hope — that the blood of Jesus has been shed on behalf of guilty sinners to save us from God's penalty of death for our sins, to save us from the present power of sin in this life after we are redeemed, and in heaven, to eventually save us from the presence of sin.

The Cross provides forgiveness of sins. How are sins forgiven? They are forgiven judicially (condemnation is removed, Christ's righteousness is given to the sinner) by the substitution of Christ ("the Just for the unjust") in place of the sinner. Without this truth, the Cross is reduced to a sentimental spectacle calculated to capture human emotions with the hope that people will turn to a better life — more kind, more caring, more self-sacrificial. But this false gospel is sentiment and warm fuzzy feelings without the substance of the reality that has transpired on behalf of mankind. Without the judicial and substitutionary Cross, the sins of sinners are left untouched, unforgiven, unatoned; the sinner is left guilty in his sins. The true Gospel says that to those who recognize their guilt and confess their need, there is blood poured out on their behalf, that they might be spared and given eternal life as a gift by his grace (Romans 6:23; 5:15). To all who will hear his voice, Jesus says, "Drink of it, all of you, for this is My blood of the covenant, which is poured out for many for forgiveness of sins" (Matthew 26:27-28, ESV).

DOCUMENT 7

Concerning the Judicial and Substitutionary Nature of Salvation

ARTICLES OF AFFIRMATION AND DENIAL

ARTICLE I

We affirm that the Christian Gospel is indispensably a message about the saving work of the historical individual, Jesus Christ,[a] who was fully God[b] and fully man,[c] whose substitutionary death upon the cross secured justification for believers against the judicial condemnation of God which rests upon sin and sinners.[d]

We deny that Christianity is merely a metaphysical abstraction, ethical program, or social movement.

> a. Luke 2:1-7; Rom. 5:18-19; 1 Cor. 15:1-8; Heb. 13:12
> b. John 1:1-3; 20:27-28; 1 Tim. 3:16; Titus 2:13; 2 Pet. 1:1
> c. Matt. 26:45; 28:9, 17; Luke 1:35; John 6:53; 14:7-11; 1 Tim. 2:5
> d. Matt. 1:1, 21; Luke 24:39; Rom. 3:21-26; 1 Cor. 6:11; 2 Cor. 5:21; Col. 1:13, 14, 22; Heb. 9:26, 28; 10:10; 1 Pet. 3:18

ARTICLE II

We affirm that the Bible presents salvation as salvation from sin's guilt and power[a] and that the measuring rod for sin is God's holy and unchanging character[b] as disclosed through the created order and man's heart,[c] but verbally revealed in the Scriptures of the Old and New Testaments.[d]

We deny that sin is defined by divinely fluctuating feeling, simply a failure in cultural standards, or a failure in man's attitudes or projects, such as self-esteem, positive perspective, affirmation of others, etc.

> a. Matt. 1:21; Rom. 3:21-26; 1 Cor. 6:11; 2 Cor. 5:21; Col. 1:22; Heb. 9:26, 28; 10:10; 1 Pet. 3:18
> b. Lev. 11:44-45; 20:7; Joel 3:17; 1 Pet. 1:14-17; 1 John 3:5-6
> c. Ps. 19:1-4; Rom. 1:18-21; 2:1, 14-16; Acts 14:17; 17:28-31
> d. Exod. 20:1-17; Deut. 6:1-7; Isa. 1:10; Hosea 1:1; Amos 7:16; John 5:39; 2 Tim. 3:16; Rev. 22:18-19; etc.

ARTICLE III

We affirm that as an affront to God's righteousness, sin fully deserves the wrath of God, who imposes the just recompense and inescapable condemnation of death either upon sinners[a] or upon an innocent Substitute who satisfies the justice of God in their place.[b]

We deny that the divine, wrathful, and just sentence of death upon sinners can be mitigated or set aside at the discretion of a holy and righteous God without the infliction of His announced penal sanction.[c]

   a. Ezek. 18:4; 1 Cor. 6.9-10, Heb. 10.26-31, Rev. 20.10-15; 21:8; 22:15
   b. Lev. 1:4; 3:2; Matt. 1:21; Rom. 3:21-26; 1 Cor. 6:11; 2 Cor. 5:21; Col. 1:20-22; Heb. 9:26,28; 10:10; 1 Pet. 3:18
   c. Ps. 49:7-9; Isa. 40:27; Ezek. 18:4; Heb. 10:26-31

ARTICLE IV

We affirm that Jesus Christ, by His death, offered a substitutionary atonement, rescuing His people from the judicial condemnation of God upon their sin by fully bearing the penalty of their sin upon the cross, the righteous dying as a sacrifice for the unrighteous and being cursed in their behalf.[a]

We deny that the death of Christ was merely a utilitarian public example of sin's ugliness and suffering, intended by God to deter others from immoral living, rather than being retributive in character.

   a. Matt. 1:21; Rom. 3:21-26; 1 Cor. 6:11; 2 Cor. 5:21; Col. 1:20-22; Heb. 9:26,28; 10:10; 1 Pet. 3:18

ARTICLE V

We affirm that the reconciling work of Christ removes God's enmity and alienation against sinners who believe in Christ by paying the prescribed penalty which rests upon their objective, legal guilt before God.[a]

We deny that Christ's saving work was merely an act of mediation or a compelling gesture of good will intended to restore communication between God and men as parties who do not trust each other.

   a. Isa. 53:4-6; Mark 16:16; John 3:18; 5:24; 1 Cor. 15:3; Eph. 1:7; 2:13-22; 3:12; Col. 2:13-14; Heb. 9:28; 1 Pet. 2:24-25

ARTICLE VI

We affirm that justification is a forensic transaction in which God not only acquits or pardons the sinner in consideration of Christ's self-sacrifice for sins, but also imputes the positive righteousness of Christ to the legal account of the sinner, this righteousness being both alien and yet constitutive, thus serving as the basis in truth of God's declared verdict of a righteous status for the believer.[a]

We deny that the atonement was merely a pathos-evoking example of God's love, intended to have a subjective moral influence in the heart of believers and leading them to live self-sacrificially by imitation. We further deny that in the teaching of the Bible God's justification of the wicked has a causative quality, that it replaces, elevates, or infuses the Adamic nature of the believer with the actual righteousness of Christ as sanctifying grace, and that it is in any way a divine assessment based upon the inward character of the believer.

a. Rom. 3:21-24; 4:1-8; 5:19; 7:18-25; 8:1-4; 10:3-10; 1 Cor. 1:30-31; 2 Cor. 5:21

ARTICLE VII

We affirm that the judicial concerns of substitutionary atonement and forensic justification are indispensable to the rich and comprehensive work of God's gracious salvation, which extends beyond the guilt of sin to its power, pollution, and consequences as well.

We deny that God's saving work of sinners is restricted to the judicial concerns of substitutionary atonement and forensic justification.

We deny any claim that God's saving work fails to encompass also the breaking of sin's power[a] and the reversing of sin's consequences in the regeneration and sanctification of men[b] and subduing of creation,[c] and in the ultimate glorification of believers[d] and re-creation of the world.[e]

a. Matt. 1:21: Acts 13:38-39; Rom. 6:12-18; Col. 1:20-23; Rev. 1:5
b. 1 Cor. 1:2,30; 6:11; Eph. 2:1-10; 5:26; Col. 3:5; Titus 3:3-8; 1 Pet. 1:22-23
c. Gen. 1:28; Rom. 8:19-22; Heb. 2:6-9
d. Rom. 8:17, 30; Eph. 1:18; 3:6; Col. 3:24; 2 Thess. 2:14; Titus 3:7; Heb. 9:15; 1 Pet. 1:3-5; 2 Pet. 3:13; Rev. 21:7
e. 2 Pet. 3:13; Rev. 21:1

TOPIC 8

The Trinity

INTRODUCTORY COMMENTS

by Dr. Jay Grimstead

The historic doctrines of the the attributes of God including the Trinity and the two natures of Christ form the essential foundation stones of Christianity on which rest many other doctrines and basic truths of Christian theology. These doctrines also provide answers to basic philosophic questions such as "the one and the many" and "the connection between the visible and the invisible worlds." If we Christians do not believe in the Biblical view of the Triune God as expressed in the Nicene Creed of AD 325, and in the two natures of Christ as expressed in the Chalcedon Council in AD 451, some of the Bible's answers to the world's foundational, philosophic questions are unanswerable. But because of these two heavenly mysteries which we cannot fathom logically and completely, we have indeed in the Bible's view of God those powerful answers for the non-Christian thinkers of the world.

It took the careful scholars of the Church over three hundred years to clarify the accurate picture of God from the Bible and we are indebted to them for working it out for posterity. For nearly 2000 years this doctrine of the Trinity and of God's attributes has been believed by the Body of Christ in every country and is still considered to be necessary if one is to be a true, orthodox Christian and to be worshipping the one true God.

Religious liberals who have rejected the Bible as their source for truth have long since given up on believing in the Trinity or the deity of Christ. But within the last century, many Bible-believing people and some conservative denominations have adopted a modern version of the "modalism" heresy from the third century AD, and as that false doctrine taught, they believe wrongly that God is not a trinity of three distinct Persons, but rather is only one divine Person who manifests Himself in any of three different modes at different times, like one Shakespearian actor playing the three different roles of Macbeth, Othello, and King Lear. This serious error has penetrated many evangelical circles and is a deadly, un-Biblical cancer which needs to be exposed and corrected. Because of this confusion among evangelicals, we have included the Trinity as one of the issues which must be addressed by this Church Council Project. We commend to the Church at large this statement on "The Trinity" to help her stay true to the historical and Biblical position held by the Church for twenty centuries and to offer her theological clarification which may help her correct some of her wayward children.

Such confusion and lack of theological clarity abounds in evangelical circles these days that a number of pastors and Christian leaders believe in the heresy of "modalism" while thinking all along they truly believe in the Trinity. Many others simply do not have enough theological interest or knowledge to even care what anyone believes about the Trinity. Thus we offer this one question as a simple test to let pastors, teachers, and church members be able to tell if a pastor or layman friend of theirs holds an errant/heretical view and needs to be exhorted and re-trained. The correct answer is "yes!" And a "no" answer or an "I don't know" answer is a signal that that person holds a mistaken view of God, and is probably a "modalist."

The question is, "Does the one true God, the God of the Bible, exist as a Trinity of three Persons wherein all three Persons are fully God and possess all the attributes of God, but the Father is not the Son or the Spirit, the Son is not the Father or the Spirit, and the Spirit is neither the Father nor the Son?" A true Biblical and historical Trinitarian will answer "yes" enthusiastically.

DOCUMENT 8

Concerning the Trinity

COPYRIGHT 2003, THE COALITION ON REVIVAL

ARTICLES OF AFFIRMATION AND DENIAL

ARTICLE I

Historic Statement on God and Christ's Deity

We affirm there is but one living and true God, everlasting, without body, parts...of infinite power, wisdom, and goodness; the Maker and Preserver of all things both visible and invisible. And in unity of this Godhead there are three Persons, of one substance, power, and eternity: the Father, the Son, and the Holy Spirit. (From the 39 Articles AD 1571)

We further affirm that there is one Lord Jesus Christ, the only-begotten Son of God, begotten of the Father before all worlds, God of God, Light of Light, very God of very God, begotten, not made, being of one substance with the Father; by whom all things were made. (From the Nicene Creed AD 325)

> Gen. 1:1; 17:1, 18:14; Exod. 3:14; 34:6-7; Deut. 6:4; Pss. 65:6-8; 145:3; Isa. 40:12-18, 21-26; Jer. 10:10; 32:27; Matt. 19:26; John 4:4; Rom. 11:33; Eph. 3:20; Rev. 4:8-11

We deny that there is any god in existence other than the one, true God of the Bible.

> Matt. 8:26-27; 13:27; 14:19; John 1:1,18; 2:1-11; 4:11; 8:58; 20:28; Rom. 9:5; Titus 2:13; Heb. 1:8; 2 Pet. 1:1; Rev. 1:8; 22:13

ARTICLE II

The Trinity Defined and Modalism and Arianism Denounced

We affirm that this one, true God exists in a Trinity of three persons and not as three separate Gods, and that we worship this one God in Trinity, and the Trinity in Unity; neither confounding the Persons; nor dividing the Substance. (Last two lines are from Athanasian Creed, fourth century.)

We further affirm that the Father, Son, and Holy Spirit are distinct Persons within the Godhead so that the Father is not the Son or the Spirit, the Son is not the Father or the Spirit, and the Holy Spirit is neither the Father nor the Son, but all three are fully God and possess all of God's attributes being equal in every divine perfection, and executing distinct and harmonious offices in the work of redemption. (Last line is from New Hampshire Baptist Confession 1833.)

Gen. 1:26; 3:22; 11:7; Ps. 110:1; Isa. 6:8; 48:16; 61:1; 63:10; Matt. 28:19; Acts 5:3-4; 1 Cor. 12:4-6; 2 Cor. 13:14; Eph. 4:4-6; Heb. 1:8; 1 Pet. 1:2; Jude 20-21

We deny that the Father, Son, and Holy Spirit are merely three different manifestations, personages, appearances, or modes of action of one single Person in the Godhead as was claimed by the heresy called Modalism (or Modal Monarchianism) of the third century AD and by certain cults today.

We further deny that anyone may properly call himself a Christian who denies this historic doctrine of the Trinity or who denies the full deity of the Son or of the Holy Spirit as did the Arians who were condemned as heretics in AD 325 and as is done by religious liberals of this century.

ARTICLE III

Distinction of the Three Persons Clarified and Mystery Acknowledged

We affirm that within the Trinity in Unity the Father is of none, neither begotten, nor proceeding: the Son is eternally begotten of the Father: the Holy Spirit is eternally proceeding from the Father and the Son. (From the *Westminster Confession* 1646)

Matt. 3:16-17; Matt. 28:19; 2 Cor. 13-14; John 1:1; 5:18; Acts 5:3

(NOTE: All the verses under Article II above apply here also.)

We deny— While we deny that God's self-revelation in Scripture is ever logically inconsistent, *we also deny* that finite minds will ever plumb the depths of all truths about God, and therefore *deny* that it is ever right or reverent for creatures to demand that their Creator satisfy all their questions about Him before they submit their wills to Him.

ARTICLE IV

Attributes of God: Old Testament God and New Testament God—the Same God

We affirm that God, in all three Persons, existed from all eternity and is omnipotent, omniscient, omnipresent, self-existent, indivisible, unchangeable, personal, and that He is perfect in His holiness, justice, love, mercy, and fatherliness in His Being and in all His activities, words, motives, and decisions.

Gen. 1:1; 17:1–18:14; Exod. 3:14; 34:6-7; Deut. 6:4; Pss. 65:6-8; 145:3; Isa. 40:12-18, 21-26; Jer. 10:10; 32:27; Matt. 19:26; John 4:4; Rom. 11:33; Eph. 3:20; Rev. 4:8-11.

(NOTE: All the verses under Article I above apply here also.)

We deny that God's infinity detracts from His Personhood or that His Personhood limits His infinity or that His holiness and justice are ever in conflict with His love and mercy.

We further deny that there is any difference between the Jehovah of the Old

Testament and the Triune God of the New Testament regarding justice and mercy or any other attribute since they are indeed the very same unchangeable God.

John 5:21-23; 8:58; 14:8-11

ARTICLE V

The Bible Our Source of Knowledge of God: Heresies Denounced

We affirm that this one, true God is indeed the God of the Bible Who is adequately and accurately, but not exhaustively, revealed in the Old and New Testaments by divine inspiration of inerrantly revealed language through God's prophets and apostles.

Ezek. 3:1-4; John 5:32-39; Rom. 1:1-4; 2 Tim. 3:16

We deny any and all views of God that negate or deviate from the traditional Judeo-Christian concept of God, including atheism, deism, finite-godism, pantheism, polytheism, or the process god of panentheism. (From "42 Articles on Historic Doctrine")

ARTICLE VI

God's Transcendence and Immanence

We affirm that God is both transcendent[a] over and immanent[b] in His creation concurrently.

a. Gen. 1:1; 18:14; Exod. 3:14; Pss. 65:6-8; 145:3; Isa. 40:12-18, 21-26; Jer. 10:10; 32:27; Matt. 19:26; Rom. 11:33; Eph. 3:20; Rev. 4:8-11
b. Gen. 2:21-22; Job 12:10; Jer. 10:12; Eph. 4:6; Col. 1:17; Heb. 1:3

We deny the Neo-Orthodox and liberal claim that, in His transcendence, God is totally *Other*[13] so that human language and logic cannot serve as an adequate and accurate connection between God's mind and our human minds.

We further deny that, in His immanence, God is ever identified with His creation as is claimed by the pantheists and by many religious liberals.

ARTICLE VII

Supernatural Intervention by God

We affirm that from time to time God supernaturally intervenes in the course of natural or human events to accomplish His sovereign and redemptive purposes.

Exod. 7:31; Deut. 6:22; Ps. 135:9; Acts 4:30; 5:12; Rom. 15:19; Matt. 11-4-5; Luke 4:36-41; John 2:23; 4:54; 20:30-31

13 See footnote 10, p. 36.

We deny any naturalistic view which rejects either a supernatural God or His miraculous intervention in nature and history.

ARTICLE VIII

The Two Natures of Christ

We affirm with the Chalcedonian Creed of AD 451 that when God the Son was incarnated into a human being through the virgin Mary, He was "perfect in Godhead and also perfect in manhood; truly God[a] and truly man,[b] of a reasonable soul and body; consubstantial with the Father according to the Godhead, and consubstantial with us according to the Manhood; in all things like unto us, without sin;... to be acknowledged in two natures, inconfusedly, unchangeably, indivisibly, inseparably; the distinction of natures being by no means taken away by the union, but rather the property of each nature being preserved, and concurring in one Person and one Subsistence, not parted or divided into two persons, but one and the same Son, and only begotten, God the Word, the Lord Jesus Christ...."

    a. John 1:1,18; 5:27; Rom. 9:5; Titus 2:13; Heb. 1:8; 2 Pet. 1:1
    b. Matt. 1:18-20; Gal. 4:4-5; Isa. 9:6; John 1:14; 5:27

We deny that Jesus Christ our Lord and Savior was any less than 100% God or any less than 100% man or that His two distinct natures, divine and human, ever resulted in Him ever being anymore than one single Person, the incarnate Son of God.

We further deny that, having taken on a human body for His work as Prophet, Priest, and King, He will ever, throughout all eternity, exist in any form other than in a glorified human body and reigning as King at the right hand of the Father.

The Trinity

EXCERPTS FROM HISTORIC CREEDS CONSISTENT WITH THIS STATEMENT

Excerpt from The Nicene Creed
(AD 325: Revised in Constantinople AD 381)

I believe in one God the Father Almighty; Maker of heaven and earth, and of all things visible and invisible.

And in one Lord Jesus Christ, the only-begotten Son of God, begotten of the Father before all worlds, God of God, Light of Light, very God of very God, begotten, not made, being of one substance with the Father; by whom all things were made;...

And in the Holy Spirit, the Lord and giver of Life; who proceedeth from the Father and the Son; who with the father and the son together is worshiped and glorified;...

The Athanasian Creed
(Fourth–Fifth Centuries AD)

1. Whosoever will be saved: before all things it is necessary that he hold the Catholic Faith:

2. Which faith except every one do keep whole and undefiled: without doubt he shall perish everlastingly.

3. And the Catholic Faith is this: That we worship one God in Trinity, and Trinity in Unity;

4. Neither confounding the Persons; nor dividing the Substance.

5. For there is one Person of the Father: another of the Son: and another of the Holy Spirit.

6. But the Godhead of the Father, of the Son, and of the Holy Spirit, is all one: the Glory equal, the Majesty coeternal.

7. Such as the Father is: such is the Son: and such is the Holy Spirit.

8. The Father uncreated: the Son uncreated: and the Holy Spirit uncreated.

9. The Father incomprehensible: the Son incomprehensible: and the Holy Spirit incomprehensible.

10. The Father eternal: the Son eternal: and the Holy Spirit eternal.

11. And yet they are not three eternals: but one eternal.

12. And also there are not three uncreated: nor three incomprehensibles, but one uncreated: and one incomprehensible.

13. So likewise the father is Almighty: the son Almighty: and the Holy Spirit Almighty.

14. And yet they are not three Almighties: but one Almighty.

15. So the Father is God: the Son is God: and the Holy Spirit is God.

16. And yet they are not three Gods: but one God.

17. So likewise the Father is Lord: the son Lord: and the Holy Spirit Lord.

18. And yet not three Lords: but one Lord.

19. For like as we are compelled by the Christian verity: to acknowledge every Person by himself to be God and Lord:

20. So are we forbidden by the Catholic Religion: to say, There be three Gods, or three Lords.

21. The Father is made of none: neither created, nor begotten.

22. The Son is of the Father alone: not made, nor created: but begotten.

23. The Holy Spirit is of the Father and of the Son: neither made, nor created, nor begotten: but proceeding.

24. So there is one Father, not three Fathers; one Son, not three sons; one Holy Spirit, not three Holy Spirits.

25. And in this Trinity none is afore, or after another: none is greater, or less than another.

26. But the whole three Persons are coeternal, and coequal.

27. So that in all things, as aforesaid: the Unity in Trinity, and the Trinity in Unity, is to be worshiped.

28. He therefore that will be saved, must thus think of the Trinity.

Excerpt from *Thirty-Nine Articles of Religion*
(AD 1571: Church of England)

I. Of Faith in the Holy Trinity.

There is but one living and true God, everlasting, without body, parts, or passions; of infinite power, wisdom, and goodness; the Maker, and Preserver of all things both visible and invisible. And in unity of this Godhead there be three Persons, of one substance, power, and eternity: the Father, the Son and the Holy Spirit.

Excerpt from Westminster Confession of Faith
(AD 1643–46)

Chapter II: Of God, and of the Holy Trinity

III. In the unity of the Godhead there be three persons, of one substance, power, and eternity: God the Father, God the Son, and God the Holy Ghost: the Father is of none, neither begotten, nor proceeding; the Son is eternally begotten of the Father; the Holy Ghost eternally proceeding from the Father and the Son.

Excerpt from New Hampshire Baptist Confession
(AD 1833)

II. Of the True God.

We believe that there is one, and only one, living and true God, an infinite, intelligent Spirit, whose name is JEHOVAH, the Maker and Supreme Ruler of heaven and earth; inexpressibly glorious in holiness, and worthy of all possible honor, confidence, and love; that in the unity of the Godhead there are three persons, the Father, the Son, and the Holy Spirit; equal in every divine perfection, and executing distinct and harmonious offices in the great work of redemption.

TOPIC 9

The Eternal Fate of Unbelievers

INTRODUCTORY COMMENTS

by Dr. Jay Grimstead

The Biblical doctrine of the existence of hell cannot be eliminated from orthodox Christianity without giving up the principles of the inerrancy of the Bible and its integrity as the authoritative, written Word of God to mankind. When a Christian turns into a "liberal religious person" and departs from the basic teachings of Christianity, the doctrine of hell is one of the first to be trashed. The English philosopher, Bertrand Russell, made these comments about hell. "There is one very serious defect to my mind in Christ's moral character, and that is that He believed in Hell. I do not feel that any person who is really profoundly humane can believe in everlasting punishment."

If God, the Creator of the universe, tells us there is a hell as punishment for those humans who do not honor Him as God and do not accept Christ's atonement for their sins, we as Christians have nothing we can say to the contrary. We have to believe that God is being just in allowing there to be a hell. The part of this doctrine that is so difficult for most or many orthodox Christians to accept is the eternal, conscious punishment of those who are in hell. We would rather have been told by some Biblical writer that hell is just for a certain amount of time until those so punished have received enough punishment for their sins and their rejection of Christ's offer of salvation from hell. Two of the teachings of sincere Christians who seek for an alternate to eternal hell are the following:

First, there are those who believe in "annihilation," claiming that at some point, either at death, or after completing his punishment by spending some time in hell, the unbeliever undergoes annihilation and no longer has any conscious life.

Second, there are those Christians who believe in "conditional immortality," and claim that immortality (eternal existence as a conscious person) is only conferred upon Christians who have been washed in the blood of the Lamb, but does not apply to those who have rejected Christ, whom they claim are annihilated when they die. To the best of our theological knowledge, neither of these positions is Biblical as we claim in this Document 9.

But since the conception of hell's punishment lasting for eternity is so horrible, and so "unthinkable" when we consider family and friends we have known being in that condition forever, many of us Christians wish the false teachings above could be true. This writer (Dr. Jay Grimstead) for one would be grateful if anyone could show him Biblical reasons how he could remain consistent with the inerrant Bible and at the same time begin believing that some lost sinners in hell can be annihilated after paying for their sins in hell for a certain time God thinks is long enough. My reason for believing in the eternal punishment of hell for lost humans is only because I believe I see that doctrine in Scripture more clearly than I see the teaching of annihilation, and my theology and life are bound by the Bible, so I believe in the orthodox view of eternal hell in spite of the fact that I would much rather not believe that it lasts for eternity for all the unsaved. Actually Scripture gives us very little information about the afterlife whether it is talking about heaven or hell. We would have to say our information about our existence after we die or after Christ returns is scanty at best. Yet this is a monumental matter—where we spend eternity!

If I am going to believe anything seriously about the Bible, I must believe also what it says about hell (or other doctrines it teaches). Since the Bible testifies of itself that it is a unity, it is not logical to take bits and pieces of it, believing certain teachings, but rejecting others; that is simply not a consistent place to stand. If what the Bible says about Jesus is true, and since Jesus testified concerning the Bible (Old Testament) that it in its entirety is true, if I am going to believe about Jesus, I must of necessity believe what the Bible says about all the doctrines it teaches, including its teachings about hell.

There are very few passages on the afterlife in the Old Testament, but perhaps Isaiah and Daniel contain the clearest pictures of hell. The last words in the book of Isaiah (66:22-24) say that when all is said and done, when the new heavens and new earth are completed, "All mankind will come to bow down before me, says the LORD. Then they shall go forth and look on the corpses of the men who have transgressed against Me. For their worm shall not die, and their fire shall not be quenched; and they shall be an abhorrence to all mankind." The picture is one of a continuing testimony throughout eternity of a recognition of the awfulness of sin, and the ongoing and complete extent of God's judgment on it. It is a picture of a battlefield where God's enemies have fallen and rotting corpses of the enemy are strewn on the ground.

Another Old Testament passage that clearly shows an aspect of hell is Daniel 12:2: "And many of those who sleep in the dust of the ground will awake, these to everlasting life, but the others to disgrace *and* everlasting contempt." Here is the resurrection which will take place on the last day (John 5:28-29; 6:39-40). We see some are raised to everlasting life, while others are raised to everlasting contempt. Both are everlasting.

The New Testament has the more complete teaching about hell. Jesus' teaching about hell in the Gospel of Matthew has been summarized by Robert A. Peterson, in his book, *Hell on Trial*, P & R Publishers. He says: Hell is real (Matthew 5:21-22, 27-30; 23:15, 33); Hell is ruled by God (Matthew 10:28; 25:41, 46); Hell involves rejection (Matthew 7:23; 8:11-12; 22:13; 25:30); Hell involves pain (Matthew 13:30, 40-43, 49-50; 18:6-9; 24:51).

In an article in *Christianity Today*, a certain pastor wrote — "Once we have given up wrath [eternal judgment/hell], can [the doctrines of] sin, judgment, or the Cross be far behind? Without the one, the others lose their meaning. Wrath measures sin, produces judgment, and necessitates the Cross." (Quoted from: William D. Eisenhower, "Sleepers in the Hands of an Angry God," *Christianity Today* 31/5, [March 20, 1987]: 26). As we saw in Isaiah, hell reveals for all eternity God's wrath (His displeasure and judgment on sin). If we remove the revelation of God's wrath from Christianity, it affects how we look on sin.

DOCUMENT 9

Concerning the Eternal Fate of Unbelievers

ARTICLES OF AFFIRMATION AND DENIAL

ARTICLE I

We affirm that only Christians will spend eternity with God in heaven and that all unbelievers will spend eternity in hell.[a]

We deny that the doctrines of universalism, annihilationism, conditional immortality, reincarnation, purgatory, and post-death conversion may be derived from Scripture or from the history of the Church.

a. Matt. 25:46; Rev. 22:11

ARTICLE II

We affirm that the doctrine of the conscious eternal punishment of the lost must be derived from the Scripture and from Scripture alone.

We further affirm that the doctrine of the conscious eternal punishment of the lost has always been the teaching of the mainstream church.

We deny that the doctrine of life after death may be based upon "near death" or "after death" experiences, or through the testimony of mediums or other supposed contacts with the dead.

ARTICLE III

We affirm that God's justice and eternal wrath are ontologically and rationally consistent with His love and mercy.

We further affirm that the wrath of the Lamb is the same as the wrath of God and that the Son is not more merciful than the Father.

We deny that it is unjust for God to grant mercy to those who believe and not to those who reject Him.

ARTICLE IV

We affirm that God is the judge of all mankind and that all humans will be resurrected and judged. Those whose names are not found in the Book of Life will be consigned to the lake of fire for eternity.[a]

We deny that there are any other options than Heaven and Hell, and *we deny* that there is any escape for those consigned to the lake of fire.

a. Rev. 20:15

ARTICLE V

We affirm that God's integrity would be violated if He did not punish sin, but *we also affirm* that God justly assigns degrees of punishment to those in hell.[a]

We deny that eternal torment in the lake of fire is inconsistent with the Bible or with the character of God.[b]

> a. Matt. 11:21-24
> b. Rev. 20:10

ARTICLE VI

We affirm that the suffering in the lake of fire is real, conscious, and without end.[a]

We deny that it is Biblical to compromise the reality of the consciousness or the unceasing character of the punishment of hell.[b]

> a. Matt. 10:28; Mark 9:43-44; Luke 16:24
> b. Rev. 20:10

ARTICLE VII

We affirm that there is no salvation for anyone apart from Christ's atonement: neither for those who have heard, nor for those who have not heard the Gospel.

We further affirm that the benefits of Christ's atonement can only be obtained during one's present life on earth.[a]

We deny that there is any salvation or escape from hell after one's death.[b]

> a. Heb. 9:27
> b. Luke 16:26

ARTICLE VIII

We affirm that the false doctrines of universalism, annihilationism, and post-death salvation diminish the importance of preaching the reality and terror of hell and the necessity of repentance in this life, and thus minimize the motivation for missions and evangelism.

We deny that these false doctrines minimize the offense of the Gospel, or that by taking away the threat of eternal punishment, the lost will more readily accept God's message of salvation.[a]

> a. Luke 16:31

DEFINITIONS FOR THIS PAPER:

"Universalism" — Adam and every human being since will eventually be saved.

"Annihilationism" — Unsaved humans will cease to exist after death at some point.

"Conditional immortality" — Immortality is only conferred upon believers.

"Post-death conversion" — Humans have a second chance to be saved after death.

TOPIC 10

The Lordship of Christ

INTRODUCTORY COMMENTS

by Dr. Jay Grimstead

The mainstream Body of Christ the last 2000 years has taught that, when the Bible calls people to come to Christ to be saved and become part of God's family, they are to come to Christ as the Lord (Master) of their lives, bowing their knees before Him as their King and living their lives for Him and in obedience to His written Word. If a person coming to Christ does not understand that he or she must take Christ as his or her Lord and Master as well as taking Him as his or her Savior, and does not sense the total appropriateness and moral requirement of allowing Christ control over one's entire life; we say that person is not coming to the real Christ of the Bible (Who, with the Father, created the universe and upholds all things by His power and to Whom every knee should bow), but rather is relating to a false image of the real Jesus Christ. If a person thinks they can come to Jesus as their Savior without coming to Him as their Lord, that person is simply not coming to the real Jesus of the Bible but is deluding himself with a false view of Christ and the Gospel. New Christians who may not understand the basic necessity of obedience to Christ as the only proper response to His salvation, need to be further discipled into the truth.

Thus, from the Bible's perspective, a human cannot have Christ as their Savior without having Him as their Lord. Now when a person comes to Christ for salvation, that person can be truly saved while he may be woefully ignorant of the majority of things he or she should eventually know about Christian doctrine, including the teaching that Christ insists that we can only connect to Him as our Savior by coming to Him as Lord. But if such a person thinks that once they are saved they can keep on sinning to their heart's content while rejecting the concept of Christ now being their Lord and Master, we can say with certainty, that person has not really come to the real Jesus so he is not really saved. Thus, ignorance of Christ's Lordship at the time of salvation is different from rebellion against His Lordship at the time of salvation.

There are some within the Church, even some prominent pastors/teachers, who teach that one need not submit to Christ the Lord to be saved. They say that sinners can accept Christ as Savior and be saved, while at the same time, consciously reject Him as Lord. They say that calling people to receive the whole Jesus Christ, the Lord and Savior, is preaching a "works-salvation," and others call it proclaiming a "lordship-salvation." This division of Christ's Saviorhood from His Lordship is a false, un-Biblical notion extremely damaging to the truth of the Gospel. It started greatly infiltrating the Church in the Western world around 1830, right at the time when dispensationalism and the "rapture-oriented gospel" were being born and promoted. We claim along with mainstream, Biblical Christianity of the past 2000 years that "We are justified by faith alone without works, but not by a faith that is alone, devoid of works."

With all true Christians we "maintain that a man is justified by faith apart from works of the Law" (Romans 3:28; see also Galatians 2:16). Yet the faith by which one is justified is a faith that bows the knee to the sovereign ruler, the Lord Jesus Christ. For the Scripture plainly says in Romans 10:9, "if you confess with your mouth Jesus as Lord, and believe in your heart that God raised Him from the dead, you shall be saved." The word "Lord" is the Greek word *kurios* and it means "Lord" in the sense of "Master," and the English Bible often translates it as "Master." *Kurios* was the title of Caesar at the time the New Testament was written, and so the early Church, who proclaimed Jesus as Lord, understood that a *kurios* is a sovereign ruler; the unbelievers also understood that the disciples were proclaiming Jesus as Lord, King, Master (Acts 2:29-36; 17:7). Most of the early martyrs who died for Christ in the first 300 years of the Church, died because they insisted upon publicly claiming that "Jesus was Lord" rather than that "Caesar was lord" when the Roman Empire gave them that either-or choice with death as the penalty for not claiming that "Caesar was lord."

This false teaching that one may have Christ as his Savior without having Him as their Lord usually comes from those who do not hold to a Biblical view of the Kingdom of God. In God's Kingdom, Christ, since His ascension to the throne of heaven, has been from that time on and now is, the KING OF THE WORLD and, as Revelation 1:5 puts it, is now at this moment "the Ruler of the Kings of the earth." A new believer does not come to the real, Biblical Christ if he does not come to Him as the King of his life Who is to be obeyed every hour of every day in every facet of life now and throughout eternity! If a new believer does not have a heartfelt, spontaneous desire from within himself to WANT to obey this marvelous, gracious, all-powerful God for Who He is and What He has done in both creation and in the salvation of sinners, he is probably not really a Christian.

Also, what most Christians do not understand about the Kingdom of God is that Christ, because of Who He is as both God the Creator and the God-Man

Savior of the world, has the right to demand total obedience from all humans on earth, Christian or non-Christian alike. In fact, our task in the Great Commission (supported by the Lord's Prayer to get *God's will done on earth as it is done in heaven*), is to bring all nations, all governments, and all humans to understand that they are obligated now, before His second coming, to bow before Him and obey Him in every area of their life 24 hours every day. He has this right and He demands it now as He claimed in Matthew 28:18, "All authority has been given to Me in heaven and on earth."

The Great Commission is essentially a command for Christ's followers to make Jesus King-Lord-Master of all nations, all governments, and all areas of life so that the principles of the Bible "govern all human existence in society and state."[14]

---

14 Dr. Jay believes that this statement from the words of Dr. Abraham Kuyper that the Bible "must govern all existence in society and state," is one of the most profound, concise, and powerful restatements of Christ's Great Commission in human language. This statement occurs in the Introduction to Dr. Kuyper's book, *Lectures on Calvinism,* (Wm. B. Eerdmans Publishering Company, 1931; reprint available as: www.cosimobooks.com/b3496_Abraham-Kuyper-1605209333-9781605209333.htm) in which he states how Biblical Christianity is to impact (and has impacted) basic areas of life including: Philosophy, Politics, Science, and the Arts. These lectures were given in 1898 at Princeton Seminary (when it still held to historic Christianity) at the invitation of Dr. B. B. Warfield. This book is recommended strongly by Dr. Jay for all the "worldchangers" for its clear vision of how to rebuild civilization on the Bible.

DOCUMENT 10

Concerning the Lordship of Christ

ARITICLES OF AFFIRMATION AND DENIAL

ARTICLE I

We affirm that for the purposes of salvation, the Saviorhood of Christ and the Lordship of Christ cannot be separated.[a]

We deny that anyone can receive Christ as his Savior while he consciously rejects Him as Lord. This is deception.[b]

>   a. Isa. 55:6-7; Matt. 6:12; 7:21-27; 10:32-33; 11:28-29; Luke 18:18-30; 19:1-10; 24:46-47; Acts 2:37-38; 3:19; 5:31; 17:30; 16:31; 20:21; Rom. 2:4; 4:23-24; 10:9; 2 Cor. 7:10; Heb. 5:9; 6:1; 1 Pet. 1:2; Rev. 3:19
>   b. 1 Cor. 6:9-11; 1 John 3:6-8

ARTICLE II

We affirm that the attempt of some theologies to define Jesus for the purposes of salvation as simply the "God-man," without any reference to the authority of His Lordship, is to present a false Christ.

We deny that repentance is simply or only a change of mind about the identity of the God-man.

ARTICLE III

We affirm that saving faith is always an instrument or means through which Christ saves a sinner.[a] It is never a meritorious basis of salvation.[b]

We deny that a person can come to saving faith unless the Spirit of the Lord draws that person.[c]

>   a. John 3:15-16, 18, 36; 5:24; Acts 10:43; Rom. 3:23-26; 10:9-10
>   b. Rom. 3:27-28; Eph. 2:8-9; Titus 3:5-7
>   c. John 6:44, 65; Titus 3:3-7

ARTICLE IV

We affirm that repentance is prerequisite to salvation[a] and entails acknowledgment of the mind and heart of the sinner concerning his sinfulness, his lost estate, and his need for turning from his sin,[b] and his coming under the ownership and lordship of Christ for obedience to His commands.[c]

We deny that one has the prerequisite repentance if he believes he can adequately deal with his sin by simply implementing a plan of reform.[d]

    a. Luke 24:46-47; Acts 2:37-38; 3:19; 5:31; 17:30; 20:21; 26:18; Rom. 2:4; 2 Cor. 7:10; 1 John 3:6-8; 2:1-6

    b. Pss. 32:5; 51:1-19; Prov. 28:13; Jer. 3:13; Ezek. 36:31; Matt. 3:6; Acts 19:18; Rom. 6:12,16; 1 John 1:9-10

    c. Jer. 31:30; Matt. 5:17-19; 7:21-23; 22:37-40; 28:19-20; John 3:36; 14:15; Acts 6:7; Rom. 1:5; 2:8; 10:9-10; 16:19,26; 1 Cor. 9:21; Phil. 2:9-13; Titus 2:14; Heb. 3:18-19; 4:2-6; 5:9; 11:8; James 1:22-2:26; 1 Pet. 1:2; 4:17; 1 John 2:4; 3:4

    d. Ps. 49:7-8; Jer. 13:23; Rom. 3:19-28

ARTICLE V

We affirm that saving faith is a gift of God's grace that involves a number of implicit elements in one event: repentance,[a] obedience to Christ's call,[b] and volitional trust in Christ alone to impart new and eternal life.[c]

We deny that salvation occurs without the elements of recognition of need for Christ or without trust and obedience in the heart.

    a. Isa. 1:16-17; Matt. 3:8; Luke 24:46-47; Acts 2:37-38; 3:19,26; 5:31; 11:18; 14:15; 17:30; 20:21; 26:18,20; Rom. 2:4; 2 Cor. 7:10-11; 1 Thess. 1:9; 2 Tim. 2:25; 1 John 3:6-8; 2:1-6

    b. Matt. 11:28-30; Luke 9:23; John 3:36; 5:39-40; 6:44; 7:37-38; Rom. 1:5; 1 Pet. 1:2

    c. John 1:12; 3:14-18,36; 5:24,38-47; 6:28-29,35-40,57-58; 7:38; 11:25; 20:31; Rom. 4:23-25; 2 Tim. 1:12

ARTICLE VI

We affirm that in sharing the Gospel with others, it is perfectly Biblical to confront an individual with the issue of his acknowledgment of the Lordship of Christ the Creator.[a]

We deny that this method of presenting the Gospel adds "meritorious works" to salvation or that yielding to the Lordship of Christ at conversion constitutes a "meritorious work."

    a. (See the other Articles of this Document and their referenced verses.)

ARTICLE VII

We affirm that the New Testament teaches the inextricable relationship of justification and sanctification. The New Testament perspective on "salvation" is that justification will issue forth in a life of gradual growth in sanctification as the believer responds to the Lordship which was accepted and begun at the time of salvation.[a]

We deny that the progress of sanctification is uniform for all believers or that it implies perfection or the absence of intermittent sin or struggle.[b]

    a. John 14:15; Acts 15:20; Rom. 6:6-7,15-23; 8:12-13; 12:1-2; 13:13-14; 1 Cor. 6:9-11; 2 Cor. 6:16-7:1; Gal. 5:16-26; Eph. 4:14-5:11; Phil. 1:6; 2:12-13; Col. 3:5-4:6; 1 Thess. 4:3; 2 Thess. 2:13; 1 Tim. 6:11-12; 2 Tim. 2:19,22; Titus 2:11-14; Heb. 5:9; 12:14; James 2:14-26; 1 Peter 1:13-23; 4:1-3; 2 Peter 1:4-11; 3:14; 1 John 1:9-2:6; 2:15-17; 3:1-10; Rev. 3:21

    b. 1 John 1:9-2:6

ARTICLE VIII

We affirm that all true Christians are at various stages of their growth in the sanctifying work of the Holy Spirit, without which there is no "salvation" at all in the Biblical, New Testament sense.[a]

We deny that the New Testament teaches two classes of Christians: (1) those who have accepted Christ as Savior but remain in a static state of immaturity or carnality (so-called "secret believers" or "carnal Christians") and (2) those who have gone on to obey Christ as Lord and thereby then become His "spiritual disciples." This distinction is an artificial expedient and false conception of the Body of Christ.

  a. Rom. 6:11-18; 1 Cor. 6:9-11; Gal. 5:16-24; Heb. 12:14

ARTICLE IX

We affirm that some may accept Christ and be saved who have not consciously focused on the issue of Christ's Lordship, but who have implicitly submitted themselves to His direction and obedience to the Scriptures.

We deny that acceptance of Christ as Lord requires the formulation of any particular verbal expression.

ARTICLE X

We affirm that some who profess acceptance of Christ, without explicitly or implicitly facing the issue of Christ's Lordship, are not saved; and we affirm that these, over a period of time, will likely, by persisting in an unregenerate way of life, make this evident.[a]

We deny that such a persistent life of disobedience to the Lord can, in fact, be the life of any true Christian.[b]

We further deny that there can be a true understanding of salvation where Christ is considered Savior apart from His being Lord.

  a. Matt. 7:21; 1 Cor. 6:9-11; Gal. 5:16-24; Heb. 10:26-31
  b. Heb. 10:26-31; 1 John 3:1-12

TOPIC 11

Unity of the Body of Christ

INTRODUCTORY COMMENTS

by Dr. Jay Grimstead

This document on the unity of the Church was not written because any false teachers were teaching that the Body of Christ should not be unified. Rather we wrote this document because there is an amazing blindness about the Church that prevails among the vast majority of real Christians of every denomination who live in the false assumption that it is appropriate and perfectly acceptable to God in heaven for Christians, pastors, and churches in general to live and operate in any town as if most of the other true, Bible-believing churches in town did not exist! The lack of even attempts at pursuing real, basic, heartfelt unity and ministry cooperation between churches made up of true Bible-believers in 99 percent of America's cities is staggering and has to be a major disappointment to our great God. Over the past 150 years we have taken it for granted that Christ's real people—our eternal brothers and sisters, whom Christ commanded us to love as co-workers and partners in the Kingdom of God tasks—do not have to be loved, communicated with, cooperated with, or sacrificed for simply because they belong to another denominational or independent church. What kind of logic is that? This lack of authentic, visible, heartfelt, cooperative unity and brotherly love between Bible-believing churches in any town is a maximum disgrace to God and to us. According to John 17:21, we can be certain the world will have no reason to believe that God sent Jesus (and that Christianity is true) until the world can see with clear evidence that we Christians in any town love each other and are united in spirit and actions. THIS HAS IMPLICATIONS FOR EVANGELISM AND FOR MAJOR SOCIETY CHANGING. So, indeed, this topic is a very important one in God's eyes and for those who care to bring forth Christ's Kingdom here on earth to some real degree before He returns in glory.

There is a unity ordained by God in Christ. It is not a unity of compromise and accommodation, but of the reality that all who are in Christ are *one people*.

When we consider this unity, we must recognize that in this respect, there are only two groups of people in the world—those who worship the Creator through Christ and those who worship and serve the creature rather than the Creator (Romans 1:25; John 5:28-29; Acts 26:18; Colossians 1:13).

This real, foundational, and eternal unity with all other Christians in the world, past-present-and-future, is established by our being connected to God through Christ into God's very family as His sons and daughters, and therefore being connected organically to all other Christians as brothers and sisters through His indwelling Holy Spirit. This essential and organic unity exists if we are truly saved even if we are unaware of it, or even if our denomination's doctrine claims that this unity cannot exist outside our own denomination. This actual unity exists because all true Christians are all actually adopted into God's family at the point of their redemption and because the third Person of the Trinity took up residence in their hearts (mind, soul, and body) at that point.

It is very much on God the Father's heart and He commands and urges that all true Christians of any local geography not only acknowledge this spiritual, real unity between churches across denominational, racial, and cultural lines, but also operate with other individual Christians, churches, and Christian organizations in such a way that this organic unity is demonstrated to the watching world. And, as Dr. Francis Schaeffer reminded us, God has given the world the right to judge the reality of our Christianity by how unified we operate locally in real time and space. The fact that most churches in most cities appear to operate with the attitude that most other Bible-believing churches in town do not even exist, tells us that the current members of the Body of Christ in most towns need a major overhaul on their thinking and attitude about demonstrating the real unity that exists among all Bible-believing churches, in spite of denominational distinctives. What needs to happen is for Bible-believing churches in any city or county to be able to tolerate the differences (or "weirdness") in other Bible-believing churches in their same city and county, and begin to cooperate so that the various churches and individuals are operating "interdependently" instead of "independently" in the work of advancing Christ's Kingdom on earth, so each is doing its own calling in serving all the other churches in town to help them do their special part as Paul tells us in Romans 12 and 1 Corinthians 12.

It is our conviction that there are many "minor" doctrinal differences between churches and denominations which we must tolerate in others as that which falls within the scope of "Christian freedom differences" and over which we should not refuse to have fellowship and a co–working relationship. However, having said that, the unity called for by Jesus, Paul, and Scripture in general assumes this unity must be based upon a basic, core of Biblical doctrine that states the essence of Christian teaching about God, Man, Salvation, Sanctification, Judgment, Eternity, etc., which it is incumbent upon all true Christian churches to believe and teach. Thus, *there must be a basic, theological unity around which the operational and fellowship unity in each locality is to be based.* The unity God seeks for His Body's expression in each geography is not to be based solely upon good feelings, compromise, and a common social problem to solve, though there are common social problems that may be solved by cooperating with churches which do not stand with historic Christianity.

We have very good news for those Christians who wish there existed a theological document which could meaningfully connect Christians of a broad diversity denominationally together around a cluster of basic, historical points of doctrine. Such a "generic statement of faith" does exist. Biblical Christians from a vast array of denominational differences have already eagerly signed such a "statement of faith" which states the basic, foundational points of main-stream, historic Christianity, but intentionally leaves unstated those more minor denominational distinctives which separate one group from another. All the Steering Committee members as well as all participants of all the conferences sponsored by the Coalition on Revival (COR) have been required to sign this generic statement of faith we refer to as the "42 Articles of the Christian World-view" which is our Document 3 in this book. The participants of these national COR conferences included Calvinists and Arminians, Charismatics and non-charismatics, high church and low church, formal and informal churches, post-millenialists and pre-millenialists, dispensational and reconstructionists, denominational and independents, etc.

Even Catholic theologians have been able to sign these 42 Articles except for the two places where this document states there are 66 books of the Bible which an honest Roman Catholic cannot sign. We thus claim that we have actually seen how a deep theological unity around Christianity's basic doctrines has already come into existence in this generation among those Christians of very wide denominational differences, and these people so theologically connected have been able to work together cooperatively in very productive ways for the Kingdom of God.

Thus there is an organic unity in the Body of Christ, that is, a unity because of what God has made the Body of Christ to be. Humans have a physical body, and the members (parts) of that body are designed to work together interdependently. As the human body must learn to use its parts (members) to walk and to communicate with intelligible language, so also the Body of Christ must learn to live out the unity for which it was designed. The Body of Christ has not yet learned well how to be unified as God intended, nor how to operate INTERDEPENDENTLY as a real BODY. Let us work and also pray that God would bring about the unity for which Christ prayed. As Jesus taught us, let us pray, "Thy Kingdom come. Thy will be done on earth as it is in Heaven" (Matt. 6:10, KJV). We know God in Heaven has willed unity in the Body. We know that He has purposed unity and that it should be attained here on earth to an extent so tangible and visible that, at some point, the world will know of a certainty that the Father has sent the Son (John 17:21 and 23).

We recommend for any Christian leader, pastor, or activist who has a heart-burden for seeing the Church globally, nationally, and locally unified around basic Biblical-theological principles, that they seriously consider using these "42 Articles of the Christian Worldview" as their "generic statement of faith" around which they attempt to gather churches together and the different parts of Christ's body locally and regionally into a unified "Team," "Body," "Church." The visible unity of the Body of Christ in any town is an essential element for both evangelism and apologetics. We commend to you John M. Frame's book, *Evangelical Reunion*, Grand Rapids: Baker Book House, 1991, which may be purchased through Amazon or downloaded free as an eBook from www.frame-poythress.org.)

DOCUMENT 11

Concerning Unity
of the
Body of Christ

COPYRIGHT 1996, THE COALITION ON REVIVAL

ARTICLES OF AFFIRMATION AND DENIAL

ARTICLE I

We affirm that the Bible, in likening the Church to a human body and its intended unity of function, includes all the believers of every level and sphere of human community.[a]

We deny that the Bible, in likening the Church to a human body and its intended unity of function, refers only to individual local congregations or only to the worldwide body of believers.

> a. Rom. 16:3-5; 12:4-5; 1 Cor. 12:1-31; Eph. 2:13-16; 4:4-6; 11-16; Col. 4:15-16

ARTICLE II

We affirm that God ordained elders and leaders within the several churches of a given locality and that they are called to show familial and bodily oneness among the churches and to teach by word, as well as by example, the divinely intended unity of all the believers in the locality.[a]

We deny that the divinely intended unity of believers in a locality necessarily implies a need for frequent large gatherings, or of community-wide sharing in all projects undertaken by believers there, or gathering all local believers under one organization, denomination, or ecclesiastical structure.

> a. John 17:20-23; Acts 1:14; 6:1-7; 15:4-29; 2 Cor. 8:23; Phil. 3:17-4:2, 9; 1 Thess. 1:2-7;
> 2 Thess. 3:6-15; 1 Tim. 4:12; Titus 2:7-8; 1 Pet. 5:1-3

ARTICLE III

We affirm that Biblical unity among congregations in a locality calls for a unified way of peacefully resolving, conciliating, or ameliorating conflicts among believers which transcend the lines of single local congregations.[a]

We further affirm that Biblical unity calls for a unified way of exercising discipline when believers are involved in serious sin with which individual congregations are unable to deal adequately without help from outside their congregations.[b]

We deny that, when some applicable agreement of cooperation with others does not exist, individual congregations are obliged to share with outside persons or jurisdictions responsibility over conflicts or sinful behavior within a congregation.

> a. Acts 15:4-29; 20:17-38; 21:18-26
> b. 1 Cor. 5:9-13; 6:1-8; Rom. 16:16-20; 2 Thess. 3:14-15

ARTICLES IV

We affirm that leaders of congregations within a locality are not realizing God's intended potential for their leadership if there exists some unaddressed great distress within the local community, or if there is some other unmet great opportunity for witness by the Body of Christ.

We further affirm that Christian laymen and laywomen exercising local leadership in government, law, business, education, and the media may often be better positioned or better gifted than local pastors and elders to bring solutions to community problems.*

We deny that it is necessarily the responsibility of leaders of congregations within a local community to give corporate attention to every problem facing the people of the community.*

ARTICLE V

We affirm that to more nearly fulfill the intent of the Biblical picture of the Body of Christ as a human body, and to realize health and purposefulness in the Body, the leaders of congregations and Christian organizations within a city or locality should together prayerfully create plans for sustained ongoing cooperative Christian ministry in and for their community, and seek with the Lord's enablement to call these plans into life among their congregations and organizations.*

We deny that the leaders of congregations and Christian para-church organizations will fully realize their callings if they fail to prayerfully and cooperatively share their gifts for unified ongoing ministry in their local community.*

ARTICLE VI

We affirm that true Christian unity must be based on a doctrinal foundation that includes historic Christian doctrine as revealed in the inerrant Scriptures and expressed in the Apostles' Creed.

We deny that true Christian unity can be divorced from the foundational truths of the Christian faith.[a]

> a. Rom. 16:17-20; 1 Cor. 11:19; Eph. 4:13-16; 2 Thess. 3:6; 1 Tim. 4:6-11; 6:3-5; Titus 1:7-10; 3:9-10; 2 Pet. 2:1-3; Jude 3

ARTICLE VII

We affirm that it is God's will for pastors to have fellowship with other Christian leaders who are committed to scriptural Christianity by getting acquainted, praying together, discussing current issues of concern, and developing a relationship of love, trust, and accountability.[a]

We deny that it is scriptural for pastors and other Christian leaders to remain personally or emotionally aloof from other Bible-believing leaders, or to operate as if the other churches in town did not exist.[b]

    a. Prov. 11:14; Zech. 8:16-17; Matt. 16:18; 1 Cor. 12:21
    b. Rom. 12:3-6; Eph. 4:15-16; Phil. 2:3-7

ARTICLE VIII

We affirm that pastors and Christian leaders in their community or local area ought to seek God's will for what He wants done in their area, and that the normative scriptural pattern is for them to do this in fellowship rather than independently.*

We deny that any one Bible-believing church or organization is capable of accomplishing all that God wills in any given area if other Bible-believing groups minister in that same area.*

ARTICLE IX

We affirm that it is wise and appropriate for God-fearing pastors and leaders of good reputation to form a local fellowship to give a united witness on what is harmful and what is wholesome and edifying in their locality.*

We deny that any agency has authority to prohibit a fellowship of Christian leaders from exercising the responsibilities God has entrusted to them, and deny that Christian leaders can rightly refuse their responsibility to work together against evil in any form.*

ARTICLE X

We affirm that national or state-wide organizations that exist to promote evangelism or to solve social and political moral evils should seek the cooperation of local pastoral fellowships before proceeding with programs locally.*

We deny that any Christian and/or para-church organization from a national or state-wide level should seek to solve local problems without receiving the input of existing pastoral fellowships, and if possible their cooperation.*

---

* See comment on the following page which applies to this and all of the noted paragraphs above.

* COMMENT: We are confident that God's Word, the Bible, teaches these principles. For reference, we encourage the reader to study the principles and examples contained in the verses given under the other Articles of Affirmation and Denial in this Document. For further study we commend to you the following passages and their contexts which contain principles and/or examples of unity: Prov. 11:14; Zech. 8:16; Matt. 16:18; 18:15-20; 21:43; John 17:20-23; Acts 1:14; 2:41-42; 2:46-3:1; 4:24-36; 5:11-12; 6:1-7; 9:31; 11:29-12:3; 14:20-23; 15:2, 4-29, 31-32; 20:17, 28; 21:18-26; Rom. 1:7; 12:4-5; 16:3-5; 1 Cor. 6:1-6; 2 Cor. 8:19; 2 Cor. 8:23; Eph. 2:13-16; 4:15-16; 4:25; Col. 1:13; 1:24; 4:15-16. The preceding is not by any means an exhaustive list. We further encourage the reader to study the principles and Scripture references in the following Coalition on Revival Articles of Affirmation and Denial papers:

DOCUMENT 3: *Essentials of a Christian World View;*

DOCUMENT 4: *The Kingdom of God;* and

DOCUMENT 14: *Christians' Civic Duties.*

TOPIC 12

Church Discipline

INTRODUCTORY COMMENTS

by Dr. Jay Grimstead

This topic, as well as the preceding topic and some others, was not written because anyone is teaching that church discipline should not be happening in local churches. Again, it is because the very basic and necessary action of church discipline in the vast majority of America's churches happens so extremely seldom. In most Bible-believing churches discipline is neither believed in nor practiced, and they do not even have a definite procedure for church discipline. Could the reason for such lack of church discipline in the American churches be because the American Christians are so Biblical and live such holy lives? Not quite. When a church excommunicates someone for committing adultery or continual theft, or all the more, if a church member is excommunicated for homosexuality, it can become a major national news item.

God requires His leaders within the Church to exercise Biblically directed discipline if church members do not live according to the pattern and standard of Biblical righteousness.

Church discipline is a very serious responsibility God has placed upon the Church and particularly upon her leaders. It is not something to be ignored. The health and safety of the Church demands that ecclesiastical leaders diligently carry out necessary Biblical discipline. They must obey Christ to carry out Biblical discipline even if there may be a danger of personal loss of friends, position, or salary. If they are unwilling to do this, they should not be in Christian leadership, and if they are pastors they should resign or take a sabbatical to rethink this whole matter, and in the process, develop enough courage to exercise church discipline as their Lord demands once they return to the pastorate.

If we would be doers of the Word and not hearers only, we must return to the Bible's teaching on church discipline. Church discipline is a very serious matter being ignored by many evangelical churches and denominations. This is to our shame and to the ill-health of the Body of Christ. It is also a disservice to the world for which we are supposed to be salt and light. It is also to our peril—for should the Church lose its salting quality, as Jesus said, *It is good for nothing but to be cast out and walked upon by men.* A child left to himself, undisciplined, will bring sorrow to the entire family; likewise in Christ's Church, when proper discipline is not exercised, the whole Church suffers.

Church discipline is to be exercised both for unrepentant, moral failure and also for believing and promoting heretical teachings which oppose the basic, foundational teachings of the Bible. And within each local, geographic entity a church member should not be able to easily and comfortably join another Bible-believing church when they have been excommunicated from a Bible-believing church. There should be inter-communication between churches in a community, so that one denomination/congregation must honor discipline exercised by another. For instance, if one congregation excommunicates a member for unrepented adultery, another congregation should not accept him as a member. Or if one congregation excommunicates a member for divorcing his wife who is guilty neither of adultery nor abandonment, another congregation should not then perform a marriage ceremony for him and his new partner.

In 1984, I called together the senior pastors of the eight largest churches in the San Jose, California, area to form a Pastors Fellowship and Prayer group which met every month for lunch and prayer and lasted for many years. Sad to say (but typical of most cities), these godly and powerful pastors hardly knew any of the other pastors personally as friends or co-workers before our first meeting; but when we met the first time, God knit our hearts together into a type of pastoral "team for the city" and many wonderful programs for that county grew spontaneously out of that fellowship of pastors over the next few years.

(A rather "spooky" thing that pulled our hearts together quickly at that first luncheon was that several of them had heard from some of their key elders and businessmen that week, that over the coming weekend a "Satanic Conference" was being held in San Jose wherein those Satanist businessmen attending were meeting for the primary purpose to "pray to their lord Satan that he would bring great disunity and conflict among the pastors of San Jose!!! That got these pastors' attention.)

I mention this group because "church discipline" was emerging spontaneously in a very Biblical way among and between these major pastors who were becoming deep and loving friends together and it worked this way. If a man was excommunicated from one of the churches because the pastor and staff did not approve of this man divorcing his wife of 30 years and marrying his cute, 25-year-old secretary just because he wanted a younger, prettier wife, that divorced man was not allowed to join any of the other seven churches if the reason for the divorce became known to the pastor whose church he was trying to join. These pastor brothers, without even organizing themselves to do so, created sort of a "closed-shop-union" among their eight churches where no sinning Christian who was excommunicated from one of their eight churches could join any of the other seven. Also for the record on how such cooperative church discipline affects the unity of the body locally, when any of these eight pastors would happen to mention in their Sunday sermon that they were praying regularly with the pastors of these seven other large churches and were sincerely enjoying that fellowship, their congregation would spontaneously erupt into boisterous applause and cheering. It is our hope that such pastors' prayer meetings and such Biblical and Kingdom active unity among pastors of various denominations could be launched in every township and city of America and beyond for the sake of both unity and church discipline, and for the greater glory of our God.

DOCUMENT 12

Concerning Church Discipline

ARTICLES OF AFFIRMATION AND DENIAL

ARTICLE I

We affirm that Christ, out of love and concern for the nourishment, concord, unity, correction, and purity of His Body, has instituted and established through His Word certain ordinances for the discipline of the Church.[a]

We deny that members of Christ's Church may be disciplined by the Church for, or that their consciences may be bound by, any human law or invention beyond what Holy Scripture requires or permits to be required.[b]

  a. (See the principles and references under Article VIII.)
  b. Matt. 15:2-3; 23:4; Mark 7:6-8; Acts 5:29; Gal. 4:9-11; 5:2-12; Col. 2:8, 18-23; Titus 1:14

ARTICLE II

We affirm that the purpose of Christian discipline in the institutional church is instruction[a] and government[b] and that this discipline encompasses the communication of the knowledge of God's will and the regulation of practice.[c]

We deny that the rigors of human discipline are sufficient to subdue the power of sin;[d]

We deny at the same time that Biblical discipline is a barrier to realization of the divinely ordained potential or destiny of any person.[e]

  a. 2 Tim. 4:2; Titus 1:13
  b. 1 Cor. 5:7-13 with 2 Cor. 2:6-8; Eph. 4:11-16
  c. 1 Tim. 5:19-20; 2 Tim. 3:16-17
  d. John 8:34-36
  e. 1 Cor. 5:7-13 with 2 Cor. 2:6-8; Heb. 12:5-13; James 1:2-4

ARTICLE III

We affirm that the purpose of admonition and discipline in the Church is at least threefold: to maintain the honor of God,[a] to restore sinners,[b] and to remove offense from the Body of Christ.[c]

We deny that the purpose of Church discipline is to impose retribution and vengeance for offenses against mere human traditions or worldly institutions within the church.[d]

a. Ezek. 36:22-23; 1 Tim. 6:1; Titus 2:10
b. 1 Cor. 5:7-13 with 2 Cor. 2:6-8; Gal. 6:1; 2 Tim. 2:25-26
c. 1 Cor. 5:4-13; 1 Tim. 1:20; Titus 3:10-11
d. Rom. 12:19

ARTICLE IV

We affirm that disciplinable offenses include both violations of the Divine Will (i.e., transgressions of a moral and ethical nature and delinquency in spiritual obligations)[a] and violations of sound doctrine, teaching, and Biblical truth (i.e., errors in belief that have the potential to dishonor God or bring offense to the truth).[b]

We deny that Church discipline is limited in scope to unethical actions involving personal relationships and/or acts of moral turpitude.

a. 1 Cor. 5:7-13; (Also see the principles and references under Article VIII.)
b. Acts 18:26; 1 Tim. 1:2-5, 20; 4:6; 6:3-5; 2 Tim. 4:2-4; Titus 1:9-11; 2:1, 7

ARTICLE V

We affirm that vigilant admonition, reproof and rebuke, loving nurture and sound teaching are necessary and crucial as "preventive" measures to safeguard members of the Church from falling into sin.[a]

We deny that churches, elders, and individual believers have fully discharged their duty to discipline if they fail to be continually vigilant in reproof, nurture, and sound teaching.[b]

a. (See the principles and references under Article IV b. and Article VIII.)
b. (See the principles and references under Article IV b. and Article VIII.)

ARTICLE VI

We affirm that discipline in all of its Biblical aspects is non-optional; that is, it is required by God and Scripture for all Church members, including leaders, and is given great weight as an ecclesiastical duty.[a]

We deny that the Church may neglect or abdicate its disciplinary duties out of fear of reprisal, threat of civil lawsuit, or any other external sanction.[b]

We further deny that the civil magistrate has any right or jurisdiction to apply sanctions against the Church for meeting its Scriptural duty to discipline its members.[c]

a. 1 Pet. 5:2; (Also see the principles and references under Article VIII.)
b. Matt. 10:28; Acts 4:20; 5:29; 1 Tim. 5:20; 2 Tim. 4:1-4; Titus 2:15
c. Acts 5:29; 1 Cor. 5:12; 6:4; Eph. 1:20-23; Phil. 2:9-10; Col. 1:18; 2:10

ARTICLE VII

We affirm that in every church disciplinary action, Biblical justice is to be maintained and truth must be carefully established by due process and strict procedural safeguards in the case of any accusation of wrongdoing.[a]

We further find and hereby advise that it is wise for churches to require consent to Biblical disciplinary procedures as part of the covenant of membership.

We deny that any charge may be accepted for adjudication by Church authorities without the corroboration of two or three witnesses and other measures of standard due process.[b]

> a. Deut. 19:15-18; Matt. 18:15-17; John 7:24; 1 Tim. 5:19
> b. (Same as a.)

ARTICLE VIII

We affirm that the components and procedures outlined in the 18th Chapter of the Gospel according to St. Matthew constitute Scripture's primary guidelines for the exercise of Christian discipline involving private sin.

We find that these components and procedures include:

1. Self-discipline (vss. 7–9)
2. Mutual discipline (vss. 15–16)
3. Church discipline (vss. 17–20)

We find further that self-discipline consists in self-examination,[a] guarding oneself against falling into temptation[b] and against enticing others away from the Kingdom of Christ.[c] *We find* that mutual discipline consists in brotherly vigilance against sin and loving confrontation of brethren in sin,[d] first in private[e] and then, if necessary, in the presence of witnesses.[f] *We find* that church discipline consists in: (1) admonition of the sinner and intercession for him by the ordained authorities and membership of the local congregation;[g] (2) adjudication of the cause against any unrepentant offender;[h] (3) appropriate rebuke, punishment, or order of restitution for offenders found guilty, including repentant offenders;[i] (4) excommunication,[j] disfellowship,[k] continued prayer, and evangelization of unrepentant offenders;[l] and (5) restoration and readmission of any offender upon repentance and evidence of sufficient spiritual growth.[m]

We deny that Matthew 18 is the exclusive Scriptural revelation concerning Christian discipline.

> a. 1 Cor. 11:28-32; 2 Cor. 13:5
> b. Josh. 6:18; Acts 15:29; Jude 1:21; 1 John 2:1, 28; 5:21
> c. Deut. 13:12-18; Matt. 18:6; Luke 17:1; 1 Cor. 8:9-13; 10:28-32; 2 Cor. 2:10-11
> d. Lev. 19:17; Ps. 141:5; Prov. 9:8; 27:5; Luke 17:3-4; Rom. 15:14; Gal. 6:1-2; 1 Thess. 5:14; 2 Thess. 3:14-15; James 5:19-20
> e. Matt. 18:15
> f. Matt. 18:16; Gal. 2:11-14
> g. Luke 17:3; Rom. 15:14; Gal. 6:1-2; 1 Tim. 5:1, 20; 2 Tim. 4:2; 1 Thess. 5:14; 2 Thess. 3:14-15
> h. Matt. 18:15-20; 1 Cor. 4:21-5:13; 6:1-6; Gal. 6:1-2
> i. Exod. 21:34; 22:3, 5-6, 11-14; Lev. 6:2-5; Num. 5:6-8
> j. Matt. 18:17; 1 Cor. 5:11-13
> k. 1 Cor. 5:11-13; 2 Thess. 3:6, 14-15
> l. 2 Thess. 3:14-15
> m. Matt. 18:21-35; 2 Cor. 2:6-11

ARTICLE IX

We affirm that active affiliation of all believers with the Church on earth is commanded by Scripture, without which membership Biblical discipline is hampered or rendered impossible.[a]

We deny that, apart from any unique or special circumstances which God may in His wisdom bring to pass, Christians can fully maintain their sanctification and spiritual growth apart from the Body of Christ.[b]

  a. Phil. 1:1; Heb. 10:24-25; Rev. 2:1-3:22
  b. Eph. 2:19 22; 4:15-16; (Also see the principles and references under Article VIII.)

ARTICLE X

We affirm that duly ordained office-bearers of the Church have God-given authority to determine and declare the status of individuals' membership within the communion of the saints, the Body of Christ.[a]

We further affirm that in making such determinations, the office-bearers of the Church act on behalf of God Himself, Who will seal in heaven those decisions made in accordance with His will and word.[b]

We deny that the authority of ordained office-holders over sinners and penitents is limited to mere fact-finding concerning guilt or innocence.

  a. 1 Cor. 5:5; 1 Tim. 1:20; 3:10; 5:22; 2 Tim. 2:17-18; Titus 1:10-16
  b. Matt. 18:18-19; 2 Cor. 2:6-10

ARTICLE XI

We affirm that public sins should be publicly exposed,[a] publicly adjudicated, and, if guilt is found, publicly punished by duly ordained and constituted Church authority.[b]

We further affirm that this authority may be vested in Church office-holders (elders, bishops, presbyters, overseers) or in councils of the Church.

We deny that public sins are adequately addressed through private or confidential disciplinary actions.

  a. 1 Tim. 5:20
  b. 1 Cor. 5:5; 1 Tim. 1:20; 3:10; 5:22; 2 Tim. 2:17-18; Titus 1:10-16

ARTICLE XII

We affirm that local congregations have a responsibility toward one another for inter-church, mutual care, and discipline, for the maintenance of purity in practice and doctrine.

We affirm further that local congregations must honor and respect one another's discipline of delinquent members, when that discipline has been carried out in accordance with the dictates of Scripture.[a]

We deny that any congregation is a totally independent entity and has no accountability elsewhere within the true universal Body of Christ. Moreover, we find reprehensible and unscriptural the common practice of certain churches to accept, without consultation and examination, members of other churches who are or have been under Biblical discipline, censure, disfellowship, or ban of excommunication in another congregation.[b]

a. 1 Cor. 1:10; 11:18-19; Phil. 1:27; Jude 1:3
b. 1 Cor. 1:10; 11:18-19; Phil. 1:27; Jude 1:3; (Also see the principles and references under Article VIII.)

ARTICLE XIII

We affirm that on the basis of the Word of God it is possible to discern the True Church of Christ and to distinguish it from the false church.

We affirm that the True Church is known by its acknowledgment of Christ as Head of the Church, by the pure preaching of the Gospel, by pure administration of the sacraments / ordinances, by faithful exercise of Christian discipline, by the management of all things according to the Word of God, and by the rejection of all things contrary thereto.[a]

We deny that a church may consider itself pure or part of the True Body of Christ if it elevates any authority above Christ and His Word, neglects the Biblical administration of sacraments/ordinances, admits the validity of non-Biblical or extra-Biblical doctrines of man, or persecutes those who live holy lives in accordance with the Word of God.[b]

a. Matt. 7:15-27; Rom. 16:17-18; 2 Thess. 3:6, 14-15; 1 Tim. 6:3-5; Titus 3:10; Gal. 1:8; 2 John 1:10-11; Rev. 2:9
b. 1 Cor. 11:1-2, 17-34; Phil. 4:9; 2 Thess. 2:15; 3:6; Rev. 2:1-3:22

ARTICLE XIV

We affirm that no true Christian believer may rightly before Christ separate himself from the True Church.[a]

We deny that a true Christian believer may rightly join himself to or remain a member of a false church. They place themselves in grave spiritual danger who, for the sake of tradition, expedience, status, convenience, or other false motives, refuse to separate themselves from the false church or to bring that church under righteous judgment.[b]

a. 1 Cor. 12:12-31; Heb. 10:25
b. 1 Cor. 15:33; 2 Cor. 6:14-7:1; 2 Thess. 3:6, 14; Rev. 2:2, 9, 14-15, 20-23; 3:14-22

TOPIC 13

Culture, Contextualization, and Missions

INTRODUCTORY COMMENTS

by Dr. Eugene Calvin Clingman

From the tiny country of Israel in about AD 33, like an overflowing fountain, the message ran forth to cover the earth. In two millennia the Gospel has fairly effaced the old pagan world and created a new "civilized" culture. This message, the Gospel, the power of God for salvation to everyone who believes, has changed the world!

The Gospel is God's message to the human race, the fallen, sinful race of Adam and Eve. Since all humans are descended from Adam, the Gospel message is universal and doesn't need to be changed from culture to culture. All Adam's descendants have the same need—that their sins be forgiven, that they be freed from the dominion of sin, and that they find acceptance with God.

If the Gospel that carries this life-giving message is changed, it is no longer the Good News, the Gospel. This is the message that changes cultures and should never itself be changed by culture.

The Gospel is trans-cultural. Change the culture with the Gospel and you have a Christian (or progressively Christ-like) culture. Change the Gospel to "fit the culture" and you have a false gospel that leaves the culture pagan, the message having been emptied of its power.

Culture surrounds a human being as water surrounds a fish. As a fish takes his environment for granted and is unaware that there are other environments in which creatures live, so we humans take for granted the way we think, dress, communicate, etc., being barely aware that there are people who are very different culturally. There are many cultures in the world, and no culture perfectly glorifies God. Our natural tendency is to feel that the way we live and think (our culture) is superior to other cultures. If a missionary is not aware of his own cultural inclinations, he may be found presenting his culture in addition to, or rather than, the Gospel of God's grace; he must learn to distinguish between the essence of the Gospel and his culture. The missionary also must not reduce, mix (syncretize), or compromise the Gospel. Paul became all things to all men, but he never altered the Gospel to do so.

Contextualization is that process of taking the Gospel received in one's own culture to a different culture and effectively communicating the unchangeable message in a form that is culturally understandable and acceptable to the receiving culture. The Gospel is not changed, but only presented in a manner that is not culturally offensive. The Gospel itself may be offensive, but we need not clothe the Gospel in American or British, etc. culture which may, in itself, be offensive to the receiving culture.

An example of failure to contextualize the Gospel is seen when missionaries to India thought it essential for vegetarian Hindu converts to eat meat. Yet eating meat is not part of the Gospel. It is not essential to eat meat in order to be saved or to progress in sanctification. Hindus can become fine Christians without ever eating meat.

An example of successful contextualizing is seen in Hudson Taylor, the great pioneer missionary and founder of the China Inland Mission. Taylor shed the British clerical garments the other missionaries continued to wear, and put on the garments of the Chinese clergy. He cut his hair like the Chinese and ate Chinese food. But because he did not compromise the Gospel, but merely clothed the message and the messenger so that the Chinese were not immediately repulsed by a message packaged in foreign attire, Hudson Taylor had tremendous success. Contextualization is a good and necessary process.

Unfortunately there are those who have twisted the concept of contextualization and in so doing, the Gospel itself. For this reason the Coalition on Revival has written the theological affirmation and denial document titled, "Concerning Culture, Contextualization, and the Gospel." Within the Church, in some Christian colleges and seminaries, and in some mission agencies there are those who hold that it is desirable, even necessary to modify the Gospel to make it meaningful to other cultures. Our affirmation and denial document contends that the Gospel cannot be changed without its becoming other than the Gospel. This document also suggests guidelines and principles for contextualization.

DOCUMENT 13

Concerning Culture, Contextualization, and the Gospel

COPYRIGHT 2003, THE COALITION ON REVIVAL

ARTICLES OF AFFIRMATION AND DENIAL

ARTICLE I

We affirm that man is a cultural being.[15]

We deny that any group of people can function apart from cultural realities.

ARTICLE II

We affirm that culture is the secondary environment men superimpose over their natural environment. Culture is the ways of thinking, willing, feeling, speaking, and acting shared by a particular people group; culture is man-made, learned, integrated, and constantly changing, and is important to all considerations having to do with an understanding and communication of truth, especially of divine truth revealed in Holy Scripture.

We deny that human interpreters of the Bible, such as missionaries, pastors, and teachers, can ever be truly culture free or that it is possible for them to transcend perfectly cultural limitations and considerations when obeying injunctions such as those having to do with studying and preaching the Word of God and with discipling the nations.

ARTICLE III

We affirm that culture is created by human beings and that all cultures reflect both the image of God inherent in mankind and the sinfulness involved in Adam's fall.

---

15 Other of the Coalition on Revival affirmation and denial documents have been notated with verses pertaining to the principles contained in them. This document, however, is not so notated. Instead we refer the reader to several documents foundational to a Christian worldview necessary for understanding the principles that pertain to the Great Commission task with which this document deals. We refer the reader to: Document 3: "Concerning the Essentials of a Christian World View"; Document 4: "Concerning the Kingdom of God"; and Document 10: "Concerning the Lordship of Christ." We suggest careful attention be paid to those principles involving the nature of man, the advance of the Gospel among the nations by means of the Great Commission, and the reality of the sovereignty and exclusivity of Jesus Christ.

We deny that there is presently any culture which conforms perfectly to God-ordained culture revealed in the Bible, or that there is any particular culture to which all others must conform.

ARTICLE IV

We affirm that the various cultures are relatively "good" or "bad" dependent upon the degree to which they reflect God's character and promote His purposes as stated in Scripture both for their members and the larger good of creation as a whole.

We deny all cultural relativity that concludes that the ideas, behaviors, and institutions of a given culture can be properly evaluated by members of that culture only, or simply on the basis of whether or not they function so as to promote its collective purposes.

ARTICLE V

We affirm that all cultures are under the judgment of the Triune God and His revealed Word, the Bible, and that therefore Christ and culture are often in conflict.

We deny that the people of any culture are exempt from the moral obligation to conduct their individual and cultural affairs in obedience to the Bible and in ways that please the one, true God.

ARTICLE VI

We affirm that God is working out His sovereign will and desires that cultures be transformed so as to operate according to the principles of Scripture in all areas of life and to thus make an optimum contribution to the ends of His divine purpose for all cultures and to the welfare of their members.

We deny that any culture has yet been fully transformed to its optimum potential, according to the pattern of God's will revealed in His Word, the Bible.

ARTICLE VII

We affirm that the primary purpose of the Church is to glorify God, and that her primary mission is to proclaim the Gospel and disciple people of all cultures so that they in turn will be salt and light in the world, and work for cultural transformation that is in agreement with God's purposes and principles, thus filling the earth with godly culture to the glory of God.

We deny that it is a primary obligation of missionaries, missions, or other Christian agencies foreign to a given culture to attempt to transform a culture by imposing change from the outside, though it is legitimate and beneficial for missionaries and agencies to do this to the degree the New Testament calls for such changes, especially when these changes are inspired by the changed people within the respondent culture.

ARTICLE VIII

We affirm that the Christian's primary loyalty and obedience is to Christ and His Kingdom and only secondarily to the Christian's own culture and civil government.

We deny that this view means the Christian is not required to be in submission to legitimate earthly powers and systems so long as they do not require him to disobey Biblical principles.

ARTICLE IX

We affirm that God's Kingdom is advanced whenever His people are governed by His authority, and by that authority promote Biblical holiness, righteousness, justice, and truth, as well as grace, mercy, love, and liberty.

We deny that God's Kingdom is coming to earth within any culture by social, political, financial, sociological, and educational action alone, without the working of the Holy Spirit through Christ's true Church.

We further deny that the goal in discipling the nations is limited to presentation of a "simple gospel" of only saving people from hell and helping them to "cope" with life until they are taken from the earth.

ARTICLE X

We affirm that in the Great Commission task of discipling the nations it is essential that the Biblical Gospel be made understandable, meaningful, and relevant to the people of any given culture by proclamation (preaching), as well as by verbal and nonverbal forms of communication normally utilized in that culture.

We deny that proclamation (preaching) is out of place in any culture.

We further deny that any other cross-cultural forms of communication foreign to the ordinary intercourse of a given culture are adequate to the task of discipling its people.

ARTICLE XI

We affirm that to attempt to influence any culture for Christ by using missionary principles, methods, or teachings which are foreign or contrary to the inerrant Scriptures as the Word of God and to historic Christian doctrine diminishes the spread of the true Gospel taught by Christ and the apostles and is destructive for individuals and for the respondent culture as a whole.

We deny that the teaching of the full, accurate message of the inerrant and infallible Bible and employing missionary principles and methods consistent with holy Scripture is ever damaging to the welfare of the people in the respondent culture, even if that message and those principles and methods are considered politically incorrect or if they cause uncomfortable confrontation or greatly alter and replace large portions of that culture and destroy long-held, local beliefs.

ARTICLE XII

We affirm that the Biblical theory of economics offers the greatest blessings to individuals and to all societies and includes the rights to own private property and the means of production; to engage in free enterprise minimally governed by civil authority, and the responsibility for the compassionate use of accumulated wealth, and the implementation of all business transactions according to Biblical justice and honesty.

We deny that any Biblical missionary or cross-cultural minister may legitimately promote socialism, Marxism, Nazism, "Liberation Theology," or the redistribution of wealth by civil governments since these philosophies and activities are un-Biblical.

ARTICLE XIII

We affirm that historic Western thought, forms, and lifestyles have developed to a great extent as a result of the influence of the Bible's worldview on Western cultures.

We deny that contextualization of the Gospel is only a disguised process of exporting Western thought forms and lifestyles in the name of Christianity.

We further deny that it is legitimate to say that Biblical Christianity is a uniquely Western system or that our definition of contextualization herein may rightly be called cultural chauvinism or paternalism.

ARTICLE XIV

We affirm that authentic Christian contextualization is primarily concerned with, though not confined to, the communication of the truth of divine revelation in the Scriptures, and as such is concerned with the translation, interpretation, and exposition of the Biblical text as understood in accordance with recognized principles of historical-grammatical interpretation.

We deny the validity of contextualization approaches based on experiences thought somehow to parallel the revelatory experiences of the Biblical writers under the inspiration of the Holy Spirit, or out of an effort merely to replicate upon contemporary respondents the impact Biblical text had upon its original hearers; or out of attempts to interpret Scripture on the basis of insights gained from the experiences, needs, and expectations of contemporary culture.

We further deny any contextualization approach that is considered to be on the same level of authority as the Holy Scriptures.

ARTICLE XV

We affirm that all truth is God's truth, the contextualization of the Gospel is greatly aided by an understanding of the various related arts and sciences, and that those contributions of disciplines such as anthropology, psychology, logic, linguistics, communications, and rhetoric that prove to be true, should not only be identified and utilized, but recognized as gifts of a gracious Creator and missionary God.

We deny that the findings of the various related arts and sciences alone provide a sufficient basis for, or can be the final determining force for, understanding, evolving, or implementing contextualization attempts.

ARTICLE XVI

We affirm that God Himself provided the best models of contextualization when He revealed His Person and plan through human language in the Old and New Testament Scripture; when He sent His Son Jesus Christ to reveal Himself to the world as a fellow human being; and when, for our learning, He informed us by the ministries of patriarchs, prophets, apostles, and others of Bible times who communicated divine messages to their contemporaries, and through the inspired text of Scripture, to all people everywhere and of all times.

We deny that models for authentic Christian contextualization may be taken from any source other than the Scriptures, except when such models parallel scriptural truth and thus elucidate and illustrate the scriptural models and truth.

ARTICLE XVII

We affirm that authentic Christian contextualization efforts convey the historical unfolding of divine revelation from Genesis to Revelation; display the centrality of Christ's person, words, and works to the plan of God; and reflect the experiences of those men chosen by God to author Scripture and otherwise communicate the Gospel to the peoples of the world.

We deny that cybernetic, dynamic equivalence, worldview, decision process, and similar models of communication and contextualization provide frameworks for Christian contextualization that are to be considered anything more than complementary to models already available in Biblical injunctions and examples.

ARTICLE XVIII

We affirm that it is critical that the contextualization task be undertaken in conjunction with representatives of the respondent culture and that, ultimately, contextualization becomes the responsibility of Christian leaders and laity indigenous to that culture.

We deny that the representatives of the respondent culture are obligated to adopt the culture of the cross-cultural worker or missionary, or that they have no responsibility to communicate Christ within and through their own culture.

ARTICLE XIX

We affirm that only those for whom the respondent culture is their first culture are in a position to understand the nuances of language and the meaning of such vehicles and aspects of communication as lifestyle, ritual, drama, architecture, media, and the like as can best be expected to avoid that which is deleterious, utilize that which is redeemable, and institute such new forms as will be contributive to Christian faith and practice.

We deny that either communication experts foreign to the respondent culture, or experts within the culture acting independently of the larger body of Christ, are well prepared and positioned to work out adequate contextualizations of the Gospel apart from the participation of the members of Christ and the local church.

ARTICLE XX

We affirm that the ultimate goal of Christian contextualization is the glorification of the Triune God Who desires to be known and is worthy of the worship of all His creatures.

We deny that Christian contextualization is designed so as to effect purely human and temporal purposes however desirable and noble.

TOPIC 14

Christians' Civic Duties

INTRODUCTORY COMMENTS

by Dr. Eugene Calvin Clingman

It was my first or second year of Bible College. I was standing outside the Chapel among a circle of upper-classmen and teachers when the discussion turned to a certain Christian leader who had written a book in which he taught that God expects Christians to be change agents in every area of culture, including government. I don't remember the words exchanged that morning, but I do remember that the man being discussed was considered by my seniors to be a liberal, because he taught that politics and government should not be left to unbelievers. This was but one experience that came from my evangelical culture that clouded my perception and cultivated in me the misconception that it is somewhat less than Christian to be involved in politics or government.

The problem is not that politics is worldly and therefore Christians should not be involved. Christians colonized North America and gave the United States a government that has been the envy of the world. About 180 years ago Christians began to acquiesce before the wicked (Proverbs 25:26), leaving politics to unbelievers. Christians who held an un-Biblical dichotomy view of the "sacred and the secular" and of "Christianity and the world" became preoccupied with the coming of Jesus and internal holiness. They forsook God's dominion mandate to Christianize the culture by discipling the nations, carrying God's holiness into every realm of every nation, including our own. Politics soon became worldly, dominated by worldly men, not because it is an unholy realm, but because Christians who should have continued to take the lead, as they had in the past, backed away. It is as if the "Christian team" left the playing field altogether (in the fields of Law, Government, Economics, Education, Science, and the Arts), went back into the locker room, and let the other team make all the scores without any opposition to societal evil. The result was that we Christians, who were supposed to be the head, became the tail. Today, all Americans suffer, as vileness rather than righteousness is exalted in our land (Psalm 12:8; Proverbs 14:34). Christians abdicated our responsibility and we, as well as our whole nation, suffer the consequences.

Is politics Christian?

The Bible says concerning the orphan and widow that they should not be oppressed, but does not stop there. It goes much farther. It instructs us to "seek justice, reprove the ruthless; defend the orphan, plead for the widow" (Isaiah 1:17; see also 1:23). The question to ask is this: How can we fulfill these commands without being involved in places of power and influence so that we can deliver the widow whose property is taxed so that she eventually loses her home, or the orphan whose father not only divorces his wife but also abandons his family financially.

Jesus taught us to daily pray, *Father, Thy Kingdom come, Thy will be done, on earth.* But the Bible nowhere teaches us to pray only. We are also to fight (strive, labor) for justice and for the delivery of the oppressed, be they oppressed by an individual, group, or by a government that overreaches its God-given authority.

Here is a one-question worldview test. The question is multiple-choice and goes like this: When there is a proposition to increase property taxes (an affliction that weighs heavily on widows and single mothers, many of whom have children orphaned by covenant-breaking fathers), what should Christians do? Choose your answer: (1) Sit by as misguided or wicked politicians set heavier and heavier burdens on the people. (2) Seek (by prayer and political effort) to elect godly people to places of decision and influence in order to promote the justice and mercy of God's law. (3) Diligently vote using righteous judgment to promote Biblical principles in our society. (4) God is not concerned with politics of this world, therefore don't be bothered; let the wicked run government; don't even bother voting; Jesus will save us out of this mess soon! If you answered (1), you are in the majority of evangelical Christians; though they would not answer verbally this way, their actions speak louder than words. If you answered (4), you are in agreement with Jehovah's Witnesses! If you answered (2) and also (3), I believe you gave a Biblical answer.

The COR topic, "Concerning Christians' Civic Duties," sets forth the Biblical perspective that Christians everywhere should promote Biblical justice within their society by faithfully voting, by running for public office or by encouraging those who run, and by being godly change-agents as much as possible within their political structure; the opportunity will vary. In a dictator-run country there is much less opportunity than in a free country such as the United States. We must use the liberty we have to promote justice and to relieve the oppressed as well as to proclaim the Gospel of the Kingdom. To truly do this, Christians must be involved in politics. By the way, are you registered to vote?

DOCUMENT 14

Concerning Christians' Civic Duty

PREAMBLE

From the beginning of time, people have gathered together in groups, starting with two in the Garden, developing into larger family groups, and finally into nations. With marvelous forethought, God has provided standards for this kind of interpersonal conduct, both for families and for venues we might label as civic arenas. These standards are found most concisely in the Decalogue given to Moses, but they are also interspersed throughout all of the Bible. The Bible therefore is our textbook for civic action. It contains principles that are valid and workable for all people, all cultures, and all time. It must be society's starting point today.

Heroes of the Church in past centuries have recognized there are different jurisdictions within society, each being directly accountable to God, and each of which has certain boundaries and its own governmental structure. Those jurisdictions are: Self-Government, Family Government, Ecclesiastical Government, and Civil (state) Government. Tyranny arises whenever any one of these jurisdictions steps beyond its own God-given boundaries and interferes un-Biblically with the legitimate action of any of the other jurisdictions or makes un-Biblical attempts to control those other jurisdictions.

Civic actions are relevant to all members of the group, because no one in society can function long without affecting others. Choices have consequences, not only for oneself, but for others also. In society we live with and in dependence on others. In order to function in this relationship, we need mutually acceptable rules to ensure that our actions are relatively predictable and fair. (1 Corinthians 12:12-31; Romans 13:1-7; 1 Peter 2:13-17).

The following statements of affirmation and denial are submitted in the context of the Coalition on Revival's (COR's) Foundation Documents, including specifically (1) "The Chicago Statement on Biblical Inerrancy," (2) the "42 Articles of Essentials of a Christian World View," and (3) the "Articles of Affirmation and Denial Concerning the Kingdom of God." This document also is consistent with the principles of the COR Worldview Documents dealing with Law, Government, and Political Action.

ARTICLES OF AFFIRMATION AND DENIAL

ARTICLE I

We affirm that God created the family as the foundation of society. (Family is defined here as single- or multi-generational units of persons related by blood, heterosexual marriage, or adoption.)[a]

We deny that healthy culture or society can be nurtured or maintained while civil government is indifferent or antagonistic toward the family, or when there is a governmental preference toward the individual which does not simultaneously maintain the integrity of the family.

>   a. Gen. 1:27; 2:22-24; 5:2; Pss. 127:1-5; 128:1-6; Ezek. 22:7; Matt. 19:4-6; Eph. 5:21-6:3; Mal. 2:16; 1 Cor. 7:10-11; 1 Tim. 3:5; 5:8

ARTICLE II

We affirm that it is the duty of civil government to strengthen and defend the family.[a]

We deny that civil government has a right to act in any way detrimental to the health and stability of the family.

>   a. Deut. 6:4-9; Rom. 13:1-4; Eph. 5:22-25; James 4:17

ARTICLE III

We affirm that the principle of civil government is a divinely established sphere, and that all citizens, especially Christians, have a stewardship role in civil government.[a]

We deny that civil government is, in itself, evil, or that Christians should avoid involvement in it.

>   a. Matt. 22:17-21; Rom. 13:1-7; 1 Pet. 2:13-17; Rev. 1:5

ARTICLE IV

We affirm that citizens under any government are accountable to God and their fellow citizens for the preservation and increase of justice, righteousness, mercy, and national stability.[a]

We deny that in a republic it is morally acceptable for the citizenry to leave government in the hands of the elite or in the hands of politicians.

>   a. Exod. 22:21-22; Isa. 1:16-17, 23; 29:13-21; 59:1-19; Jer. 5:28-29; 7:5-7; 22:1-3; 32:17-19; Zeph. 3:1-8; Zech. 7:9-10; Mal. 3:5; Matt. 12:18 with 28:20; 23:23; 1 Tim. 1:8-11

ARTICLE V

We affirm that in a society based upon representative government citizens share responsibility for the actions of their leaders.

We deny that in a society based upon representative government the citizenry is held blameless for the actions of those whom they elect.

>   Josh. 7:24-25; Dan. 9:5-6, 8; Zeph. 3:1-8; Rom. 5:12-19

ARTICLE VI

We affirm that God holds all persons, especially Christians, responsible to establish and maintain righteous civil government.[a]

We deny that Christians may avoid involvement in civil government and remain blameless.

> a. Exod. 22:21-22; Isa. 1:16-17, 23; Jer. 5:28-29; 7:5-7; 22:1-3; Zeph. 3:1-8; Zech. 7:9-10; Mal. 3:5; Matt. 12:18 with 28:20; 23:23; Rom. 12:18, 21

ARTICLE VII

We affirm that any and all concepts of law and civil government have their basis in ideological principles which are moral and religious.[a]

We deny that it is possible for either law or civil government to be strictly secular or divorced from ideologies which, in their essence, are religious and moral.

> a. Gen. 1:27 with Rom. 1:18-22; Exod. 20:2 as a preface of Exod. 20:3-17; Rom. 13:3-4; Mic. 6:16

ARTICLE VIII

We affirm that every law and every concept of civil government is the implementation of a group's or individual's religious and moral ideology.[a]

We deny that either law or civil government exist apart from religious and moral ideologies.

We further deny that either law or civil government are amoral, or non-religious.

> a. (See Article VII, a.)

ARTICLE IX

We affirm every civil government holds some single religious and moral ideology above other competing ideologies, and is thus partial to that reigning ideology.[a]

We deny that it is possible for all religious and moral principles to be represented equally by any civil government, or that civil government is able to function value-neutral.

> a. Gen. 1:27 with Rom. 1:18-22; Lev. 18:2-4; Ps. 115:2-8; Isa. 44:9-20; Hab. 2:18-20; 2 Thess. 2:3-4

ARTICLE X

We affirm that God, in the Bible, teaches principles related to man's civic responsibilities and rights, and that these precepts apply to all men, Christian and non-Christian.[a]

We deny that any man is morally free to govern or enact laws at variance with the truth of the Bible.

> a. (These things are evident in the Biblical passages listed under the other Articles.)

ARTICLE XI

We affirm that civil government will function most beneficially for all citizens when it is based on Biblical principles.[a]

We deny that there are principles superior to those found in the Old and New Testaments of the Bible on which civil government and civilization may be founded.

> a. Deut. 4:5-8; 29:18-28; Pss. 19:7-9; 82:1-8; 89:14; 119:144, 160, 172; Ezek. 33:10-19; Jon. 3:6-10; Micah 6:8-16; Zech. 5:3-4

ARTICLE XII

We affirm that Jesus Christ, to whom all authority in Heaven and in Earth is given, has the supreme right to rule in every earthly state and institution by submission of its people and civil government to the principles of the Bible in both the Old and New Testaments.[a]

We deny that any man or system has a lawful or moral right to cast off the government of Jesus Christ, or to rule over men in either their consciences or their bodies in opposition to the principles of the Bible, or Jesus Christ.[b]

> a. Pss. 2:1-12; 72:8; 110:1-7; Matt. 28:18; Luke 19:11-27; Eph. 1:20-23; Col. 1:16-18; 3:17; Rev. 1:5
> b. Acts 4:19-20; 5:20; Rom. 13:4

ARTICLE XIII

We affirm that God created church and state as separate entities.[a]

We deny that either the Church should rule over the state, or that the state should rule over the Church.

> a. Deut. 31:9; Josh. 8:33; 20:4; 2 Chron. 26:17-20; Matt. 22:21; Acts 4:19-20; 5:20; Rom. 13:1-2; 1 Pet. 2:13-17

ARTICLE XIV

We affirm that the Church should influence the state toward moral goodness, justice, and mercy, and should hold the state accountable to the principles of the Bible.[a]

We deny that the Church has no duty or right to speak into the civil sphere; and,

We deny that it is moral for the Church to remain silent while civil government violates Biblical principles.

> a. Deut. 17:18-20; Prov. 24:11-12; Jer. 4:1-2; 12:14-17; 22:1-5; Mal. 2:7-9; 3:13-18; Rom. 13:4; 2:12-16; 1 Tim. 1:8-11; Rev. 1:5

ARTICLE XV

We affirm that the Great Commission includes the mandate to disciple all nations into Christianity, so that both its institutions and its people come into agreement with Biblical concepts of civil government.[a]

We deny that the Great Commission includes no mandate to influence the civil realm toward Biblical principles and activities.

> a. Isa. 2:1-4; 42:5-8 with Acts 13:47; Isa. 45:22-24; Hab. 2:13-14; Matt. 12:18 with 28:18-20

ARTICLE XVI

We affirm that the Church is responsible to teach its people principles of Biblical civil government, and encourage their involvement in civil government to the degree of their individual callings.[a]

We deny that the teaching responsibilities of the Church can be fully discharged without Biblical instruction in the principles and duties of a Christian's participation in civic responsibilities under Christ's Lordship.

   a. Lev. 20:22-23; Deut. 1:15-17; 5:31; 6:1,7; 11:19; 1 Pet. 4:11; Rev. 1:5

ARTICLE XVII

We affirm that Christians should seek political office at every level in order to help guide their nation toward Christian principles.[a]

We deny that every Christian should seek political office, or that Christians who are elected should seek to aggrandize power for personal gain rather than Christian principles.

   a. Esther 10:3; Prov. 14:34; 1 Cor. 12:12-14; 1 Tim. 2:1-4

ARTICLE XVIII

We affirm that all men are morally obligated to obey the laws of God rather than the laws of man when they conflict.[a]

We deny that anyone is released from moral obligation to God's laws by submitting himself to man's law.

   a. Exod. 1:15-21; Dan. 3:16-18; 6:6-10; Acts 4:19-20; 5:29

TOPIC 15
Biblical Economic Systems
INTRODUCTORY COMMENTS
by Dr. Eugene Calvin Clingman

We created this document because a significant portion of liberal-leaning evangelicals, such as Jim Wallis of *Sojourners Magazine*, are now promoting socialism and claim it is a Biblical economic system. Dr. Grimstead asked Dr. David Ayers, a sociology professor at Grove City College, to create a white paper on this topic. He did that and our COR team boiled down that paper into the affirmation and denials document titled "Biblical Economic Systems."

God gave man stewardship dominion over the earth and this assignment has never been withdrawn. To fulfill his stewardship, God made man with creativity and resourcefulness.

Economic activity is a major area in which man's stewardship and gifts are exercised to the glory of God, for one's own provision, and for the good of others.

The Bible does not teach socialism as a legitimate economic system; socialism is an un-Biblical and wicked philosophy and system. This COR document was written because of the trend of the modern church toward socialism.

Liberation Theology

A major movement that has its roots in the Latin American Roman Catholic Church is called "Liberation Theology." Liberation Theology teaches what Dr. R. J. Rushdoony calls "a sentimental form of Marxism." [16]

1. Dr. Rushdoony also says, "Catholic and Protestant seminaries and missionary agencies are too often cesspools of liberation theology." [17]

2. Liberation Theology claims Biblical support while it also seeks to overthrow the ruling ideology, usually the overthrow of Christianity. They say Christianity is a façade for multinational corporations as they take advantage of the poor and gain wealth through systematic control of society. This Latin American philosophical movement has become a pattern and

---

16 Article: "Wealth and the State," by Rev. R. J. Rushdoony. https://chalcedon.edu/resources/articles/wealth-and-the-state.
17 Ibid.

inspiration for other forms of liberation theologies that "find contemporary expression among blacks, feminists, Asians, Hispanic Americans, and Native Americans." [18]

3. The "Black Liberation Theology" of Rev. James Cone (founder) and Rev. Jeremiah Wright (Barack Obama's former longtime pastor) is the same Marxism as the Liberation Theology of South and Central America. Black Liberation Theology claims Biblical support for their effort to overthrow the rich so that wealth may be divided equally among all. They say capitalism is oppressive by nature and socialism is compassionate and just. The average American is perpetually bombarded by the socialistically leaning media and school system (especially at university level but also down to K–12). Government in America, Europe, and other places has grown increasingly socialistic, taking from some people by force.

4. In the U.S., what is unjustly taken by government force is given to others, so that a growing percentage of the American population is on either the government payroll or government-supported welfare programs.

The Wealth of Nations

In contrast to socialism, Adam Smith (1723–1790), a Scottish philosopher and economist, wrote one of the most influential books ever written, *An Inquiry into the Nature and Causes of the Wealth of Nations* (1776); it is a study of life, political institutions, law, and ethics.

Smith showed that national wealth was more than the country's stock of gold and silver. In his time, nations devised systems, tariffs, subsidies, and protections for its own country and industries. The goal: keep gold and silver at home and cause more of it to come to the home nation. Smith showed that this system is counterproductive. Smith argued that free trade would benefit both parties of trade transactions, thereby increasing the prosperity of the participating nations.

He further showed that a society would prosper best economically if it was not controlled by government (the reigning theory of that day), and that freedom and self-interest, rather than creating chaos, would bring prosperity. He wrote that self-interest includes the necessity to protect one's neighbor and deal fairly with him since one's own welfare is bound up in the welfare of his neighbor. Self-interest, provided there is open competition and no coercion, is a force for good. Adam Smith's *The Wealth of Nations* greatly influenced politicians and became the intellectual fuel by which the industrial revolution (1750–1850) was expanded into the nineteenth century.

18 *Evangelical Dictionary of Theology*, Grand Rapids: Baker Books, 1984; see article by D.D. Webster, pg. 635.

Today, nations once guided by Smith's principles of freedom and free trade, loose controls, and right to ownership of property, both real and personal (and also John Locke's principles), feel the tentacles of socialism squeeze ever more tightly as they depart from those principles.

The Bible teaches an economic system compatible with the words, *Thou shalt not steal,* and with these words, "He will have compassion on the poor and needy, and the lives of the needy he will save" (Psalm 72:13). In other words, the Bible teaches the right to own and hold personal property even while teaching the compassionate use of wealth. Everyone who owns property is responsible to use his wealth in a compassionate and God-honoring way.

Limitations on Civil Government and Voluntary Giving

Civil government, however, is not authorized by God to force people to give to those in need. Civil government is also required by God to follow the command, *Thou shalt not steal.* Stealing is unlawful whether done by a single individual or by a group of individuals who compose a government.

Compassionate use of wealth is to be voluntary. It is not to be by threat of a gun, jail, or confiscation of one's property; such compulsion is theft. God has not authorized any person or entity to take the individual's wealth in order to distribute it to others.[19]

Each man is responsible before God as a steward, and will be held accountable by God for the use of his wealth. Civil government has a legitimate sphere and jurisdiction, and there are taxes appropriate in order to carry out its functions. But civil government is outside its God-ordained jurisdiction when it redistributes wealth, controls wealth, limits or regulates wealth or economic activity, and taxes its citizens for such items as: INCOME, PROPERTY, INHERITANCE, etc. Such taxation is by force, and as it were, at the point of a gun and threat of incarceration; for if one does not pay such required, albeit socialistic, taxes, the IRS (America) will show up at the doorstep of that reluctant citizen to secure the "just taxes" they intend to give to those who need it more than he.

The Bible teaches that the one who works has the right both to enjoy the fruit of his labor and to direct its use. The opportunity to gain is a primary motive for man's economic activity, and God has ordained it so. The Bible teaches that economic activity calculated to make a profit, if done righteously, is good and

---

19 See the short but excellent and concise book *The Law* by Frederic Bastiat (1801–1850). He clearly spells out that it is "Legal Plunder" for rulers and civil governments of any kind to pass laws that take from some and give to others by government decree. It is the same as theft or stealing (according to the Ten Commandments, *Thou shalt not steal*), and socialistic to take property owned by some and mandate redistribution of it to others. Long before, John Locke always affirmed the same principle that required "Life, Liberty, and Property" to be protected and encouraged in a free society founded upon God's Law of Liberty. See also *John Locke, Philosopher of American Liberty: Life, Liberty, and Property,* by Mary-Elaine Swanson, Nordskog Publishing, 2012, www.nordskogpublishing.com.

righteous. The same Bible teaches that using one's profit only for oneself is unrighteous.

All men are created equal in rights, dignity, and God-likeness, yet are not created equal in their natural endowments. One man's abilities, creativity, or intellectual capacities vary from another's. These giftings are bestowed by God who is sovereign over such things. All men, therefore, are not created equal in their economic opportunities. The more gifted, other things being equal, have an economic advantage. Men and nations should obey God's commands and statutes, being content with such things as they have, and rejoice with King David who worshiped the Lord saying, "Both riches and honor come from Thee, and Thou dost rule over all, and in Thy hand is power and might; and it lies in Thy hand to make great, and to strengthen everyone" (1 Chronicles 29:12).

DOCUMENT 15

Concerning Biblical Economic Systems

INTRODUCTION

This statement was developed by the Steering Committee of the Council on Revival. It contains affirmations and denials of truth concerning the Christian position on Biblical economic systems. It presents what we believe are the essential points of the orthodox and Biblical position on this topic.

For the glory of the One who is light, truth, and love, and in a spirit of humility, and a concern for doctrinal purity, and unity, we present this document to the Body of Christ worldwide for feedback and reasoned debate. We invite any Christian brothers and sisters who might disagree with the points made by this document to submit feedback to us.

ARTICLES OF AFFIRMATION AND DENIAL

DEFINITION: Economics is the study and the implementation of principles for the production, distribution, and consumption of goods and services.

ARTICLE I

We affirm that God created man and the earth in which man lives, and that man is given stewardship responsibility over the earth by the Creator.

We deny that man is no longer responsible to God as steward of earth's resources.

Gen. 1:28; 2:15; 3:23; Pss. 8:4-8; 24:1-2; 104:14; Heb. 2:8; Rev. 11:18

ARTICLE II

We affirm that man's creativity and resourcefulness are a reflection of God's own image, in which man was created, and that a key area in which these traits are evidenced is in economic activities.

We deny that economic activities and efforts are in opposition to either man's or God's nature, or to the moral laws of the universe.

Gen. 1:26-31; Pss. 8:4-8; 104:14-15; Prov. 16:11; 31:22; Eccles. 2:24; 3:13; 4:9; 5:18-19

ARTICLE III

We affirm that the Bible teaches that individuals have the right to hold private property.

We deny that the Bible teaches an economic system in which all property belongs to the community or the state.

> Exod. 20:9, 15, 17; Lev. 19:13; Prov. 13:22; James 5:4

ARTICLE IV

We affirm that the opportunity for the individual to profit from his labors, and to produce wealth through his just and lawful endeavors, is a primary motivator in the production of wealth, and a key ingredient to a society's economic health and stability.

We deny that wealth, economic prosperity, or technological advancement may be significantly achieved apart from the individual's opportunity to personally gain from his lawful efforts.

> Deut. 8:18; Prov. 3:22; 1 Tim. 5:8

ARTICLE V

We affirm that the Bible is the sufficient source for learning the fundamental economic principles which both please God, and lead to economic prosperity and stability.

We deny that the Bible is inadequate to teach fundamental economic principles which please God, and lead to prosperity and economic stability.

> Ps. 111:10; Prov. 11:1; Isa. 8:20; 2 Tim. 3:16-17

ARTICLE VI

We affirm that the Bible contains those economic principles which are moral and just, principles which ought to be followed by all people, all societies, and all states.

We deny that it is morally acceptable for any person, state, or institution to pursue economic gain in opposition to Biblical principles.

> Lev. 18:2-5, 24-30; 19:35-37; 20:22-23; Deut. 4:8; 16:18-19; Ps. 119:75, 106, 160; Prov. 13:18; Rom. 13:8-10; 2 Tim. 3:16-17

ARTICLE VII

We affirm that, for the Christian, the primary incentive for the production of wealth, is to be his attitude of stewardship to God.

We deny that a mature Christian attitude is one that seeks economic gain for selfish reasons.

> Deut. 8:11-20; Prov. 30:8-9; Hab. 2:13-14; Luke 12:16-21; 16:9-13; 1 Cor. 10:31; Eph. 6:5-9; Col. 3:23-24

ARTICLE VIII

We affirm an economy will prosper to the degree in which its entrepreneurs honor the stewardship-before-God principle.

We deny that a healthy economic or social environment may long be maintained without a practice of the stewardship-before-God principle.

Exod. 23:24-26; Deut. 28:1-68; 2 Chron. 24:20; Prov. 13:11; Isa. 65:11-16

ARTICLE IX

We affirm that earning profits and gaining wealth in the process of serving the market with goods or services is a good and moral thing when pursued in accordance with Biblical principles.

We deny that profitability which results from serving a free market in accordance with Scriptural principles is inherently wrong or merely self-serving.

Deut. 8:18; Prov. 12:11; 13:11; Eccles. 2:24; 3:13; 4:9; 5:18-19

ARTICLE X

We affirm that one role of civil government is to create an infrastructure, and a climate of justice and order, in which individuals are encouraged to create, develop, and produce products and services helpful to mankind, and to the earth's creatures and environment.

We deny that civil government's function is to manipulate, manage, or control economics or the productivity of its citizens.

Exod. 20:15; Deut. 1:16-17; 16:18-20; Ps. 125:3; Prov. 29:2; Rom. 13:3-4; Eph. 4:28

ARTICLE XI

We affirm that economic prosperity grows out of the freedom of the individual to labor and to receive for himself the rewards of his labor, and that history demonstrates that this is true.

We deny that civil government has the ability to produce lasting wealth through the organized production, or by the implementation of Marxist, communistic, or socialistic principles.

We further deny that there is any example in history where civil government organized production or where Marxist, communistic, or socialistic principles have inured to the long term benefit of its people or to the production of wealth.

(No Scripture references as the proof is by the testimony of history, not the Bible.)

ARTICLE XII

We affirm that though all men are created equal in regard to their rights and liberties, yet they are not created equal in their intellectual, creative, or physical abilities, and that these inequities are a factor in an individual's ability to produce wealth.

We deny that all people have the same intellectual or physical ability, or that all people should expect to enjoy the same level of productivity or wealth.

Lev. 19:15; Prov. 17:5; 22:2; Mark 14:7; Luke 19:12-27; Acts 10:34; Rom. 12:6-8; 1 Cor. 12:12ff; Gal. 3:28

ARTICLE XIII

We affirm that the Christian is called to the compassionate use of wealth which includes a call to sacrificial giving to assist the poor and needy.

We deny that a Christian worldview allows for the selfish use or hoarding of wealth.

Exod. 22:25; Deut. 15:7-8, 11; 24:14-15; Ps. 68:10; Prov. 14:21, 31; 19:17; 2:16; 28:8; Eph. 4:28; Col. 3:5; 1 Tim. 6:10, 17-19

ARTICLE XIV

We affirm that God gives the individual the responsibility to make choices as to how he will use his wealth.

We deny that civil government has the duty or right to redistribute wealth or to direct the individual in the use of his wealth, so long as the individual is not acting immorally.

Exod. 20:15; Prov. 10:15-16; 22:16; Eccles. 2:24-25; Matt. 25:14-30; 2 Thess. 3:10-15

ARTICLE XV

We affirm that it is the responsibility of the Church to teach the fundamental principles of Biblical economics and to equip its people to discern between Biblical and un-Biblical economic activities and systems.

We deny that the learning of, or practice of, Biblical economics is optional to the Christian, or that the ministry of the Church may be deemed successful without diligent training of its people in Biblical economics.

Deut. 28:1-68; Ps. 119:142; Rom. 1:20; 2 Tim. 3:16-17; Heb. 4:12

ARTICLE XVI

We affirm that tithing (which is 10%) is a fundamental Biblical economic principle.

We deny that tithing does not apply to Christians today or that a Christian's economic duty is fulfilled when tithing is not practiced.

Gen. 14:18-19; Lev. 27:30-32; Mal. 3:8-12; Matt. 23:23; Heb. 7:9-10

ARTICLE XVII

We affirm that every man who practices Biblical economics may expect God's blessing of provision and increase upon his labors, and that God is ultimately sovereign in economics and may for his own purposes withhold economic blessing.

We deny that man should labor without hope, or that there is any formula that will automatically and without fail inure to economic prosperity, or that God's sovereignty is excluded from the realm of economics.

Job 1:21; Prov. 22:29; Eccles. 9:11; Hag. 2:15-19; Matt. 5:45; 20:11-16; 21:33-43; 1 Cor. 9:9-10; Heb. 11:32-40

ARTICLE XVIII

We affirm that there is only one legitimate economic theory for all people of all cultures, which is the Biblical economic theory.

We deny that there are multiple valid economic theories.

Deut. 8:18-20; Prov. 14:34, 20:10; Ezek. 5:5-8; John 16:13; 17:17; Rom. 1:18-22; 2:14-16; 1 Tim. 6:3-6; James 4:1-10; Rev. 20:12-15

TOPIC 16
Concerning Marriage, Divorce, and Remarriage

INTRODUCTORY COMMENTS

by Dr. Eugene Calvin Clingman

God's Purpose in Marriage

We say again that this topic was not written because divorce and remarriage was being actively promoted in Christian circles, but because divorce among evangelicals was becoming far greater than the small percentage that would fall under Biblically allowable divorce.[20] Mr. Garry Moes, the Developer at Greenville Seminary and director of World-Com Communications, did the early stage, primary work on this document before we boiled it down as a team into our regular creedal form of affirmations and denials.

Although God could have created one sexless creature, He made male and female. The Bible reveals that God's primary intention for creating the sexes is to bring male and female together in marriage: (1) to form the family and, (2) produce godly children to populate the world. Regarding marriage God says through Adam, "For this cause a man shall leave his father and his mother, and shall cleave to his wife; and they shall become one flesh" (Genesis 2:24; see also Matthew 19:4,5). And regarding godly children, God says through Malachi, "Did he not make them (man and wife) one, with a portion of the Spirit in their union? And what was the one God seeking? Godly offspring." (Malachi 2:15, ESV). For family and for godly children God made male and female.

Human beings need revelation in order to know what is real. The Bible is God's clearest revelation and map of reality for living in all areas of life. The serpent in the Garden led our first parents into a fantasy world. The serpent led them to decide that it was more important for them to discover for themselves what reality is, rather than listen to God. God had told them, *In the day you*

---

20 When Ronald Reagan signed the nation's first No-Fault Divorce legislation as governor of California in 1969, he did not suspect this policy innovation would lead to a dramatic increase in divorce rates and a consequent plunge in marriage rates with sky-rocketing increase of live-in-partners who never marry. Reagan later told his son Michael that imposing No-Fault Divorce on California was "one of the worst mistakes he ever made in public office." Michael Reagan, *Twice Adopted* (Nashville: Broadman & Holman, 2004), 44.

eat you will surely die. The serpent said, *You will not surely die.* (Genesis 3:3-4) Our parents had two options:

1. They could choose to hold to the words spoken by the One who created the reality in which they lived and who alone was capable of knowing what would happen if they ate from the God-created Tree of the Knowledge of Good and Evil.

2. They could reject God's revelation to them and choose an alternate path in an attempt to assert that another reality was possible, a reality of their own making.

As we know, they rejected God's revelation and chose for themselves the option of DECIDING FOR THEMSELVES what is good and evil.

Today, as in that day, in the measure we live outside God's revealed Word, we too live in a fantasy world. To whatever extent we do not bring "every thought captive to the obedience of Christ" the Creator (2 Corinthians 10:5), we live in a world of our own making, a fantasy world that does not comport with God's created reality. Since God made the world and all things, He is the only One in a position to tell us what life is about, what the things around us really mean, why they are there, what defines good and evil, and what the consequences are of one action or another.

The human race has lived in unreality since the Fall. The Bible calls this unreality "darkness" (Acts 26:18 and Colossians 1:13). In principle, those who accept and follow Christ are delivered from darkness and have the light of life who is Jesus. But to whatever extent we Christians live outside the Bible, God's revealed Word, we continue to be darkened (Isaiah 8:20). Jesus and His apostles admonish us to *walk in the light* (John 12:35; Ephesians 4:17,18; 1 John 1:7). As in any other area of life, when it comes to "Marriage, Divorce, and Remarriage," we must have God's Word to orient us to reality so that we may not live in darkness.

In this document, you will find that God says you can divorce! But only in certain situations. There is lawful divorce. You will also discover when God permits remarriage and when it is forbidden.

God says, "I hate divorce!" The passage in which this statement appears is the one in which God explains that He created marriage for the purpose of raising godly children (Malachi 2:14-16). The implication is that divorce thwarts the successful raising of the kind of children God wants—godly children.

An article I read on the Ohio State University Website asserts that children from divorced families are on *average* somewhat worse off than children who have lived in intact families. These children have more difficulty in school, more behavior problems, more negative self-concepts, more problems with peers, and more trouble getting along with their parents. As important as these things might be, I would go on to ask — are these the only criteria to measure the damage divorce can bring to the children? Ohio State overlooks the reality of God's world when they limit their study to such things. What factors then should be considered? What about the fact that parents who divorce for un-Biblical reasons have broken covenant? Does this set up the children for the likelihood of treating covenants as optional; the most significant of which are covenant with God and covenant with spouse? What about the fact that in the illegitimate divorce parents are setting God's Word aside in favor of disobedience for the sake of their feelings and desires? Could this predispose the children to follow the same pattern of rejecting God's Word when it doesn't suit their desires?

And, isn't such a course the road to hell? What about the fact that the husband who unrighteously divorces his wife is rejecting his responsibility to love his wife as Christ loves His Church? Doesn't that tell the daughters that the love of a husband should not be counted on, and that she should not seek refuge and security in marriage partnership with a godly man? Doesn't it tell sons that they also do not need to love their wives as Christ loves His Church? And doesn't it also convey the message to both daughter and son that just as father has broken covenant with wife and family, it is likely God also is not in the business of keeping covenant? Does it predispose the children to believe that just as they were treated as unimportant, so their own children are not of much value? A wife could unrighteously divorce her husband which would bring similar repercussions. The truth is that divorce sets children up for these things and more. God hates divorce, and so should we.

There is also forgiveness and restoration! This document deals with these things as well.

DOCUMENT 16

Concerning Marriage, Divorce, and Remarriage

ARTICLES OF AFFIRMATION AND DENIAL

ARTICLE I

We affirm that sexual distinction is a part of the essence of humanity and marriage.[a]

We deny that members of the same sex can be married, in God's eyes.[b]

    a. Gen. 1:27-28; 2:20-25; Matt. 19:4-5
    b. Gen. 2:20-25; Lev. 18:22; 20:13; Matt. 19:4-5; Rom. 1:26-27; 1 Cor. 6:9-11; 1 Tim. 1:8-11

ARTICLE II

We affirm that marriage is designed to be a lifelong union.[a]

We deny that marriage is less than a lifelong union or that it is simply a temporary state based upon faithfulness to a mutual contract between partners.

    a. Exod. 20:14, 17; Mal. 2:14-16; Matt. 19:4-6

ARTICLE III

We affirm that companionship is integral to the marriage relationship.[a]

We deny that companionship is the only purpose of marriage.

    a. Gen. 2:18; Mal. 2:14

ARTICLE IV

We affirm that sexual intercourse is an integral part of marriage. Indeed, according to Scripture, it is an obligation of marriage, a debt which must be paid to one's spouse, because it is the seal of marriage's essential quality, the "one-flesh" union of a man and a woman.[a]

We deny that marital partners should remain sexually abstinent, except by reason of physical handicap or mutual, voluntary consent for temporary spiritual devotion or service.

    a. Gen. 2:24 with 1 Cor. 6:16; 1 Cor. 7:3-5

ARTICLE V

We affirm that procreation of children is normally an integral part of marriage, and that children are to be received as desired issue of a marriage and welcomed as blessings of the Lord.[a]

We deny that marital partners should remain permanently childless by choice or that marital partners should attempt, by unscriptural means, to limit the hand of God in granting children to them.[b]

    a. Gen.1:28; 4:1; 28:3; 30:1; Pss.113:9; 127:3-5; Prov.17:6
    b. Same as a.

ARTICLE VI

We affirm that the covenantal marital relationship is symbolic of and of the same essence as Christ's relationship with His Bride, the Church ("True Israel") of all ages.[a]

We deny that the marital relationship has no transcendent model or symbol.

    a. Eph.5:25-32; Rev.21:2,9

ARTICLE VII

We affirm that commitment to God has priority over all other familial commitments.[a]

We deny that the marital relationship takes precedence over the partners' relationship to God.

    a. Deut.33:8-9; Matt.10:37; Luke 14:26; Col.3:18

ARTICLE VIII

We affirm that the marriage bond is broken at the death of either partner.[a]

We deny that the marital relationship continues beyond death.[b]

    a. Rom.7:2-3; 1 Cor.7:39
    b. Matt.22:25-30

ARTICLE IX

We affirm that the call to celibacy may be a gift of God for the purpose of increased devotion to God's service.[a]

We deny that celibacy makes one holy or, in itself, elevates the celibate's holiness above that of other saints[b] or that a married person may practice celibacy.[c]

    a. 1 Cor.7:7,32-35
    b. 1 Cor.7:7; 1 Tim.4:1-3
    c. 1 Cor.7:3-5

ARTICLE X

We affirm that the Bible condemns adultery, fornication,[a] incest,[b] homosexual behavior,[c] rape,[d] bestiality,[e] and physical and emotional abuse.[f]

We deny that the Bible accepts or is indifferent concerning these and all other sexual sins.

    a. Exod.22:16; Ps.50:16-18; Mal.3:5; 1 Cor.6:9; Heb.13:4
    b. Lev.18:6-18; 20:11-12,17,19-21; Deut.22:30; 27:20,22-23; Ezek.22:11; 1 Cor.5:1
    c. Lev.18:22-24; 20:13-16; Rom.1:24-32; 1 Cor.6:9-11; 1 Tim.1:8-11
    d. Deut.22:25-27
    e. Exod.22:19; Lev.18:23; 20:15-16; Deut.27:21
    f. Exod.21:24; Lev.19:18; 24:20; Deut.19:21; Mic.2:9; Matt.5:21,27,43; 22:39

ARTICLE XI

We affirm that God prohibits believers from entering into marriage with unbelievers.[a]

We deny that Scripture requires that believing spouses who come to the faith subsequent to marriage must leave or divorce unbelieving spouses who desire to remain in the marriage.[b]

> a. 1 Cor. 7:39; 2 Cor. 6:14
> b. 1 Cor. 7:12-14

ARTICLE XII

We affirm that, as Christ is the head of man, the husband is the head of the wife; as the Church is subject to Christ, the wife is to be subject to her own husband.[a]

We deny that a husband may exercise tyranny over his wife or subject her to any role that diminishes her divinely ordained position as a complementary partner for her husband in the cultural mandate.[b]

> a. 1 Cor. 11:3; Eph. 5:22-24
> b. Gen. 1:27-28; Eph. 5:25-33; 1 Pet. 3:7-8

ARTICLE XIII

We affirm that the effects of the Fall of mankind into sin include: impure and guilty sexuality, unjust domination in the marital relationship, and increased pain in childbirth.[a]

We affirm, nevertheless, that the essential authority of the husband as federal head of the wife existed in the marital relationship prior to the Fall.[b]

We deny that the results of the Fall include God placing the wife under the headship of her husband.

> a. Gen. 3:16; Mic. 2:9; Rom. 1:22-32; 1 Pet. 3:7-8
> b. 1 Tim. 2:11-13; 1 Cor. 11:3, 7-9

ARTICLE XIV

We affirm that God hates divorce.[a]

We deny that man may lawfully "put asunder" what God has "joined together" or that divorce is part of God's perfect plan for humankind.[b]

> a. Mal. 2:16; Luke 16:18
> b. Matt. 19:6-9; Rom. 7:2-3

ARTICLE XV

We affirm that there are no more than two Biblical grounds for divorce: (1) fornication, narrowly defined as to include nothing more than sexual sin outside of marriage,[a] and (2) the desertion of a believing spouse by an unbelieving partner or desertion by a partner living in such a state of unrepentant sin as qualifies him or her to be viewed as an unbeliever in the eyes of the Lord and the Church.[b]

We deny that spouses may Scripturally divorce for any reason other than those stated by Christ in Matthew 5:32 and 19:9 and by St. Paul in 1 Corinthians 7:15 (as rendered in the original Greek, certain modern translations being unreliable).

    a. Matt. 5:31-32; 19:9; Mark 10:1-12; Luke 16:18
    b. 1 Cor. 7:10-15

ARTICLE XVI

We affirm that men and women are commanded by God to repent of marital sins and to forgive and reconcile with their marital partners upon Scriptural grounds.[a]

We deny that God ever commands divorce.

    a. 1 Cor. 7:10-15; Matt. 6:12; Eph. 4:32; Col. 3:13

ARTICLE XVII

We affirm that new male Christians in polygamous societies should not divorce their wives.[a]

We deny that believers are permitted to newly enter into polygamous relationships.[b]

    a. Exod. 21:10; Mic. 2:9
    b. Matt. 19:5; Mark 10:8; Eph. 5:31; 1 Tim. 3:2; Titus 1:6

ARTICLE XVIII

We affirm that remarriage is permitted by God for persons divorced under Biblical grounds[a] and for surviving partners of spouses who die.[b]

We deny that divorced persons who marry and subsequently divorce other spouses may then remarry their original spouse.[c]

    a. Matt. 5:31-32; 19:9
    b. Rom. 7:2-3; 1 Cor. 7:39
    c. Deut. 24:1-4; Jer. 3:1

TOPIC 17

Biblical Distinctives between Males and Females

INTRODUCTORY COMMENTS

by Dr. Jay Grimstead

As our theologians approached this topic, I felt that the Church needed to address the threat of extreme feminism in the Church, along with the abdication of masculine leadership. It was decided the scholarly work on this topic was already well done by "The Council on Biblical Manhood and Womanhood" in their landmark document, the "Danvers Statement," which committee was headed up by Dr. Wayne Grudem and Dr. John Piper.

These two scholars also edited their committee's 566-page book containing the 26 scholarly white papers on this subject created by their committee members which papers form the back up arguments that support their "Danvers Statement." The book's title is, *Recovering Biblical Manhood and Womanhood: A Response to Evangelical Feminism,* John Piper and Wayne Grudem (Wheaton, IL: Crossway Books, 1991). We obtained the written approval from this committee to use and republish their Danvers Statement as the statement we wished to have represent our thoughts about manhood and evangelical feminism, and to include it among our list of theological white papers dealing with controversial issues within evangelicalism.

Here is an interesting fact that connects "The Council on Biblical Manhood and Womanhood" and the ICBI (International Council on Biblical Inerrancy). In a conversation with Wayne Grudem, I was pleased to hear him say that when they formed their committee, they decided to use how we organized our ICBI in the 1970s as their model for proceeding with their task.

He said they thus decided to:

A. Gather a group of leading and respected evangelical scholars from a variety of denominations to deal with this issue;

B. Have a number of those scholars write a white paper on various subtopics dealing Biblically with the issues of manhood and feminism in evangelicalism.

C. Combine these papers into an edited book that would stand as a landmark, conservative Biblical statement on the subject;

D. Hold a major summit type meeting for the greater evangelical world where the book would be released and a number of plenary speeches and smaller seminars presented to offer the logical Biblical arguments, the hermeneutics, and the historical position on each sub-point;

E. And maintain a standing committee into the future to keep promoting the Biblical truth on this matter and keep dealing with issues that emerge on this topic in the future.

We highly recommend this book, *Recovering Biblical Manhood and Womanhood: A Response to Evangelical Feminism* as the definitive, Biblical statement on men and women within the evangelical churches.

We think every Christian leader dealing with this scourge of evangelical feminism and its counterpart, masculine abdication, should have this book in his library's arsenal. We also recommend supporting their committee, The Council on Biblical Manhood and Womanhood, and using some of their committee members to come speak to your church or organization on this topic.

In a nutshell, those who hold to the inerrancy of the Bible are generally in strong agreement that God tells us clearly in His authoritative Word for His good reasons, that His plan calls for having male headship and leadership both in the home and in the church. God knows that because of how He created the universe and how He created man and woman, it is bad for the marriage, bad for the children, and ultimately bad for society to have females, however gifted, strong, and holy (Proverbs 31:10-31), be the head over their husbands or to exercise leadership over men in the Body of Christ. Only as wives submit willingly to Christ first and their husband's headship and decisions can they model how the Church is supposed to submit to her Lord Christ as in Ephesians.

And only as husbands love their wives with a sacrificial, protective love, can they model how Christ loves and sacrifices for the Church. To have women be in charge of their husbands spoils this beautiful illustration and tends to undermine the marriage. We urge all Bible-believing pastors to honor and obey God's Word in 1 Timothy 2 and 1 Corinthians 11 and thereby not allow or encourage their wives or any godly woman in their church, no matter how capable, to have spiritual or pastoral authority over the men in their church.

In many Christian families, the easy abdication by the husbands of their God-created responsibility to lead and provide has forced women to shoulder a burden that was not originally assigned to them by God, causing injury to the whole family. On the other hand, families have also been damaged by the influences and effects of feminism.

Feminism has pervaded the American culture with the false notion that a woman's dignity and fulfillment come with a career, making the maximum use of her talents outside the home, and that homemaking and childrearing responsibilities are less meaningful, less dignified, and less fulfilling. Christian husbands must find God's grace to create the opportunity and atmosphere needed to help their wives fulfill their role as their husband's God-ordained helper (helpmeet) and partner. It is not right for any Christian to usurp Biblical mandated roles or God-given callings of another.

The evangelical feminists assert there are no God-ordained differences between men and women. The truth is that the differences between the male and female body are but a signal and a parable of differences at the very center of our beings as male or female. On every cell of our body is stamped "male" or "female." We believe the Bible is unambiguously clear that God requires male headship in the home and in the church.

In the home the marriage relationship is to be a reflection of Christ the groom and the head of the Church, to whom the bride gladly submits as to her loving leader and head, the Lord Jesus Christ. God also created the man for headship in the Church. It is also clear in 1 Timothy 2 that God commands women to keep silent in the churches and not to teach men or have authority over men in the church. We have found no place in Scripture where women are pastors in the Christian churches, although Paul clearly recognized the contribution of women for instance in Romans 16:1-7. Though women are not designed by God or ordained by Him to carry leadership or teaching positions over men, there are multiple, worthwhile, productive opportunities for service in the church for women. The Church in the twentieth and twenty-first centuries has been greatly damaged, misdirected, and hindered in its Kingdom work by allowing anti-Biblical secular principles to be widely absorbed and influential, not only in the theologically liberal churches (which would be expected), but also in many Bible-believing evangelical and charismatic churches. We see inappropriate roles for men and women in many of the churches which travel under the name of "evangelical."

This issue is somewhat controversial—a touchy topic, but one which must be addressed and confronted. Feminism and masculine abdication of leadership roles are dangerous and self-destructive and should be addressed and confronted. If the men of the Church would extend more healing, comfort, and supportive care and leadership to all men and women, this would encompass the globe with healing and would attract many men and women to the Gospel. It would also strengthen the Body of Christ.

[NOTE: The Danvers Statement Council did not include denials, nor call their points "articles" with Roman numerals. Publisher decided to add the word "Article" and use Roman numerals to be consistent with the other documents in this book.]

DOCUMENT 17

Biblical Distinctives between Males and Females

THE DANVERS STATEMENT

COPYRIGHT 1991 BY
THE COUNCIL ON BIBLICAL MANHOOD AND WOMANHOOD

Rationale

We have been moved in our purpose by the following contemporary developments which we observe with deep concern:

1. The widespread uncertainty and confusion in our culture regarding the complementary differences between masculinity and femininity;

2. The tragic effects of this confusion in unraveling the fabric of marriage woven by God out of the beautiful and diverse strands of manhood and womanhood;

3. The increasing promotion given to feminist egalitarianism with accompanying distortions or neglect of the glad harmony portrayed in Scripture between the loving, humble leadership of redeemed husbands and the intelligent, willing support of that leadership by redeemed wives;

4. The widespread ambivalence regarding the values of motherhood, vocational homemaking, and the many ministries historically performed by women;

5. The growing claims of legitimacy for sexual relationships which have Biblically and historically been considered illicit or perverse, and the increase in pornographic portrayal of human sexuality;

6. The upsurge of physical and emotional abuse in the family;

7. The emergence of roles for men and women in church leadership that do not conform to Biblical teaching but backfire in the crippling of Biblically faithful witness;

8. The increasing prevalence and acceptance of hermeneutical oddities devised to reinterpret apparently plain meanings of Biblical texts;

9. The consequent threat to Biblical authority as the clarity of Scripture is

jeopardized and the accessibility of its meaning to ordinary people is withdrawn into the restricted realm of technical ingenuity;

10. And behind all this the apparent accommodation of some within the church to the spirit of the age at the expense of winsome, radical Biblical authenticity which in the power of the Holy Spirit may reform rather than reflect our ailing culture.

Purposes

Recognizing our own abiding sinfulness and fallibility, and acknowledging the genuine evangelical standing of many who do not agree with all of our convictions, nevertheless, moved by the preceding observations and by the hope that the noble Biblical vision of sexual complementarity may yet win the mind and heart of Christ's Church, we engage to pursue the following purposes:

1. To study and set forth the Biblical view of the relationship between men and women, especially in the home and in the church.

2. To promote the publication of scholarly and popular materials representing this view.

3. To encourage the confidence of lay people to study and understand for themselves the teaching of Scripture, especially on the issue of relationships between men and women.

4. To encourage the considered and sensitive application of this Biblical view in the appropriate spheres of life.

5. And thereby

   • to bring healing to persons and relationships injured by an inadequate grasp of God's will concerning manhood and womanhood,

   • to help both men and women realize their full ministry potential through a true understanding and practice of their God given roles,

   • and to promote the spread of the Gospel among all peoples by fostering a Biblical wholeness in relationships that will attract a fractured world.

AFFIRMATIONS
BASED ON OUR UNDERSTANDING OF BIBLICAL TEACHINGS, WE AFFIRM THE FOLLOWING:

ARTICLE I

Both Adam and Eve were created in God's image, equal before God as persons and distinct in their manhood and womanhood (Genesis 1:26-27, 2:18).

ARTICLE II

Distinctions in masculine and feminine roles are ordained by God as part of the created order, and should find an echo in every human heart (Genesis 2:18, 21-24; 1 Corinthians 11:7-9; 1 Timothy 2:12-14).

ARTICLE III

Adam's headship in marriage was established by God before the Fall, and was not a result of sin (Genesis 2:16-18, 21-24; 3:1-13; 1 Corinthians 11:7-9).

ARTICLE IV

The Fall introduced distortions into the relationships between men and women (Genesis 3:1-7, 12, 16).

- In the home, the husband's loving, humble headship tends to be replaced by domination or passivity; the wife's intelligent, willing submission tends to be replaced by usurpation or servility.

- In the church, sin inclines men toward a worldly love of power or an abdication of spiritual responsibility, and inclines women to resist limitations on their roles or to neglect the use of their gifts in appropriate ministries.

ARTICLE V

The Old Testament, as well as the New Testament, manifests the equally high value and dignity which God attached to the roles of both men and women (Genesis 1:21-27, 2:18; Galatians 3:28). Both Old and New Testaments also affirm the principle of male headship in the family and in the covenant community (Genesis 2:18; Ephesians 5:21-33; Colossians 3:18-19; 1 Timothy 2:11-15).

ARTICLE VI

Redemption in Christ aims at removing the distortions introduced by the curse.

- In the family, husbands should forsake harsh or selfish leadership and grow in love and care for their wives; wives should forsake resistance to their husbands' authority and grow in willing, joyful submission to their husbands' leadership (Ephesians 5:21-33; Colossians 3:18-19; Titus 2:2-5; 1 Peter 3:1-7).

- In the church, redemption in Christ gives men and women an equal share in the blessings of salvation; nevertheless, some governing and teaching roles within the church are restricted to men (Genesis 3:28; 1 Corinthians 11:2-16; 1 Timothy 2:11-15).

ARTICLE VII

In all of life Christ is the supreme authority and guide for men and women, so that no earthly submission—domestic, religious, or civil—ever implies a mandate to follow a human authority into sin (Daniel 3:10-18; Acts 4:19-20, 5:27-29; 1 Peter 3:1-2).

ARTICLE VIII

In both men and women a heartfelt sense of call to ministry should never be used to set aside Biblical criteria for particular ministries (1 Timothy 2:11-15, 3:1-13; Titus 1:5-9). Rather, Biblical teaching should remain the authority for testing our subjective discernment of God's will.

ARTICLE IX

With half the world's population outside the reach of indigenous evangelism; with countless other lost people in those societies that have heard the Gospel; with the stresses and miseries of sickness, malnutrition, homelessness, illiteracy, ignorance, aging, addiction, crime, incarceration, neuroses, and loneliness, no man or woman who feels a passion from God to make His grace known in word and deed need ever live without a fulfilling ministry for the glory of Christ and the good of this fallen world (1 Corinthians 12:7-21).

ARTICLE X

We are convinced that a denial or neglect of these principles will lead to increasingly destructive consequences in our families, our churches, and the culture at large.

～

[*The Danvers Statement* was prepared by several evangelical leaders at a CBMW meeting in Danvers, Mass., in December, 1987. It was first published in final form by the CBMW in Wheaton, Ill., in November, 1988. We grant permission and encourage interested persons to use, reproduce, and distribute the "Danvers Statement." Please contact CBMW for the cost of additional copies of this brochure: CBMW, 2825 Lexington Road, Louisville, KY 40280, https://cbmw.org/uncategorized/the-danvers-statement/#affirmations.

An impressive list of Christian leaders, theologians, counselors, and pastors have joined the CBMW Council; their names and positions are listed at the end of Document 17 at the COR Website which is www.ChurchCouncil.org, or may be obtained from CBMW.]

TOPIC 18
Homosexuality
INTRODUCTORY COMMENTS
by Dr. Eugene Calvin Clingman

To even have to write a document for the Church of Jesus Christ declaring that homosexual sex is both a clear-cut sin of fornication and, beyond that, one of the behaviors God thinks of as "abominable" seems as if it should be unnecessary. But so far has our culture, and parts of the "visible church," sunk into depravity and an anti-Biblical perspective, that it sadly has become necessary to clarify this fact which should be obvious to all Christians. We asked Dr. Ed Welch, a professor of counseling at Westminster Seminary East, and a director of the Nouthetic Counselling Center, to write the white paper from which our team extracted the principles that we boiled down into the affirmations and denials for this topic. For more on this topic, see the peer-reviewed articles at Family Research Institute: www.familyresearchinst.org.

The Living God had good reason to stop homosexuality in its tracks by judgment on two entire cities of unrepentant homosexuals. The spirit behind the homosexual movement appears insatiable. Nothing less than the power of God in revival can stop it.

If capital punishment for heterosexual adultery had continued in America beyond its early stages in the 1600s and early 1700s, there would probably be no homosexual movement for equal marriage rights as we have today. Homosexual non-Christians have a legitimate gripe with our relativistic culture if we allow heterosexuals social and moral freedom to commit fornication but do not extend that freedom to homosexuals as well. It is clear that a culture's acceptance of homosexuality is an indication of serious cultural decline and the pending death of that society at the hands of God's judgment. America is at this moment of history undergoing God's remedial judgment for our intentional sins and for departing from the Biblical foundations on which our nation was originally built by the Pilgrims, Puritans, and Founding Fathers. If a portion of the Church of Jesus in America does not arise, repent, undergo a new Reformation of Bible-obedience, and begin living as Christ commands us to live, we can be certain that America will undergo more intense judgment of God, starting with the Church itself for allowing this culture to deteriorate to this degree by not being the proper "salt and light" we should have been over the past 150 years. The Church is primarily to blame for the fact that America's

culture, laws, and governments have deteriorated to this point of massive sickness and is now at this critical point of self-destruction tottering at the edge of
the cliff of a full-blown, anti-God tyranny.

The Church is faltering before Jezebel! Compromise in the culture is leaking
into the Church in ever widening streams. "The fact is, the division within the
visible church over homosexuality is representative of almost all that is troubling
Christianity today. It inescapably involves the issue of Biblical authority, the
nature of church ministry, the scope of church discipline, and the church's
responsibility and relationship to the civil sphere." [21] For these reasons the
Coalition on Revival decided to address the homosexual issue explicitly and so
an affirmation and denial document was created.

Later, during the Western Hemisphere Consultation on Theology (WHCT)
at Knox Seminary in Fort Lauderdale, FL, August 6-9, 2003, news broke that
a practicing homosexual had just been ordained an Episcopal bishop. At that
point, a number of Consultation delegates took up the task of creating "A
Statement on Homosexuality." That document was signed by all delegates,
stating their perspective on homosexuality. As part of our introduction to the
Coalition on Revival affirmation and denial document which follows on page
162, we now present the entire "A Statement on Homosexuality" signed by all
the delegates of the WHCT:

A STATEMENT ON HOMOSEXUALITY
CREATED AND SIGNED BY THE DELEGATES OF THE WESTERN HEMISPHERE
CONSULTATION ON THEOLOGY, AUGUST 6-9, 2003, FT. LAUDERDALE, FL

"Woe to those who call evil good, and good evil" (Isaiah 5:20).

Sin is the breaking of God's laws revealed in the Bible. All sexual sins
are condemned by God, including heterosexual adultery, homosexual
sex, lesbianism, and bestiality. All sex outside of monogamous, heterosexual
marriage is immoral.

The Bible claims that no one has a right to call himself a Christian who
chooses a lifestyle which includes these sins or any other sins including murder,
stealing, perjury, etc.

To ordain men to the Christian ministry and place them in leadership in
God's Church who deliberately and regularly commit such sins as kidnapping,
rape, theft, perjury, or any of the sexual sins mentioned above would be an
extreme foolishness that tramples on God's commandments and holds God
and His honor in contempt.

The recent elevation of an unrepentant homosexual to the holy office of
Bishop is an aberration; it is both dishonoring to God and a betrayal of the

---

21 *Unnatural Affections: The Impuritan Ethic of Homosexuality and the Modern Church* by George
Grant and Mark Horne. Legacy Press, 1991, 9,10.

historic Faith of Christianity. The ordination of a practicing homosexual to any church office contradicts the clear mandate of the first Jerusalem council (Acts 15) led by the original leaders of the Church, Christ's Apostles. We urge the churches to remove from office all practicing homosexuals, to call them to repentance, and then accompany them on the difficult road of restoration.

The Bible declares that homosexuals must repent of and forsake their homosexual practices and turn to Jesus in order to be saved. The Bible describes the good news of Christ as the gift of His grace. He gives His children the power to turn away from sin. As sinners we know that perfect goodness is found only in Jesus Christ.

We welcome as brothers and sisters all who call on the name of Christ and repent of their sins and homosexual practices. We are compelled by God's love to extend an extra measure of compassion to people wounded by any form of sexual addiction.

The Apostle Paul wrote, "Do you not know that the unrighteous shall not inherit the kingdom of God? Do not be deceived; neither fornicators, nor idolaters, nor adulterers, nor effeminate, nor homosexuals…shall inherit the kingdom of God. And such were some of you; but you were washed, but you were sanctified, but you were justified in the name of the Lord Jesus Christ, and in the Spirit of our God" (1 Corinthians 6:9-11).

Also history shows us that every Christian society of the past has condemned the practice of homosexuality. Every state of the United States of America outlawed sodomy until recently. The history of Greece and Rome shows that the acceptance of homosexual practice is one of the last steps before the collapse of civilized societies.

We exhort pastors to read from their pulpits, and heads of families to discuss in their homes, this statement and the relevant Bible passages. We exhort all mature Christians to show compassion toward the sexually broken and actively demonstrate the love and compassion of our Redeemer God.

The Bible, which is the Word of the Living God, speaks clearly regarding homosexuality: Romans 1:24-28; 1 Timothy 1:9-10; Jude 7; Exodus 18:20; Leviticus 18:22-25; 20:13; 1 Kings 14:24.

DOCUMENT 18
Concerning Homosexuality

ARTICLES OF AFFIRMATION AND DENIAL

ARTICLE I

We affirm that Scripture describes homosexuality, in thought[a] or behavior,[b] as sin.

We deny that Scripture's discussion of homosexuality is culture-specific,[c] or relevant only to non-committed or "unnatural" homosexual relationships.*

   a. Matt. 5:27-28
   b. Gen. 18:20-21; 19:5-7, 13, 24-28; Lev. 18:22-24; 20:13-16; Judg. 19:22; 1 Kings 14:24; Rom. 1:24-32; 1 Cor. 6:9-11; 1 Tim. 1:8-11; Jude 1:7
   c. Ps. 119:89; Matt. 5:18-19; Isa. 8:20

ARTICLE II

We affirm that the Holy Spirit empowers homosexuals to change,[a] meaning that, by the grace of Christ, those who were homosexual can learn holy love[b] for both men and women.

We further affirm that sanctification in Christlikeness is progressive[c] and all Christians struggle against their inherent sinful nature until they reach heaven.[d]

We deny that a person is truly converted to Christ if he or she continues on in any homosexual practice.[e]

   a. 1 Cor. 6:9-11
   b. Rom. 13:8-10
   c. Heb. 12:14; 2 Pet. 3:18; Heb. 5:12-6:1; 1 Thess. 4:2-8
   d. Gal. 5:5; 5:16-6:9; Rom. 6:12-23; Pss. 17:15; 51:1-19
   e. 1 Cor. 6:9-11; Matt. 16:24-27; Lev. 20:13-16; Rom. 6:23

ARTICLE III

We affirm that spiritual change affects the whole person:[a] behavior, imagination, motives, beliefs, and affections.[b]

We deny that spiritual change targets behavior alone.[c]

   a. John 3:3
   b. Eph. 4:17-5:12; Col. 3:5-14
   c. Heb. 10:16; Jer. 32:38-40; 31:33-34; Titus 1:15-16

---

* It is our general understanding from Scripture that all of Scripture's condemnation of fornication applies as well to homosexual sex. And it is apparent that Scripture looks at homosexual sex not only as sin deserving judgment, but also sees it as "an abomination" (Lev. 18:22).

ARTICLE IV

We affirm that, like any sin, homosexuality can be influenced by innumerable factors, such as biology,[a] early homosexual molestation,[b] cultural values,[c] opportunities for homosexual experimentation.[d] However, those who are homosexual are so because they have made decisions to be homosexual.[e]

We deny that homosexuality is ultimately caused by biology or life circumstances. *We also deny* that homosexuality is something other than a moral choice.[f]

>   a. Lev. 21:18-21
>   b. Ezek. 20:18 19; Exod. 2015 6; Num. 14:18; Deut. 5:9-10
>   c. 1 Kings 14:24; 2 Kings 16:3; 21:2
>   d. Gal. 5:13; 1 Cor. 15:33; Prov. 13:20
>   e. Rom. 1:24-32; Lev. 20:13
>   f. Lev. 20:13; 1 Cor. 6:9-11

ARTICLE V

We affirm that we should devote as much attention to how we speak with love and grace to homosexuals as to what we speak.[a]

We deny that the clear teachings of Scripture on homosexuality must be muted in order to reach homosexuals in a compassionate manner.[b]

>   a. Prov. 22:11; 19:22; Col. 4:5-6
>   b. Zech. 8:16; John 8:45; Eph. 4:15

ARTICLE VI

We affirm that the preaching of the doctrines of grace and the fervent worship of the Triune God should attract homosexuals to the church,[a] that they might learn to trust, worship, and obey Jesus Christ.[b]

We deny that homosexuals who claim to be believers in Jesus Christ, and who are committed to practice their homosexual behavior, should be allowed to continue as communicant members of the church of Christ,[c]

>   a. 2 Cor. 2:14-17; Acts 2:46-47; Ps. 22:27
>   b. 1 Pet. 1:2; Rom. 1:5; Eph. 4:20-24
>   c. 1 Cor. 5:9-13; 2 Cor. 6:14; Eph. 5:11; 2 Thess. 3:6

ARTICLE VII

We affirm that the Bible teaches that practicing homosexuals will not inherit the Kingdom of God.[a]

We deny that the Bible offers any hope of salvation to an unrepentant, practicing homosexual.[b]

We further deny that one who is a practicing homosexual is following Jesus Christ, or that such a one may properly be called Christian.[c]

>   a. 1 Cor. 6:9
>   b. 1 Cor. 6:9
>   c. Matt. 16:24-27; Acts 11:26; Lev. 20:13 with Matt. 5:17-19

ARTICLE VIII

We affirm that repentant homosexuals who, recognizing the reality of their sin, call upon Jesus Christ for His salvation, leaving off homosexual practices, and become born again, are saved from eternal judgment, including judgment for homosexual sin, and may confidently expect to spend eternity with God and His saints in Heaven.[a]

We deny that practicing homosexuals have any Biblical reason to suppose they are born again, or that they will not be condemned for their sins, or that they have any reason to expect to spend eternity with God, but may only reasonably expect to spend eternity in hell, separated from God and His saints who are in Heaven.[b]

    a. 1 Cor. 6:9-11
    b. Rev. 22:14-15; 1 Cor. 6:9-11

ARTICLE IX

We affirm that the Gospel of Jesus Christ holds promise of eternal life for all repentant homosexuals.[a]

We deny that there is no hope for homosexuals, or that homosexuals cannot be forgiven if they are repentant and leave off homosexual practices.[b]

    a. 1 Tim. 1:15-16; Mark 2:17; Luke 15:2; 19:10; Acts 2:40-41
    b. Rom. 10:13; 1 Tim. 1:15-16

ARTICLE X

We affirm that God has called heterosexual men and women into leadership in Christ's Church.[a]

We deny that a practicing homosexual may be a pastor, a teacher, or hold any other office of service in Christ's Church,[b] or be a communicant member.[c]

    a. 1 Tim. 3:2-10; Titus 1:5-9; Gen. 1:27
    b. 1 Tim. 3:2-10; Titus 1:5-9; Deut. 17:14-15
    c. 1 Cor. 5:1-13; 2 Cor. 6:14; Eph. 5:3-12; 2 Thess. 3:6; Rev. 22:15

ARTICLE XI

We affirm that Christians and Christian churches ought to eagerly share Christ's love for the homosexual, urging them to repent and be washed from their sins by the blood of Jesus Christ.[a]

We deny that Christians ought to hate or reject homosexuals,[b] or that Christians ought to ignore homosexual sin as if it were a sin not needing repentance.[c]

    a. Mark 16:15-16; 2 Cor. 5:19-6:2; Eph. 1:7-8; 1 Pet. 1:2
    b. Luke 6:36; 1 Cor. 6:11; Eph. 5:1-2
    c. 1 Cor. 5:1-7; Rom. 13:12; 2 Cor. 6:16-7:1

TOPIC 19
A Biblical Approach to Counseling

INTRODUCTORY COMMENTS

by Dr. Eugene Calvin Clingman

Since the 1950s, various secular approaches to counseling and psychology such as Freudianism, Rogerianism, and Skinnerism have infiltrated Christian seminaries, churches, and organizations to such a degree that now thousands of well-meaning pastors and Christian counselors have been offering less-than-Biblical counseling to their parishioners and patients and thinking all along that they are representing God's Biblical truth as they do so. Dr. Grimstead asked Dr. David Powlison, who is a professor of counseling at Westminster Seminary East and a director of the Nouthetic Counseling Center, to create a white paper on "A Biblical Approach to Counseling" and he graciously wrote such a paper for us. Our team boiled the main points down into the creed-like statements of this present document on Biblical Counseling.

For the record we will mention that the founder of this Nouthetic Counseling Center was Dr. Jay Adams, who was also one of the ICBI Advisory Board members recruited by Dr. Grimstead in 1977.

One of the high points of folly in our modern world is that secular psychology has systematically excluded the knowledge of God from its study and practice. A counselor cannot truly help another human being without recognizing him to be a creature made in God's image, responsible to that God and His moral standards (God's law), and who is required to live in love toward God and people. When the Bible is rejected, when it is not taken as foundational to the understanding of who and what man is, the counselor is left to himself and to the prevailing winds of opinion and psychological fads, focused on getting the client the greatest measure of happiness, and thus begins his task immensely unprepared to help any hurting human. Some so-called Christian counselors are basically secular-pscyhology trained and use that viewpoint and those methods, for instance, that man is good and problems are brain chemistry, environment, experience, and/or behavior. True Christian counseling is really, or should be, Christian ministry, typical of what the church is supposed to always be doing, by a strong mature wise Christian or minister of the Gospel, whose approach is not man-focused but Christ-centered.

The Bible says there are only two possibilities for the source and standard of truth—God or man. The Bible says each human being is created in God's image with an eternal soul that will either abide forever in fellowship with God, experiencing all that humanness was meant to be—eternal bliss and fellowship with other redeemed humans and the holy angels, or he will live forever a death that never dies, his eternal soul cast away from God and every other rational creature, experiencing forever loneliness, regret, guilt, sadness, and despair.

The first necessary paradigm for competent counseling is this—the source of truth and understanding of man and his relationship to God and others must come from the Bible.

A second necessary paradigm for competent counseling is the understanding that man is a sinner. A sinner is one who has failed morally by failing to keep God's law standard.

A third necessary paradigm is that God has provided redemption and forgiveness for the sinner through Jesus Christ. Christ is truly the answer to the counselee's need, whether that need be forgiveness and restoration for his own sins committed, or help dealing with having been sinned against by others, or coping with the difficulties of everyday life.

The answer for each of these areas is found in Christ and His word. For a counselor to approach counseling with less than these necessary paradigms foremost in his mind is like a doctor eagerly coming to help his patient, not knowing his medicine is laced with arsenic and his surgical instruments coated with cyanide. He may sincerely wish to help his patient, but his remedies are loaded with poison that will surely diminish the possibility of recovery.

Christian bookstores are filled with racks of self-help books. But human beings were not designed to seek their own happiness as their primary goal. Man was designed by God to bring glory to God, and in so doing, enjoy Him forever and in so enjoying, find his greatest happiness and fulfillment. Seeking God, His glory, and His will are primary and necessary to a joyful and productive life. He who seeks to save his life will lose it, and he who loses his life for Jesus sake and the sake of the Kingdom of God, will find it. In His presence is fullness of joy and at His right hand there are pleasures forevermore.

Christian counseling should seek to give the counselee understanding of who he is in God's eyes, (a sinner responsible for his thoughts and actions, with unlimited possibilities of help, joy, and fulfillment in Jesus Christ), and fill the mind of the counselee with pertinent Biblical solutions, perspectives, goals, and hopes. In this way Christian counseling is an avenue of witness to those who are lost and a help for maturing Christians.

DOCUMENT 19

Concerning a Biblical Approach to Counseling

COPYRIGHT 2003, THE COALITION ON REVIVAL

ARTICLES OF AFFIRMATION AND DENIAL

ARTICLE I

We affirm that the Bible is the only basis of true knowledge about God, human existence, relationships between God and man, and relationships between people.[a]

We deny that man, his psyche, or his relationships with other people may be understood apart from the authoritative knowledge contained in the Bible.[b]

    a. Gen. 1:1; Deut. 29:29; Ps. 19:7-11,14; Prov. 1:7; Isa. 8:20; Col. 2:8; 2 Tim. 3:16
    b. Same as a. above.

ARTICLE II

We affirm that the Bible, by precept and example, is sufficient to provide a systematic approach to counseling and provides a sufficient basis for understanding all personal and situational problems.[a]

We deny that the Bible is inadequate to provide either wisdom for the counselor or comfort, reproof, correction, and training in right actions and thoughts to the counselee.[b]

    a. Deut. 29:29; Pss. 19:7-11,14; 119:98-100; Col. 2:8; 2 Tim. 3:16
    b. Same as a. above. Also Ps. 119:9,11

ARTICLE III

We affirm that the Biblical approach to counseling is fundamentally distinct from other counseling methods and is superior to any other method.[a]

We deny that all counseling methods produce the same results or that there is any method superior to Biblical instruction and counseling.[b]

    a. Ps. 119:98-100; Isa. 8:20
    b. Prov. 14:12

ARTICLE IV

We affirm that all human beings are created by God[a] and are morally accountable to Him for their choices,[b] for the things they believe,[c] and for how they live.[d]

We deny a non-moral universe and the concept of non-moral human beings.

We deny that human beings are guiltless in their choices and that they are the unwitting products of environment.

a. Gen. 1:1, 27
b. Hosea 6:7; Rom. :23; 5:12
c. Isa. 59:7; Jer. 4:14; Matt. 5:28; Rom. 1:5, 18-25; 16:26; 2 Cor. 10:5; Col. 2:8; Rev. 21:8
d. Isa. 1:28; 55:7; Rom. 1:28-32; 1 Cor. 6:9-10; Gal. 5:19-21; Rev. 21:8

ARTICLE V

We affirm that each person is required to love God supremely,[a] and his neighbor as himself,[b] and that psychological problems and immoral actions stem from failure to fulfill this requirement of love.[c]

We deny that psychological problems or immoral actions are the result of evolutionary immaturity, psychological preconditioning, or environment alone.

a. Deu. 6:5
b. Lev. 19:18
c. Rom. 13:8-10; Gal. 5:19-26

ARTICLE VI

We affirm that problems labeled "psychological," behavioral," "adjustment," "mental," "relational," and, "emotional" are "spiritual" problems.

We deny that "psychological," behavioral," "adjustment," "mental," "relational," and, "emotional" problems fall under a category outside the realm of spiritual problems.

ARTICLE VII

We affirm that sin hinders or severs relationship toward God[a] and toward our fellow human beings.[b] Sin is defined as failure to live up to God's moral requirements which are summed up in the two Great Commandments.[c]

We deny that human beings can live successfully and fruitfully when sin impairs relationships with God and others.[d]

a. Gen. 2:17 with 3:1-24; Ps. 51:4, 11; Matt. 27:46 with 2 Cor. 5:21
b. Gen. 6:11; Ezek. 16:21; Gal. 5:19-21
c. Matt. 22:36-40; 1 John 3:4
d. Pss. 1:1-6; 9:5-6; 11:6; 37:18-20; Zech. 5:4

ARTICLE VIII

We affirm that the image of God in man is a reflection of God's own nature deposited and imprinted on human personhood,[a] making each human life significant,[b] and that this image of God in man is the basis of, and reason for, the Ten Commandments and all social morals.

We deny that human life is on a par or near-par with animal life,[c] or that social morals ought to be derived from group consensus or social pragmatism.[d]

a. Gen. 1:27
b. Gen. 9:6
c. Gen. 1:27; Heb. 2:6-8
d. Exod. 23:2; Deut. 13:1-18

ARTICLE IX

We affirm that the Bible defines the ideal for human functioning in terms such as: to be renewed in the image of God,[a] to walk as Jesus walked,[b] to have the mind of Christ,[c] to live by faith,[d] to obey the law of God,[e] to bear the fruit of the Holy Spirit,[f] to glorify God,[g] to be wise,[h] to be holy as God is holy.[i]

We deny that any other standard or goal is worthy of human dignity, or true to the nature of man or his needs.[j]

    a. Phil. 2:15; 1 John 3:1-2
    b. Eph. 4:1-6, 17-24; 5:2; Col. 1:10; 2:6; Phil. 3:13-19; 1 John 2:6
    c. 1 Cor. 2:16; 2 Cor. 10:5
    d. Rom. 1:17; Gal. 2.20; Heb. 10:36-39
    e. Matt. 5:19; 2 Cor. 6:14; Heb. 8:10; 2 Cor. 6:14; 1 John 3:4
    f. Rom. 8:6; Gal. 5:22-26
    g. 1 Cor. 6:20; 1 Pet. 4:16
    h. Eph. 5:15; 1 Cor. 10:15; James 3:13
    i. Eph. 1:4; 5:27; 1 Pet. 1:15
    j. Gen. 1:27; Ps. 106:20; Rom. 1:22-23

ARTICLE X

We affirm that what the Bible calls sin is what is fundamentally and pervasively wrong with people,[a] and that counseling should be approached with this presupposition foremost in the mind of the counselor who should seek to bring the counselee into this same understanding.[b]

We deny that Christian counseling should rest on the presupposition that man's fundamental flaw is sociological, environmental, or psychological, or that such a presupposition is ultimately helpful to the counselee.

    a. Isa. 1:4-6; 55:7; Rom. 3:10-18, 23
    b. Pss. 1:1-6; 119:98-100; Isa. 8:20

ARTICLE XI

We affirm that all humans are capable of infinite self-deception.[a]

We deny that any human is capable of infallibly knowing his own heart.[b]

    a. Jer. 17:9; Matt. 15:14; Eph. 4:17-19,22; Titus 3:3; 2 Tim. 2:25-26
    b. Same as a. above.

ARTICLE XII

We affirm that the good news of redemption through Jesus Christ, as set forth in the Bible, is the solution for what troubles all people, spiritually, physically, and emotionally.[a]

We deny that any other solution or therapy, whether psychological, psycho-therapeutic, medical, philosophical, quasi-religious, or religious, actually addresses the real problem or cures souls.[b]

    a. Acts 10:38; 26:18; Cor. 6:11
    b. Isa. 8:20; Jer. 6:14; 8:11

ARTICLE XIII

We affirm that Christian counseling deals not only with personal sin, but also with suffering, being sinned against, enemies, temptations and trials, hardships, evil companions, lies from the cultural surround, etc., that is with the whole of human experience.[a] [22]

We deny that Christian counseling is limited to needs engendered by personal sins.[b]

> a.Ps. 19:7-11,14; 2 Tim. 3:16-17
> b. Same as a. above.

ARTICLE XIV

We affirm that the goal of Christian counseling is to aid in the process of Biblical conversion and sanctification,[a] which process progressively restores human beings to the image in which man was originally created, and ultimately into the image of Christ.[b]

We deny that self-actualization, individuation, self-fulfillment, the meeting of supposed psychological needs, etc., describe the goal of Christian counseling.

> a. Matt. 28:20; Acts 26:18; Eph. 4:20-32; 1 Thess. 4:3-8
> b. Rom. 8:29; Eph. 5:1-2; Heb. 2:11; 1 Pet. 1:14-17,23

ARTICLE XV

We affirm that in order for persons to be renewed in their thinking, choosing, emotions, and relationships, they must learn to progressively put off old ways of thinking and acting, and be renewed in the spirit of their mind, and put on the new self, which in the likeness of God has been created in righteousness and holiness of the truth.[a]

We deny that any process which attempts to lead a person to improve, modify, or reconstruct life without Biblically-based identification with Jesus Christ has a place in Christian counseling.[b]

> a. Rom. 12:1-2; Eph. 4:20-5:2; 2 Pet. 3:17-18
> b. Isa. 8:20; Matt. 28:20; Col. 2:8,18-19

ARTICLE XVI

We affirm that the Church is commissioned by God to the task of maturing believers into the image of Christ,[a] and therefore counseling is an important restorative function of the Church.[b]

We deny that any person or entity has the right to demand that counseling be reserved for the mental health professional to the exclusion of the Church.

> a. See Article XIV, a. and b.; 2 Cor. 3:17-18; Col. 1:28-29; Heb. 5:12-14
> b. Isa. 11:2 with John 20:22 and 2 Cor. 5:20; Eph. 4:11-16

---

22 Jesus Christ dealt with the whole person, with all his needs, felt and real. Christian counseling deals with the whole of the inner man, the soul of man.

ARTICLE XVII

We affirm that the Scriptures contain the framework of ultimate meaning and values for every sphere of life.[a]

We deny that the Bible is inadequate to provide the ultimate meaning and values for every sphere of life.

> a. Gen. 1:1; Ps. 119:98-100; Prov. 1:7; 8:1-36; Isa. 8:20; 2 Tim. 3:16-17

ARTICLE XVIII

We affirm that some counselees may need medical treatment or other practical helps (educational, vocational, financial) as supplements to Biblical counseling in the overall process of progressive sanctification.

We deny that alleviating medical or social problems alone is the answer to anyone's spiritual problems; and

We deny that Biblical counseling should be neglected in cases where medical or social actions are also needed.

ARTICLE XIX

We affirm that secular counseling disciplines that do not begin with Biblical principles are fundamentally and presuppositionally distorted.[a]

We deny that there is any counseling method not beginning with Biblical principles that is anything less than fundamentally flawed in its ability to arrive at real and lasting solutions for the counselee.[b]

> a. Gen. 1:1, 27; Prov. 1:7; Isa. 8:20
> b. This has been established in the preceding Articles of Affirmation and Denial.

ARTICLE XX

We affirm that some observations and practices of secular psychologists (and other non-Christians) may be helpful in Christian counseling when reinterpreted and reconfigured in light of Biblical presuppositions.

We deny that any theory or technique which does not flow from Biblical presuppositions is faithful to the realities of human nature or human needs.

> This has been established in the preceding Articles of Affirmation and Denial.

ARTICLE XXI

We affirm that Bible-based counseling is a significant opportunity to lead people to the forgiveness of sins through knowledge of and relationship with Christ.[a]

We deny that the Christian counselor should refrain from challenging people to receive Christ and His ways.[b]

> a. Matt. 28:20
> b. Same as a. above.

ARTICLE XXII

We affirm that some Christians are called to serve in institutions and ministries, both Christian and non-Christian, which serve people's counseling needs, in order both to help needy individuals and to influence professions and institutions with the Biblical worldview.[a]

We deny that either this profession or its institutions should be avoided by Christians, or that Christians serving in this profession or its institutions should suppress their Biblical worldview in order to conform to the secular viewpoint of this profession or its institutions.[b]

    a. Matt. 5:13
    b. Matt. 5:15-16; Phil. 2:15-16

TOPIC 20

Israel and the Church

INTRODUCTORY COMMENTS

by Dr. Jay Grimstead

The committee for this paper was headed up by a Messianic Jewish scholar whom we love and respect, Dr. Daniel Juster, Director of Tikkun Ministries. There is a very large interest among Bible-believing Christians in both the land of Israel and the present day Jews in particular, and there are an increasing number of "Messianic Christian Congregations" being called into existence.

We believe this paper will offer the greater Body of Christ a balanced and Biblical perspective that will, on the one hand, encourage non-Jewish Christians to appreciate the heritage of the Jews, the great amount which Christians owe to the Jews, and to greatly help eliminate anti-Semitism. On the other hand, we hope this paper will help some Jewish-oriented Christians and Messianic congregations and organizations not to over-emphasize their "Jewishness" so that they sometimes present to outsiders the appearance of unbalanced attitudes and approaches.

There is one particular un-Biblical view about the Jews that we should address that has risen out of a theology called dispensationalism which many godly, sincere Christians believe, and which appears to be believed and taught by some Christian Messianic congregations. That view claims that, in God's perspective about life on this planet, He sees the nation of Israel as a third category of human beings, as if there were: (1) believers (saved), (2) unbelievers (lost), and (3) Israel (another special category). This document clearly and Biblically states that there are fundamentally only two types of humans: (1) the saved, and (2) the lost; and from the time of creation on to the return of Christ, there will only and always be only these two categories of humans in God's mind. So each individual Jewish person is either saved or lost, but they are not in a special third category of human beings. Israel is a nation (a people group) to whom God made special promises, some yet to be fulfilled. All God's promises have their answer in Jesus Christ the Messiah, including those given to Israel as a nation.

DOCUMENT 20

Concerning Israel and the Church

COPYRIGHT 2003, THE COALITION ON REVIVAL

ARTICLES OF AFFIRMATION AND DENIAL

ARTICLE I

We affirm that by virtue of divine election,[a] the preservation and ultimate engrafting of Jewish people demonstrate God's mercy and faithfulness to His Word and serves the purpose of the conversion of the Gentiles just as the engrafting of the Gentiles serves the purpose of the conversion of the Jews.

We deny that this "divine election" implies the salvation of individual Jews without their repentance and conversion through the Gospel.

> a. Rom. 11:1-2, 25-26

ARTICLE II

We affirm that Christians of all nations are called to show love and mercy to Jewish people and to call them to repentance as with other peoples as part of their witness.[a]

We deny that seeking to bring Jews to the knowledge of Jesus the Messiah is demeaning, disrespectful, or unloving.[b]

> a. Rom. 11:30-31
> b. Rom. 11:14; 9:3

ARTICLE III

We affirm that Christians of all nations are indebted to the Jewish people for preserving the Scriptures and especially to the saved remnant of ancient Israel who were faithful to the covenants and brought the Gospel to the world.[a]

We deny that this gives ground for Christians to idolize the Jewish people who will also be indebted to Christians of other nations at the end of the age for their salvation.[b]

> a. Rom. 9:4-5; 11:18
> b. Rom. 11:14, 30-32

ARTICLE IV

We affirm the legitimacy of Jewish followers of Jesus remaining part of their people, whether individually or in Messianic Jewish congregations, or in Messianic Jewish cell groups in the structure of the larger Church.

We deny the validity of forming congregations with exclusive physical descent membership policies or sectarian attitudes of separation from the larger Body of Christ[a] or that maintaining Jewish cultural expressions should be required.

> a. Gal. 3:28; Eph. 2:14-18

ARTICLE V

We affirm the unity in the Messiah of Jew and Gentile as one new man and the spiritual seed of Abraham.[a]

We deny that this precludes uniquely Jewish or other cultural/ethnic expressions of New Covenant faith or differences of calling among people in the Body of Christ.[b]

> a. Gal. 3:28-29; Eph. 1:6-7
> b. Rom. 11:29; 1 Cor. 1:2; 7:17-24

ARTICLE VI

We affirm that the return of the Jewish people to the land of Israel may or may not be part of God's prophetic fulfillment in working to bring all elect "Israel" to Himself.

We further affirm that Jews who believe in Christ will be grafted back into the "Olive Tree" in which all followers of Jesus find their sustenance.[a]

We deny that this gives Israel the right to treat Gentiles in the Promised Land with injustice or give an unqualified right and mandate to take by military force at the present time the land promised to Abraham.

> a. Rom. 11:23-26

ARTICLE VII

We affirm that all forms of anti-Semitism are contrary to Christian faith.

We further affirm that the Jewish people as a people are rich in cultural contributions to the world, a culture with significant praiseworthy elements.[a]

We deny that Rabbinical Judaism is an adequate faith for the salvation of the Jewish people.[b]

> a. Gen. 12:1-3; Rom. 9:15
> b. Rom. 10:1-3

ARTICLE VIII

We affirm that, with regard to salvation, God has always had only two categories of people: those who are His people and are saved, and those who are not His people and are lost.

We deny that the Jewish people comprise a third category of humanity as if there are the saved, the lost, and the Jews.

ARTICLE IX

We affirm that the "middle wall of partition"[a] has been broken down and there is now "one new man" in Christ, which comprise God's people.

We deny that God seeks to have all people groups dissolve into a homogeneity or that God may not have purposes for varieties of people.

    a. Eph. 2:14

TOPIC 21

Concerning the Education of Christian Children

INTRODUCTORY COMMENTS

by Dr. Eugene Calvin Clingman

It was in 2004 at a gathering in Dr. Jay Grimstead's living room that I brought up the possibility of creating a COR document on the education of Christian children. Our friend Mark Rushdoony (son of Dr. R. J. Rushdoony) and others were there, all of us with our wives. I had mentioned this issue to Jay before, but this time it sprang to life in Jay's mind. We agreed that a paper was needed that would deal with one of the most significant problems of our time, the giving of Christian children to the state for indoctrination by the government school system (AKA public schools).

Because I had a great concern for this issue, Dr. Grimstead assigned me to create the first set of principles which would be discussed, edited, then boiled down into the affirmations and denials for the document that would be titled Concerning the Education of Christian Children.

This important document focuses on two fundamental concepts:

1) Scripture commands parents to train their children in the nurture and admonition of the Lord into a Christian worldview,

2) Though civil government is a God-ordained jurisdiction, God has not given civil government any jurisdiction over the education or indoctrination of children.

Such a document needed to be written for the Church because the statistics tell us two tragic facts about America's youth who grow up in church:

1. Almost 90 percent of all children who attend church also are students in the public school system.

2. More than 80 percent of these government-schooled Christian children cast off their Christian faith during high school, college, or shortly thereafter!

These horrible statistics tell us there is major blindness in the Church. There is a great need for the Church to make a change.

The Southern Baptist Council on Family Life reported to the 2002 Annual Meeting of the Southern Baptist Convention that 88 percent of the children raised in evangelical homes leave church at the age of 18, never to return. Is there something wrong with this? Is this the plan and purpose of our God who told us He would be God to us AND to our children, if only we would obey Him and also diligently train our children into a Biblical worldview (Deuteronomy 6:6-9)?

The statistics presented in this introduction are based on America. Yet because much of the developed and developing world is unfortunately influenced by and following the U.S. in educational philosophy and goals, the document in the pages that follow was written for the international Church; it is by no means for the U.S. only.

In the years my generation attended government schools, America and its institutions (including the public school system) were still operating under the influence of what Dr. Francis Schaeffer called the "memory of Christian principles," which lasted up through the 1940s, 1950s and into the early 1960s and even beyond. In those days, it was not anywhere near as dangerous or disastrous to send Christian kids to public schools as it is now, although it was always better for their early philosophical training to send them to a private Christian school or to home school them. Today, after America's social-political-moral revolution largely beginning in 1964, the forces of intentional, anti-Biblical, humanistic thought and raw paganism have been increasingly forced upon the public school students in ever heavier doses. By the 1990s it was becoming clear that sending Christian kids to public school was essentially moral and philosophical suicide. The government public school system is purposefully calibrated to indoctrinate children through each subject into humanism, socialism, and amoral/situational ethics while Christ and Christian principles are mocked and exiled from the classroom. How did we get to this point?

The Common Schools were the predecessors of what has become the modern public school system. These common schools were begun by committed Christians who knew that in order to preserve a Christian civil order and culture, the people needed to be able to read the Bible so as to know Christ the Savior. These schools were begun with the primary intention to teach children to read so they could read the Bible. In 1647 a law called the Old Deluder Satan Law was passed in the colonies that required a town of 50 or more families to provide an elementary school where reading, writing, and Bible were taught. These once Christian schools were eventually hijacked by the Unitarians. In process of time influential educational thinkers like John Dewey put these public schools on a path purposely leading away from Christianity and the Bible. The public school system of today is finely tuned to remove Christianity from the student and the culture. And if this is the measure of its success, it is succeeding phenomenally!

Education is inherently religious; the subject matter being taught cannot be taught from a religiously neutral point of view, it is always couched in a worldview and worldviews are by nature religious. Evolution is held by faith; in other words evolution is religiously held; evolution is a religion. Humanism, the belief that there is nothing higher than man, is held by faith; humanism is a religion.

We should ask ourselves, would it have been acceptable to the God of Israel for the Jews to take their children to the priests of Baal to be trained and intellectually groomed for their future lives as Jewish adults? What about taking the Israelite children over to the Philistines so the priests of Dagon could train them? Or maybe bus them back to Egypt to attend Egyptian schools! To each of these the answer is clear! Yet close to 90 percent of Christian children in the U.S. also attend schools of a faith other than the faith of Christ, the Creator and Sustainer of all things. These schools are overseen primarily by those who teach a worldview just as opposed to Christianity as Dagon worship was to the worship of the God of Israel.

The evolutionistic-humanistic religion of the government school will allow no other religion. This is why Christianity is banned. Religious beliefs are always exclusive. It is evolutionary-humanism that reigns in the government school system, in spite of the fact that many Christian teachers and administrators are employed by the system.

The quintessential question every worldview answers is this — "Is there a God?"

The next question that must be answered is "Who is that God; is it the God of the Bible?"

The government school system in America emphatically insists that there is no God and is particularly emphatic on insisting that the God of the Bible does not or could not exist. Sometimes this is done by outright denial of God, other times by subtly ignoring the reality of God who is all around them and who speaks to them in every fact and experience they encounter in the God-created environment in which they live and move and have their being!

The worldview of the government school education is the religious faith of evolutionary-humanism. Evolutionary-humanism believes there is no God. The public school system is therefore foolish, for "the fool has said in his heart, 'There is no God'." Scripture assures us that "He who walks with wise men will be wise, but the companion of fools will suffer harm" (Proverbs 13:20). Indeed, 88 percent demise in the faith of Christian children demonstrates the harm that is suffered.

The humanist establishment understands the religious nature of the battle and is deliberately using the government schools to destroy Christianity.

This comes to light in such statements as this:

"I am convinced that the battle for humankind's future must be waged and won in the public school classroom by teachers who correctly perceive their roles as the proselytizers of a new faith: a religion of humanity that recognizes and respects the spark of what theologians call divinity in every human being. These teachers must embody the same selfless dedication as the most rabid fundamentalist preachers, for they will be ministers of another sort, utilizing a classroom instead of a pulpit to convey humanist values in whatever they teach, regardless of the educational level — preschool, day care, or large state university."

John Dunphy, *The Humanist Magazine* (Jan/Feb 1983)

Humanism has a comprehensive and dedicated program to promote itself. God tells Christian parents, indeed He tells the whole Church:

"Now this is the commandment, and these are the statutes and judgments which the LORD your God has commanded to teach you, that you may observe them in the land which you are crossing over to possess, that you may fear the LORD your God, to keep all His statutes and His commandments which I command you, you and your son and your grandson, all the days of your life, and that your days may be prolonged.... And these words which I command you today shall be in your heart. You shall teach them diligently to your children, and shall talk of them when you sit in your house, when you walk by the way, when you lie down, and when you rise up."

Deuteronomy 6:1-2, 6-7 (NKJV)

Can we honestly say we are training our children "diligently," as God commands, if they spend 30 or so hours a week with the priests of another faith? Isn't it presumptuous to hope a few hours of Sunday school, church service, and youth group will repair the damage?

We should understand that the work of the Church and of every Christian ministry is effective into the future only as the good results of present efforts are carried into the future by the next generation. Any progress we make in this generation, that gets God's will done on earth, as in heaven, will be established or lost depending to a great extent on the generation that follows. We can build and restore, teach and disciple, but only as the next generation has a clear vision of what it means to be Christian, and how Christianity should work itself into society as salt and light — only then can the progress survive.

It is the firm conviction of the COR Board and Steering Committee that education is an assignment given by God to parents and the Church. God has not assigned to civil government the business of indoctrinating (educating) children. We urge Christian parents to remove their children from the public school system and give them some form of Christian education. It is our earnest prayer and desire that the readers of this document Concerning the Education of Christian Children be blessed by the Lord to this end.

DOCUMENT 21

Concerning the Education of Christian Children

ARTICLES OF AFFIRMATION AND DENIAL

CopyRight 2006, The Coalition on Revival

PREFACE

We refer the reader to two documents that are foundational to these Affirmation and Denial statements. They are Document 1: "Biblical Inerrancy" and Document 10: "The Lordship of Christ" in this book, and are also downloadable for printing out at our Website, www.ChurchCouncil.org. The statements set forth in this document assume what is set forth in them.

A. Foundational Biblical Principles and the Myth of Neutrality

ARTICLE I

The Bible is our absolute guide for all life and all education.

We affirm that the Bible—being God's own inerrant, written Word—is the ultimate standard by which all other truth-claims are to be judged,[a] and thus offers mankind the clearest, most complete picture of all reality and the only logically coherent worldview,[b] and is the only authoritative standard and guide for living and pleasing God.[c]

We further affirm that though knowledge sources other than the Christian Bible such as reason, research, tradition, and experience are all valuable tools in gaining wisdom and knowledge of God, mankind, and the universe, all such tools are always to be judged and informed by the Bible rather than them standing in judgment on the Bible's truth. The Bible tells us that the fear of the Lord is the beginning of wisdom but not the end of wisdom.

We further affirm that the Bible sufficiently sets forth God's requirements for the education of Christian children.[d]

We deny that there is any source of truth higher than, or equal to, the Bible or that the Bible may be judged by any other standard.

We further deny that the Bible is either silent or neutral on the subject of the education of Christian children, or that it is insufficient in setting forth requirements for the training of Christian children.

>   a. Num. 23:19; Pss. 111:7; 119:89, 151, 160; Matt. 24:35; John 17:17; 2 Tim. 3:16-17; 2 Pet. 1:20-21
>   b. Isa. 8:20
>   c. Josh. 1:8; Ps. 119:9; Eccles. 11:9-10
>   d. 2 Tim. 2:16-17

ARTICLE II

All education is religious education.

We affirm that all education is foundationally religious — for the assumptions of every educator, educational system, and curriculum rests upon non-provable faith presuppositions (i.e., religious presuppositions) about reality, the nature of history, the being of man (metaphysics), the nature of knowledge (epistemology), and of morality (ethics).

We deny that educators, child development theorists, ethicists, curriculum writers, etc., are religiously, metaphysically, epistemologically, or ethically neutral, for they all live and work on the basis of either the Christian worldview or some non-Christian worldview, and interpret all facts in light of their worldview and their presuppositions.

We deny that anyone is or can be religiously, metaphysically, epistemologically, or ethically neutral — having no presuppositions, no view of truth, no view of right and wrong, or no worldview.

ARTICLE III

Christians are required to live in obedience to their Lord Jesus and the Bible.

We affirm that Jesus is Lord of every area of life including education, and that every human,[a] especially Christians, are required by God's Word to submit themselves and all persons and things under their care to the Lordship of Christ and the teachings and requirements of the Bible.[b]

We deny that education is outside the jurisdiction of Christ's Lordship or the Bible's teaching.

We further deny that a person may reject either the Lordship of Jesus Christ or the Bible's instruction for educating our children and be a mature and wise Christian.

>   a. Phil. 2:10-11; 2 Cor. 10:5; Col. 2:2-3
>   b. Deut. 6:25; Matt. 5:19; 16:24-26; 1 Cor. 6:20; 1 John 5:2-3

B. The Biblically Mandated Jurisdictions of Family, Church, and Civil Government

ARTICLE IV

The Bible clarifies three God-ordained jurisdictions; the Family, the Church, the Civil Government.

We affirm that in the Bible God clearly designates three major areas of jurisdiction for the healthy, productive, and just operation of human society, and gives each of these jurisdictions specific authority and well-defined duties for society, which jurisdictions are: the Family, the Church, and the civil government.[a]

We further affirm that tyranny occurs and society's self-destruction begins whenever any of these three jurisdictions attempts to exercise authority or control within the boundaries of either of the other two jurisdictions. Both life and liberty may only be truly attained for individuals and society through the knowledge of our Lord Jesus Christ and glad submission to the principles of the Bible.

We further affirm that the family is the basic building-block of strong, healthy societies and that undermining families or interfering with the family's jurisdiction is a fast way to deteriorate and destroy any society.

We deny that the Family, the Church, or the civil government in a society may take authority and control in either of the other two jurisdictions without that particular society moving in the direction of self-destruction and injustice.

We deny that these three distinct jurisdictions are rightly or fully maintained if either the civil government or the church controls the education of children.

a. Gen. 18:19; Deut. 6:1–9, 20–25; 11:19–22; Ps. 78:3–6; Prov. 1:8; 2:1f; 3:1; 4:1–4, 7, 20; 6:20–22; 22:6; 31:1; Eph. 6:1–4

ARTICLE V

Parental jurisdiction over their children and their children's training and education —

We affirm that God has given parents custody, jurisdiction, and authority over their children, as stewards to raise them as servants of Christ, to seek to discern their calling, and to train, discipline, and educate them in the Biblical worldview. Parents may not rightfully yield their jurisdiction or authority to the civil government.[a]

We deny that, Biblically, the civil government has ownership, jurisdiction, or authority over children, or that the civil government has authority to usurp the stewardship to raise or educate children given by God to the parents.

We further deny that the civil government or the church may interfere with a parent's education of their children except in some matters of abandonment or criminal justice, or may impose requirements, standards, or methods for training, educating, or disciplining their children.

We further deny that the civil government has a right before God to impose compulsory attendance laws, licensure of teachers of private schools, or curriculum requirements for home and private schools.

> a. Ps. 127:3-5; Gen. 18:19; Eph. 6:4; Deut. 12:28; 1 Sam. 3:13

C. *Christian Education of Christians' Children Is Biblically Mandated*

ARTICLE VI

The obligation of Christian parents to give their children a Biblically based education —

We affirm that the Bible provides the only adequate and coherent worldview and foundation for all philosophy, ethics, law, government, science, the arts, and education[a] and that Christian parents are obligated by God to guide and educate their children to think, decide, feel, and act in all areas of life according to the worldview presented in the Bible[b] and may not righteously allow their children to be educated in worldviews which oppose the Biblical worldview.[c] "The fear of the Lord is the beginning of wisdom."[d]

We further affirm that Christians are required by God to train their children for their greatest possible impact for Christ's purposes on earth[e] and to find their special destiny in God,[f] to train further for that destiny if needed,[g] and to fulfill that special calling with all their heart and with a passionate love and obedience to their Lord Christ[h] and to extend God's Kingdom here on earth.[i]

We deny that education can be evaluated as good or successful if it does not purposefully train the child into the Christian worldview and assist the child in bringing all thoughts captive to the obedience of Christ, or is not cognizant of, and tailored to, the individual gifts and calling of each child.

> a. Gen. 1:1
> b. Rom. 12:1-2; 2 Cor. 10:5; Isa. 8:20
> c. Prov. 13:20; 1 Cor. 15:33; Deut. 12:30; Ps. 106:34-36
> d. Ps. 111:10
> e. Gen. 1:28; 18:19; Deut. 10:12-13
> f. 1 Peter 4:10
> g. 2 Tim. 2:15
> h. Deut. 6:5; Col. 3:23-24; Heb. 9:14
> i. Matt. 28:18-20; Hab. 2:13-14

ARTICLE VII

Anti-Biblical educators are incompetent to teach the children of Christians.

We affirm that educators who stand opposed to God and the principles of the Bible and who believe any of the unfounded, foolish, modern myths that: (1) there is no personal, Creator God, (2) all morals are relative, (3) the universe came into being out of impersonal matter-energy by chance, (4) man is just an animal, (5) mankind is not corrupted by the Fall, (6) there is no afterlife or final judgment by God, (7) Christ is not the incarnate God who died as a sacrifice to redeem the elect, (8) the civil government is our highest authority and owns the children, (9) the Bible is not God's inerrant, written Word to mankind…do not have the philosophical, moral, or personal competence to properly educate Christian children.[a]

We deny that there is a Kantian-type dichotomy and disconnect between the visible world and the invisible world and that: (1) there is no logical or linguistic connection possible between the invisible "upper story" and the visible "lower story," (2) that human language is inadequate to bridge the gap between these two realms, (3) that there are some areas of life that are outside of God's control or plans or interest, (4) this false, dichotomy thought-form may be pursued without tending toward government tyranny, the disintegration of society, and attacks upon Christianity.

We further deny that there is any area of thought, life, or culture outside the scope of the Bible's Creation Mandate (Genesis 1:28; 9:7), the Lord's Prayer (Matthew 6:10), or the Great Commission (Matthew 28:18-20).

We further deny that Christian parents may righteously choose educational options for their children that do not purposefully and faithfully affirm the Lord Jesus as present King of the universe and promote or encourage His righteous, Biblical purposes for all mankind, or place their children under teachers and mentors, with peers, or under the influence of a curriculum that would tend to lead them into a secular, anti-Christian, un-Biblical worldview or into moral compromise.

We further deny that teachers, mentors, and other students have a neutral effect on a child's educational, moral, or spiritual development.

    a. Ps. 14:1; Prov. 13:20; 1 Cor. 6:1-6; 15:33; Isa. 2:6; 8:20; Deut. 12:30; Ps. 106:34-36

D. What Constitutes True Education in the Biblical Worldview?

ARTICLE VIII

The ingredients of a Christian education —

We affirm that a Biblical education in the Christian worldview will have these ingredients:

(1) parental-controlled teaching,[a] (2) a Biblical curriculum,[b] (3) Biblical goals for the education,[c] (4) Biblical standards,[b,d] (5) Biblical methods,[e] and (6) Biblical motivations for accomplishing the child's education.

We deny that education is Biblical or Christian if parental responsibility, parental presence, and parental participation are not involved and if the ultimate goal is not to glorify God and enjoy Him forever.

We further deny that education is Biblical or Christian if its ultimate standard in theory and practice is not the Bible itself, and if its priority is the impartation of facts to the neglect of the formation of Christ-like character and a Christian way of life or if the subservient motivations it uses are inconsistent with Scripture.

a. Gen. 18:19; Deut. 6:1–9, 20–25; 11:19–22; Ps. 78:3–6; Prov. 1:8; 2:1ff.; 3:1; 4:1–4, 7, 20; 6:20–22; 22:6; 31:1; Eph. 6:1–4
b. Deut. 6:1-9; 30:10, 17-20; Josh. 1:8; Isa. 2:6; 8:20; Eph. 6:1-4; Rom. 12:1-2; 2 Cor. 10:5
c. Gen. 1:28; 9:1; Hab. 2:13-14; Matt. 28:18-20; John 12:26; Rom. 12:1-2; 2 Cor. 6:14-7:1; 10:5; Eph. 6:1-4; 1 John 2:15-17
d. Prov. 13:20; 1 Cor. 15:33; 2 Cor. 6:14-7:1
e. Deut. 6:1-9; Luke 6:40
f. Deut. 28:1-68; Hab. 2:13-14; Matt. 22:37-40; Rev. 20:11-21:11

ARTICLE IX

Generational thinking and our covenant with God —

We affirm that Christians are required to think in terms of generational faithfulness regarding how their training of their children will be passed on to their children's children and how families are to develop solidarity, mutual commitment to Christian family goals, interdependence and a model for a Biblical family functioning in all phases of life.[a]

We further affirm that giving a comprehensive, Christian education to their children is a vital aspect of Christian parents keeping covenant with God, operating generationally, soundly training, productive citizens for their society's future and receiving the covenant blessings of God.

We deny that Christian parents or church staff and elders are properly fulfilling their leadership role if they fail to teach and model the Biblical necessity of Christians to educate their children into the Christian worldview and the necessity of shielding their children from indoctrination by the civil government, or into any but the Christian worldview, or if they are not teaching and modeling generational thinking among those they influence.

a. Exod. 32:13; Deut. 6:1-9; Ps. 78:1-11; Eph. 5:22-6:9

ARTICLE X

Only the Bible presents a true perspective of history and all reality.

We affirm that a correct view of history can be achieved only by accepting that there was a beginning when all things out of nothing were created by God,[a] that man is fallen and in need of a redeemer,[b] and that Redeemer has come — the Lord Jesus Christ,[c] and that earth's history will end with the final judgment of all who have ever lived in history.[d] History is linear,[e] heading in a definite direction that is sovereignly guided by God.[f] History is not cyclical.[g]

We deny that history can be understood apart from a firm knowledge of its basics which are: Creation, Fall, Redemption, and Judgment, or that one can understand the context of reality for any subject apart from seeing Christ as the centerpiece of all reality and the lens of perspective through which all people are to view all things in life.

We further deny that man is basically good, or that avoiding or obfuscating the fact of sin and the Fall or its effects on the human race can lead to true education, or that true education can take place when the reality of God Who created all things out of nothing is denied.

a. Gen. 1:1-31
b. Gen. 3:1-24
c. Matt. 1:20-23; 1 Tim. 1:15
d. 2 Cor. 5:10; Rev. 20:12-15
e. Gen. 1:1; 1 Cor. 15:24
f. Amos 3:6; Matt. 10:29-31; Acts 2:23
g. Gen. 1:1; Rev. 21:1; 22:3-4

ARTICLE XI

Imparting worldview is impossible for the teacher to avoid.

We affirm that every fact taught to a student is necessarily couched in the worldview of the school, its curriculum and methodology, and the teacher, and therefore both facts and worldview are passed from the teacher to the student in the teaching and learning process.[a]

We further affirm that the words of Jesus: "a disciple … will be like his teacher" (Luke 6:40, NKJV), recognize that the process of education includes the passing of knowledge and character from the teacher to the student and that the usual outcome of education makes the student like the teacher in both knowledge and character to some degree.

We deny that facts may be taught to students from a neutral viewpoint or that the teacher's worldview is ever removed from the teaching and learning process.

We further deny that education takes place without passing both knowledge and character from the teacher to the student.

a. Prov. 13:20; Luke 6:40; 1 Cor. 15:33; 2 Cor. 6:14-17

ARTICLE XII

How the Church can help parents educate their children.

We affirm that the church may assist parents in the education of their children by establishing Christian schools, and that righteous options for educating Christian children include home schooling and church sponsored or privately run Christian schools.

We deny that by establishing Christian schools the church is given jurisdiction over the education of children other than that which the parents delegate temporarily and partially to the school.

We further deny that any K through 12 civil government schools (aka, public schools) which are not thoroughly committed to God's inspiration of the Bible, to teaching Biblical principles, and to advancing the Kingdom of Christ on earth are a righteous choice for Christian parents to make for their children.

TOPIC 22

The Sanctity
of Human Life

INTRODUCTORY COMMENTS

by Dr. Jay Grimstead

Jesus taught us to pray daily, *Thy Kingdom come, Thy will be done,* ON EARTH *as it is in heaven!* For the Christian who is thinking Scripturally, it is plain to see that it is *not* God's will for babies to be cut to pieces or burnt alive with salt water in their mother's womb!

The Coalition on Revival began to take on the issue of the Sanctity of Human Life after it was first urged upon the COR Board of Directors by Board Member Jerry Nordskog (Nordskog Publishing Inc.) whose heart it had weighed upon for some time. The COR Board approved Jerry's recommendation. The document created is scientifically informed and always guided by the queen of sciences, Biblical theology. This is truly an issue that calls for Christian involvement!

Dr. Jay Grimstead assumed the task of architect to take this document through its various stages of writing and editing to its completion. Again there was a review committee that helped mold it along the way, and its content bounced back and forth between us as we considered various approaches and how much to deal with the philosophy of truth and epistemology within this document.

The primary theologian who offered the most direction about its content and our need to deal with the epistemological question of "How do we know Truth at all?" was Dr. Robert Fugate who directs "Thy Word Is Truth" ministries. He is on our COR Steering Committee and is one of COR's major theologians. Thanks to him, this document is, in itself, an outstanding worldview study from the basement to the top floor. "The Bible is truth!" is the opening proposition and it builds from there.

This paper states in terms unequivocal that abortion is murder (Article XII Affirmation), and that God requires the civil government to execute murderers (XIII). Civil government is the only institution authorized (required) by God to use the death penalty; no individual or group has this authority (XX). A society that does not deal properly with murderers will itself be judged by God (XIV).

It also addresses the oft-presented excuse, What if the life of the mother is at risk? (XVIII).

This topic, more than any that the Coalition on Revival is dealing with, requires consulting not only the Bible, but also medicine and psychology. For this reason there are a large number of footnotes and an extensive appendix with footnotes and source references. There is also a section by the Elliot Institute (AfterAbortion.org) that shows recent research of abortion's harm to women, life-threatening dangers of abortion, and psychological risks. (Some excerpts of this material are included in this book as Appendix O, pp. 286-296; our Website, www.ChurchCouncil.org, has this document with complete appendices.) It was Dr. Fugate who put us in touch with the Elliot Institute and their impressive work which makes this Appendix such a valuable tool. *There is enough medical, legal, and psychological information in this Elliot Institute Appendix that any pro-life activist group would be able to lay the foundation for a winnable legal case that could possibly put many abortion clinics out of business just by getting women who have been deeply damaged (physically, psychologically, financially, socially, etc.) to work with a sharp, pro-life lawyer to bring charges against such abortion clinics and sue them out of business, once the local, personal testimonies of major damage from abortions have been recorded.*

The Coalition on Revival sets forth this document with the belief that the Bible is clear on abortion. We urge the Church of Jesus Christ to awaken and hold forth God's standard within her sanctuaries and also carry the message to the public square, becoming active in the political and cultural arenas to apply the brakes until a full stop comes to the vicious murder of unborn children and euthanasia of the youngest and oldest among us. One of the very disturbing facts which needs to be brought out into the open sunlight for all to see, with statistics backing up such research, is that a very high percentage of teenage and college-age girls in Christian churches, including daughters of pastors and deacons, have secretly had abortions and their parents and church leaders have intentionally kept this quiet so that necessary repentance, healing, and even possible revival in a church has stopped dead. In such cases, the Church proves itself unworthy to be the solution to the abortion problem because the Church is part of the problem itself.

We trust this document will become a tool and a weapon for the purpose of repentance, revival, and reformation of the Church, and then help the Church around the world in rebuilding laws and governments upon the principles of the Bible on which they should be founded. May God be gracious to us, and grant us REPENTANCE, REVIVAL, and REFORMATION.

DOCUMENT 22

Concerning the Sanctity of Human Life

ARTICLES OF AFFIRMATION AND DENIAL

A. Foundational Biblical Principles.

ARTICLE I

The Bible is truth.

We affirm that the Bible — being God's inspired, inerrant, written Word — is truth in its entirety, and as such, is the ultimate standard by which all other truth-claims are to be judged,[a] and thus offers mankind the clearest, most complete picture of all reality and the only logically coherent worldview.

We deny that there is any source of truth higher than, or equal to, the Bible or that the Bible's truth may be judged by any other standard.

   a. John 17:17; Pss. 1:1; 111:7; 119:89, 128, 151, 160; Matt. 24:35; Num. 23:19; 2 Tim. 3:16–17; 2 Pet. 1:3; 1 Cor. 3:19

ARTICLE II

Science, medicine, and law are part of a worldview.

We affirm that no one is religiously, metaphysically, epistemologically, or ethically neutral — having no presuppositions, no view of truth, no view of right and wrong, and no worldview by which to see reality and filter all data. All humans live and work on the basis of either the Christian worldview or some non-Christian, anti-Biblical worldview.

We further affirm that modern history declares that scientists, medical researchers, and medical practitioners (including psychiatrists and psychologists) who are not submitted to the absolutes of the Christian worldview have often become very dangerous weapons in the hands of a totalitarian state.

We deny that non-Biblical worldviews can provide an adequate basis for the sanctity of human life.[a]

   a. See Appendix, "Non-Biblical worldviews provide no basis for the sanctity of human life."[*]

[*NOTE: The full appendix to this Document is not in this book. See Appendix O, p. 286 for selected excerpts. The document with its complete appendix can be accessed at www.ChurchCouncil.org.]

ARTICLE III
God created humans in His own image.

We affirm that the infinite, personal, Triune God of the Bible created man in His image[a]; thus human beings reflect and represent God to some degree and are qualitatively distinct from and superior to all the rest of creation.[b] Since man is the image of God, each human life is of inestimable value from conception to death.[23]

We deny all views that would undermine the absolute and eternal Creator-creature distinction or that claim man is divine or can ever become divine.

We further deny the rationality and morality of any attempt to distinguish persons from non-persons within the human race.

    a. Gen. 1:26f; 5:1,3; 9:6; 1 Cor. 11:7; James 3:9; cf. Ps. 8:5
    b. Gen. 1:27–30; 2:19f; 9:1–3; Job 35:10; Ps. 8:6–8; Eccles. 7:29; Matt. 12:11ff

ARTICLE IV
The fall of man disrupted, but did not destroy, the image of God.

We affirm that, after the fall of man, sin disrupted and marred God's image, but fallen man still bears the image of God, however distorted it may become.[a]

We deny that, after the fall, man no longer retains any aspects of the image of God, including his original, God-ordained value that makes him superior to all animals, vegetables, minerals, or galaxies.

    a. Gen. 5:1ff; 9:6; 1 Cor. 11:7; James 3:9

ARTICLE V
Humans were created for God's glory, pleasure, and purposes.

We affirm that the triune God, Who reveals Himself in the Bible, created mankind for Himself, and thus all people, Christian and non-Christian alike, are obligated to exist primarily for God's own glory, pleasure, and purposes.[a]

We deny that people have a right to exist for the purpose of serving their own pleasures, security or prestige, or that any human may rightly deny God's existence and not live in grateful obedience to God's Biblical commands.[b]

    a. Col. 1:16; Rom. 11:36; Rev. 4:11; 1 Cor. 10:31
    b. Rom. 1:18–21ff

---

23 "Scripture never defines the image of God in terms of specific qualities or abilities. Instead, Scripture teaches that human beings as such are individually created in God's image (Genesis 1:26ff.; 9:6, 1 Corinthians 11:7; James 3:9) and that a 'human being' is anyone who belongs to the race of Adam and bears God's image (cf. Genesis 5:1-3ff.). Because being the image of God is the Scriptural ground for having the rights of a person (Genesis 9:6; James 3:9), we can say that Scripture equates 'being God's image' with 'being a person.' ... In Genesis 6:9 and in James 3:9, Scripture commands us to respect the image of God. And the context of these verses absolutely excludes any attempt to distinguish persons from non persons within the human race" (John M. Frame, *Medical Ethics: Principles, Persons, and Problems.* Phillipsburg, NJ: P&R Publishing, 1988, 35).

ARTICLE VI

God's plan and providential control of life

We affirm that: God is the ultimate giver[a] and owner[b] of human life, and therefore He alone can determine and delegate the lawful means for bringing new human life into existence.

We further affirm that as the Creator, God has the right to take human life[c] and determine and delegate what is the lawful means for ending a human life.[d]

We further affirm that God opens and closes the womb and thus is active in the conception process[e], and that children are a gift from God.[f]

We deny that the forming of new life, or that the control over human beings, belongs to man to do as he wishes, independent from God's written law-Word.

We further deny that the formation of a new human life should introduce seed or eggs beyond that of the husband or wife.[g]

We further deny that any person or state has the right to take human life in violation of God's written law-Word.[h]

    a. Gen. 2:7; 4:1; Deut. 32:39; Job 33:4; 32:8; Eccles. 12:7; Isa. 42:5; 57:16; Zech. 12:1; Heb. 12:9
    b. Ezek. 18:4; Ps. 24:1; Num. 16:22; Heb. 12:9; Dan. 5:23
    c. Deut. 32:39; 1 Sam. 2:6; 2 Kings 5:7; Job 1:21; 14:5; Ps. 68:20; Rev. 1:18
    d. 2 Kings 14:6; Acts 25:11
    e. Gen. 16:2; 20:18; 30:2, 17–24; Exod. 23:25ff.; 29:31ff.; 30:22ff.; Ruth 4:13; 1 Sam. 1:5ff., 10, 19ff.
    f. Gen. 17:16; Pss. 127:3–5; 128:3f
    g. Mal. 2:14ff.; 1 Tim. 5:14

ARTICLE VII

God's absolute sovereignty over the time-space universe and over all history

We affirm that God works all things according to His sovereign, all-wise, and all-comprehensive plan.[a]

We further affirm that (though we may not understand why) God's plan includes physical and mental defects,[b] debilitating diseases,[c] calamities,[d] the extent of each person's financial resources,[e] and God's plan exercises control over the sinful acts of every person.[f]

We further affirm that God has His own good purposes for human suffering, and gives people grace to endure it, and that suffering is never meaningless.[g]

We deny that anything or anyone is outside the scope of God's sovereign plan and providential control.

We further deny that there are any "accidents" from God's perspective; that God has no future knowledge of all things; and that there is any real thing called "chance" in this universe.

    a. Eph. 1:11
    b. Exod. 4:11; Isa. 45:9–11; John 9:1–3

c. John 11:4; Exod. 15:26
d. Amos 3:6; Job 1:21
e. Job 34:19; 1 Sam. 2:7; Deut. 8:18
f. Gen. 50:20; 2 Sam. 16:10; 24:1; Ps. 76:10; Acts 3:13; 4:27ff.; Rom. 11:32
g. Job; Rom. 5:3ff.; 2 Cor. 1:3–6; 12:7–10; James 1:2–4; Rom. 8:28; 1 Cor. 10:13

ARTICLE VIII

God is in control of all death.

We affirm that God has ordained human mortality[a] and that — though death[24] is an enemy[b] — dying is not always to be resisted.[c]

We further affirm that — though life is a gift from God — life is not to be worshipped and that God's will includes some self-sacrifice — sometimes even to death.[d]

We further affirm that the Biblical definition of death is God's separation of the human body from its spirit, and that the physical criterion for death is the coagulation of the blood so it can no longer circulate the "breath of life."

We deny the errors that: death is the end of human existence; death is an illusion; and death, in itself, is a good thing.

We further deny that the continuation of an individual human life is always the highest good or that it is always God's will.

We further deny that the recent technological definitions of death (other than that stated above) are either adequate or ethical.

a. Gen. 2:16ff.; 3:19; Job 14:5; Ps. 90:10; Eccles. 3:2; Rom. 5:12; Heb. 9:27
b. 1 Cor. 15:26
c. Gen. 49:33; Matt. 27:50; Acts 21:13; 25:11; Rom. 14:7ff.; Phil. 1:21
d. John 10:11; 15:13; Rom. 5:7ff.; 1 Cor. 13:3; 2 Cor. 4:7–18; 2 Cor. 11–12; Phil. 1:20–26; Heb. 11; 1 John 3:16; cf. Esther 4:16; Dan. 3:17ff.

ARTICLE IX

Stewardship: A person's body and soul belong to God, not to the person.

We affirm that people are God's creation,[a] and they belong to Him in their entirety[b] — bodies[c] and souls.[d]

We further affirm that, since we are the Lord's, no one has a right to live or die to himself.[e]

We deny that a person's body belongs to oneself, and that one has a right to do with it whatever one wishes.

a. Ps. 100:3
b. Ps. 24:1
c. 1 Cor. 6:15–20; 7:4
d. Ezek. 18:4
e. Rom. 14:7f

24 Death is not merely a biological event; it is also a spiritual event. Death occurs when a human spirit leaves its body (Eccles. 12:7, James 2:26) and goes either to heaven (Luke 23:43; 2 Cor. 5:6,8; Phil. 1:23; Rev. 7:9-17; Eccles. 12:7) or to hell (Luke 16:22-17).

ARTICLE X

Human knowledge is finite.

We affirm that, because man's knowledge is finite,[a] apart from the Bible, there
is no logically coherent standard for ethics[b] and no adequate standard for
determining human value, the purpose of human life, or the usefulness or
the quality of someone's life.

We further affirm that finite human knowledge, coupled with the depravity of
the human mind and will, is incompetent to control life and to develop a
superior form of humanity.

We further affirm that — though the Bible speaks truth — the truth we humans
know is finite and will always be so — even in heaven.

We deny that man, starting from himself, has the right, or the mental or moral
competence, to develop his own ethical standards,[c] to control life, or to
determine whether someone's life has no purpose.

We further deny that people can know with absolute certainty who is incurable,
or that they can know all of God's purposes in allowing suffering.[d]

a. Deut. 29:29; 1 Cor. 13:9,12; Rom. 11:33f; Ps. 139:6; Isa. 55:8ff.
b. James 4:12; Exod. 20
c. John 9:1–4; Job 38–41
d. Job 1–2; Ps. 44

B. God Safeguards Human Life with Biblical Laws

ARTICLE XI

Normative ethics for all humans

We affirm that God reveals His absolute ethics to man through the Bible and
that the Bible's ethics and principles are binding upon everyone, everywhere,
for all time.

We further affirm that normative ethics, the "ought," cannot be derived from
what "is."

We deny that ethics is relative and that ethics may be personally, culturally,
pragmatically, or statistically determined.

We further deny that, because man is scientifically and technologically able to
do something, it is necessarily morally right for him to do so.

ARTICLE XII

Murder

We affirm that murder is the intentional killing of a human being in violation
of God's law.

We deny that murder includes: accidental manslaughter;[a] killing in self-defense;[b]
Biblically-authorized capital punishment; or killing combatants in a just war.[c]

a. Exod. 21:13ff.; Num. 35:11–15, 22–25; Deut. 19:4–6, 10; Josh. 20:1–9; with the exception of Exod. 21:22f
b. Exod. 22:1
c. 1 Kings 2:5ff.

ARTICLE XIII

God decrees that all convicted murderers must be executed.

We affirm that, because all humans bear the image of God, God forbids murder and commands and exemplifies in the Bible that all murderers must be executed by legitimate civil governments[a] as swiftly as reasonably possible.

We deny that the New Testament overturns capital punishment and that any state, legislature, or court may rightfully dispense with capital punishment for murder.[b]

We further deny that the Church has ever been given authority by God to execute capital punishment.

a. Gen. 9:5ff.; Exod. 21:12–14; Num. 35:16–21, 30–33; Lev. 24:17; Deut. 19:11–13; 21:1–9
b. Matt. 15:3 (citing Exod. 21:17; Lev. 20:9); Rom. 1:32; 13:4; Acts 25:11, 25; 26:31; Rev. 13:10; cf. 1 Tim. 1:8–10; Matt. 5:17–19

ARTICLE XIV

Failure to execute murderers brings God's judgment on such societies.

We affirm that when a murder occurs the land is polluted,[a] and the murderer's family,[b] his city[c] and his nation[d] share the guilt of the murderer[e] until the murderer is justly executed.

We further affirm that God will judge nations that fail to execute murderers,[f] but He will bless cities and nations that obey Him in this matter.[g]

We deny that God holds guiltless cities and nations that fail to execute murderers.[h]

We further deny the erroneous belief that God brings no judgments within history.[i]

a. Num. 35:33ff.; Gen. 4:10ff.
b. 2 Sam. 21:4–6; 2 Kings 9:26
c. Deut. 21:1–9; Jer. 26:15
d. Deut. 19:10, 13
e. Deut. 21:7ff.
f. Jer. 2:34–37; Hosea 1:4; 4:1–5
g. Deut. 19:13
h. Amos 1:11–15; Nah. 3:1
i. Gen. 6:13; 19:24; 1 Chron. 16:14; Ps. 105:7; Jer. 18:7; Dan. 2:21

Various forms of murder

We affirm that abortion (i.e., the intentional killing of an unborn human baby) — at any stage of his or her development, regardless of motive — is murder.

We further affirm that:

infanticide (i.e., the intentional killing, by act or omission, of a human infant);

euthanasia/"mercy-killing"/assisted suicide[a] (i.e., the intentional killing, by act or omission, of a human being, whose life is deemed not worth living or too painful);[25]

suicide (i.e., the voluntary and intentional killing, by act or omission, of oneself; self-murder);[b, 26]

hastening death to obtain fresh organs;

birth control involving the destruction of fertilized human embryos (e.g., IUD, progestin "minipill," progestin injections, high estrogen "morning after pill," etc.);[27]

destruction of fertilized human embryos when using reproductive technologies (including freezing human embryos, much in vitro fertilization, human embryonic stem cell research, human cloning, etc.);[28]

human embryonic and fetal experimentation resulting in death;

reckless actions causing physical injury to a pregnant mother that directly results in the death of her baby,[c]

— are all forms of murder by God's standards.

We further affirm that mercifully allowing natural death may be right in cases of imminent and irreversible[29] death from incurable disease, fatal injury, or

---

25 Patients and their families normally have a moral obligation to receive available medical treatment that is clearly effective in restoring their health and saving their life. Cf. the *Westminster Larger Catechism*'s positive requirement to save life implied in the Sixth Commandment (Q. 135-136).

26 Thus suicide does not include acts of self-sacrifice in which persons do not directly will their own death, but are prepared to accept death as a possible consequence of performing some act of charity, justice, mercy, or piety to which God has called them. Such acts of self-sacrifice may include: attempting to save the lives of others during a military campaign or rescuing someone during a natural disaster; defense of family or friends unjustly attacked (Esther 4:16); ministering to the infectious sick; and bearing witness to Christ in times of persecution and martyrdom (Dan. 3:17ff.; 1 Cor. 13:3); cf. John 15:13; Rom. 5:71ff.

27 Franklin E. Payne, *Making Biblical Decisions* (Escondido, CA: Hosanna House, 1989), 38.

28 In this paper no distinction is made between the terms "zygote" (the cell formed by the joining of the male sperm and the female egg), "embryo," and "fetus." The term "embryo" is commonly used to denote the first eight weeks of human development, and the term "fetus" often denotes human development from the beginning of the third month of pregnancy through the ninth month.

29 "A condition is 'irreversible' from a human perspective when there are no known available medical means to correct the injury or disease process leading to death. In other words, there is no medical hope for recovery, and it is only a matter of time before a person dies. Medically, this means that

old age—without unnatural, life-sustaining equipment, unless the person desires such heroic measures and has financial means to pay for them.

We deny that patients and their families have a moral obligation to receive medical treatments for which they have no righteous means of paying.[30]

We further deny that it is the state's God-given responsibility to provide for, or to fund, medical care;[31] that civil magistrates may enact legal definitions of death that are un-Biblical,[32] for the purpose of furthering organ harvesting, without becoming an accessory to murder; and that the end justifies the means.[d]

We further deny that birth control methods that do not prevent conception, but prevent implantation of a fertilized human egg in the uterus are not murderous.

We further deny that it is ever proper to withhold basic care and love for those who are dying[e] or that laying down one's life to save the lives of others is murder or unlawful suicide.[f]

a. 2 Sam. 1:6–16
b. (Every instance of suicide and assisted suicide in the Bible is directly associated

---

even the best unnatural (mechanical) means will not stop death" (Norman L. Geisler, *Christian Ethics: Options and Issues* (Grand Rapids: Baker, 1989), 169. Cf. John J. Davis, *Evangelical Ethics*, 3d Ed., (Phillipsburg, PA: P & R, 2004), 192ff.

30 Furthermore, the responsibility to save one's life must be balanced against other Biblical responsibilities, such as: providing for one's family (1 Tim. 5:8), leaving an inheritance to children (2 Cor. 12:14; Prov. 19:14) and grandchildren (Prov. 13:22), supporting spiritual leaders (1 Tim. 5:17ff.), etc. (cf. Franklin E. Payne, *Biblical Healing for Modern Medicine* (Augusta, GA: Covenant Books, 1993), 43,58,70,97). Furthermore, does the Old Testament limitation of debt to six years apply to contemporary debt incurred for medical services?

31 There is no Biblical basis for the state paying for medical expenses—except the medical expenses for diseases and injuries acquired in the "line of duty" by military personnel, policemen, firemen, and other civil servants. (See Franklin E. Payne, *Biblical Healing for Modern Medicine*, 169.) There is no inherent right to medical treatment.

32 The term (physical) "death" denotes the total and permanent (i.e., without possibility of resuscitation or recovery) cessation of all the vital functions and signs of any organism. In determining a Biblical definition for physical death the following concepts are relevant:
• the life is in the blood (Gen. 9:4; Lev. 17:11,14; Deut. 12:23; cf. John 6:53ff.);
• the breath of life (Gen. 2:7; 6:17-7:15,22; Job 7:7; 12:10; 27:3; 33:4; Isa. 2:22; Ezek. 37:5-10; Acts 17:25; Rev. 11:11);
• to cease breathing is to die (Gen. 25:8,17; 35:29; 49:33; Josh. 10:40; 11:11,14; 1 Kings 15:29; 17:17; Ps. 104:29; Mark 15:37,39; Luke 23:46; Acts 5:5,10); and
• the heart is the wellspring of life (Prov. 4:23) (metaphorical usage).
Since life is in the blood/circulatory system, we must not treat a person as dead as long as his blood continues to provide oxygenation (the "breath of life") to the cells. Once the blood dies (i.e., is coagulated), the person can be treated as dead. this encapsulates the cardio-pulmonary definition of death (i.e., irreversible cessation of circulatory and respiratory functions), since the blood carries the oxygen (the "breath of life") to the person's body cells.
Thus "brain-death" alone is not a sufficient criterion of physical death. A medical definition of "death" should include the irreversible loss of heart, lung, and perhaps brain function—making each a "necessary criterion and all three together the sufficient criteria for declaring someone to be dead." Other criteria, such as body temperature, color, kidney function, etc., may be used by way of confirmation (John M. Frame, *Medical Ethics: Principles, Persons, and Problems*, 58-62,75-81). Note that a human embryo does not have brain waves or brain function until 6–7 weeks after conception, but he or she is most definitely alive.

by the Biblical authors with the person's spiritual collapse and disobedience against God.) (Judg. 9:52–57; 1 Sam. 31:3–6; 1 Chron. 10:3–6; 2 Sam. 1:6–16; 17:23; 1 Kings 16:15–20; Matt. 27:5; Acts 1:18)

c. Exod. 21:22ff.[33]

d. Rom. 3:8

e. Prov. 13:6; Job 29:13 with 31:19; Matt. 25:35–45

f. John 15:13; 1 John 3:16

ARTICLE XVI

The fetus is a human person, distinct from its mother.

We affirm that the Bible is unambiguous in teaching that a fetus[34] is a human person, a living child,[35] distinct from its mother.[a]

We further affirm that the fetus has its own unique set of genes and chromosomes, brain waves, and fingerprints.

We deny that it is either Biblical or scientific to claim that the fetus is merely a part of the mother's body or that it is simply "tissue."

a. See Appendix "Evidence that a fetus is a person: Biblical evidence," which discusses the following verses: Gen. 16:11; Exod. 21:22; 2 Sam. 11:5 NKJ; Isa. 7:14; Exod. 21:22; Luke 1:41,44; Gen. 25:22; Job 3:3; Luke 1:36; Luke 1:15; Luke 1:41,44; Luke 2:12,16; Acts 7:19; 1 Pet. 2:2; Luke 18:15; 2 Tim. 3:15; Job 3:13; 31:15; Pss. 22:9ff.; 139:13–16; 51:5; Isa. 49:1,5; Jer. 1:4ff.; 20:17ff.; Hosea 12:3; Job 10:8–12; 31:15; Pss. 119:73; 139:13–16; Jer. 1:5; Ps. 78:5ff.; Exod. 21:22ff.; cf. Gen. 9:5ff.; Gen. 25:23; Exod. 21:22ff.; Luke 1:15,36,41–44; Gal. 1:15; Ps. 51:5; Rom. 5:12ff.; Job 3:13–15; Luke 1:15; Luke 1:41,44; Ps. 51:5; Luke 1:41,44; Gal. 1:15ff.; Judg. 13:3,5,7; Isa. 49:1,5; Jer. 1:5; Rom. 9:11ff.; Heb. 10:5; Matt. 1:20; Luke 1:35; Luke 1:31; Matt. 1:20; Luke 1:31; Heb. 2:17,14; cf. Ps. 22:9ff.; Isa. 49:1,5; Luke 3:23–38; Hosea 9:14; Job 3:10–16; 10:18ff.; Eccles. 6:3; Exod. 23:26

ARTICLE XVII

Birth defects, rape and incest

We affirm that the Bible teaches that children must not be punished for the sinful lifestyle or crimes of their parents.[a]

We deny that it is not murder to abort a baby for reasons of birth defects,[b] rape, incest, lifestyle choice, overpopulation, or financial or personal stress.

a. Deut. 24:16; Ezek. 18

b. Exod. 4:11; Isa. 45:9–11; John 9:1–3; 11:4

---

33 H. Wayne House, "Miscarriage or Premature Birth: Additional Thoughts on Exodus 21:22-25," *Westminster Theological Journal* 41:1 (Fall 1978), 109-123. John M. Frame, "Abortion from a Biblical Perspective," in *Thou Shalt Not Kill: The Christian Case against Abortion*, ed. Richard L. Ganz (New Rochelle, NY: Arlington House, 1978), 51-57. Umberto Cassuto, *A Commentary on the Book of Exodus* (Jerusalem: Magnes, 19678), 275,277.

34 "Fetus" is a Latin word meaning children (of human beings) or offspring (of animals); it is used for both the young already born and the young still in their mother's womb (P G. W. Glare, ed., *Oxford Latin Dictionary*. Oxford: Clarendon Press, 2004, 695).

35 Personhood must not be confused with personality. Personhood is an ontological category; personality is a psychological concept.

ARTICLE XVIII

The life of the mother

We affirm that, in very rare cases in which pregnancy directly threatens the physical life of the mother, the doctor has two patients, the mother and the baby, and his efforts should be to save both.

We further affirm that, in the process of seeking to save the lives of both mother and child, it is not murder if medical science is unsuccessful in saving the life of one or both.

We deny that it is morally right for a doctor to care for a pregnant mother and neglect attempting to save the life of her unborn baby.

ARTICLE XIX

Non-lethal violations of the sanctity of human life

We affirm that eugenics[36] (now expanded through the technologies and use of sperm banks, artificial insemination by donor, surrogate mothers, in vitro fertilization, genetic engineering, cybernetics, nanotechnology, etc.) is a violation of the sanctity of human life.

We further affirm that:

Forced sterilization; torturing prisoners of war, or torturing for any reason; dangerous medical experiments with humans;[37] un-Biblical buying and selling human beings, including: kidnapping people to sell them and buying kidnapped people;[a] buying or selling human sperm or human eggs for the purpose of producing human embryos; a woman renting her womb as a surrogate mother; buying and selling one's sexuality (e.g., prostitution, pornography); bestiality;[b] racial prejudice;[c,38] and imprisonment as punishment for crime — are all non-lethal violations of the sanctity of human life.

We deny that any of the above acts can be justified by the Bible.

a. Rev. 18:11, 13; Exod. 21:16; Deut. 24:7
b. Exod. 22:19; Lev. 20:15ff.

---

36 The term "eugenics" denotes the scientific and social attempt to produce "superior" offspring by processes of selective breeding of humans, encouraging childbearing among those deemed most "fit," and impeding or preventing parenthood among those deemed "inferior."

37 In such scientific or medical experiments, the risks to the participant or patient outweigh possible benefits to him or her.

38 Racism may be defined as the belief that one race is inherently superior to another race(s), and that the superior race has the right to dominion over the other(s). Biblically, individual acts of racial prejudice (e.g., refusing to hire or to conduct business with a person of another race) are sins, but they are not crimes to be punished by the state.

c. Contrast the racial solidarity of all mankind in: Creation (Gen. 1:26–28, God created all mankind in His image; Acts 17:26); Fall (Gen. 3:15–19; Rom. 5:12; 1–3); and Redemption — including: the atonement (John 3:16; 1 Tim. 2:4; 1 John 2:2); the preaching of the Gospel (Matt. 28:18ff.; Acts 1:8; 2:8–11; 10:15, 34ff.); and union with Christ and unity in Christ's Church (Mark 11:17; 2 Cor. 5:17; Gal. 3:8, 28ff.; Eph. 2:13–19; Col. 3:11; Rev. 5:9ff.; cf. Luke 10:33).

ARTICLE XX

Citizen's obligations to obey God where man's laws contradict God's laws in the Bible

We affirm that individual citizens and civil magistrates are not Biblically-bound to obey human laws or court rulings that violate the laws or commands of God's written Word.

We further affirm that people must disobey any unjust law (as Biblically defined) whenever obedience to that law would cause them to disobey God's written Word.

[NOTE: The complete document contains endnotes, an index, statistics from the Elliot Institute, and an extensive scholarly appendix. The document with full appendix may be obtained from www.ChurchCouncil.org.]

TOPIC 23
God's Law for All Societies

INTRODUCTORY COMMENTS

by Dr. Eugene Calvin Clingman

"This is love, that we walk according to
His commandments." (2 John 6, NKJV)

In 2010, I suggested to Dr. Grimstead and the COR board that we should probably create a document dealing with God's Law and its present applicability to the Church and the world. We decided to proceed with this idea and we began putting our thoughts on paper. Before long, Dr. Grimstead took the responsibility for organizing the main structure and content for this topic, and received much good input from the Review Committee. That Review Committee for this topic was composed of Dr. Robert Fugate, Dr. Jay Grimstead, Col. Robert Hieronymus, Dr. Phil Kayser, and me.

"When the righteous are in authority, the people rejoice;
But when a wicked man rules, the people groan" (Proverbs 29:2, NKJV).

"When the righteous rejoice, there is great glory;
But when the wicked arise, men hide themselves" (Proverbs 28:12, NKJV).

It is clear from these two verses that God speaks to societal issues. Two things are evident in our society today:

1. The righteous are not in authority.
2. Wicked men have arisen.

What is the answer? The answer is for the Church to return to God's Law and to lead the nation to return to God's Law.

I am not talking about becoming justified or made righteous through the Law; it cannot be done; righteousness is obtained through faith in Christ and His atoning work. What I am talking about is the fact that the Law, written upon the heart of New Covenant people (Jeremiah 31:31) is the standard of righteousness God requires for individuals and nations (Romans 2:14-16); this is the same moral law given by God in the Ten Commandments and its accompanying case laws. The Christian standard of the Law is love, and love is the fulfillment of the Law (Romans 13:10). But love is not something less than what the Law requires. In other words we cannot say, "I am walking in love, therefore the Law does not apply to me!" But we may say, "I am walking in love which causes me to fulfill the Law and more besides. And if I fail to fulfill the righteous requirements of the Law, it is evidence that I am not walking in love, and that I have failed to attain in my actions, speech, or thoughts that standard God has written upon my New Covenant heart." Clearly the standard of the Law is never discarded or abrogated, and even when one is walking in love it is fulfilled, never set aside.

I want to be careful also to make clear that I am not suggesting we subjectively look into our New Covenant heart to discern what the Law of God is. We need an objective external law to look to in order to understand the Law written on our hearts. God's written laws in the Bible are the only absolute and objective laws for us human beings since those same laws of God written on our hearts are capable of misinterpretation or misapplication because of our fallen and self-deceptive human nature.

The Law cannot be discarded — because it is a *reflection of the righteous character of God*. And God's righteous character does not fluctuate and is never altered. Because His Law is a reflection of His righteous character, His Law is the standard required of all human beings. The Church has often failed to comprehend these things. The Law is often set aside in evangelical circles and considered of no account for the Christian; and because it is of no account for the Christian, it is also, in their minds, of no account for the general culture. This is wrong thinking!

Unfortunately, the Biblical view of the Law of God (Ten Commandments and its case laws) has been greatly distorted by some teachings of dispensationalism. Dispensationalism teaches that Old Testament law does not apply to the New Testament dispensation. And since the Old Testament law allegedly does not apply, Christians are free from obedience to the law. They say that if a law principle is not repeated in the New Testament, it does not apply. If this were true, bestiality would be permissible for the Christian since laws against this abomination are not repeated or restated in the New Testament.

Contrary to dispensationalism's errors, we are certain that Old Testament law is continuous with the New Testament dispensation and applicable to Christians unless the New Testament abrogates it such as in the case of "clean" and "unclean" foods and the sacrifice of animals for our atonement.

The Law of God has been written upon the heart of man (Romans 2:14-15). Because it pertains to every human being individually, it pertains to every collection of human beings, and because to every collection of human beings, to every nation.

There is one standard and only one. God's Law is for all societies and nations, always.[39]

> "Remove from me the way of lying,
> And grant me Your law graciously" (Psalm 119:29, NKJV).

> "To the law and to the testimony!
> If they do not speak according to this word,
> It is because there is no light in them" (Isaiah 8:20, NKJV).

> "But he who looks into the perfect law of liberty
> And continues in it, and is not a forgetful hearer
> But a doer of the work,
> This one will be blessed in what he does" (James 1:25, NKJV).

---

39 See the book, *God's Ten Commandments: Yesterday, Today, Forever* by Francis Nigel Lee, Ventura, CA: Nordskog Publishing, 2007. See also *Historical and Theological Foundations of Law*, in 3 Volumes, by John Eidsmoe, Ventura, CA: Nordskog Publishing, 2016.

DOCUMENT 23

Concerning God's Law for All Societies

ARTICLES OF AFFIRMATION AND DENIAL

ARTICLE I

We affirm that the tri-personal God[a] of the Christian Bible is the only ultimate and proper Lawgiver and Judge in this universe[b] Who alone determines and defines truth,[c] good and evil,[d] justice and injustice,[e] liberty and enslavement.[f]

We deny that there is any other legitimate foundation for law than that given by the God of the Christian Bible.[g]

> a. Matt. 28:19; Isa. 48:16; 2 Cor. 13:14; Eph. 2:8; 1 John 5:7; Rev. 1:4-6; Gen. 1:1-3,26; 3:22; 11:6-8; Ps. 45:6-7; Isa. 44:6; 48:12-16; John 1:1-2; Heb. 1:8,6,10
> b. James 4:12; Gen. 18:25; Isa. 33:22; 45:5-12
> c. Truth is an attribute of God (Deut. 32:4; Ps. 31:5; Isa. 61:8; John 14:6; 1 John 5:6). Consequently, God's Word is truth (Ps. 119:160; Isa. 8:20; Dan. 10:21 NKJV; John 17:17).
> d. Gen. 2:9; Isa. 5:20; Jer. 18:11; Ezek. 36:13. Goodness is an attribute of God (1 John 4:16), which He reveals to mankind through His Word (Rom. 7:12,16) and deeds.
> e. Deut. 32:4; Prov. 29:26; Justice is an attribute of God, which He reveals through implanting His Law in all mankind (see Article II, Affirmation) and through imposing His spoken and written laws (Gen. 2:16ff.; Exod. 20; Ps. 19:7ff.; Rom. 7:12; Heb. 2:2).
> f. Exod. 20:2; Deut. 28; Ps. 119:45; Isa. 61:1ff.; Luke 4:18ff.; John 8:32-36; James 1:25; 2:12; Rom. 6:16ff.; 1 Cor. 7:21-23
> g. Isa. 8:20; Deut. 4:5-9; Neh. 9:13; Ezek. 20:24-25; 1 Tim. 1:8-11

ARTICLE II

We affirm that the Moral Law of God is a reflection[a] of God's immutable,[b] holy,[c] righteous[d] and good nature.[e] The knowledge of the conduct required by the moral law is written on the hearts of all mankind,[f] and was later codified in the Ten Commandments,[g] which is a summary of God's Moral Law,[h] and in the case laws which are applications and extensions of the Ten Commandments.[i]

We deny that the Moral Law was not in effect prior to the giving of the Ten Commandments through Moses.[j]

We further deny that the Ten Commandments apply to only a portion of the human race[k] or are limited to only a portion of world history.[l]

a. Lev. 11:44-45; 1 Pet. 1:16
b. Matt. 5:17-19; Luke 16:17; Deut. 29:29; Pss. 111:7-8; 119:152, 160
c. Lev. 19:2; Rom. 7:12; 2 Pet. 2:21
d. Deut. 4:8; Pss. 19:9; 119:142; Rom. 7:12; 8:4; Heb. 2:2.
e. Neh. 9:13; Pss. 12:6; 19:7ff.; Rom. 7:12, 16, 21; 1 Tim. 1:8
f. Lev. 18:27-28; Rom. 1:18, 32; 2:14-15; 3:19-20; 4:15; 5:13
g. Deut. 4:13; 10:4; Exod. 34:1-4
h. Exod. 34:38; Rom. 13:8-10
i. As an example, many case law applications are given in Deuteronomy 6-26; first commandment (6:1-11:32), second commandment (12:1-32), third commandment (13:1-14:29), fourth commandment (15:1-16:17), fifth commandment (16:18-18:22), sixth commandment (19:1-22:12), seventh commandment (22:13-23:14), eighth commandment (23:15-24:22), ninth commandment (25:1-19), tenth commandment (26:1-19). Exodus and other passages give other similar case law applications.
j. Gen. 18:19; 26:5; Lev. 18:24-30; 20:22-23; Rom. 2:15; 4:15; 5:13; Gal. 3:19
k. Lev. 18:24-30; 19:15; 20:22-23; 24:22; Deut. 1:16-17; Ezra 7:25; Pss. 2; 9:8; Eccles. 12:13; Isa. 51:4; Jer. 46:1ff.; Dan. 4:27; Amos 1:3-2:3; Matt. 5:14
l. Deut. 11:1; 19:9; Ps. 119:44, 142, 152, 160; Isa. 42:4; 2 Pet. 2:6-8; Matt. 7:23; Titus 2:14

ARTICLE III

We affirm that God revealed His Laws for all mankind in the Christian Bible[a] by means of inerrant, verbal inspiration[b] and that those written Laws are absolute and universal and therefore are to be obeyed by all mankind; they apply to Christians, to unbelievers and to all social orders in all places at all times. Man is required always and everywhere to reverence God and obey His Law Word.[c] The Christian Bible defines "sin" as "lawlessness."[d]

We further affirm that God's Moral Laws which He deposited in the Christian Bible are sufficient to guide any society at any period of history into being just, prosperous, strong and healthy, and those laws should be enacted into public policy by all leaders of nations.[e]

We deny that God intends His Laws in the Christian Bible to apply only to Christians or to those who choose to obey those Biblical laws.[f]

We further deny that there is any epistemological, theological, or ethical "neutral ground"[g] in this universe where mankind may stand without being always and absolutely accountable to His Creator, and under obligation to humble himself before God the Creator in the obedience of faith and worship.[h]

a. Ezek. 20:11; Jer. 9:24-26; Rom. 3:29-31
b. Pss. 33:4; 119:160; John 17:17; Matt. 5:18; 2 Tim. 3:16-17; 2 Pet. 1:20-21; Gal. 3:16
c. Rom. 2:12-16; Matt. 28:19-20 with 5:17-19; Rom. 1:18-32
d. 1 John. 3:4 (see Matt. 7:23; Rom. 4:7; 6:19; 2 Cor. 6:14; Titus 2:14; Heb. 10:17)
e. Deut. 28; Luke 3:12-14 (based on the 6th, 8th, 9th, 10th Commandments of the Decalogue); 1 Tim. 1:8-10 (Paul's list of civil crimes is based on the Ten Commandments); Rev. 9:2ff. (based on Commandments 1-2, 6-8, 10). The Great Commission is to disciple nations — and a key component of any nation is its civil government (with its legal and judicial system) and its economic system.
f. Lev. 18:24-30; 19:15; 20:22-23; 24:22; Deut. 1:16-17; Ezra 7:25; Pss. 2; 9:8; Eccles. 12:13; Isa. 51:4; Jer. 46:1ff.; Dan. 4:27; Amos 1:3-2:3; Matt. 5:14; This is graphically illustrated by God's judgments on Sodom and Gomorrah, the Canaanite nations, and many

other nations indicted by the Old Testament prophets. God's judgments fell on these cities and nations precisely because they trampled God's Moral Law. Furthermore, God warned Israel that if she fell into the sins of the Canaanites, God would dispossess her also (Lev. 18:24–30; 20:22ff.; Deut. 8:19–20). The same moral law applied to Israel and to the Gentile nations.
g. Matt. 12:30
h. Matt. 12:36; Rom. 14:12; Heb. 4:13

ARTICLE IV

We affirm that God's Laws are to be obeyed by all Christians, not as a basis for justification,[a] but as the standard within which the "justified-by-faith-Christian" lives when he lives in love, for "love is the fulfillment of the law."[b] Loving others is a Biblical command[c] and God's Law tells how to love God and other people.[d]

We further affirm that the Law of God applies to the unbeliever as the continuing and eternal standard for all morality and justice in all cultures[e] because God's Law reflects God's own, unchanging, moral character.[f]

We deny that a person can be walking in love and at the same time be disobeying God's Moral Law.[g]

We further deny that either Christians or non-Christians have the right to disobey God's Moral Law or God's requirement of love toward God and neighbor,[h] or that by obeying God's Moral Law they are justified.[i]

a. Rom. 3:27; 9:32; Gen. 15:6; Acts 13:39; Rom. 1:17; 3:22, 25–30; 4:3, 5, 9, 11; 5:1; 9:30, 32; 10:4, 6, 10; Gal. 2:16; 3:6, 8, 11, 24; 5:5; Phil. 3:9; Heb. 11:4, 7, 33; James 2:23; 2 Pet. 1:1
b. Rom. 13:10; James 2:8, 14-26; Matt. 22:37–40 (citing Deut. 6:5 and Lev. 19:18); Luke 11:42; Gal. 5:14
c. Lev. 19:18; John 13:34; John 13:34; 14:15, 21; 15:10, 12; 1 John 2:7ff.; 3:23ff.; 4:21; 5:2ff.; 2 John 5ff. Lawlessness drives out love (Matt. 24:12).
d. Rom. 13:10, See footnote 23.
e. Rom. 2:12-16; See footnote 19–20.
f. Ps. 119:172; Mal. 3:6; Isa. 33:22; Jer. 12:1; Dan. 9:4-11; Rom. 2:5; 2 Thess. 1:5; Rev. 16:5-6
g. Matt. 24:12; John 14:15, 21, 23, 24
h. Col. 3:6; Heb. 4:11
i. Acts 13:39; Rom. 3:20, 28; Gal. 2:16; 3:11, 24; 5:4

ARTICLE V

We affirm that the points of morality, justice and social order which any society institutes into their civil codes of law flow directly out of the religion and worldview of the official or unofficial leaders who control the power centers of that society.[a]

We deny that civil laws do or can flow out of neutral, objective, non-religious sources or are uninfluenced by the worldview of the leaders of said society.[b]

a. Ps. 135:15-18; Isa. 2:6-22
b. 2 Sam. 23:3; 2 Kings 17:37; Pss. 19:9; 111:10; Prov. 1:7; 8:15-16; 9:10; 16:6

ARTICLE VI

We affirm that the basic foundations of God's Moral Law in the Christian Bible are set forth in His Ten Commandments in Exodus 20,[a] and those Ten Commandments are explained, expanded, and applied in what is called the Biblical "case laws" such as we see in Exodus 21-23 and Deuteronomy 6-26.[b]

We further affirm that Western Civilization with its attending social, financial, scientific, and juridical benefits owes its development to the Christian Bible and to Christian society's commitment over the centuries to basing their societies' laws upon the Ten Commandments which resulted in the development of just and righteous laws and law systems such as the English "Common Law."

We deny: that an individual or society can remain strong,[c] just,[d] prosperous,[e] creative[f] or rational[g] when that individual or society ignores or hates the God of the Christian Bible or disobeys His Biblical commands[h] and history testifies profusely to this denial.

  a. The "Ten Commandments" (Exod. 34:28; Deut. 4:13; 10:4) are considered to be such a summary of the law that they are called "the words of the covenant" (Exod. 34:28).
  b. For example, Deuteronomy 5:1-22 reiterates the Ten Commandments, and then proceeds to give a detailed exposition of each commandment in chapters 6-26: first commandment (6:1-11:32), second commandment (12:1-32), third commandment (13:1-14:29), fourth commandment (15:1-16:17), fifth commandment (16:18-18:22), sixth commandment (19:1-22:12), seventh commandment (22:13-23:14), eighth commandment (23:15-24:22), ninth commandment (25:1-19), tenth commandment (26:1-19). Exodus and other passages give other similar case law applications. An example of the Ten Commandments being further defined is Deut. 19:4-13 wherein the case law there defines "You shall not murder" as being neither an accidental killing nor capital punishment.
  c. Isa. 14:12
  d. Isa. 42:4; 51:4; Hab. 1:4
  e. Deut. 29:9; Josh. 1:7-8; 1 Kings 2:3; 2 Chron. 31:21; Ps. 19:11
  f. Ps. 19:7-11
  g. 1 Sam. 13:13; Pss. 19:7-11; 111:10
  h. Pss. 2:8-12; 33:10-12; 94:1-23; Prov. 24:15-16; Isa. 2:6; Jer. 6:19; 18:17-10

ARTICLE VII

We affirm that there is a distinctive and identifiable Christian worldview[a] that includes a distinctive and identifiable Christian view of law,[b] and that at the heart of the Christian worldview stands the Almighty, Sovereign God of the Universe,[c] Who reveals Himself most clearly and completely in the Christian Bible.[d]

We deny that there is no distinctive and identifiable Christian worldview or view of law, and that any views are authentically Christian if they center on anything other than the Almighty, Sovereign God of the Universe revealed in the Christian Bible.[e]

  a. Prov. 14:18; Luke 1:17; 1 Cor. 1:20, 21, 24; 2:5-7; 3:19; Col. 2:1-23
  b. Jude 1:3; Isa. 33:22; Luke 1:17

c. Luke 11:49; 1 Cor. 1:21, 24

d. 1 Cor. 4:6; 2 Tim. 3:16-17; Jude 1:3; Heb. 1:1-4

e. Pss. 14:1; 53:1; See an earlier document, "Christian Worldview of Law," COR, 1989, Affirmations and Denials 2, at www.Reformation.net.

ARTICLE VIII

We affirm that the tri-personal[a] God[b] of the Christian Bible is the only ultimate Lawgiver and Judge.[c] This of necessity means that all human authority must be delegated,[d] limited,[e] specified,[f] and directly accountable to God.[g]

We further affirm that all three God-appointed jurisdictions of family,[h] church,[i] and state[j] must inevitably choose between conflicting law orders.[k] The laws they choose reflect the God or gods they submit to.[l] To acknowledge God's Lordship over all of life[m] inescapably calls for submission to His Law's authority over all of life.[n]

We further affirm that the Biblical Law order is vastly superior to all alternatives.[o]

We deny that there is any other legitimate foundation for law than that given by the one true God in the Christian Bible.[p]

a. Gen. 1:1-3, 26; 3:22; 11:6-8; Ps. 45:6-7; Isa. 44:6; 48:12-16; John 1:1-2; Heb. 1:8, 6, 10

b. Deut. 6:4; 32:39; Isa. 43:10; 45:5; Zech. 14:9; Mark 12:29, 32; Gal. 3:20; 1 Tim. 2:5

c. James 4:12; Gen. 18:25; Isa. 33:22; Ps. 2; Matt. 28:18

d. 2 Chron. 13:5; Dan. 2:37, 38; 7:6, 12; Matt. 8:9; 21:23, 27; 28:18; Rom. 13:1-2; John 19:11

e. John 19:11; 2 Cor. 10:13; Rom. 13:1 [literally, "there is no authority if not from God"]

f. Deut. 5:32; 17:20

g. Luke 16:2, 10-13; Rom. 13:1-6; 1 Cor. 9:13

h. Gen. 2:21-25; 12:3; 28:14; Acts 3:25; Eph. 5:22-33

i. Matt. 16:18; 1 Cor. 12:28; Eph. 5:24-33; Col. 1:18; Heb. 12:23; Rev. 2-3

j. Gen. 9:6-7; 2 Sam. 23:3; Ps. 2:10-12; Rom. 13:1-7

k. Deut. 30:19; Josh. 24:14; Ps. 119:173; Isa. 7:16; Matt. 6:24

l. Deut. 11:28; 28:14; Josh. 23:16; 1 Kings 9:6; 11:10; 2 Kings 17:41; Jer. 16:11

m. Ps. 47:7; Matt. 28:18; 11:25; Acts 10:36; Acts 17:24

n. Deut. 32:46-47; Matt. 4:4; 28:18-20; 2 Tim. 3:15-17

o. Deut. 4:6-8; 28; Ps. 119:72; Rom. 7:12; 2 Tim. 3:15-17; 1 Tim. 1:8

p. Deut. 4:2; 1 Kings 18:18; 2 Chron. 24:20; Pss. 94:20; 119:118, 128; Prov. 29:26; Ezek. 20:25

ARTICLE IX

We affirm that it is the vital and unavoidable responsibility of the truly Biblical Christian community in every society to seek in every Biblically consistent way to hold its society's views of law true to Biblical principles,[a] and that when societies choose anti-Biblical views of law, they can expect few long-term blessings from God and many adverse consequences and divine curses.[b]

We deny that the Christian community properly fulfills its calling to make disciples of every nation and to be salt and light to the world when it fails to do everything within its Biblically-defined, God-ordained jurisdiction to hold its society's views of law true to Biblical principles.[c]

We further deny that any church, mission, or Christian organization is accurately proclaiming the Gospel of Jesus which does not teach that Christ is at this very moment, and ever since His ascension to the throne at the right hand of the Father, ruling over the earth as the King of Kings and Lord of Lords, Who has commissioned us to get His will done "on earth as it is in heaven," and to work to have His kingdom come "on earth as it is in heaven," and to see His name hallowed on earth as it is hallowed in heaven.[d]

a. 2 Chron. 7:14; Ezra 7:10; Neh. 2:10; Hos. 10:12; Amos 5:6; Zeph. 2:3; Matt. 5:13
b. Gen. 12:3; Exod. 20:2; Deut. 28; Jer. 18:7-10
c. Matt. 28:20 with Matt. 5:17-19
d. Matt. 6:9-13; 28:16-20; See an earlier document, "Christian Worldview of Law," COR, 1989, Affirmations and Denials 2, at www.Reformation.net

ARTICLE X

We affirm that the rejection[a] or reduction of God's Laws[b] in the Christian Bible and disobedience to those laws[c] are probably the most debilitating defects in the Body of Christ today[d] and are the primary issues that have tragically reduced a majority of the Church to her present condition of being self-serving,[e] materialistic,[f] theologically confused,[g] antinomian,[h] and culturally impotent.[i]

We deny that rejection or reduction of Biblical Law by the Body of Christ is of no consequence,[j] or that such rejection or reduction will produce Biblically strong individuals, families, churches or nations.[k]

a. 2 Kings 17:15; Ps. 119:18; Is. 5:24; Jer. 6:19; 1 Thess. 4:7-8
b. Deut. 4:2; 12:32; Rev. 22:19
c. Ezek. 5:7; Eph. 5:6; Col. 3:6; Heb. 2:2; 4:11
d. Isa. 1:4-6; Matt. 7:23; 24:12; 1 Cor. 6:14; Titus 2:14; 1 John 1-5; Jude
e. Eccles.; Phil. 3:19; Jude 12
f. Pss. 39:6; 62:10; Eccles. 2:4-11
g. Deut. 28:20; 32:5-6; Rom. 2:17-24; Titus 3:5
h. Rom. 6:1-3, 15-16; 8:7; Titus 2:14
i. Deut. 28:13; Matt. 5:13-16
j. Prov. 8:36; 10:16; 11:19; Isa. 3:11; Gal. 6:7-8
k. Deut. 28; 1 Cor. 10:1-22; 11:30-32; 1 Pet. 3:8-12; etc.

ARTICLE XI

We affirm that antinomianism (the disregard or dismissal of God's Moral Laws as being applicable to people today) is a modern day curse and sickness[a] within many professed, Bible-believing churches that must be corrected before such churches can accomplish their God-appointed destinies in fulfilling the Great Commission and in bringing forth God's Kingdom on earth in all areas of society to whatever degree this may be accomplished before Christ's return.[b]

We further affirm that God's Law and Justice are not opposed to God's grace and mercy, but rather that both sides express two aspects of God's goodness since both aspects originate from the heart of God and meet in perfect and full expression at the cross of Christ.[c]

We deny: that the following antinomian statements are Biblical or are beneficial to the Church or to any society, but rather that these false beliefs are destructive, demonic, and damnable:

A. Old Testament Moral Laws and principles do not carry over into the New Testament period.[d]

B. Some of the Old Testament Moral Laws and principles stand in opposition to the Moral Laws and principles of the New Testament or participate in some kind of "inferior" type of spirituality or morality.[e]

C. The "law of Christ" is substantially different than the Old Testament Moral Law.[f]

D. It is not God's intention that either the Old Testament's or the New Testament's Moral Laws and principles should be institutionalized into civil law for any and all societies on earth today.[g]

E. An individual's personal understanding and sense of right and wrong (enlightened by that person's understanding of how the Holy Spirit is guiding their life) is superior to the Christian Bible as a guide to issues of right and wrong.[h]

    a. Ps.34:1-22; Isa.1:4-6
    b. Isa.61:4-9; Matt.16:18-19; 2 Thess.1:11-12
    c. Pss.85:10; 89:14; 101:1; 119:77; Isa.16:5; 30:18; Hos.2:19; Matt.23:23; Titus 2:14
    d. But see Matt.5:17-19; Is.42:1-4; Rom.3:31; 8:4; Titus 2:14; Rom.13:8-10; etc.
    e. But see Matt.5:17-19; Rom.7:12,14; Gal.5:14; 1 Tim.1:8-10; 1 John 2:7; 3:11; 3:5
    f. But see Matt.5:17-19; Rom.13:9
    g. But see Matt.5:17-19; 15:3-9; John 18:36; Acts 25:11,25; 26:31; Rom.1:32; 13:1-4; 1 Tim.1:9-10; Heb.2:2
    h. Pss.93:5; 111:7; 119:118; Isa.8:20; John 10:35; Rom.1:18; 1 Cor.4:6; Eph.2:20; 2 Tim.3:16-17; 2 Pet.1:18-21

ARTICLE XII

We affirm that all commands of the Moral Law in the Old Testament are to be "Maintained unless Modified" by the New Testament.

We further affirm that the principles of the Old Testament case laws are to be "Maintained unless Modified" by the New Testament.[a]

We deny that any of the Moral Law in the Old Testament is "Rescinded unless Repeated" in the New Testament.[b]

We further deny that, after the inauguration of the new covenant, Christians are obligated to keep the Old Testament ceremonial laws.[c]

    a. Matt.5:17-19 upholds all moral and case laws of the Old Testament, including "the least of these commandments"—a reference to Deut.22:6. Note that the apostles repeatedly told their hearers that they were under obligation to the Old Testament moral and case laws: Eph.6:2-3; Rom.13:9-10; 2 Cor.6:16-18; 13:1; James 2:8,11; 1 Pet.1:16; 3:9-12; etc., reminding them that the Old Testament blessings for obedience (Heb.13:5-6; Eph.6:2-3; 2 Cor.6:16-18) and curses for disobedience (Heb.10:30,38; 12:5,6; James 2:9-12; 1 Pet.3:12) continue to apply. For many years the

only Bible of the early church was the Old Testament (Acts 8:32,35; 17:2,11; 18:24,28; Rom. 16:26; 2 Tim. 3:15-17).
b. Deut. 4:2; 12:32; Matt. 4:4; 5:17-19; Gal. 3:15; Rev. 22:18
c. Rom. 14:5; Gal. 4:10; Col. 2:11-23; Heb. 9:10

ARTICLE XIII

We affirm that a prominent feature of the New Covenant is that God writes His same Moral Law on the minds and hearts of all His People,[a] causing them to delight in obeying God's Law.[b]

We further affirm that faith and love produce obedient works[c] thereby establishing the Law of God[d] and fulfilling the righteous requirements of God's Moral Law.[e]

We deny that the New Covenant, grace, or saving faith[f] abrogate the obligation to obey the Moral Law of God.[g]

    a. Jer. 31:31–33; Heb. 8:8–10; 10:16; Ezek. 36:26ff.
    b. Ps. 119:24,70,77,92,97,159,174; Rom. 7:22,25
    c. James 2:17–20; Gal. 5:6; Eph. 2:9-10; Titus 2:11-14; 3:8,14; Heb. 10:22-24
    d. Rom. 3:31
    e. Rom. 2:26; 8:4
    f. Rom. 3:31
    g. Titus 3:8; James 2:17-20, 22, 26; Rev. 2:19

ARTICLE XIV

We affirm that the sovereign God of the Christian Bible providentially directs the course of human history, including civil law, which is a vital part of that history;[a] that with the consummation of history, including legal history, will come the final, eternal triumph of God's law, when eternal, universal, and perfect justice will prevail;[b] and this assurance gives Christians of all eras ultimate hope even in the midst of the rampant violations of God's Law at any point in history, and imparts real meaning and eternal significance to man's response to God's Law in this present life.[c]

We deny that history, including legal history, is a merely purposeless sequence of events; and,

We deny that there will be no final, eternal triumph of God's Law, or that eternal, universal and perfect justice will never prevail.[d]

    a. Isa. 42:1-4; Gen. 49:10; Ps. 2; Isa. 2:2-4; 9:8-7; Mic. 4:1-3
    b. Isa. 9:7; 11:9; Jer. 31:34; 1 Cor. 15:23-28,15-58; Heb. 2:8
    c. Ps. 37:11; Matt. 5:5; Rom. 8:18-39; 1 Cor. 15:58; Gal. 6:9
    d. Matt. 12:20; 1 Cor. 15:54-58; 1 John 5:4; See also above, Article IV, Affirmations and Denials.

ARTICLE XV

We affirm that, in giving us His infallible[a] and sufficient written Word,[b] God has once-for-all revealed[c] good and evil,[d] justice and injustice,[e] liberty,[f] and the role of the state,[g] etc.

We further affirm that since "every transgression and disobedience received its just punishment" (Heb. 2:2, NKJV),[h] God's justice should be applied and implemented by all legislative bodies.[i]

We deny that Scripture teaches that God ever authorized any nation, society, or social institution to govern itself by natural revelation or natural law alone.[j]

We further deny that legal positivism (the doctrine asserting that there is no higher authority than the state, and law is whatever the state says it is)[k] is Biblical.[l]

  a. Ps. 19:7; 119:160; John 10:35; 17:17. Consider the following syllogism:
   • God cannot lie (Titus 1:2) and therefore all that He says must be intended to be true.
   • God is omniscient (Heb. 4:13) and therefore He can never say anything that is a mistake.
   • All Scripture is God's Word (2 Tim. 3:16; 1 Thess. 2:13)
   • Therefore, all Scripture is inerrant.
  b. 2 Tim. 3:16-17; 2 Pet. 1:3
  c. Jude 3
  d. 1 Kings 3:9; Eccles. 12:14; Isa. 5:20; Matt. 19:17
  e. Deut. 32:4,21; Ps. 89:14; 97:2; 99:4; 111:7; Prov. 8:15; Isa. 30:18; 33:5; 40:14; 42:4; 51:4; 58:2; Zeph. 2:3; 3:5; 7:9; Matt. 12:18,20
  f. Isa. 61:1; Luke 4:18; 2 Cor. 3:17; Gal. 5:1; James 1:25; 2:12,19
  g. Deut. 4:1-8; 17:14-20; Prov. 8:15
  h. See also Isa. 8:20;
  i. Isa. 42:4; Mic. 4:2
  j. Isa. 8:19-20; Mic. 4:2; Deut. 5:32-33; 17:11,20; Isa. 65:2. Both before the Fall and after, man was and continues to be dependent upon special revelation from God (i.e., God's spoken and written words). Isa. 8:20; 2 Sam. 23:3
  k. Legal positivism is the basis for civil law in the US and virtually all modern countries. Since legal positivism is un-Biblical and God never authorized natural law to function as the basis for civil law (i.e., apart from God's Word), Biblical law is the only viable source of law today.
  l. Isa. 10:1; 24:5; Pss. 82:1ff.; 94:20; Ezek. 45:9; Luke 18:6,2,4; 2 Thess. 2:3; Rev. 13; Exod. 12:49; Lev. 18:5,6

ARTICLE XVI

We affirm that God blesses individuals, families, churches, cities, and nations that honor, love, and obey His laws and brings historical judgments upon these to the degree that they rebel against His laws.[a] On the final judgment day, each of these entities will be judged by the perfect law of Scripture.[b]

We deny that individuals, families, churches, cities or nations can avoid God's sanctions or that they will be judged by some standard other than by the revelation of Scripture, i.e., the Christian Bible.[c]

  a. Gen. 12:3; 22:18; 26:4; 28:14; Pss. 33:12; 72:17; Jer. 4:2; Acts 3:25
  b. Deut. 27:11-28:68; 1 Sam. 2:30; Prov. 14:34; Ps. 2; Jer. 4:2; 18:7-10; Jon. 1:1-2; 3:5-9
  c. Pss. 2; 56:7; 67:4; 96:10; Isa. 2:4; Ezek. 39:21; Matt. 23:33; Rom. 2:3; 1 Thess. 5:3; Heb. 2:3; 122:25

TOPIC 24

The Biblical Perspective of Environmental Stewardship:
Subduing and Ruling the Earth To the Glory of God and the Benefit of Our Neighbors

INTRODUCTORY COMMENTS

by Dr. Jay Grimstead

We asked Dr. E. Calvin Beisner, Founder and National Spokesman of The Cornwall Alliance for the Stewardship of Creation, to draft our affirmations and denials on "Environmentalism" because he has been a leading scholar assessing environmentalism from a Biblical perspective for nearly twenty-five years. A coalition of theologians, pastors, ministry leaders, scientists, economists, policy experts, and committed laymen, the Cornwall Alliance is the world's leading evangelical voice promoting environmental stewardship and economic development built on Biblical principles. Founded in 2005, its mission is to magnify the glory of God in creation, the wisdom of His truth in environmental stewardship, the kindness of His mercy in lifting the needy out of poverty, and the wonders of His grace in the Gospel of Jesus Christ. Through its educational ministry it promotes simultaneously,

- Biblical earth stewardship—godly dominion over the Earth, enhancing its fruitfulness, beauty, and safety,
- economic development for the world's poorest, and
- the proclamation and defense of the Gospel of Christ,

—all in a world permeated by an environmental movement whose worldview, theology, and ethics are mostly anti-Biblical, whose science and economics often are poorly done, whose policies therefore often fail to benefit ecosystems and the species that inhabit them but prolong human poverty, and whose doctrines of

God, creation, humanity, sin, and salvation often contradict those of the Bible, making environmentalism an alternative religion in its own right.

The worldwide environmental movement is many faceted, with adherents differing widely in terms of worldview, theology, ethics, science, economics, and politics. Environmentalists come from all of the world's major religions. Some are atheist materialist secularists; some pantheists, panentheists, or animists; some monotheists; some worshipers of Gaia or proponents of revived paganism and indigenous religions.

As Dr. E. Calvin Beisner writes, the word "environment" derives from the French *environner*, "surround," and simply means "surroundings." It thus implicitly encompasses everything and so tends to generate totalitarian, utopian political visions compatible with socialism and global government such as those embodied in the United Nations' Agenda 21[40] and Framework Convention on Climate Change, or the International Council for Local Environmental Initiative (founded to implement Agenda 21 by providing model legislation and regulation to municipal, county, and regional governments, bypassing citizen input and consent, and compromising national sovereignty). We encourage you to visit www.cornwallalliance.org to learn more about environmentalism and how Christians should respond to it.

Environmentalism tends to undermine liberty and limited, constitutional government—federalism (with its preference for concentrating government at the local level), and the maintenance of sovereign states. Much environmentalism also rejects the Biblical doctrines that mankind alone is created in God's image, is therefore distinct from and more valuable than any other species, and has a mandate from God to subdue and rule the Earth (Genesis 1:28) for God's glory and human benefit.

---

40 Most Biblical Christians need to examine and become aware of the comprehensive, socialistic, global-control initiative launched by the U.N. in 1992 called "Agenda 21" and what they refer to as "Sustainable Development" which is an effort to use the pseudo-science of environmentalism as a means to control governments starting at the city-county level. This plan is unconstitutional, destructive, and frightening and has made great inroads already into many U.S. counties. Wherever Christians and constitutionalists become aware of Agenda 21, it is emphatically opposed. I wish to call your attention to another Website and source: www.FreedomAdvocates.org; http://americanpolicy. org/deweese-report; email: deweesereport@americanpolicy.org, American Policy Center, 53 Main Street, Box 3640, Warrenton, VA 20188-3640, 540-341-8911.

DOCUMENT 24

The Biblical Perspective of Environmental Stewardship:

Subduing and Ruling the Earth To the Glory of God and the Benefit of Our Neighbors

COPYRIGHT 2013, THE COALITION ON REVIVAL

PRIMARY AUTHOR: **Dr. E. Calvin Beisner**

REVIEW COMMITTEE: **Dr. Jay Grimstead, Dr. Robert Fugate, Dr. Eugene Calvin Clingman**

ARTICLES OF AFFIRMATION AND DENIAL

ARTICLE I

We affirm that the Earth is the LORD's, and the fullness thereof (Psalm 24:1).

We deny that the Earth or anything else is the result of impersonal, blind chance over time.

ARTICLE II

We affirm that the Bible — the 66 books of the Old and New Testaments — is the sole, absolute, inerrant epistemological basis for mankind for all knowledge of all things, seen and unseen, and that all claims of truth and moral duty that contradict it are false and harmful.

We deny that the physical universe and human observations of it justify truth claims contrary to those of the Bible, and that liberty, justice, and human dignity can be sustained while rejecting Biblical truth and law.

ARTICLE III

We affirm that the only true God — a spirit infinite, eternal, and immutable — revealed Himself in creation (which He made out of nothing and includes both physical and spiritual things), the Bible, and His one and only Son, Jesus Christ, and that though God reveals His wisdom and power in the creation, He is, always has been, and always will be absolutely distinct from and transcendent over creation, which He rules at all times and places.

We deny atheism (there is no God), pantheism (everything is God), panentheism (God is to the universe as the human soul is to the human body), animism (there are many gods, and they indwell and animate physical objects as human souls indwell and animate human bodies), and any other view that denies the Creator/creature distinction, because those who hold them exchange the truth about God for a lie, and worship and serve the creature rather than the Creator, who is blessed forever (Romans 1:25).

ARTICLE IV

We affirm that human dignity, freedom, and justice can be sustained only insofar as a society affirms the Creator/creature distinction and embraces the truth of Scripture, and that those who deny it become futile in their thinking, and their foolish hearts are darkened (Romans 1:21).

We deny that societies built on atheism, pantheism, panentheism, animism (also called spiritism), or any other rejection of the Creator/creature distinction can flourish intellectually, morally, aesthetically, and materially.

ARTICLE V

We affirm that the creation includes persons — conscious spirits capable of reason, moral judgment, and affection, and therefore morally accountable for their actions — and that some of these persons are bodiless (immaterial, e.g., angels and demons) and some embodied (combinations of spirit and body, e.g., humans).

We deny that the material cosmos — "nature" and its parts, the created world of time and space, matter and energy, planets and stars, energy and material elements — is personal, either in its whole or in its parts; hence we deny that forests and trees, mountains and rocks, oceans and lakes and streams, and animals are persons.

ARTICLE VI

We affirm that God made man, male and female, in His own image (Genesis 1:26–27).

We deny that any other terrestrial life form bears the image of God or is of equal value or priority with human beings (Matthew 10:29–31).

ARTICLE VII

We affirm that though the Earth is the LORD's, He has also given it to men (Psalm 115:16) and mandated that they be fruitful, multiply, fill the Earth, subdue it, and have dominion over everything that lives in it (Genesis 1:28).

We *deny* that human dominion over the Earth is, in principle, sinful, and that the possibility of its abuse negates the righteousness of its proper use.

ARTICLE VIII

We *affirm* that the Earth and all its physical and biological systems are the effects of God's omniscient design, omnipotent creation, and faithful sustaining, and that when God completed His creative work it was "very good" (Genesis 1:31).

We *deny* that an infinitely wise Designer, infinitely powerful Creator, and perfectly faithful Sustainer of the Earth would have made it susceptible to catastrophic degradation from proportionally small causes, and consequently *we deny* that wise environmental stewardship readily embraces claims of catastrophe stemming from such causes.

ARTICLE IX

We *affirm* that by God's design Earth and its physical and biological systems are robust, resilient, and self-correcting.

We *deny* that they are fragile.

ARTICLE X

We *affirm* that godly human dominion over the Earth means men and women, created in the image of God, laboring freely and lovingly together to enhance Earth's safety, fruitfulness, and beauty, to the glory of God and the benefit of our neighbors.

We *deny* that godly human dominion entails humans' being servants rather than masters of the Earth.

ARTICLE XI

We *affirm* that when God had created Adam, He placed him in the Garden of Eden to cultivate and guard it (Genesis 2:15, GNT).

We *deny* that the Garden of Eden represents the whole Earth and that the instruction to "cultivate and guard" the Garden ought to be reinterpreted to mean either that man is to "serve and protect" the Garden or the Earth, or that man is to "worship and protect" the Garden or the Earth, or that man is to "worship and hear" God either directly or through the Earth or its parts.

ARTICLE XII

We *affirm* that a comprehensive understanding of the relationship between God's placing Adam in the Garden to cultivate and guard it (Genesis 2:15) and God's commanding Adam and Eve to be fruitful and multiply and fill the Earth and subdue it and rule everything in it (Genesis 1:28) entails a growing population that spreads out from the Garden to till the whole Earth

and transform it from wilderness to garden and ultimately to garden city
(Revelation 21:2; 22:1–3).

We deny that Biblical Earth stewardship, or godly dominion, is limited to
keeping Earth in the condition in which man finds it, i.e., *we deny* that, as
many environmentalists put it, "Nature knows best" and its transformation
by humans is in principle wrong or harmful.

ARTICLE XIII

We affirm that the Bible normally associates wilderness or wildness with
divine judgment and curse (Exodus 23:29; Leviticus 26:22; Deuteronomy 7:22;
1 Samuel 17:46; Isaiah 5:2–4; 13:19–22; 34:1–17; Jeremiah 50:39; Leviticus 16:21–22).

We deny that wilderness is the best state of the Earth.

ARTICLE XIV

We affirm that God placed minerals, plants, and animals in and on the Earth
for His pleasure, to reveal His glory and elicit man's praise, and to serve
human needs through godly use (Genesis 2:5–16; 4:22; Numbers 31:21–23;
Job 38–41; Psalm 19:1–6; Psalm 104).

We deny that recognizing instrumental value in the Earth and its various
physical and biological components dishonors God or is idolatrous.

ARTICLE XV

We affirm that one way of exercising godly dominion is by transforming raw
materials into resources and using them to meet human needs.

We deny that leaving everything in the Earth in its natural state is proper
Biblical stewardship (Matthew 25:14–30).

ARTICLE XVI

We affirm that because of man's fall into sin, sinful human hearts often fall prey
to materialism, the covetous love of money, and the selfish accumulation of
possessions (Luke 12:16–21; 1 Timothy 6:10; Colossians 3:5).

We deny that the temptation to materialist idolatry entails that the production
of wealth, whether material from the Earth or immaterial from the human
mind, is sinful in and of itself.

ARTICLE XVII

We affirm that man is accountable to God's judgment in all he does with the
Earth.

We deny that man's accountability to God justifies abolishing private property
(Exodus 20:15, 17), adopting collectivist economic institutions, or delegating
to civil governments—whether local, national, or global—ownership or
control of land, natural resources, or private property.

ARTICLE XVIII

We affirm that man's fall into sin (Genesis 3) entails the possibility and indeed the historical reality of human abuse of the Earth and of fellow humans.

We deny that man's fall into sin completely destroys the possibility of godly dominion.

ARTICLE XIX

We affirm that in response to man's sin God cursed the ground so that it would not, as before sin, yield easily even to godly dominion/cultivation, let alone to ungodly, abusive domination (Genesis 3:17–19), and indeed subjected the whole cosmos to decay and corruption until He restores it partially in history by obedience to the dominion mandate (Genesis 1:28), whether by the unregenerate through common grace (Matthew 7:11) or by the regenerate through special grace (Romans 8:18–24), and fully in the New Heavens and New Earth of the *eschaton* (Revelation 21:1–3, 22–27; 22:1–5), all secured by the redeeming work of Christ (Colossians 1:14–20).

We deny, due to God's faithfulness to His covenant, in which He proclaimed, after the Flood, that He would sustain the cycles on which terrestrial life depends for as long as the Earth endures (Genesis 8:22), that God's curse on the Earth negates either the dominion mandate (Genesis 1:28) or the robustness and self-correcting resilience of the God-sustained Earth.

ARTICLE XX

We affirm that human multiplication and filling of the Earth are intrinsically good (Genesis 1:28) and that, in principle, children, lots of them, are a blessing from God to their faithful parents and the rest of the Earth (Psalms 127; 128).

We deny that the Earth is overpopulated; that "overpopulation" is even a meaningful term, since it cannot be defined by demographic quantities such as population density, population growth rate, or age distribution; and that godly dominion over the Earth requires population control or "family planning" to limit fertility.

ARTICLE XXI

We affirm that when the Bible speaks of God's judgment on human societies because they have "polluted the land," the "pollution" in mind is consistently not chemical or biological but moral — the pollution of idolatry, adultery, murder, oppression of the weak, and other violations of the moral law of God expressed in the Ten Commandments (Psalm 106:38; Jeremiah 3:1–10; 16:18).

We deny that Biblical prophets' concerns about the pollution of any land focus significantly on chemical emissions from agriculture or industry, although prudent study of the risks those pose to human and ecosystem health is a worthy task and can lead to proper efforts to balance risks and benefits.

ARTICLE XXII

We affirm that cost/benefit analysis (Luke 14:28) is a proper and critically important aspect of godly dominion over the Earth (Proverbs 14:4).

We deny that cost/benefit analysis is unprincipled pragmatism or indicates a lack of faith in God.

ARTICLE XXIII

We affirm that, pursuant to sin and the curse, risk is inherent in every human activity (Hebrews 9:27) and therefore that it is lawful in principle to balance risk against risk.

We deny that the mere existence of risk in an activity makes it immoral in principle.

ARTICLE XXIV

We affirm that proper environmental prioritization will address greater risks before lesser risks and take into account the opportunity costs of fighting various risks — i.e., that it will recognize that since resources spent to reduce one risk cannot be used to reduce another, it is wise to allocate resources where they will achieve the greatest risk reduction.

We deny that spending vast resources to reduce small risks, when those resources could be spent to reduce greater risks instead, is good environmental stewardship.

ARTICLE XXV

We affirm that environmental policies that address relatively minor risks while harming the poor — such as opposition to the use of abundant, affordable, reliable energy sources like fossil fuels in the name of fighting global warming; the suppression of the use of safe, affordable, and effective insecticides like DDT to reduce malaria in the name of protecting biodiversity; and the conversion of vast amounts of corn and other agricultural products into engine fuel in the name of ecological protection — constitute oppression of the world's poor.

We deny that the policies named, and many others like them, are morally justified.

ARTICLE XVI

We affirm that, because a clean, safe, healthful, beautiful environment is a costly good, wealthy societies can better afford environmental protection and restoration than poor societies.

We deny that economic development is, per se, a threat to environmental quality.

ARTICLE XXVII

We affirm that private ownership of land and other resources, because it harnesses God-given human incentives to overcome the "tragedy of the commons," is the best institutional system for environmental protection.

We deny that collective economic systems are equally good at protecting or improving natural environments.

ARTICLE XXVIII

We affirm that local, constitutionally limited, responsive governments by the consent of the governed are better suited to environmental stewardship than central, unlimited governments without regard to the consent of the governed.

We deny that socialism, fascism, communism, and other forms of collectivist, expansionist government offer better solutions to environmental risks than limited, free, constitutional governments with market economies.

ARTICLE XXIX

We affirm that truth-telling is a moral obligation and that sound environmental stewardship depends on it.

We deny that intentional exaggeration, as practiced by many environmental advocacy organizations, or minimization, as practiced by many industries, of environmental risks or of the effectiveness of various means of addressing them is righteous.

ARTICLE XXX

We affirm that godly dominion is a responsibility for everyone at all times.

We deny that the expectation of divine judgment, in whatever eschatological framework, negates the need for Biblical Earth stewardship.

Closing Words

The documents in this book represent countless thousands of hours of some of the best theological minds from several nations. This time and effort has been invested because theology, being foundational to all of life, is crucial to every Christian; and the theology in this book is especially needed at this moment in the history of the Church. These are not the only critical issues, but they represent battlefronts; they are areas where the Church in many quarters is confused or compromised. We believe that, regarding these 24 controversial issues, if the Body of Christ in any country can come to agreement with these 24 Documents, that nation's Church will believe Biblically and be God's salt and light to their nation. And to the degree the Body of Christ in any nation disregards or opposes the teachings of the Bible, to that degree will they be a destructive force and find themselves incapable of being the Biblical salt and light to their nation as our Lord commands them to be. We pray and trust that this book, along with the effort of COR and its International Church Council Project, will make some good difference toward a more pure, complete, and quality Christianity for this twenty-first century.

Regarding our own nation, the U.S.A., I feel compelled to offer this following perspective. Because of much of the American Church's disobedience to the Bible, and apathy, lack of courage, and poor judgment over the past 100 years, she has, by default, allowed the global forces of atheism, socialism, and moral relativity to capture control of all of America's major institutions such as: government, the courts, the media, economics, and education, and even large portions of the institutional church. As a tragic result America is a divided nation, split into two irreconcilable parts which are now at odds with each other in what we call "the war of worldviews."

The ultimate question to be decided is this: "Which worldview and basis for all law will govern America and the other nations of the world: a Biblical worldview or an anti-Biblical worldview?" When we understand the ultimacy of this all-embracing question, we can then appreciate the Biblical fact that the Church on earth is commissioned by Christ to lead and teach the whole world that all of its social institutions mentioned above and all individuals on earth are to operate under the wise, Biblically-just governorship of Jesus who is King of the universe and has been since His resurrection from the dead, and that the Church is called to administer Christ's Kingdom on earth. Thus, all mankind is moving towards a planet either governed by the God-hating forces of Satan, or governed by the wise, workable principles of the Bible as taught by the

Bible-obeying Church of King Jesus. These are the only two options presented to mankind at any point in history. Only to whatever degree the Church in any nation acknowledges this perspective on this cosmic spiritual battle, and this either-or choice before her, will she be able to begin making Christ King of her own affairs and eventually King of all the nations and their people.

We heartily invite all Christians on this planet who desire to live in obedience to the Bible in all areas of life at all times, to form themselves and their local churches into "United Spiritual Armies" at the city and county levels, and to establish a network with other such churches and "spiritual armies" at their state and national levels with the goal of making Christ King of their cities and nation. We invite you to join with us in applying these 24 Documents to the life of the Church and in making 2 Corinthians 10:5 a reality. By that we mean that together we are called by God to destroy "speculations and every lofty thing raised up against the knowledge of God, and we *are* taking every thought captive to the obedience of Christ."

As a closing encouragement — observe how Christianity is growing faster than any other religion in the world. Christian sociologists working with the U.S. Center for World Mission in Pasadena, CA have shown that the ratio of non-Christians to Christians continues to decrease. By AD 100, 70 years after the Early Church was born, there were 360 non-Christians to every Christian. By AD 1000 the ratio was 270 to one. After the Medieval Church, in AD 1500 the ratio was approximately 85 to one. This trend continued so that by 1900, the ratio was 21 to one, and in 1980, 13 to one. And by 2010 there were approximately 7.3 non-Christians for every one Christian. It is clear that King Jesus continues to bring more and more of the world's population under His gracious dominion century after century. Trusting this rate will continue as it has the past 2000 years, the ratio between non-Christians and Christians will soon be one-to-one and beyond. We have reason to hope and to labor with prayerful, confident optimism as we press forward in the Great Commission, remembering that our labors are not in vain in the Lord!

At this very critical and exciting period of history, we can expect the God described in the Bible to be eager to answer our prayers "to move mountains" (Mark 11:22-23) as we follow the courageous example of those heroes of the faith who have gone before us and paved the Church's highway of history with their actions, their writings, and their blood, such as the sound advice given to us by William Carey, "Attempt great things for God, expect great things from God." May we be as faithful for future generations of Christians as they were for us.

— JAY GRIMSTEAD

Appendices

APPENDIX A
Documents, Theologians, and Reviewers* Chart

DOCUMENTS
A. HISTORIC DOCTRINAL ISSUES #1-9
1. BIBLICAL INERRANCY
2. BIBLICAL HERMENEUTICS
3. FORTY-TWO ARTICLES OF THE CHRISTIAN WORLDVIEW
4. THE KINGDOM OF GOD
5. THE OMNISCIENCE OF GOD
6. PELAGIANISM
7. JUDICIAL, SUBSTITUTIONARY SALVATION
8. THE TRINITY
9. THE ETERNAL FATE OF UNBELIEVERS
B. CURRENT CHURCH ISSUES #10-15
10. THE LORDSHIP OF CHRIST
11. UNITY OF THE BODY OF CHRIST
12. CHURCH DISCIPLINE
13. CULTURE, CONTEXTUALIZATION, AND MISSIONS
14. THE CHRISTIAN'S CIVIC DUTIES
15. BIBLICAL ECONOMIC SYSTEMS
C. SOCIAL & FAMILY ISSUES #16-24 (+ Israel & the Church & Environmentalism)
16. MARRIAGE, DIVORCE, AND REMARRIAGE
17. BIBLICAL DISTINCTIVES BETWEEN MALES AND FEMALES
18. HOMOSEXUALITY
19. BIBLICAL COUNSELING
20. ISRAEL AND THE CHURCH
21. EDUCATION OF CHRISTIAN CHILDREN
22. SANCTITY OF HUMAN LIFE
23. LAW OF GOD FOR ALL SOCIETIES
24. ENVIRONMENTALISM

LEAD THEOLOGIAN AND SOME REVIEW CONTRIBUTORS*

LEAD THEOLOGIAN	REVIEW COMMITTEE
A. HISTORIC DOCTRINAL ISSUES #1-9	
1. Dr. Jay Grimstead	(ICBI Document; No Review Committee)
2. Dr. Henry Krabbendam	(ICBI Document; No Review Committee)
3. Dr. Jay Grimstead	Two key theologians who helped create this document did not wish for their names to appear in this chart.
4. Jay Grimstead	Dr. William Mikler, Dr. D. James Kennedy, Dr. David Chilton, Mr. Gary DeMar, Dr. Larry Walker
5. Dr. E. Calvin Beisner	Dr. Paul Lindstrom, Dr. Roger Nicole, Dr. Kenneth Talbot
6. Dr. E. Calvin Beisner	Dr. Henry Krabbendam, Dr. Harold O. J. Brown
7. Dr. Greg Bahnsen	Dr. George Grant, Dr. Joe Kickasola
8. Dr. Jay Grimstead	Dr. Robert Fugate, Dr. Phil Kayser, Dr. Eugene Clingman
9. Dr. David Ayers	Dr. Jay Grimstead, Dr. Gary Amos
B. CURRENT CHURCH ISSUES #10-15	
10. Dr. Marc Mueller	Dr. Ted Baehr, Dr. Jay Grimstead, Dr. Larry Walker
11. Dr. Jay Grimstead	Dr. Bernie Ogilvy, Mr. Doug Daugherty, Dr. Dan Juster
12. Mr. Garry Moes	Mr. Art Cunningham, Dr. Mark Dalbey, Dr. Wellington Boone
13. Dr. David Hesselgrave	Dr. Eugene Clingman, Dr. Henry Krabbendam
14. Mr. Robert Hieronymus	Mr. Dan Smithwick, Colonel John Eidsmoe, Dr. Dan Juster
15. Dr. Ronald Nash	Dr. David Ayers, Mr. Garry Moes, Dr. Charles Wolfe, Dr. Jay Grimstead, Mr. Dan Smithwick
C. SOCIAL & FAMILY ISSUES #16-24 (+ Israel & the Church & Environmentalism)	
16. Mr. Garry Moes	Dr. David Powlison, Dr. Jay Grimstead
17.	(This document is by the Council on Biblical Manhood and Womanhood; no COR review committee)
18. Dr. Ed Welch	Dr. Bob Simonds, Dr. Gary Amos, Dr. Robert Dugan, Dr. Eugene Clingman
19. Dr. David Powlison	Rev. Craig Hill, Dr. Dan Juster, Dr. Bob Schlosser
20. Dr. Dan Juster	Mr. Robert Hieronymus, Dr. Eugene Clingman
21. Dr. Eugene Clingman	Dr. Jay Grimstead, Dr. Robert Fugate
22. Dr. Jay Grimstead	Mr. Robert Hieronymus, Dr. Robert Fugate, Dr. Eugene Clingman, Dr. Phil Kayser
23. Dr. Jay Grimstead	Dr. Eugene Clingman, Dr. Robert Fugate, Dr. Phil Kayser
24. Dr. E. Calvin Beisner	Dr. Jay Grimstead, Dr. Robert Fugate, Dr. Eugene Clingman

*During the years, these committees often numbered from 7 to 10 theologians and Christian leaders. In the final stages of a document's creation, we assigned a few men to be a "Review Committee," some of whom are listed here.

APPENDIX B

2014 COALITION ON REVIVAL AND INTERNATIONAL CHURCH COUNCIL PROJECT

Executive Board

Dr. Ted Baehr
Chairman;
Christian Film & TV Com.

Mr. Jerry Nordskog
President,
Nordskog Publishing Inc.

Bishop Wellington Boone
President,
Fellowship of Int'l. Churches

Mr. Victor Rivera
President, Integrity
Document Solutions Inc.

Dr. Jay Grimstead
Director, Coalition on Revival
Mrs. Donna Grimstead
Pharmacist

Dr. Robert Simonds
Citizens for Excellence
in Education/
NACE

Steering Committee

Dr. David J. Ayers, Prof.,
Grove City College

Dr. Ted Baehr, Chr.,
Christian Film & TV Com.

Rev. Mark Beliles, Pres.,
Providence Foundation

Bishop Wellington Boone, Pres.,
Fellowship of Int'l. Churches

Dr. James Borland, Prof.,
Liberty University

Dr. Eugene Clingman, Ex. Admin.,
Int'l. Church Council Project

Rev. Geoffrey Donnan, Pres.,
International Christian Ministries

Colonel John Eidsmoe, Alabama
State Defense Force, Pastor, Attorney,
Author, Worldview Speaker

Dr. Robert Fugate, Director,
Lord of the Nations

Dr. George Grant, Pres.,
King's Meadow Study Center

Dr. Jay Grimstead,
Dir., Coalition on Revival

Dr. Peter Hammond, Pres.,
Frontline Fellowship, South Africa

Dr. David Hesselgrave, Former Exec.
Dir., Evangel. Missiological Society

Rev. Craig Hill, Pres.,
Family Foundations International

Dr. Daniel C. Juster, Director,
Tikkun Ministries

Dr. Henry Krabbendam,
Professor, Covenant College

Bishop William Mikler, Senior
Minister, St. John's Abbey

Mr. Garry J. Moes, Director of
Development, Greenville Seminary

Mr. Jerry Nordskog,
Pres., Nordskog Publishing Inc.

Dr. David Powlison, Prof.,
Westminster Theol. Seminary

Mr. Victor Rivera,
Integrity Document Solutions Inc.

Dr. Thomas Schirrmacher, Prof.,
Martin Bucer Seminary, Germany

Dr. Robert Simonds, Citizens for
Excellence in Education/NACE

Mr. Dan Smithwick, Pres.,
Nehemiah Institute

Dr. Joseph Tson, Pres. Romanian
Missionary Society, Romania

Dr. Larry Walker, Prof.,
Beeson Divinity School

Dr. Ed Welch, Prof.,
Westminister Seminary-East

Advisory Board

Dr. Gary Amos,
Author, Lawyer

Dr. Paul Chappell, Exec. Vice Pres.,
The King's Seminary

Mr. Art Cunningham,
Retired Mgr., Hughes Aircraft

Dr. Mark Dalbey, Pres.,
Covenant Theol. Seminary

Mr. Doug Daugherty, Pres.,
Chattanooga Resource Foundation

Dr. Kenneth Gentry,
GoodBirth Ministries

Dr. Joseph Kickasola,
Prof., Regent University

Mr. Bernie Ogilvy,
Pres., Master's Institute

Dr. Kenneth Talbot, Pres.,
Whitefield Theol. Seminary

Dr. Rodman Williams,
Prof., Regent University

Dr. Charles Wolfe,
Restore the Republic

APPENDIX C

THE 1986
STEERING COMMITTEE
OF THE
COALITION ON REVIVAL

The 113 members of the COR Steering Committee (62 pictured here plus the other 51 listed) networked with each other to encourage the overall goals of COR for promoting "Bible Obedience" in the Body of Christ. The 62 members pictured were speakers at COR's 1986 "Continental Congress on the Christian Worldview III" in Washington, D.C. on July 2-4, at the Shoreham Hotel, and these pictures are taken from the conference brochure for that event.

This was the culminating conference of two previous ones wherein each of 17 committees, working all three years, completed their work on creating the Worldview Documents on how the Bible applies to the various areas of life such as the fields of: Law, Government, Economics, Business, Education, the Media and Arts, Science and Technology, Medicine, and Counseling. The last day of this conference on July 4, they all gathered at the steps of the Lincoln Memorial and held a National Solemn Assembly to repent and commit to rebuilding American civilization on the Bible. At that Solemn Assembly, various members of the Steering Committee read aloud at the microphone COR's entire "Manifesto for the Christian Church" which states the kind of Christianity Christ is calling His Church to proclaim and model in order to fulfill the Great Commission.

Mr. Ray Allen
President
ACT Ministries, Inc.
Faith without Activism Is Dead

Dr. Gleason L. Archer
Professor of Old Testament
Trinity Evangelical Divinity School
*Proper Procedures for Solving
Bible Difficulties*

Mrs. Virginia Armstrong
Ex. Dir., Blackstone Institute
of Public Law and Policy
*The Christian System of Law,
Definitions and Defenses*

Dr. Ted Baehr
Pres., Good News Communication
*How to Communicate The
Gospel Effectively and with
Power through the Media*

Dr. David W. Balsiger
Publisher-Editor
Biblical News Service/
Presidential Biblical Scoreboard

Mr. John Beckett
President
Intercessors for America
*Nehemiah and The Fortune
500*

Dr. E. Calvin Beisner
Editor, Benton County Times
*Changes to Watch for When
Biblical Economics Is
in Place in America*

Rev. Luther J. Blackwell Jr.
Pastor, New Life Fellowship
*The Kingdom of God and the
Black Community*

Dr. Charles Blair
Pastor, Calvary Temple
*Renewal through the Local
Church*

Dr. Richard Bliss
Dir., Curriculum Development,
Institute for Creation Research
*The Menace of Humanism &
Evolutionary Indoctrination*

Mr. Ron Boehme
Director, Youth with a Mission
*Why Is God Being Merciful
to America?*

Bishop Wellington Boone
Pastor & Founder, Manna
Christian Fellowship Churches
*Occupying as Priests —
Ruling as Kings*

Mr. Daryl Borgquist
Associate, National Council for
Educational Research
*That the Poor May Live
with You*

Mr. Arthur Cunningham
Pres., Hughes Aircraft Bible Club
*Using Company Resources to
Evangelize Employees*

Mr. Gary DeMar
President, American Vision
*The Theology of Christian
Activism*

Mrs. Gladys Dickelman
Exec. Dir., National Day of Prayer
*Prayer Penetration: Strategy
and Prototypes of Dynamic
Prayer Mobilization*

Rev. Peter Doane
Pastor, South Bay Covenant
Church
*Discipleship, God's Tool for
Maturity*

Mr. Colonel Doner
President, American Christian
Voice Foundation
*A Practical Strategy for
Repossessing Our Government*

Rev. Marshall Foster
Pres., Foundation for Christian
Self-Government
*Strategy for Saving the Constitution
— Our Last Hope for the Republic*

Rev. Joseph L. Garlington
Pastor
Pittsburgh Covenant Church
*The Need for a Biblical
Black Movement*

Mr. Peter Gemma
Exec. Dir., National Pro Life
Political Action Committee
Abortion in America:
The Fight for Life

Dr. D. James Kennedy
Pastor
Coral Ridge Presbyterian Church
Reclaiming America for God

Rev. John Gimenez
Pastor
Rock Church
Unity in Christ's body

Dr. Paul Kienel
President, Association of
Christian Schools, Int.
The Leader and His Family

Dr. Duane Gish
Vice President
Institute for Creation Research
The Scientific and Biblical
Evidence for Creation

Dr. Henry Krabbendam
Professor of Biblical Studies
Covenant College
The Fear of God as the Starting
Point of All Knowledge

Dr. Robert G. Grant
Board Chairman, Christian Voice/
Coalition for Religious Freedom
The Church Under Assault:
Religious Freedom Crisis

Dr. Richard Lappert
Consultant, Connecticut State
Department of Education
The Last Chance for
American Education

Dr. Jay H. Grimstead
Founder & Director
Coalition on Revival
The Vision and the Task
of COR

Dr. Walter Maier
Prof., Old Testament
Concordia Theological Seminary
Fallacies of the Historical
Critical Method of Bible
Interpretation

Mr. Ron Haus
Pres., 1st Cen. Communications
The Power and Possibilities of
Revolutionizing Today's Media

Mrs. Connie Marshner
Editor, *Family Protection Report*
How Christian Unity Could
Change the Country

Dr. Ronald A. Jenson
President
International School of Theology
Unifying and Mobilizing the
Body of Christ

Mr. Robert Martin
General Manager
Fieldstead and Company
Compassion, A Biblical
Response to Poverty

Mrs. Dee Jepson
Public Liaison, White House
The Influence of Godly
Women in This Generation

Mr. Ed McAteer
President
Religious Roundtable
Personal Witnessing for Christ

Mr. Roy Jones
Director, Legislative Affairs, Liberty
Federation
The Polarization of American
Politics

Dr. R. E. McMaster
Editor, *The Reaper*
Why Government Is Always
Religion Applied to Economics

Mr. Ray Joseph
Editor, Christian Statesman
National Reform Association
Christian Civil Government,
Part II

Bishop John Meares
Bishop
Evangel Temple
Worship and the Oppressed

Rev. Lou Montecalvo
Pastor, Redeemer Temple Southeast
Church
*Renewing Your Pastoral
Ministry*

Dr. T. M. Moore
Pastor
Church of the Savior
*The Reforming of
Evangelicalism*

Rev. Bob Mumford
President
Life Changers
The Battle for Life

Dr. Gary North
President
Institute for Christian Economics
*Why God Has Waited for
World Revival Until Now*

Dr. Ed Payne
Prof. & MD, Dept. of Family
Medicine, Medical College of
Georgia
Critical Issues in Modern Medicine

Mr. Dennis Peacocke
President
Covenant Outreach Ministries
Cultural Evangelism

Dr. John M. Perkins
President & Founder
Voice of Calvary Ministries
I Have a Dream, II

Mr. Jerry Regier
President, Family Research Council
of America
*Strenthening the Family
through Public Policy*

Dr. George Rekers
Prof., University of South Carolina,
School of Medicine
*Family Building in the Last
Quarter of the 20th Century*

Dr. R. J. Rushdoony
President
Chalcedon Foundation
*Christian Conquest of the
World*

Dr. E. Michael Rusten
Business Consultant
*Mobilizing Christians for
Social Action*

Mr. Herb Schlossberg
Author, Financial Advisor
*Idolatry: Biblical and
Contemporary*

Dr. Robert L. Simonds
Pres., National Association of
Christian Educators
*How Public Education's
Worldview Has Destroyed the
American Family*

Mrs. Carolyn Sundseth
Assoc. Dir., Office of Public
Liaison, The White House
*Christian Women in
Government*

Rev. Larry Tomczak
Editor, *People of Destiny*
magazine
*The Church at the Close of
the Twentieth Century*

Dr. Joseph Tson
President
The Romanian Missionary Society
*Partners with Christ in His
Suffering*

Mr. Peter Waldron
President
Contact American
*Destroying a Political Trojan
Horse*

Dr. Larry L. Walker
Prof., Old Testament,
Mid-America Baptist Seminary
*Retaining and Revitalizaing
Christian Colleges and
Seminaries*

Rev. Robert Weiner
President
Maranatha Ministries
*World Dominion through
God's Glorious Church*

Dr. John W. Whitehead
President
Rutherford Institute
Priorities for the Eighties

Rev. Al Whittinghill
Evangelist
Ambassadors for Christ
Spiritual Warfare—The Real
Battle

Mr. Don Zoller
Chairman
Outreach Ministries, McLean Bible
Church
The Church in America—
The Next 25 Years

OTHER COALITION ON REVIVAL
STEERING COMMITTEE MEMBERS

Dr. Joseph Aldrich
President
Multnomah School of the Bible

Dr. William Barker
Editor
Presbyterian Journal

Mr. Russ Bixler
President
WBCB-TV

Dr. Bill Bright
Founder and President
Campus Crusade for Christ International

Dr. Harold O. J. Brown
Professor of Biblical and Systematic Theology
Trinity Evangelical Divinity School

Dr. Glen Cole
Pastor
Capitol Christian Center

Dr. Lawrence J. Crabb Jr.
Director, Institute of Biblical Counseling,
Grace Theological Seminary

Mr. Ted DeMoss
President
Christian Business Men's Comm. of USA

Dr. James Draper
Pastor
First Baptist Church of Euless

Mr. Robert Dugan
Director
NAE-Public Affairs

Dr. Michael Farris
Legal Counsel
Concerned Women of America

Dr. Paul Feinberg
Professor of Biblical and Systematic Theology
Trinity Evangelical Divinity School

Dr. Arthur Gay
Pastor
South Park Church

Dr. Armin Gesswein
President
Revival Prayer Fellowship

Mrs. Melody Green
President
Last Days Ministries

Dr. E. V. Hill
Pastor
Mount Zion Baptist Church

Rev. Dick Hillis
President Emeritus
Overseas Crusade

Dr. David M. Howard
General Director
World Evangelical Fellowship

Rev. Dick Iverson
President
Portland Bible College

Col. Glen A. Jones (Ret.)
National Director of the Military Ministry
Campus Crusade for Christ

Dr. Jay L. Kessler
President
Taylor University

Rev. Mike Kiley
Pastor
The Home Church

Dr. Tim LaHaye
President
American Coalition for Traditional Values

Mrs. Beverly LaHaye
President
Concerned Women of America

Dr. Harold Lindsell
Editor Emeritus
Christianity Today

Dr. Allan A. MacRae
President Emeritus
Biblical Theological Seminary

Rev. Ronald Marr
Editor & Publisher
Christian Enquirer

Rev. Josh D. McDowell
President
Josh McDowell Ministries

Dr. Robertson McQuilkin
President
Columbia Bible College

Mr. Robert Metcalf
Founder
Christian Studies Center

Rev. James Morriss
Pastor
Rocky Mountain Fellowship

Rev. Ian North
President
Ambassadors for Christ

Dr. Raymond D. Ortlund
President
Renewal Ministries

Dr. J. I. Packer
Professor of Systematic Theology
Regent College

Dr. Luis Palau
President
Luis Palau Evangelistic Team

Mr. Archie Parish
President
Serve International

Dr. William Reed
President
Christian Medical Foundation

Rev. Marvin Rickard
Pastor
Los Gatos Christian Church

Dr. Adrian P. Rogers
Pastor
Bellevue Baptist Church

Rev. Ron Sadlow
Director
Church Resource Ministries, Tennessee

Robert L. Saucy
Chairman, Department of Systematic Theology
Talbot School of Theology

Mr. Franky Schaeffer
President
Franky Schaeffer V Productions

Mrs. Edith Schaeffer
Author, Speaker
L'Abri Fellowship

Rev. Mark D. Siljander
Congressman
Michigan-4th District

Dr. John Sparks
Professor of Law and Economics
Grove City College

Dr. Paul Toms
Pastor
Park Street Church

Dr. Jack Van Impe
President
Jack Van Impe Ministries

Mr. Donald Wildmon
President
National Federation for Decency

Mr. Jimmy Williams
Executive Director
Probe Ministries

Rev. John Wimber
Pastor
Vineyard Christian Ministries

Dr. Ralph Winter
General Director
U.S Center for World Mission

APPENDIX D
THE 1978 LIST OF THE ICBI
(INTERNATIONAL COUNCIL ON BIBLICAL INERRANCY)
EXECUTIVE COUNCIL AND ADVISORY BOARD

Previously published in the ICBI book, *The Foundation of Biblical Authority*, 1978, page 12.

The ICBI was a "theological army" composed of 53 world-respected evangelical theologians and heads of Christian organizations which gathered into a global team to stand together in proclaiming that the Bible's inerrancy was "an essential element for the authority of Scripture and a necessity for the health of the church," and that the Bible's inerrancy was what Jesus and all the Bible's inspired human authors, and all of the first 1900 years of the Church's teachers and heroes believed and taught. By contrast, the liberal theologians ensconced within many evangelical churches, schools, and organizations taught the falsehoods that one can have an authoritative Bible which is partly true and partly false (not inerrant), and that the doctrine of the Bible's inerrancy was only a recent falsehood invented within the last 300 years of the Church's history.

Executive Council

Gleason L. Archer
James M. Boice
Edmund P. Clowney
Norman L. Geisler
John H. Gerstner
Jay H. Grimstead
Harold W. Hoehner
Don E. Hoke
A. Wetherell Johnson
Kenneth S. Kantzer
James I. Packer
J. Barton Payne
Robert D. Preus
Earl D. Radmacher
Francis A. Schaeffer
R. C. Sproul

Advisory Board

Jay E. Adams
John W. Alexander
Hudson T. Armerding
Greg L. Bahnsen
Henri G. Blocher
William R. Bright
W. A. Criswell
Robert K. DeVries
Charles L. Feinberg
William N. Garrison
D. James Kennedy
Jay L. Kesler
Fred H. Klooster
George W. Knight
Harold Kuhn
Samuel R. Külling
Gordon R. Lewis
Harold Lindsell

John F. MacArthur
Josh P. McDowell
Allan A. McRae
Walter A. Maier
Roger R. Nicole
Harold J. Ockenga
Raymond C. Ortlund
Luis Palau
Adrian P. Rogers
Lome C. Sanny
Robert L. Saucy
Frederick R. Schatz
Joseph R. Schultz
Morton H. Smith
Ray C. Stedman
G. Aiken Taylor
Merrill C. Tenney
Larry L. Walker
John F. Walvoord

APPENDIX E
THE DECLARATION OF BIBLICAL TRUTH

We declare that the 24 documents of Affirmations and Denials of the Coalition on Revival represent well, however imperfectly,* what the Bible teaches on those 24 topics and also reflect what the mainstream Body of Christ has generally believed over the past 2000 years.

We urge all Christians who believe in the inerrancy of the Bible to study these 24 documents, and then join with us in signing this Declaration of Biblical Truth and in promoting and teaching these Biblical principles to all who will listen.

We further declare that to the degree the Scriptural principles reflected in these Affirmations and Denials are neglected, rejected, or opposed by individual Christians, churches, schools, or organizations, to that degree will those people wittingly or unwittingly lead the Church into further deterioration, confusion, self-destruction, and irrelevance, thus rendering Her less capable of being God's salt and light to a lost and sinful world.

---

*If you have minor reservations regarding some wording of the Documents, see below.

Name_____Date_____	
Postal Address _____	
City _____ State _____ Zip _____	
Email_____ Signature_____	

This Declaration of Biblical Truth was created and signed by the participating theologians, pastors, and Christian leaders who took part in the Western Hemisphere Consultation on Theology held at Knox Theological Seminary in Ft. Lauderdale, Florida, USA, August 6-9, 2003. The delegates discussed and then affirmed the first 20 (topics 1-20) of these theological documents at that time. (As a point of information: All 2,000 plus of the members of the Evangelical Theological Society were invited to participate in this Consultation.) In the intervening years since 2003, the COR team of theologians created another 4 (Topics 21-24) documents which have been added to the original 20.

We are creating a global list of signers in order to "draw a line in the sand" which we trust will make evident the truly Christian position on each topic, the position that stands with the inerrancy of Scripture and with the mainstream theology of the Church of the past 20 centuries. We invite all Christians world-wide, leaders and people alike, to sign this Declaration of Biblical Truth and become a part of the growing family standing together, presenting a united front for Biblical truth and opposition to un-Biblical error.

To be registered as a signer of the Declaration of Biblical Truth, please go to the ICCP Website at www.ChurchCouncil.org, or you may photocopy these two pages, fill out, sign, and mail to: COR, P. O. Box 1139, Murphys, CA 95247. (All 24 COR Documents are available and printable at the Website.)

MINOR RESERVATIONS?

If you think you generally agree with these 24 Theological Documents, but have minor reservations about certain wording in some documents you would like to see discussed and changed, you may sign below with minor reservations.

When theologians ask other Christian leaders to sign a declaration stating they agree with over 100 pages of concentrated theology dealing with 24 controversial issues dividing the Church, one would expect that some would have minor reservations regarding some portions. For this reason we make available the form below.

Name_____	Date_____	
Postal Address _____		
City _____	State _____	Zip _____
Email_____	Signature _____	

STATEMENT OF AGREEMENT WITH MINOR RESERVATIONS

In signing this Declaration of Biblical Truth, I am declaring that I am in substantial agreement with the main points of the 24 Coalition on Revival Affirmations and Denials Documents. However, I wish to offer to the Steering Committee my suggestions in writing for minor wording changes within the 24 documents that I believe would provide a more Biblical perspective on portions with which I have minor reservations. Doing so will allow me to sign the Declaration with a sense of theological integrity.

In registering such minor reservations on a separate sheet of paper, identify the name of the document and the number of the Affirmation or Denial under consideration, then offer the minor wording changes you wish to suggest and mail them along with your signed Declaration of Biblical Truth to the Coalition on Revival office at the above address. These minor reservations and suggestions will be kept on file and will be given consideration at our global church councils in 2017, 2019, and 2020. What is to be finally done with these suggestions will represent the consensus wisdom of Christian leaders from many nations and many denominations and perspectives from all five continents. By 2021 we are hoping a major portion of the Bible-believing, global Body of Christ will have together committed to a united Biblical-theological standard of doctrine which is consistent with the mainstream theology of the first 20 centuries!

APPENDIX F

Twenty-Question Survey on the Inerrancy of the Bible

Dr. Jay created these 20 Questions to be used by him and his co-workers in the ICBI in the late 1970s and early 1980s to survey evangelical colleges, seminaries, pastors and organizations which had followed the trend to move into a neo-orthodox, relativistic, less-than-Biblical perspective on the Bible (and some historic Christian doctrines), so those people could be confronted about their liberal tendencies and an honest evaluation of their growing liberalism could be documented and made public.

However, some leaders within the ICBI were opposed to "confrontation of evangelicals who had gone liberal" and did not want to identify those who were turning liberal because the Christian culture at that time they said "was not comfortable with confrontation of anyone or debates and battles over truth." So as a young, "still wet behind the ears," reformer, my 20 Questions were rejected as a tool for clarifying which evangelicals were standing with the Bible and which had gone neo-orthodox, and I did not have the courage at that time to stand alone and confront those who needed confrontation. So these 20 Questions are being brought out again today 35 years later in hopes that a younger generation of "Reformers" will have the courage to lose friends and popularity if necessary, and confront falsehood and deception within evangelicalism as Christ wants it confronted and exposed.

It is important to realize that these 20 Questions identify most of the exact falsehoods which are being taught at this moment in many "evangelical" colleges and seminaries. When an evangelical theologian goes liberal, he goes liberal on most of the points listed in these 20 Questions so they are a "precision tool" for identifying those turning liberal in their view of the Bible. We encourage any Christian who needs to know if a professor at their child's college, or a pastor, or any Christian leader in any organization or mission agency had turned liberal, to use these 20 questions as a survey of those leaders in question. Our estimate is that probably 50% or more of the evangelical Christian church has gone liberal in their view of the Bible, and many of them do so without even knowing they are turning against Christ's own teaching about the Bible. You may photocopy these pages or download these 20 questions at our COR Website: www.Reformation.net.

TWENTY QUESTIONS
14 Questions on the Inerrancy of the Bible
6 Inerrancy related questions on Theology

14 QUESTIONS WHICH CAN REVEAL
ONE'S VIEW OF THE BIBLE'S INERRANCY

TRUE *FALSE*

1. Did Moses write the first 5 books of the Bible (with the exception of the account of his death in Deuteronomy 34)? ☐ ☐

2. Did God make Eve out of a rib from Adam's body and did the entire human race descend from that first pair of human beings as described in Genesis chapters 2-5? ☐ ☐

3. Should the account of the fall of Adam and Eve in Genesis 3, the account of Noah and the flood and distribution of families over the earth in Genesis 6-9, the plagues of Egypt in Exodus 4-15, and the fall of Jericho in Joshua 6 be taken as serious, actual history the way we take the signing of the Declaration of Independence in 1776 as actual, time-space history? ☐ ☐

4. Did God actually give the Ten Commandments and the other laws to Moses in the word-for-word way they are recorded in Exodus 20-23 (in the original Hebrew language) and the instructions for building the tabernacle and furniture the way those instructions are recorded in Exodus 25-27? ☐ ☐

5. Did Isaiah the prophet write the whole book of Isaiah in the eighth century BC and was the book of Daniel written in Daniel's time in the sixth century BC? ☐ ☐

6. Did all the miracles recorded in Matthew, Mark, Luke, John, and the Acts happen exactly the way they are recorded in those five books? ☐ ☐

7. When Christ and the apostles cast out demons, were personal demonic beings actually making an exit from those victims and is there a real, personal Satan who is bent on deceiving and destroying human beings and whose activities in actual history with Job are recorded in Job 1 and 2? ☐ ☐

8. Is Paul's hierarchical teaching in Ephesians 5 (that wives are to live in submission and obedience to their husbands as the Church should in relation to her Lord Christ) to be taken as normative teaching ☐ ☐

which is absolute and is binding on the Church in the twentieth century as it also was in the first century?

TRUE *FALSE*

9. Is the entire Bible (Genesis through Revelation) inerrant in its statements about matters of interest to science, history, anthropology, psychology and ethics as it is inerrant regarding matters of faith and practice, Heaven and the unseen World? ☐ ☐

10. Is the Bible synonymous with and identical to the written Word of God so we may accurately say, "The words and sentences of the Bible (in the original manuscripts) are the very words and sentences God wanted written into the Bible...." and so we may say, "What the Bible says, God says."? ☐ ☐

11. Did Jesus and Paul believe and teach the view of the inerrancy of Scripture which was later defended by Augustine, Luther, Calvin, Spurgeon, Hodge, Warfield, Machen, and recently Francis Schaeffer? ☐ ☐

12. Is the Historical-Critical Method (and the JEDP theory as it is generally applied) a liberally biased, destructive, non-neutral tool because of its anti-supernatural presuppositions that should not be followed by Bible-believing scholars? ☐ ☐

13. Is the view of Scripture as it was taught by Hodge, Warfield, Machen, and Francis Schaeffer more Biblical, more logical and more like the view taught by the heroes of church history the first 18 centuries than that view of Scripture taught by the neo-orthodox theologians Karl Barth, Emil Brunner, and the later G. C. Berkouwer? ☐ ☐

14. Do you agree with the 19 Articles of the Chicago Statement on Biblical Inerrancy (Doc. 1) created by the ICBI and do you consider that statement to accurately reflect the Bible's teaching about its own inspiration and the approach to Scripture of the mainstream scholars of church history during the first 18 centuries of the church? ☐ ☐

6 QUESTIONS ON THEOLOGY WHICH CAN REVEAL ONE'S VIEW OF THE BIBLE'S INERRANCY

15. Was Jesus' death a substitutionary payment of the death penalty for men's sins to propitiate God's wrath and offer a legal, forensic justification for those humans who willingly come under Christ's blood atonement? ☐ ☐

16. Will the entire human race be separated into only two categories: those who respond properly to God and Christ's atonement to spend ☐ ☐

eternity with God in heaven; and those who respond improperly to be separated from God for eternity in hell?

TRUE *FALSE*

17. Are abortion-on-demand, adultery, homosexual sex and pornography condemned by God in the Bible for all people for all time so involvement in any of these practices would be scripturally and morally sinful for any Christian? ☐ ☐

18. Do socialism, Marxism, and "Liberation Theology" stand in opposition to the principles of the Bible and its teachings about man, law, government, economics, and general reality? ☐ ☐

19. Should all secular psychology including that taught by men such as Freud, Skinner, Rogers and Maslow be informed by, interpreted by, and judged by Scripture for its conformity to truth and reality rather than Scripture's view of man and reality being informed and judged by secular psychology? ☐ ☐

20. Were Calvin, Knox, Bradford, Witherspoon, Spurgeon, Warfield, and Francis Schaeffer correct in claiming that in the Bible, God calls all kings, governors and civil magistrates to govern the people justly as servants of God on earth as justice is defined in the Bible, and that those magistrates also must live under those principles of justice at all times as private persons or public officials? ☐ ☐

APPENDIX G
Survey Questions for Parents to Ask of Their Children's College Professors

A huge percent of Christian colleges and seminaries have left the Biblical view of Scripture and have moved into a liberal and neo-orthodox, relativistic view of the Bible and other orthodox doctrines. This set of 44 survey questions about 20 issues is a tool any parent (or student or donor or reporter) may use to find out what a professor or administrator in any so-called Christian college really believes if the professor will answer the questions honestly. Before any parent pays for and sends their student to any "Christian" college, they should survey some of the professors to get a reading on the school.

It is a fact that many professors feel they have no responsibility to be held accountable for what they teach and thus they deeply resent anyone conducting any kind of survey of their positions, so many professors will refuse to answer such survey questions. A good book explaining the fact that a number of Christian colleges have turned liberal on issues such as the Bible, Evolution, and Creation is *Already Compromised* by Ken Ham and Greg Hall, published by Master Books, and we recommend you purchase that book if you are a parent or student.

1. THE BIBLE
   Are the very words and sentences of the Bible (in the original manuscripts) all selected and inspired by God through the human authors so that we may honestly say that:
   A. "What the Bible says, God says" and "The very words of the Bible are God's Words"; and,
   B. "The Bible is co-authored by God and the human writers so that it was written 100% by God and 100% by man in the same way that Jesus was both 100% God and 100% man at the same time; and,
   C. The Bible is true not only in matters of the unseen, spiritual world ("the upper story"), but also wherever it touches on matters of interest to history and science, time and space...?
2. GOD'S OMNISCIENCE/FOREKNOWLEDGE
   A. Is God's knowledge of all things in the future as certain as His knowledge of all things in the past, and does God's knowledge of the future specifically include the future choices of all free agents including Himself; and,

B. Do you believe that God's moral character is infinitely, eternally, and immutably holy, righteous, and good, ensuring that His choices will always be holy, righteous, and good? □ □

3. THE ATONEMENT

Was Christ's death on the Cross as the Lamb of God a substitutionary Atonement for man's sin to rescue His people from the judicial condemnation of God because of their sin, so the penalty for sin could be legally paid by Christ and man could be counted righteous as he stands clothed in Christ's righteousness? □ □

4. THE TRINITY

Does the God of the Bible exist as a Trinity of three Persons wherein all three Persons are fully God and possess all the attributes of God, but the Father is not the Son or the Spirit, the Son is not the Father or the Spirit, and the Spirit is not the Father or the Son? □ □

5. HEAVEN AND HELL

Do all true Christians spend eternity with God and His people in Heaven and are all those who reject Christ's salvation separated from God and Heaven for eternity? □ □

6. THE LORDSHIP OF CHRIST

Do you agree that one cannot have a relationship with the real, Biblical Christ as their Savior if they do not also take Him eagerly as their Lord, Master, and King of their lives, Who has the right to call them up to a life of obedience to Him and the Bible the rest of their lives? □ □

7. UNITY OF THE BODY OF CHRIST

Do you agree that:

A. True, Biblical Unity of the Body of Christ must be based upon a doctrinal foundation that includes historic Christian doctrines as revealed in the inerrant Scriptures and expressed in the Apostles Creed; and, □ □

B. Local Biblical unity would lead the leaders of congregations and Christian organizations within a city or county together to prayerfully create plans for sustained, ongoing, cooperative Christian ministry in and for their community, and seek the Lord's enablement to call these plans into life together whether it is for evangelism, education, mercy ministry, or righteous political activity...? □ □

8. CHURCH DISCIPLINE

Do you agree that:

A. The purpose of Church Discipline is: to maintain the honor of God; to restore sinners; and to remove offense from the Body of Christ and thus warn others to avoid sin; and, □ □

B. Disciplinable offenses include both violations of the Divine Will stated in the Bible, and violations of sound doctrine and Biblical truth; and, □ □

C. All Church Discipline is non-optional for churches wishing to operate by the Bible...? □ □

9. CULTURE, CONTEXTUALIZATION, AND MISSIONS

TRUE FALSE

Do you agree that:

A. Various cultures are relatively "good" or "bad" dependent upon the degree to which they reflect God's character and promote His purposes as stated in Scripture both for their members and the larger good of creation as a whole; and,

B. The Christian's primary loyalty and obedience is to Christ and His Kingdom and only secondarily to the Christian's own culture and civil government; and,

C. In the Great Commission task of discipling all nations, it is essential that the Biblical Gospel be made understandable, meaningful, and relevant to the people of any given culture by proclaiming (preaching), as well as by verbal and nonverbal forms of communication normally used in that culture without compromising the Gospel or diminishing its message out of fear of displeasing that respondent culture…?

10. THE CHRISTIAN'S CIVIC DUTIES

Do you agree that:

A. The principle of civil government is a Divinely established sphere, and that all citizens, especially Christians, have a stewardship role in civil government: and,

B. Citizens under any government are accountable to God and their fellow citizens for the preservation and increase of justice, righteousness, mercy, and national stability: and,

C. That in a constitutional republic based upon representative government, citizens share responsibility for the actions and decisions of their elected leaders…?

11. SOCIALISM

Do you agree that:

A. God appointed mankind as steward over the earth and that the Bible teaches that individuals have a right to hold and manage their own private property: and,

B. The opportunity for an individual to profit from his labors and to produce wealth through his just and lawful endeavors is a primary motivator in the production of wealth, and a key ingredient to a society's economic health and stability: and,

C. The Bible is the sufficient source for learning the fundamental economic principles which both please God and lead to economic prosperity and stability, and contains economic principles which are moral and just, principles which ought to be followed by all people, all societies, and all states: and,

D. Earning profits and gaining wealth in the process of serving the market with goods or services is a good and moral thing when pursued in accordance with Biblical principles; and it is the responsibility of the Church to teach that the fundamental principles of Biblical economics and that Biblical economic theory is the only legitimate economic theory for all people of all cultures…?

TRUE FALSE

12. DIVORCE AND REMARRIAGE

Do you agree that:

A. In the Bible God has given all mankind three, moral absolutes for marriage which are:

1. Marriage partners are to have exclusive sex with each other but no one else; ☐ ☐

2. Marriage is to be a partnership and commitment between one man and one woman for life; ☐ ☐

3. In Eph. 5:22-33, God tells us the marriage is to reflect and be an example of the relationship between Christ and His Bride the Church, wherein the husband is to model the role of Christ by his willingness to lovingly sacrifice his life for his bride, and the wife is to model the Church's obedience and submission to Christ by her obedience and submission to her husband. ☐ ☐

B. The Bible offers us only two possible legitimate reasons for divorce which are:

1. Physical adultery on the part of one of the marriage partners; (Matt. 5:31-32) and, ☐ ☐

2. Desertion/abuse on the part of one of the partners (1 Cor. 7:10-15) ☐ ☐

C. The Bible prohibits believers from entering into marriage with unbelievers (1 Cor. 7:39; 2 Cor. 6:14)…? ☐ ☐

13. BIBLICAL DISTINCTIVES BETWEEN MALES AND FEMALES

Do you agree that:

Though both male and female humans are endowed by God with His image and are therefore of more value than all other created things in the universe, the Bible makes it clear that God has commanded males, not females, to carry the role of headship and leadership in both the home and in the Church, and that these distinctions are built-in and commanded by God and are not just the result of cultural mores? ☐ ☐

14. HOMOSEXUALITY

Do you agree that:

A. The Scriptures describe all homosexual practice as sin, and all Scriptures condemning fornication apply directly to homosexual sex as well, but also the Bible calls homosexual sex "an abomination": and, ☐ ☐

B. The Holy Spirit, when one is born again and washed by the atoning blood of Christ's sacrifice, is able to empower homosexuals to learn a holy love for both men and women and overcome their perverted sexual desires and have a normal, heterosexual marriage: and, ☐ ☐

C. The Bible offers no hope of salvation for practicing homosexuals who claim to be Christians, and churches which attempt to be Biblical should not allow practicing homosexuals to continue as communicant members. ☐ ☐

TRUE FALSE

15. BIBLICAL APPROACH TO COUNSELING

Do you agree that:

A. The Bible is the only basis of true knowledge about God, human □ □
existence, and healthy human relationships, and has sufficient wisdom to provide a systematic approach to counseling and provides
a basis for understanding all personal and situational problems:
and,

B. Every human is required to love God supremely, and his neighbor as □ □
himself, and psychological problems and immoral actions stem from
failure to fulfill this love command, and sin (as a failure to live up to
God's moral requirements) hinders, or severs, relationships with God
or our fellow human beings.

16. CHRISTIANS EDUCATING THEIR CHILDREN

Do you agree that:

A. Christians are required by God in the Bible to live in obedience to □ □
their Lord Jesus, and thus are called by God to see that their children
are intentionally and systematically taught the Biblical Worldview.
God has given parents custody, jurisdiction, and authority over their
children, as stewards to raise them as servants of Christ, to seek to
discern their calling and to train, discipline, and educate them in that
Biblical Worldview: and,

B. Anti-God and anti-Biblical public school educators or curriculum □ □
developers are an unwise choice for preparing Christian children to
become wise, Bible-obeying, Jesus-loving, mature servants of God in
their adult lives who see all of life through the grid of the Biblical
Worldview. In fact, the public school system and teachers at this point
in history generally teach just the opposite of the Biblical Worldview,
therefore we strongly urge Christian parents and their church's leadership to either home school their children or send them to a clearly
Christian school, but not to the government schools…?

17. THE SANCTITY OF HUMAN LIFE

Do you agree that:

A. Human beings are all created by God with God's own image imbed- □ □
ded within their soul and spirit, therefore they are all of immeasurable value to be valued far above all animals, vegetation, or material
wealth and are to be treated as God commands us in His Bible:
and,

B. Abortion of the fetus and infanticide are cold-blooded murder of the □ □
child and can do (and usually does) untold damage to the aborting
mother, therefore abortion should again be a criminal offence with
clear, legal, civic penalties as it was in the past: and,

C. Societies which condone abortion are judged by God for countless □ □
murders in the land, so such societies need to either repent and change
their laws or expect God's severe judgment.

18. GOD'S LAW FOR ALL SOCIETIES

Do you agree that:

TRUE FALSE

A. God revealed His Laws for all mankind in the Christian Bible by ☐ ☐
means of inerrant, verbal inspiration and that those written laws are
absolute and universal and therefore are to be obeyed by all mankind:
they apply to Christians and unbelievers and to all social orders in all
places at all times: and,

B. A human cannot be walking in love and at the same time be disobey- ☐ ☐
ing God's Moral Law and neither Christians nor non-Christians have
the right to disobey God's requirement of love toward God and one's
neighbor: and,

C. God's Bible is the ultimate standard by which all other laws, books, ☐ ☐
ideas, morals, actions, or people are to be judged or valued...?

19. ENVIRONMENTALISM

Do you agree that:

A. In the Bible, God has given his obedient people who love His laws and ☐ ☐
His actions, the task of stewardship of the earth and all its resources,
mines, vegetation, and animals, and wants the societies of all mankind
to operate within this stewardship according to His laws and principles
stated in the inerrant Bible: and,

B. It is apparent that the socialistic version of the environmentalist ☐ ☐
movement is both hostile to God's eternal, absolute principles for
how life is to be lived on this planet, and has fallen into the hands of
global socialists who wish to use their pseudo-scientific mandates as
a means of tyrannical control over the nations of the earth.

20. EVOLUTION

Do you agree that:

A. The theory of Evolution, including Theistic Evolution, is a logically ☐ ☐
and scientifically false and unfounded concept which offers no actual
evidence for its theories in the real fossil records or geological records
or in any established facts from any field of science, and that the laws
of probability show that the vast complexity of the human body cell
(plus many other biological facts) render evolution impossible to all
except those who believe it irrationally as a kind of "religious presupposition" and hold to it in spite of the facts rather than because of
the facts?

APPENDIX H
QUESTIONS FOR PASTORS FOR SELF-EXAMINATION

Most historically aware Christian leaders lay the blame for the deterioration of the Church over the past 100 plus years, and the resultant disintegration and decadence of our secular culture, on the average local pastors of the churches who have not had the courage or clarity of doctrine to call their people up to a true "obedient to the Bible" kind of Christianity. To the degree any area or region has pastors who are willing to give their lives for Christ and advancing His Kingdom on earth, to that degree is there a high probability that churches in those areas can undergo a Revival and a Reformation of Biblical theology and obedience to the principles of the Bible in daily living. Our estimate is that most Bible-believing, Jesus-loving pastors will have to tell themselves "NO" to many of these 10 questions. Please offer this set of questions to pastors you know with discretion and gentleness as we believe most pastors need to ask themselves these very questions. These questions should also be answered by any church elders, deacons, or staff. We encourage you to photocopy them from these two pages in this book to use with pastors or other Christian leaders for their self-examination.

QUESTIONS FOR PASTORS

1. Do I have more "fear of God" than I have "fear of man," especially in regard to fearing what my own congregation and my denomination/association/associates think, feel, and say about me?

2. Am I willing to regularly, publicly, and from my pulpit, require every member of our local church (from within their own heart's motivation), to desire and intentionally attempt to live in hourly obedience to the Bible's commands and principles in every area of their daily lives?

3. Am I willing, if Biblically necessary, to excommunicate from our church, any of my elders, deacons, staff, or closest friends or their adult children, if they persist in unrepentant, obvious sin?

4. Is glorifying and pleasing God and obeying Christ and the Bible and fulfilling His purposes and destiny for my life my highest priority more so than my concerns about my own prestige, financial security, and comfort?

5. Do I believe I am willing to physically die for Christ and the establishment of His Kingdom on earth, and willing to lose my friends, finances, and

comforts if necessary to please and glorify God and to obey His clear will for my life if it comes to that?

6. Am I willing to be held personally accountable for my own obedience to the Bible in every sphere of life daily (as stated in Matt. 18) by some of my own elders, deacons, or Christian friends, and by at least one other pastor within our local geography?

7. If I believe that our nation's public school system from grades K to 12 at this point in history has become philosophically and morally corrupt, sick and self-destructive for human beings, will I be bound by my Christian beliefs to publicly urge all our church members to pull their children out of public school and educate them in a distinctively Christian school situation?

8. Am I willing, with my elders, deacons and staff, to design and execute a long-range church plan wherein all of our adult church members (plus teenagers) are systematically and intentionally taught, trained, led, and encouraged to grow up to the level of Biblical Christian maturity, and to discover their own Spirit-endowed gifts so they may take their place in serving the greater Body of Christ and walk in their own appointed destiny as a productive, active Body member?

9. Am I willing to allow some of our church members and church leaders or staff to organize small, voluntary, fellowship groups ("Growth Groups") within our church to meet regularly for the purpose of:
    A. Honest Sharing of their inner lives and to pray for each other and family members;
    B. Holding each other mutually accountable to live in obedience to the Bible daily in every area of their lives;
    C. Making a commitment to the well-being of the other group members physically, spiritually, emotionally, financially, and in matters regarding their families?

10. Am I willing to become part of a local Pastors' Fellowship wherein we meet regularly to:
    A. Pray for each other's lives and ministries;
    B. Hold each other mutually accountable for living in obedience to the Bible hourly;
    C. Cooperate together as God may lead us in coordinated efforts at: Evangelism, Educational Seminars, United Worship Celebrations, Mercy Ministry, and speaking out with a united voice in the public media against social immorality and injustice?

APPENDIX I
INGREDIENTS OF CHRISTIAN MATURITY
by Dr. Jay Grimstead

Most Christians and most pastors seem to be unaware of the fact that God in the Bible calls all Christians without exception to become "mature Christians," and not to wallow around for years in an immature state of Christianity (where many Christians may be living far below their potential).

We invite you to photocopy this set of "Ingredients of Christian Maturity" and encourage people in your church or Christian group to examine their lives in light of these 10 "ingredients."

Please also check out the short teaching at the end explaining the meaning of the Greek word "Teleios" and the passages in which that term is used.

THE MATURE CHRISTIAN WILL HAVE
THESE THINGS OPERATING IN HIS/HER LIFE:

1. He has the lordship of Christ settled in his own mind and life, knowing the essence of the Christian life is obedience to Christ, and no longer struggles with whether or not Christ will really be His Master over every area of life.
   (Rom. 12:1-2; John 14:21; 1 Pet. 1:14-16)

2. He feeds himself regularly on the written Word of God without having to be pushed or "bottle fed" by his pastor and systematically reads through the Bible over and over.
   (Ps. 1:2-3: 1 Pet. 2:2)

3. He knows the basic content of the Word and can explain generally what is in each book of the Bible and what the foundational doctrines of Christianity are, so he cannot easily be led astray into false doctrine.
   (Eph. 4:13-15; 2 Tim. 3:16-17)

4. He has prayer and praise as a regular and important part of his life and takes some special times for prayer and reflection on his life-ministry-goals, etc.
   (Eph. 6:18-19; Phil. 4:6)

5. He is experiencing what some of us call "New Testament Fellowship" regularly with a group of Christians where there is:
   A. Honest sharing of his inner heart and life;
      (Eph. 4:15)
   B. Serious commitment to the life and well-being of others in the group; and
      (Acts 2:42-47)
   C. Mutual accountability (holding each other accountable) for living in obedience to Christ and the Bible.
      (Matt. 18:15-17)

6. He has a Biblically ordered family life, and while answering to God first before men, takes responsibility to serve faithfully in authority and under authorities God places over him that are not un-Biblical, inappropriate, nor violate his conscience toward God, whether the sphere be marriage commitment, parenthood, the local church, work, or civil government.
   (Matt. 8:9-10; Acts 5:29; Eph. 5:21; Eph. 6:7; Rom. 13:1; Eph. 5:22-31; Eph. 6:1; Eph. 6:5-8; Heb. 13:17)

7. He is increasingly demonstrating the Fruits of the Spirit (Christlikeness) and knows how to overcome sin in his life and how to receive forgiveness when he does sin.
   (Gal. 5:22-23; 1 Cor. 10:13; 1 John 1:9)

8. He is aware (or is becoming aware) of his gifting, calling, and his place and task in the Body, and is functioning energetically in that place (or is on his way there).
   (2 Tim. 1:7; Rom. 1:1)

9. He is able to lead others to the Lord and get them started "walking with the Lord."
   (2 Tim. 2:2)

10. He is generally an emotionally and socially mature human being and is not driven or controlled by un-Biblical fears, anger, addictions, etc.
    (Col. 4:5-6; Ps. 1:1-3, 1 Tim. 3:2-7)

THE GREEK WORD "TELEIOS"

In the New Testament, the Holy Spirit has given us the Greek word "teleios" which is translated to mean "mature," "complete," "adult," and "perfect." The texts for this message are these key passages using "teleios." (*Emphasis added.*)

Col. 1:28 "...teaching every man with all wisdom that we may present every man *complete* in Christ."

Eph. 4:13 "Until we all attain to the unity of the faith, and of the knowledge of the Son of God, to a *mature* man, to the measure of the stature of the fulness of Christ."

Heb. 5:13-14 "For everyone who partakes only of milk is not accustomed to the word of righteousness, for he is a babe. But solid food is for the *mature*, who because of practice have their senses trained to discern good and evil."

The Bible thus makes a distinction between the mature and the immature "babes in Christ" Christians. Our growth, development, and maturing in Christlikeness does not have to be a vague, measureless, fuzzy journey. Rather our journey into Christlikeness is composed of certain measurable milestones, indicators, and "yardsticks" that can tell us how far we have progressed and whether or not we are mature in Christ. In a nutshell, Christian maturity is simply Christlikeness along our own, God-given, personality lines, and Christlikeness is measured primarily by one's obedience and conformity to the Bible's commands and teachings.

Clearly, it appears in these texts that Christian maturity is not optional, but rather is required of all believers. That is, we do not have the right or the option to stagnate in Christian immaturity year after year but are obligated to press on to maturity in our own lives so we radiate Christ and do His will from the heart; all Christians without exception are thus obligated.

APPENDIX J
AN EVERLASTING KINGDOM
by Jay Grimstead

The Kingdom of God appears to be one of the most misunderstood Biblical topics among evangelicals. At 79 years old I now believe I have a fairly accurate grasp on the Kingdom of God. But for the first thirty years of my adult Christian life and for the first 23 years of my professional ministry life, and after getting a masters and doctorate at an evangelical seminary, I hardly had a clue as to what the Kingdom of God was all about and what we Christians were to do about making it functional on earth here and now. It is my belief that the vast majority of Bible-believing, sincere Christians are even now living in the theological fog about the Kingdom of God in which I lived for 30 years. I hope in this short article to contrast the differences between the Biblical view of the Kingdom of God and the less-than-Biblical view I see held by most evangelicals I have ever met.

In January of 1989, I called together a group of about 20 evangelical theologians to create a formal, creed-like, doctrinal statement about the Kingdom of God, which we did over an intense three-day period in Washington, D.C., for the purpose of helping to clear up the theological fog surrounding this topic. We were pleased with the results and sensed God led us in our discussions and editing. The result is now Document 4 here in the book on pp. 46–55, and is downloadable and printable from the Website, www.ChurchCouncil.org. This appendix will be referring to and quoting that Document we call "The 25 Articles on the Kingdom of God." I recommend any student of the Kingdom of God obtain it for their own study. The Scriptural references backing up each article are included at the end of each of the 25 articles.

Following are some of the major points I believe the leadership of the global Church must come to understand before we have any hope of accomplishing the Great Commission. And most of these points which will appear revolutionary will involve a major "paradigm shift" in the minds of the Church's leaders if they care to consider and eventually accept this view of the Kingdom of God at all, which we believe is completely Biblical.

1. **CHRIST'S KINGDOM IS ACTUALLY HERE ON EARTH NOW** — and has been functioning on earth with Christ as the legal, actual "King of Heaven and Earth" in this age ever since Christ ascended to the right hand of the Father

2000 years ago. Therefore we do not need to wait for His second coming for the Kingdom to be inaugurated! (Article IV)

2. THE KINGDOM OF GOD IS NOT ONLY SPIRITUAL BUT IS ALSO FUNCTIONING IN HISTORY — at this moment politically, legally, physically, artistically, scientifically, and culturally wherever His obedient servants join together as a team to bring forth the Kingdom of God on earth through their families, schools, businesses, churches, organizations, law firms, legislatures, etc.; in any country in any society. We deny that God's rulership is limited to transforming only the private lives of individuals. (Article VI)

3. THE LORD'S PRAYER IS PRIMARILY ASKING GOD TO GET HIS KINGDOM TO COME TO EARTH AND HIS WILL TO BE DONE ON EARTH AS IT IS DONE IN HEAVEN NOW STARTING WITH THE FIRST CENTURY — No serious scholar will attempt to convince anyone that what Jesus really had in mind (when He gave this model prayer in Matthew 6 was that, though His disciples should pray that kind of prayer daily, they should really pray it with the understanding that God's Kingdom coming to earth and His will being done on earth was not to happen for 2000-plus years, nor expect that prayer to be answered until after His second coming. (Article XIV)

4. THE GREAT COMMISSION (Matthew 28:18-20) WAS ESSENTIALLY A COMMAND TO MAKE BIBLE-OBEYING DISCIPLES OF ALL NATIONS AND GET THEIR NATIONS TO LIVE IN FULL OBEDIENCE TO EVERYTHING GOD SAID IN THE BIBLE IN ALL AREAS OF LIFE AND OFFICIALLY BOW TO CHRIST AS KING OVER THEIR LIVES, GOVERNMENTS AND SOCIETIES AS THE ROMAN EMPIRE AT THAT TIME BOWED TO CAESAR — What the Great Commission was not, was a commission to only go and get souls saved so those souls could go to heaven at some point in the future. (Articles X, XI, and XIII)

5. CHRIST, NOT SATAN, IS THE RULER OF THIS EARTH NOW EVER SINCE HIS ASCENSION — We deny that Satan is the ruler of this world in any sense that undermines the recognition of the rightful rule of Christ over the earth during this present age. We further deny that Christ will ever be given any more power by the Father over the earth than He was given at his first coming. The apostles were, as we are, given the task to get the inhabitants of all nations to recognize the historic and legal fact that God had made Christ the new "emperor" of the planet and that all logic, morality, and good sense required all men to repent of their sins and fall before Christ as Creator, Sustainer, Judge, Saviour, and King over all people on earth and that not to do so is to live in evil rebellion and in a psychotic state of unreality. The world does not have to get worse and worse. Christ commanded us to make

the world better and better century by century. And every nation (except France) where serious Christians united to change their nation and bring forth the Kingdom of God on earth were successful to a measurable degree to which history clearly attests. (Articles VIII, IX, and X)

6. THE BIBLE IS THE PLUMB LINE FOR ALL NATIONS AS TO HOW THEY ARE TO GOVERN THEIR COUNTRIES — which laws to impose as civil law, how they are to run their courts, families, economics, what morals to require of their societies, and what worldview (philosophy) should undergird their culture, this being true whether a culture is historically Christian, Moslem, Hindu, or atheistic! This is so because God created them and the rest of the universe and requires this of all men. That same God came to earth as Jesus, the incarnation of the Trinity's second Person, and became "the last Adam" and the Lamb of God and Saviour, so people may now be right with God for time and eternity. He also came as the genetic heir of King David's throne to be King of earth now. (Article XVIII)

7. THE KINGDOM OF GOD IS TO GAIN WILLING SUBJECTS INCREASINGLY ON EARTH OVER THE CENTURIES SO GREAT PORTIONS OF THE PLANET ARE CHRISTIANIZED WHEN JESUS DOES RETURN — That this is the actual trend of history can be shown by Christian sociology statistics from the U.S. Center for World Mission in Pasadena, California. At the end of the first century only one out of every 360 people was Christian. By AD 1000 the ratio was one Christian to every 270 non-Christians. By 1900, it was one to 21. By 1970, the ratio was one to 13. And by 2010 it was one Christian to every 7.3 non-Christians. At this rate, the ratio could soon be one to one! We have actually been gaining much ground in numbers and in many fields of life over the past 2000 years. And for the record, the Church over the ages has never adopted a universally accepted position regarding eschatology, thus, no group of Christians should make any eschatolotical view a test for orthodoxy, whether that be from the perspective of premillennialism, postmillenialism, or amillennialism, since Scripture leaves all three of those positions open for people to accept. (Articles XV, XVI, and XXV)

In closing, I would urge those who may find this information disturbing to study the Kingdom document which supports this. Few doctrines are as critical to our evangelism of the world as the doctrine of the Kingdom of God and it is my opinion that many of the evangelical church denominations have held less-than-Biblical views on this topic since approximately 1830.

APPENDIX K

How Kant's Epistemology Birthed Neo-Orthodoxy

Out of the 24 theological positions presented in this book, by far the topic of the Inerrancy of the Bible is the most foundational and the most important both for accurate theology and for Christlike living. The inerrant, authoritative Bible is not only the basis and source of all other doctrines of Scripture, but is also the basis for all knowledge that all humans, Christians and non-Christians alike, are capable of knowing in every field of life.

In the Bible, God has communicated to all mankind what is reality and truth about the universe and how it works, and society and how it works best, and how the unseen world and the visible world impact each other. In the Bible He has given mankind the absolute standards for how humans can discern the differences between truth and error, right and wrong, reality and unreality, and these standards do not change with time or culture or geography. In the field of Philosophy, two of the first and foundational questions to be asked and answered are these (for which the Bible has excellent, rational answers):

1. "What is reality?" This field of philosophical inquiry is called "metaphysics."

2. "How can we know reality and truth and differentiate it from unreality and falsehood?" This field of philosophical inquiry is called "epistemology." During the twentieth century epistemology was the major topic of the philosophers of the world.

When a so-called Christian goes "liberal" and begins considering that the Bible is part true and part false, that Christian almost certainly has been looking at the Bible through the eyes of an un-Biblical "epistemology" which he or she has absorbed from our culture. That liberal also sets himself up as "judge" over the Bible regarding what he thinks it ought to say, rather than allowing the Bible to be "judge" over him and all his thinking.

Kant and Pure Reason

Most theological liberals have accepted without question the false epistemology of Immanuel Kant (1724–1804), expressed first in his world-shaking book from 1781, *Critique of Pure Reason*. When Kant wrote this book, the secular, non-Christian philosophers of the world had reached a major "dead end" in atheistic philosophy because David Hume (1711–1776), a British empiricist, had convinced them that, based upon their atheistic assumptions which

Hume accepted, the atheistic philosophers not only had no real proof that God and the invisible world existed—Hume demonstrated that they also had no real proof that the physical world of science existed or that the philosophers themselves existed. (What a terrible plight!!) So Kant set out to solve this problem and in so doing, Kant felt that he had successfully saved both the existence of God and the existence and value of science and the physical world.

Kant's Two Disconnected Worlds

The unreasonable and very un-Biblical mental trick that Kant put forth to try to save the philosophers' ability to have "true knowledge" of the existence of both the physical world of time and space, and of the invisible world of spirit and thought, was to create a false "DICHOTOMY" between the visible world and the invisible world. He did this by claiming in his new philosophy that there exists an absolute and eternal and impassable barrier (like a 20-foot thick concrete wall 100 feet high) between the visible world and the invisible world and no communication or knowledge which uses either language or logic may penetrate that wall between the visible world and the invisible world. What this means is that Kant was claiming that *God could not create a Bible using human language and logic to communicate with mankind even if God wanted to!* It also meant that humans could therefore have no certain knowledge about God through the Bible's language and logic, but only through emotional, "spiritual" experiences with God that were indefinable and unexplainable by either logic or language.

Thus Kant tried to mentally create for his fellow non-Christian philosophers this new dichotomy which placed the invisible world of God, angels, heaven, religion, etc. in a hermetically sealed, air-tight, leak-proof spiritual "compartment" which could not have any logical or language connection or penetration whatsoever with the other air-tight, leak-proof "compartment" containing the physical world of time and space, matter and energy, science, history, and human bodies.

Kant felt that by creating this absolute dichotomy between those two opposite worlds, he had saved both religion and God in the invisible world and he had also saved the physical universe for science and history. What our dear readers need to realize about this very new and very un-Biblical, esoteric development in Kant's work, is that by 1850, all the major universities in Europe had wholeheartedly accepted Kant's dichotomy view of reality. It is this dichotomy which is the philosophical basis of an estimated 99% of all theological liberal thought as well as the basis of all secular philosophy since Kant. The entire history of secular (un-Biblical) philosophy divides itself into pre-Kantian philosophy and post-Kantian philosophy as the secular, atheistic philosophers had nowhere else to turn from the dead end to which their assumptions had led them up through the time of David Hume the Empiricist. Atheistic thinkers will go to extreme and foolish lengths to try to avoid, at all costs, accepting the Bible's view of all reality and its view of good and evil, of time and eternity, history and God.

Before the writings of Kant, Hegel (1770–1831) and Kierkegaard (1813–1855), most all secular philosophers (who had rejected the Bible as Truth) still hoped for and assumed that their thinking could eventually lead to forming "a unified field of knowledge" wherein all facts and details of the universe (both visible and invisible) could logically be related to all other facts and details of the universe. Without God's revealed information in human language in the Bible about both the visible and the invisible portions of the universe, it is close to impossible to arrive at "a unified field of knowledge."

Kant's "solution" was to give up all hope of ever discovering a logical "unified field of knowledge" and instead offered his "radical dichotomy" wherein there is zero logical connection between the visible and the invisible worlds. Hegel took this even further by changing the rules of epistemology on how one arrives at true "knowledge," and Kierkegaard poured these concepts into an "existential" framework.

Most all liberal (non-Biblical) theologians in the 1800s and 1900s accepted the anti-Biblical philosophies of Kant, Hegel, and Kierkegaard. Karl Barth was trained in Kantian philosophy and liberal theology and believed that God is totally "other" or only transcendent. After he met Christ he wrote his commentary on the book of Romans in 1919, and became the "father of Neo-Orthodoxy." The neo-orthodox movement was based upon Kant's dichotomy of reality and attempted to proclaim *some* orthodox doctrine but based that doctrine upon a Bible they, as liberals, still believed was only partly true and was partly false, containing many human errors.

On the other hand, Christian philosophers call the Bible the *"epistemological basis of our faith and of all knowledge about all things."* Most conservative theologians agree. Belief in the inerrancy and total inspiration of the entire Bible is the only logical and proper starting place for all truly Biblical discussions on any topic. The mainstream, orthodox Body of Christ from all denominations for the past 2000 years has stood squarely upon the same Biblical positions on controversial issues that we state in each document. These issues would not have been controversial in the first place if all evangelical leaders and writers were committed to the total truthfulness of the Bible.

For a deeper explanation, see Chapter 3 of Francis Schaeffer's book, *Escape from Reason.* For fuller definition of neo-orthodoxy and other relevant terms like epistemology, metaphysics, and transcendent, see our Glossary on pp. 309–314.

APPENDIX L

How a Neo-Orthodox, Liberal View of the Bible Infiltrated and Corrupted Evangelical Churches and Schools

Though we touch on this topic in the Introduction to this book on p. 6, a clear explanation of neo-orthodoxy and how it infiltrated and corrupted evangelicalism is included in this Appendix. To understand the 17 falsehoods which a liberal and neo-orthodox view promotes, one needs only to look at the ICBI Chicago Statement on Biblical Inerrancy (Document No. 1) and see what Articles 3 through 19 teach. Our ICBI Statements in these 17 Articles are combating actual neo-orthodox falsehoods now being taught in many so called "evangelical" seminaries and Christian colleges.

Liberalism under the name "Neo-Orthodoxy" Infiltrates and Corrupts Evangelicalism

by Dr. Jay Grimstead

Modernism Challenges the Historic View on Inerrancy

Just as the Church's understanding of the full deity of Christ and the Trinity awaited the Arian controversy and the Council of Nicea in AD 325; and just as the full understanding of Justification by Faith and the Priesthood of every Believer awaited the 1500s when it was clarified by Luther and Calvin, so the doctrine of the Inspiration of Scripture awaited the twentieth century for its full debate and delineation. Up until the twentieth century, all branches of Christianity accepted the basic inerrancy view of inspiration except for the secular philosophers and the liberal theologians, and so a full-scale debate was unnecessary until then.

By the end of the liberal-fundamentalist doctrinal battles of the 1920s and 1930s, large portions of previously sound major denominations were infected with a liberal view of the Bible. The evangelicals and fundamentalists within those denominations generally pulled out and started their own new denominations, seminaries, and mission societies and stood firm on the historical view of the Bible taught by Moses, Jesus, Paul, and the heros of the faith the past 2000 years. By that time, almost all the theological schools and theologians of Europe had gone liberal. America and Canada, which are usually from 25 to 60 years behind Europe in their philosophical disintegration, were just starting to "catch up" with Europe theologically in their move toward liberalism.

As Francis Schaeffer stated so eloquently, courage for confrontation over matters of truth and righteousness in the hearts of Christian leaders in North America was replaced by a kind of "knee-jerk" response committed to accommodation and "peace at any price" which sadly still reigns supreme within most evangelical circles today. This is one major reason things have disintegrated so far and so fast. At the same time, the relativistic view of truth and a dichotomy worldview (that segregates the spiritual world from the material world into two separate air-tight compartments) that came from philosophers such as Hume, Kant, and Hegel had all but completely captured the university intellectuals of the entire world.

Neo-Orthodoxy Infects the Evangelical Ranks

This was the kind of academic atmosphere that prevailed during the 20 years from 1947 to 1967 when many evangelical seminaries and colleges sent their bright young scholars to European universities to get their doctorates. A large percentage of these young scholars were infected with liberal and neo-orthodox views of the Bible, and then returned to their evangelical schools to teach a neo-orthodox view of the Bible (what they sincerely believed were the "latest, most scholarly" views) to their students.

These partially "corrupted" young professors did not openly challenge their denomination's or institution's historic view of inspiration of the Bible. It was more subtle than that and less obvious than the open battle over the Bible of the 1920s and 1930s. Most of these young professors were infected with neo-orthodoxy, the then fashionable "reformed" liberalism of Swiss theologian Karl Barth. Neo-orthodoxy claims that the human words of the Bible are not the very words of God, but rather are a fallible human "witness" to the words of God and are therefore in a sense, the "Word" of God to man. In some cases they claim that the words of the Bible "become" the Word of God to man at a particular existential moment when that man senses God speaking to him. Others have spoken of the Bible "containing" the Word of God.

Neo-Orthodoxy Undermines the Reliability of Scripture

Since most neo-orthodox theologians attempt to honor God's word in some sense, their presentation to their students of their existential and relativistic re-interpretation of the Bible does not appear to be, nor is it intended to be, an attack upon the Bible. But since most neo-orthodox men accept most of the higher critical theories of theological liberalism and since they usually believe (with Kant and Barth) that human language is incapable of communicating absolute, unchanging, and inerrant truth from God to man, therefore they are essentially liberals in their view of Scripture.

In addition, most neo-orthodox "evangelicals" believe they cannot count on the Bible being absolutely true in matters of time and space, science and history, or ethics and anthropology (that is, areas that are open to scientific verification or falsification), but they do comfort themselves by saying they believe the Bible may be capable of communicating undistorted truth in "spiritual" matters such as eternity and heaven, faith and salvation, or piety and theology (areas that are not open to objective empirical verification). Thus they ask us to believe the Bible in those areas of "faith and practice" that cannot be verified, and to also believe the Bible is not totally reliable in matters of history and science: that is, in those areas which ARE verifiable.

Can you see here the illogical foolishness of this neo-orthodox view?

Here is the logical problem. If we are unable to believe in the history and accuracy of what the Bible tells us about visible, tangible areas capable of verification and falsification, what reason have we to believe when it tells us about invisible things we cannot verify? What foolishness this is!

Document No. 1, "The Chicago Statement on Biblical Inerrancy," deals with this neo-orthodox foolishness in Article XII when it states: "We deny that Biblical inerrancy and infallibility are limited to spiritual, religious, or redemptive themes, exclusive of assertions in the fields of history and science." It may be noted that the older liberals who rejected both the Bible's history and the Bible's statements about the invisible world, were more logical than the neo-orthodox liberals at this point.

In a nutshell, a liberal and neo-orthodox view of Scripture considers the original Greek and Hebrew manuscripts of the Bible to be part true and part false and that their theological experts must help us determine what parts of the Bible are true and what parts are false. That is the essence of theological liberalism under whatever name it travels even if it goes by the name of "evangelicalism." Thus, a professor infected with a neo-orthodox view of Scripture will tend not to believe that Moses wrote all five books of the Pentateuch; or that Isaiah wrote the whole book of Isaiah; or that Daniel was written in Daniel's time; or that the flood of Noah was a universal flood covering the whole earth; or that all of present mankind came from Noah's family; etc., etc. They will also tend to teach students that neither Jesus nor the Church Fathers believed the inerrancy view of Scripture that was indeed taught by Jesus, Paul, Augustine, Calvin, Wesley, Spurgeon, Hodge, Warfield, Machen, and Schaeffer. They teach that the inerrancy view is a late development in church history.

Neo-Orthodoxy Entrenches Itself in Evangelical Institutions

Since the 1960s, many evangelical seminaries and colleges, denominations and organizations have been infected by the prevailing fog of neo-orthodoxy. Many sincere evangelicals, including many pastors and professors, are neo-orthodox liberals in regard to Scripture and don't even know there is anything wrong with their view. In light of all this, we felt we had to launch the International Council on Biblical Inerrancy in 1977.

By 1976, a neo-orthodox and liberal view of Scripture and therefore a relativistic view of doctrine and morals had permeated much of evangelicalism. The prevailing mood among educated people was openness to the liberalized view of Scripture and a general fear of being labeled a "narrow inerrantist" who still believed the old, "unscholarly and medieval" view that Scripture was inerrant. If some Christians in many evangelical circles really believed in the inerrancy of the Bible, they tended to remain "in the closet."

Furthermore, we, who felt God wanted us to stand up for the traditional, inerrancy view of Scripture and call our churches and organizations to be consistent with the statement on Scripture in that organization's founding documents, were often attacked as troublemakers and told to be quiet or to go away. Almost no one wanted to face up to an honest, open evaluation of how far a church or organization had slid down the slippery slope towards increasing liberalization. Christian leaders then, who believed in the inerrancy of the Bible, found themselves becoming lonely warriors who were misunderstood, feared, and sometimes gently persecuted. Almost no one seemed to be willing to make it a national Christian issue and get it settled if it meant losing friends or a position in their organization.

The Battle for the Bible Explodes

In 1976, Dr. Harold Lindsell came out with his bombshell book, *The Battle for the Bible*, which exposed the massive infiltration of liberalism and neo-orthodoxy into nearly every denomination and seminary that considered itself evangelical. Lindsell's book was very accurate in exposing the deterioration and it was scholarly in its presentation. As far as we can tell, none of Lindsell's charges were ever refuted in any substantive manner by the institutions in question. The accused schools merely fumed and spoke harsh things against Dr. Lindsell. At that time, few leaders besides Dr. Lindsell and Francis Schaeffer were attempting to make the inerrancy of the Bible an issue, though many were still faithfully teaching inerrancy.

The general response to *The Battle for the Bible* among the evangelical leadership of America was that it was "divisive" and that Lindsell was too "harsh" and "unloving" in exposing the factual situation within evangelical institutions. Thus, the Church was neither ready nor willing to go to battle over the watershed issue of inerrancy. Many of the inerrantists were in the "closet" and the anti-inerrantist, neo-orthodox theologians were having a field day making fun of the old-fashioned view in the various evangelical periodicals and journals. (I want to make it clear at this point that the Fundamentalists and most Pentecostals stood firmly for inerrancy during this period). It was in this context that the ICBI was born.

APPENDIX M
DR. JAY'S LETTER TO R. C. SPROUL THAT CONCEIVED THE ICBI AND EVENTUALLY LED TO COR AND ICCP

SOUTH PENINSULA
AREA DIRECTOR – CHRIS HAUGEN
SOUTH PENINSULA STAFF – JAY GRIMSTEAD, KRISTINE TAYLOR
TRAINING STAFF – PATTI DOBBS, MIKE DUNKLE, FRED CHAY
ADMINISTRATIVE AIDE – SHERI HOPKINS

October 6, 1976

Dr. R. C. Sproul
Ligonier Valley Study Center
Stahlstown, Penn. 15687

Dear R. C.,

An idea has been germinating in my mind since last spring and it's taken a concrete enough form by now so that I want to share it with you and get your opinion and have you bounce back any comments you may have about this idea. You're the first person I'm really mentioning this to because I don't really foresee going ahead with something of this magnitude if you aren't excited about it yourself.

The general idea is to arrange a yearly conference for Christian scholars, theologians, apologists, and Biblical scholars who stand for the traditional view of scripture that you and Gerstner and Warfield and I believe. That is, I'm not thinking of setting up a dialogue thing or a broad thing for men of various evangelical stripes to get together, but to take those who stand for traditional orthodoxy, for the Biblical reformational view of scripture. <u>I see the purposes for such a gathering being these</u>: <u>First</u>, to strategize what needs to be written and taught for the next year or two or three years and perhaps keep in touch with an ongoing ten-year strategy, to teach and inform and encourage the Christian church along orthodox lines of believing and living. Within this strategy session I could see us talking about where the pressure points are, what articles need to be answered, what books need to be answered, what tapes need to be produced. <u>Secondly</u>, and in conjunction with whatever strategy we arrive at for written materials, scholars would assign themselves various tasks and perhaps even co-authoring books, men would buy into the action as they felt they needed to, in order to catch their piece of the front line battlefield action. It's easy for scholars to get excited about a two-hundred page dissertation on the vocalized schwa or some point about Ugaritic. This all needs to be done sometime by someone, but I would guess that the whole health of the Christian Church in America and abroad would be greatly helped by a concerted focused coalition effort of orthodox scholars, rather than letting all these orthodox scholars buy into a piece of the action periodically and as they happen to think of something that needs written or said. A third reason for getting together men at a yearly conference (even if they didn't come every year) would be general encouragement in a very lonely position and general information sharing as scholars and as men concerned about the state of the church and what to do about it. A fourth reason would be to have a united front openly or not; that is, I see a difference between a united effort and a united front. Or rather I see a difference between a low profile united front and a high profile united front and I'm not at all sure we'd want a high profile united front, though that may be desirable. There are probably other reasons, but those are the ones that come to my mind and this is the thing I've been running around in my mind for six months.

I think the reason this idea has come to mind is this, R. C. It's apparent to me that evangelical Christianity actually is divided right down the middle between those that hold to the traditional view of scripture and truth on the one hand, and those on the other hand who have been affected by Barth and Berkouwer in their view of truth and epistemology and scripture and all the resulting doctrines that get diminished as a result.

This is something that neither Hubbard nor the archangel Gabriel can rightly accuse you or Schaeffer or Lindsell of causing. The division has only this last couple of years made itself apparent even though it has been coming for probably the last twenty years. I think it's foolish to say the division is not there and I think it's even more foolish to say as, for example Hubbard is trying to say (and Guder is trying to say and many theologians are trying to say), that what we need is an evangelicalism broad enough to straddle Warfield on one side and Berkouwer on the other. With their spongy view of truth and their great tolerance for logical disharmony within systems, they're able to think that way sincerely and to really think it can be done and should be done. On the other hand, we with the traditional view of truth and scripture know that there's a watershed here and that a choice has to be made. That this is one of those either-or situations rather than a both/and. Here's the kind of thing I mean. This is in a letter from Hubbard that I received three days ago, in response to my letter of sharing with him all the liberal stuff I found at Fuller. It's interesting that of all the points I brought up, he did not deal with even one of them. It's as if political astuteness and love can cover every heresy that ever raises its head. I mention this to you in confidence so that you will be careful who you share this information with, but the quote I wanted to share with you is as follows:

"I've had further discussion with Geoffrey Bromiley on these matters and I'm inclined to agree with him that we need to seek some kind of middle ground between Warfield's rationalist response to nineteenth century criticism and what may be Berkouwer's tendency to lean too far to the side of Barth."

So I take the division of evangelical Christianity into two major camps, theologically, as a fact we have to live with something that cannot be ignored and something which cannot be reconciled. So my interest in a yearly conference of orthodox scholars is based on the fact of that sure division. I would hope what could be accomplished through a yearly conference of this sort would be to inform those who stand with orthodoxy (laymen and pastors and young people), what the issues really are and that it is an either-or choice and why orthodoxy is the most Biblical and the true reformation view, and the most rational view. Also that this view is worth being lonely for and worth suffering for, and even worth dividing over if necessary, not that any of us want division, but it's just that some of us realize there are sins in the church worse than division. On the other hand I would hope for this conference to produce enough convincing arguments and enough strategic writing that those laymen and pastors who are in the other camp by default or because they haven't thought through the issues would, as it were, defect and come over to true orthodoxy. I have to say that I have very little hope for scholars who know what it's all about and have made a deliberate choice, such as Jewett and I would include Guder. I say I have very little hope of changing their minds or swinging them over. From what I see, most of the Christians in America are grossly ignorant of the true foundational issues underlying the Biblical debate on inerrancy. To me, inerrancy as an issue is like the tip of an iceberg with nine-tenths of the discussion underneath the water in the area of presuppositions and epistemology and an understanding of philosophy.

So I see education as a major task for people on our side of
the fence. Strategically, my guess is that those redefinition
evangelicals or neo-evangelicals, or whatever they're to be
called, do not really want people to be thoroughly educated
on these issues philosophically, historically, Biblically. This
may be an overly harsh judgment, but I really think if people
see the facts of what Calvin and Luther really taught, if
they could really understand something of Kant and Kirkegaard
and the noumenal-phenomenal world, then they would, in an
overwhelming way, see that we're speaking the truth and the
other side is speaking falsehood; that we're seeing clearly
and the other side is seeing through confused and foggy
glasses. In short, I see that education of the masses will
help our side and it will not help the other side. What will
help the other side are the two things that they're already
doing; first, stressing a focus on fellowship over clear
doctrine and labeling some of us divisive, narrow, unloving,
etc., and secondly,--and again this may be overly harsh--
secondly, a deliberate reinterpretation of the facts as we see
Jewett's rewriting of the reformer's doctrine in his bulletin,
"The Divine Word in Human Words." I really don't know whether
Jewett's bulletin was written that way out of sheer confusion
or deliberate effort to misrepresent the facts. That's for God
to say. The truth of the matter is that you and I know that
it definitely misrepresents the facts, and people who believe
him will be believing a lie rather than the truth.

So, my gut level feeling is that guys like Jewett don't
really want to face the issues head on in open debate. This
is one reason I think a massive concentrated focused effort
where we could renew our strategy each year and build it
as we go each year would be the way to go for the orthodox
side. I think we're a minority. I think the whole cultural
and religious situation is such that left unattended, the
weight will all be thrown on the side of the redefinition
evangelicals. I think that most Christians, on whichever side
of this issue they stand, are so negatively loaded to the
idea of fighting for truth or taking an unpopular stand on
doctrinal issues, having lack of courage, etc., that people
have to be quite well educated and motivated to stand for
where we have to stand. At best, I think we probably have a
losing battle. But I think if we organize and strategize and
get our scholars focused and coordinated in working together
as a united front, we'll have a much better chance to affect
the whole Christian Church than if we just let everybody take
a little piece of the action as he sees it and feels it, and
as it comes to him in the midst of his regular pursuits.

Practically, what I envision is having this conference be hosted by Pittsburgh one year and San Francisco the alternate year, and going back and forth. On our side out here, I think I could get my hands on enough Christians who could provide free housing and a lot of board free to any scholars or conferees who happen to be coming. The transportation would be the only serious cost in something like this. I envision the thing being a week long where the scholars are talking to each other and perhaps anybody else who's listening in. For four or five days strategizing and assigning themselves tasks, etc., and then having the thing culminate in a weekend conference for the public that people would fly in to or drive in to a conference like Mt. Hermon Grounds that would hold five hundred people. At that point we could charge people an extra ten or fifteen dollars for the fee and take in $6,000 each year to defray the cost of the scholars' air fare. I don't know if this should officially be a joint venture of the Ligonier and the Reformation Study Center or if we should just be a catalyst in this thing, if you like the idea. I would guess it would be better to have a broad base of orthodox churches. What I would fear at the outset is that such a thing would eventually take into its governing group men who truly were not orthodox in their views of scripture and then we would be right back to where the redefinition evangelicals want us to be. I would really like to get the response from you and your cohorts and board there at Ligonier, because if this is a viable idea, if this is something God would have us do, I'd like to begin shooting for a conference in '78. I might try to reach you by phone within ten days, just to get your initial reaction.

We're grateful that you exist and have set this example for us. God bless you guys as you carry on. My love to Jim and Tim and those tremendous wives.

In Christ,

Jay

APPENDIX N

A MANIFESTO FOR THE CHRISTIAN CHURCH

(PLUS THE LIST OF SIGNERS)

At our third and final annual working conference held in Washington, D.C. July 2-4, 1986, where we were completing our creation of COR's "Worldview Documents" on how the Bible applies to the various fields of life, (Law, Government, Business, Education, Media, etc.), our Steering Committee approved COR's "MANIFESTO FOR THE CHRISTIAN CHURCH" and signed it in a "National Solemn Assembly" held that July 4th at the Lincoln Memorial.

We believe this Manifesto explains the kind of Biblical Christianity our Lord Jesus Christ calls for in the Bible and requires of Christians today who are concerned about fulfilling His Great Commission and rebuilding civilization upon the principles of the Bible, and holding local "Solemn Assemblies"[41] for Christians to repent as God is requiring at this time of great decadence. We believe any version of Christian living which is opposed to the statements and standards outlined in this *Christian Manifesto* will further deteriorate the Body of Christ and render it less capable of being the "salt and light" Christ calls us to be to our confused and darkened society.

A list of respected Christian leaders who signed this Manifesto in 1986 (including Steering Committee members) is provided so Christians today can be encouraged to sign it again at this critical time of world history during organized, local Solemn Assemblies. Because this Manifesto is a covenantal document in which sins are confessed and necessary unity of the local Body of Christ acknowledged and set forth as the model in which we Christians must participate and for which we must strive, the authors strongly urge that this document be signed along with other local churches as a united spiritual army and that when doing so the repentance called for in this document be genuine. Experience has shown that to sign this document without participating in the unity for which it calls or to sign it superficially with known and hidden sin, is to invite God's judgment and to open the doors of satanic attack upon individuals and participating churches. *"Put on the full armor of God, that you may be able*

---

41 Please inquire at: COR-ICCP@goldrush.com for the "National Solemn Assembly Committee," which offers instructions, program ideas, and outlines for the group wanting to hold their own local Solemn Assembly for the Church to repent and call down God's mercy on His people and on their nations at this urgent moment in history.

to stand firm against the schemes of the devil" Eph. 6:11 ff. "Greater is *He Who is in you than he who is in the world"* 1 John 4:4. *"Submit therefore to God. Resist the devil and he will flee from you"* James 4:7.

That said, individuals are indeed called upon to take to heart the principles, to make the confessions their own so far as they apply, and to join in the resolutions as a faithful follower of Christ. This document clearly marks the lines between Biblical Christianity on the one hand, and on the other hand, both the secular world which is opposed to God's principles and "status quo" kinds of "Christianity" which are not committed to living in full obedience to Christ's Bible.

A Manifesto for the Christian Church

Declaration and Covenant
July 4, 1986

An Act of Contrition and Humble Repentance
A Solemn Covenant
A Statement of Essential Truths and a Call to Action

Dr. Jay Grimstead, D.Min., General Editor
Mr. E. Calvin Beisner, M.A., Assistant to the General Editor

PREAMBLE

To promote Biblical obedience, peace, unity, love, joy, and compassion among all men, and to secure for ourselves and future generations the blessing of God Almighty, we hereby enter into a Solemn Covenant, grounded in the following declaration:

> *God, eternal Creator, Author of liberty, has spoken with reason, accuracy, and clarity concerning justice, truth, and reality in Heaven and on Earth.*

In bold defiance of God's Word—the Bible, the fallen race of man has perverted justice, truth, and reality, leaving a painful legacy of negligence, confusion, chaos, and exploitation; and, thus, has created a compelling need for correction and redemption by our merciful God. In this twentieth century, evil has so multiplied that all life and liberty are at risk of destruction by the godless or by the judgment of God.

The Church of Jesus Christ, now grown lukewarm and indifferent in pursuing its redemptive priestly ministry and corrective prophetic authority, largely has tolerated or participated in the dominant evils and error of this sin-filled age, further adding to our planetary crisis.

That future generations of God's children and nations yet unborn may learn of righteousness and judgment without suffering the cost of repeated sins, we declare with brokenness the record of our grievous transgression of the Divine Law.

AN ACT OF CONTRITION AND HUMBLE REPENTANCE

We humbly and openly confess that too often, as a people and as individuals:

1. We have failed to care adequately for the souls of men who will spend eternity in the fires of hell if they fail to receive for themselves the atoning blood of Christ, bowing their knees before Him as Lord of their lives and King of the universe;

2. We have disobeyed God's clear commands in Scripture;

3. We have built our own egos rather than advancing the Kingdom of Christ;

4. We have all too often fallen short of the integrity, faithfulness, and total honesty with each other that God requires of us before the watching world;

5. We have failed to confront falsehood and unrighteousness consistently in the Church or in the world because of our fear of man and of losing prestige or security;

6. We have been content to reduce the power of the transcendent Gospel to

mere creedal form devoid of spiritual content or present reality by our harlotry with the idols of personal peace and affluence;

7. We have neglected our God-ordained duties to be the world's salt, light, teacher, and example; as a result, the world is in desperate trouble and western civilization stands on the brink of self-destruction;

8. We and our fathers have settled for a substandard, false version of Christianity in our local churches and denominations;

9. We have tolerated sin within our ranks when we should have administered church discipline and excommunication;

10. We have allowed heresies to creep into our churches and institutions of higher learning, failing to demand of our teachers that they teach and stand upon the faithful and inerrant written Word of God;

11. We have heaped to ourselves teachers and pastors to tickle our ears with pleasant falsehoods and entertaining fables rather than convicting us of sin and demanding that we live righteous lives of obedience to the Bible;

12. We sold our children's minds and souls to the godless influence of secularized education and the media;

13. We have allowed our churches to become irrelevant, powerless ghettos while those who hate or neglect God and His righteous standards for society have stolen the America of our founding fathers out from under our slumbering eyes;

14. We have allowed misguided policies, flagrant sins, and hideous atrocities to be enacted by our elected and appointed officials — legislative, executive, and judicial — without rising up en masse and demanding that they be corrected in the name of God and for the sake of justice;

15. We have permitted both Christian and non-Christian men of our society to fail in leadership, becoming emasculated, tamed, dependent, self-centered, and soft; and, in the opposite extreme, we have allowed some men to abuse their authority by their lack of sacrificial love for their families;

16. We have lived beyond our means by misusing credit, so trading our liberty for financial bondage;

17. We have adopted the covetousness and materialism of our surrounding culture, seeking the approval of men and neglecting the fear of the Lord;

18. We have been caught up in a self-centered, false version of Christianity, focusing on our own needs and desires rather than on God's glory and on sacrificing ourselves for the needs of our Christian brothers and fellow humans;

19. We have concerned ourselves more with Heaven, the future, and escaping this world at Christ's Second Coming, than with preparing His Bride to be spotless, beautiful, glorious, and pleasing to Him when He comes;

20. We foolishly have allowed Satan to divide us from other members in His Body through pride, jealousy, and competition, through a lack of humble serving of one another, and by concentrating on divisive minor issues rather than the clear Biblical articles of faith upon which we agree;

21. We have rested, idle and uncaring, while Satanically inspired Marxist communism and a revival of pagan religions has enslaved two-thirds of our planet, causing massive, needless suffering to the peoples under their sway;

22. We have failed to conduct our lives or manage our affairs in the conscious certainty that God's eternal standards for personal and social righteousness are unchanging and inexorable in their absolute cause-and-effect relationships, thus dishonoring God and playing the fool in our personal lives and social policies;

THEREFORE:

1. In brokenness and humility, we cast ourselves before the throne of Almighty God beseeching Him to forgive these sins of ours and our fathers that we have so grievously and callously committed against Him, against each other and against the dying world. We call upon our Father in Heaven to apply to these our sins the purifying, atoning blood of our Lord and Savior, Jesus Christ.

2. In repentance, shame, and sorrow we ask our fellow Christians—all whom we have offended, ignored, and despised; before whom we have not been honest, open, vulnerable and tender; and whose ministries we have falsely believed we could do well without—to forgive us in the name of Jesus and for the sake of His glory and the unity of His Body. We hereby declare that we forgive all Christian brothers and sisters who have so treated us.

3. In shame and sorrow, we ask forgiveness of those fellow humans who have not bowed their knee to Jesus as King of the universe or yet come under the saving power of His shed Blood.

   - Forgive us for caring so little for your souls that we have not ministered more aggressively and lovingly to you about your eternal destiny and your fear of death.
   - Forgive us for our attempts to evangelize you that have been impersonal, mechanical, or insensitive.
   - Forgive us for displaying before you ugly, uninspiring lives devoid of God's integrity, compassion, and power.

- Forgive us for being such poor examples of Christ's love by our dis-unity that you have rejected both Him and us, to your own spiritual impoverishment.
- Forgive us for our failure to demonstrate to you Biblical answers for your difficulties and problems in life.
- Forgive us for failing to occupy our proper position as servants in the affairs of law, government, economics, business, education, media, the arts, med-icine, and science as the Creator's salt and light to the world, so that these spheres of life might offer you more help, justice, hope, peace, and joy.

We have failed you miserably and we beg you to forgive us in the name of the great God who created us all for His glory.

> And now, O God, forgive our willful disobedience, hardness
> of heart, and selfish indulgence. Hear our prayers, forgive our
> sin, and heal our land, O Lord, thus fulfilling the merciful
> promise of your Word.
> "O Lord, hear! O Lord, forgive! O Lord, listen and take
> action! For Thine own sake, O my God, do not delay,
> because...Thy people are called by Thy name." (Daniel 9:19)

A Solemn Covenant

Now, for the Glory of God, having repented of our sin and counted the cost of true discipleship, willing either to be martyred or to reign with Him, we hereby solemnly covenant with Almighty God and with one another, to live henceforth in full, serious obedience to all the Bible's commands that apply to us today, to the best of our ability and in dependence on the power of the Holy Spirit, from now until the day we die, so help us God.

We hereby voluntarily invite others in the family of God to hold us accountable to live in full obedience to the Bible, and to show us with demonstrated love whatever discrepancies they observe between our lives and what is written in the Bible. We submit in advance to Biblical church discipline as described in Matthew 18:15-20.

We commit ourselves, in the presence of God Almighty and of our Christian brothers and sisters:

- to live to glorify God and to enjoy Him forever—the chief reasons for our existence in time and eternity;
- to offer ourselves as living sacrifices to be used as God wills to build up the Body of Christ on earth that it may become Biblical, holy, strong, coura-geous, unified, and effective in fulfilling its commissioned task on earth;

- to do all we can, in the lives of our fellow humans and in the societies in which we live, to see God's will done on earth as it is in heaven, insofar as that is possible between now and the physical return of our great God and Savior Jesus Christ.

A STATEMENT OF ESSENTIAL TRUTHS AND A CALL TO ACTION

Whereas, our souls are burdened with the un-Biblical, Laodicean state of the Church in our age; and,

Whereas, the Body of Christ on earth has failed to be the salt, light, and teacher of a dark and dying world; and,

Whereas, we believe that we, the sleeping, uncaring, uncourageous, and unholy members of the Body of Christ bear much of the blame for the fact that our own society and Western civilization are on the brink of self destruction;

WE THEREFORE DECLARE:

That a broad acceptance by the Bible-believing Church of the basic Biblical affirmations stated herein should be considered essential, primary, foundational, and non-negotiable by all Christians who wish to work and pray toward the revival of the Church and the reformation of society; and,

That the Body of Christ, in order to fulfill her Lord's Great Commission to make Bible-obeying disciples of all nations, needs to commit itself to the following statements of truth and plans of action:

A. The Church Must Learn What Is Reality.

1. Inerrancy of the Bible.

We affirm that the original manuscripts of the Old and New Testaments of the Bible were so inspired by God, that the human authors wrote the exact words and sentences God inspired them to write without error and without misrepresenting God, history, or the created world in any way. What the Bible says, God says. Those inside and outside the Christian Church who teach that the Bible is partly true and partly false, and that it is up to us humans to decide which parts are which, stand in opposition to the view of the Bible held by Moses, David, Jesus, Paul, the early Church, the Reformers, and all of mainstream Christianity down to the last century, and are, by their destructive teaching, undermining the faith of the next generation.

2. The Bible Is the Final Test of All Truth Claims.

We affirm that this God-inspired, inerrant Bible is the only absolute, objective, final test for all truth claims, and the clearest verbal picture of reality that has ever come into the hands of mankind. By it, and it alone, are all philosophies, books, values, actions, and plans to be measured as to their consistency with reality, visible and invisible. Whatever statements or values are in opposition to the statements and values of the Bible err to the degree of their opposition.

3. **The Bible States Reality for All Areas of Life and Thought.**

   We affirm that the Bible is not only God's statements to us regarding religion, salvation, eternity, and righteousness, but also the final measurement and depository of certain fundamental facts of reality and basic principles that God wants all mankind to know in the spheres of law, government, economics, business, education, arts and communication, medicine, psychology, and science. All theories and practices of these spheres of life are only true, right, and realistic to the degree that they agree with the Bible. The Bible furnishes mankind with the only logical and verbal connection between time and eternity, religion and science, the visible and invisible worlds.

4. **Cause and Effect Relationships of God's Commandments.**

   We affirm that God built the universe and man in accordance with the laws of His own Being in such a way that there is a cause and effect relationship between obeying the laws and commandments deposited in His Word and being blessed by God. Those people or nations that live in opposition to Biblical laws and commandments will, sooner or later, be cursed and destroyed. This is not to say that we can force God's hand to bless us, but rather that it is always best for us to obey His will.

   It is, therefore, to the great benefit of all mankind, Christian and non-Christian alike, to bring every society's judicial and legal systems into as close an approximation to the laws and commandments of the Bible as its citizens will allow.

5. **World View.**

   We affirm that the Bible presents God's own world view, which is consistent and practical and answers all of the basic life questions of man. To function properly in the Church and in the world, Christians must seek to understand, to the best of their ability, the full theological world view presented in the Bible. They must be willing to measure all points of their own theology by the Bible and, in submission to the Bible, to make whatever changes are called for in their own theology.

6. **The 42 Articles of the Essentials of the Christian World View.**

   We affirm that The Coalition on Revival's 42 Articles of the Essentials of the Christian World View states the basic doctrines of historic Christianity and can serve as a theological test and guardrail to keep an individual or a church from heresy.

B. The Christian Church Must Live under the Lordship of Jesus Christ and, Therefore, in Full Obedience to the Bible.

7. Lordship of Christ Non-Optional.

We affirm that living under the total Lordship of Jesus Christ in every area of life is not optional for those who would call themselves Christians. Though obedience to the Bible's commands does not earn or retain salvation, still the Bible is clear in its teachings that no one who lives a life of deliberate, consistent disobedience to the Bible's commands ought to call himself a Christian. We are saved by faith alone, but not by a faith that is alone, devoid of obedience.

8. Living above Deliberate Sin.

We affirm that it is possible and expected by God that Christians will and must live above conscious, deliberate choices to sin. We are capable of this because of our new nature, the indwelling Holy Spirit, and the ability of Christ's shed blood to break the power of canceled sin. This is not to say that the most holy of us do not need daily to say, "Forgive us our debts as we forgive our debtors."

9. The Great Commission.

We affirm that the Great Commission is a mandate by our Lord to go forth into all the world and make Bible-obeying disciples of all nations. Getting men's souls saved is only a preliminary part of fulfilling the Great Commission. Our work is incomplete unless we teach them to obey all He commanded. The words of the Lord's prayer for God's will to "be done on earth as it is in heaven" are another way to state the essence of the same Great Commission.

10. Christ's Lordship Extends to the Entire Universe.

We affirm that a full understanding of the Lordship of Christ is to realize that, when Jesus stated, "All authority in heaven and earth has been given to Me," He was declaring that whatever power Satan held over the world was broken by His death on the cross and His victorious resurrection. As Son of God and representative man, Jesus regained authority over the earth which Adam, as representative man, lost. This is the meaning of His being seated at the right hand of God. When Jesus returns, He will gain no greater authority over this earth and the forces of Satan than He had from the moment He ascended to and sat upon His throne, though He will exercise His authority in full power, then in a way He is not fully exercising it now.

11. Christian Maturity.

We affirm that all Christians must be nurtured by those who are their spiritual leaders if they are to reach their full level of Christian maturity. No Christian or group of Christians has the right before God to live year after year on a spiritual plateau, stagnating in Christian immaturity. Christian maturity is capable enough of definition so that the apostles categorized their people as either mature or immature. It is measured by the extent of one's conformity to the image of Christ, made visible by Biblical obedience in every area of life.

12. The Necessity of Human Accountability.

We affirm that because of our infinite capacity for self-deception, all of us who strive for Christian maturity and a Biblically obedient life need to be held accountable to live in obedience to the Bible by living, trustworthy brothers and sisters. Apart from this our obedience must always fall short of its potential. This brother-to-brother accountability should be entered into mutually by voluntary association.

13. The Need for Confrontation.

We affirm that in a life where there exists "the world, the flesh and the devil," there is need for living confrontation over matters of falsehood and unrighteousness in the Church and in the world. It is impossible for any group of people to live truly obedient lives without applying to each other regular confrontation, exhortation, rebuke, and church discipline. Church discipline must be an on-going part of any congregation that chooses truly to live according to the Bible.

C. Churches Must Live in Love and Unity with Each Other.

14. Only One Body.

We affirm that although there are many denominational and theological divisions within the body of Christ, in reality there exists only one Body of Christ to which all true Christians of all denominations belong. This central fact must be exemplified by churches and pastors at a local level and in a visible way. The desire in Christ's heart is that His Body demonstrate visible, real Body unity, love, and interdependence.

15. Local Pastors' Prayer Fellowships.

We affirm that the unity of the Body of Christ must be demonstrated and can be greatly aided by local pastors praying together in honest fellowship for each other's lives and ministries. Their prayer and fellowship must go deep, to the point of sincere love, sacrifice, and experiencing joy at each other's success.

16. Humility Required.

We affirm that before local body unity will be real or have a large effect, pastors and Christian leaders must be willing to allow others to get credit for, or have control of joint projects, and to work in programs under the name of another church or leader. Humility and faithful servanthood are essential for true body unity, locally and nationally.

17. Loyalty and Support of Leaders in the Body.

We affirm that within any local church or para-church organization there must be a real and visible unity of spirit, purpose, and leadership. Struggles for power and poorly defined organizational chains of command must be seen as problems not to be tolerated, except for temporary periods, until the unity around the proper leadership can be defined and established. A pastor or para-church leader needs his staff and board to be deeply loyal and unified around his leadership, without his vision being forced to compete with other visions within the church or organization.

D. The Christian Church Must be Salt and Light to the World.

18. Light and Salt Are to Influence the World.

We affirm that to be salt and light to the world means to influence it for good and to show it the way to live and conduct its affairs. In short, it means getting God's will to "be done on earth as it is in heaven" and to "make disciples of all nations, teaching them to obey whatsoever I have commanded you." Christ instituted the Church as the world's teacher. The world will not know how to live or which direction to go without the Church's Biblical influence on its theories, laws, actions, and institutions. To be salt and light, the Church cannot exist in a Christian "ghetto" or have a dichotomous view that falsely divides life into the spiritual versus the physical-historical-measurable.

19. Storming the Gates of Hell.

We affirm that part of the task of the bearers of the Christian Gospel is to identify, find, cast out, and break the Satanic power of demons over those to whom we minister. All Christian ministers inside and outside the institutional church must know how to deal with and overpower demons that oppress or harass people in their care. They must do this in the name of Christ and by the power of His presently effective blood.

20. Social Evils to Oppose.

We affirm that all Bible-believing Christians must take a non-neutral stance in opposing, praying against, and speaking against social moral evils such as the following:

A. Abortion on demand, infanticide, and euthanasia.

B. Adultery, fornication, homosexuality, bestiality, and other forms of sexual perversion.

C. Pornography, prostitution, sexual entertainment, rape, and other crimes of exploitation and physical, emotional, or sexual abuse.

D. Drug abuse.

E. Unjust treatment of the poor and disadvantaged.

F. Criminal injustice.

G. Racial discrimination.

H. Theft, fraud, and violence not in self-defense.

I. State usurpation of parental rights and God-given liberties.

J. Statist-collectivist theft from citizens through devaluation of their money and redistribution of their wealth.

K. Atheism, moral relativism, and evolutionism taught as a monopoly viewpoint in public schools.

L. Communism/Marxism, fascism, Nazism, and the one-world government of the New Age Movement.

NOW THEREFORE:

In hope of God's mercy and blessing upon His Church and a needy world, we humbly call on all who name Jesus Christ as Lord and Savior and every Bible-believing church on earth to join us in these acts of repentance, in ratifying this covenant with God and His Church, and in embracing these fundamental and non-negotiable truths and mandates, to the great end that God might be glorified and His will might be done.

Benediction

May we live to glorify God. May we fellowship with Him eternally. May we offer ourselves a living sacrifice to God and our fellow men. May we be salt and light in the world. May the fruit of our labor, as much as is possible, be the working of God's will on earth as it is in heaven.

May God give us His strength, wisdom, holiness, justice, love, and power in full measure. And may God multiply those who enter herein.

Christian Leaders Who Signed
A Manifesto for the Christian Church
in 1986

The following Christian leaders signed A Manifesto for the Christian Church in 1986. Among these Christian leaders are some who have since passed on.

Dr. Joseph Aldrich, Pres.
Multnomah School of the Bible

Rev. Ray Allen, President
ACT Ministries, Inc.

Dr. Gary Amos, Professor
Law and Public Policy-CBN University

Rev. Francis Anfuso, President
Christian Equippers Int'l.

Dr. Gleason Archer, Ph.D., Professor, O.T.,
Trinity Evangelical Divinity School

Dr. Virginia Armstrong, Ph.D., Exec. Director
Blackstone Institute of Public Law and Policy

Dr. Theodore Baehr, J.D., President
Good News Communications

Dr. David W. Balsiger, L.H.D.,
Publisher-Editor
Biblical News Service

Dr. William Barker, Th.D., Editor
Presbyterian Journal

Rev. Ern Baxter, President
Ern Baxter Ministries

Mr. John Beckett, President
Intercessors for America

Dick Bernal, Pastor
Jubilee Christian Center

Mr. E. Calvin Beisner
Author, Editor

Rev. Dick Benjamin, Pastor
Abbotts Loop Christian Center

Rev. Luther Blackwell, Pastor
New Life Fellowship

Dr. Charles Blair, D.D., Pastor
Calvary Temple

Dr. Richard Bliss, Ed.D., Director of Curriculum
Institute for Creation Research

Mr. Ron Boehme, Director
Youth With a Mission; Revive America

Rev. W. Wellington Boone, Pastor & Founder
Manna Christian Fellowship Churches

Dr. Harold O. J. Brown, Ph.D., Professor
Bibl. & Sys. Theo., Trinity Evangelical Divinity
School

Dr. Emanuele Cannistraci, Pastor
Evangel Christian Fellowship

Rev. Jack Carter, Professor
Biblical Studies — C.F.N.I.

Rev. David Chilton, Pastor
Church of the Redeemer

Mrs. Evelyn Christenson, President
Evelyn Christenson Ministries

Dr. Glenn Cole, D.D., Pastor
Capital Christian Center

Dr. Robert Coleman, Professor
Trinity Evang. Free Div. School

Dr. Lawrence Crabb, Ph.D., Director
Inst. Bibl. Counsel, Grace Theological Seminary

Mr. Art Cunningham, Manager
Hughes Aircraft

Mr. Gary DeMar, President
American Vision

Mr. Ted DeMoss, President
Christian Business Men's Committee

Mrs. Gladys Dickelman, Executive Director
National Day of Prayer

Mr. Colonel Doner, President
Christian Action Network

Rev. Jeff Donnan, President
Christians for Justice, International

Dr. Robert Dugan, Director
NAE-Public Affairs

Mr. Laury Eck, Attorney
Christian Mediation

Dr. Ted Engstrom, President
World Vision International

Mr. Michael Farris, President
Home School Legal Defense Association

Mr. Roger Flemming, Asst. U.S. Director
The Navigators

Rev. Marshall Foster, President
Mayflower Institute

Rev. Gerald Fry, Pastor
Clavary Community Church

Mr. Bill Garaway, President
Business with a Purpose

Dr. Arthur Gay, D.Min., Pastor
South Park Church

Mr. Peter Gemma, Executive Director
National ProLife Political Action Co.

Dr. Duane Gish, Ph.D., Vice President
Institute for Creation Research

Mr. Jose Gonzales, President
Semilla, Inc.

Dr. Charles Green, President
Network of Christian Ministries

Rev. Dan Greenlee, Pastor
Calvary Cathedral

Col. Robert Grete, Principal
Rocky Bayou Christian School

Dr. Jay Grimstead, D.Min., Found. Dir.
Coalition on Revival

Rev. Ronald Haus, President
1st Century Broadcasting

Dr. Lewis Hicks
Physician

Dr. Dick Hillis, D.D. Pres. Emeritus
Overseas Crusades

Dr. Steven Hotze
Physician

Dr. David Howard, L.H.D., Gen. Director
World Evangelical Fellowship

Rev. Dick Iverson, President
Portland Bible College

Dr. Ron Jenson, D.Min., President
International Leadership

Mrs. Dee Jepsen, Chairman
Board of Regents, CBN University

Col. Glen Jones, National Director
Military Ministry, Campus Crusade

Mr. Roy Jones, Coalitions Director
Republican Senatorial Committee

Rev. Raymond P. Joseph, Pastor
Southfield Presbyterian Church

Dr. D. James Kennedy, Ph.D., Pastor
Coral Ridge Presbyterian Church

Joseph Kickasola, Professor
Law & Public Policy-CBN University

Dr. Paul Kienel, Ed.D., Pastor
Association of Christian Schools Intl.

Dr. David Kiteley, Pastor
Shiloh Christian Fellowship

Dr. Henry Krabbendam, Ph.D., Professor
Covenant College

Dr. Tim Lahaye, D.Min., President
American Coalition for Traditional Values

Dr. Richard Lappert, Ph.D., Consultant
Connecticut State Department of Education

Dr. Harold Lindsell, Ph.D., Editor Emeritus
Christianity Today

Dr. Paul Lindstrom, Director
Christian Liberty Academy

Dr. Allan MacRae, Ph.D., Pres. Emeritus
Biblical Theological Seminary

Rev. Ronald Marr, Editor & Publisher
Christian Enquirer

Dr. Peter Marshall
Author, Lecturer

Mrs. Connaught Marshner, Director
Child & Family Protection Institute

Rev. Bob Martin, Exec. Bd. Member
Maranatha Christian Churches

Mr. Robert Martin, General Manager
Fieldstead & Company

Mr. Ted McAteer, President
Religious Roundtable

Dr. Josh McDowell, D.D., President
Josh McDowell Ministries

Mr. R. E. McMaster, Jr., Editor
The Reaper

Dr. Robertson McQuilkin, D.D., President
Columbia Bible College

Bishop John L. Meares, Pastor
Evangel Temple

Mr. Robert Metcalf, Founder
Christian Studies Center

Rev. Lou Montecalvo, Pastor
Redeemer Temple Southeast Church

Rev. Joseph Morecraft, Pastor
Chalcedon Presbyterian Church

Rev. Bob Mumford, President
Lifechangers

Dr. Gary North, Ph.D., President
Institute for Christian Economics

Dr. Raymond Ortlund, D.D., President
Renewal Ministries

Dr. J. I. Packer, Ph.D., Professor
Systematic Theology, Regent College

Dr. Luis Palau, President
Luis Palau Evangelistic Team

Dr. Ed Payne, M.D., Professor
Medical College of Georgia

Rev. Dennis Peacocke, President
Strategic Christian Services

Dr. John Perkins, D.D., President
Voice of Calvary Ministries

Dr. William Reed, M.D., President
Christian Medical Foundation

Mr. Jerry Regier, President
Family Research Council

Dr. George Rekers, Ph.D., Professor
University of S.C. School of Medicine

Dr. Adrian Rogers, Pastor
Bellevue Baptist Church

Dr. R. J. Rushdoony, Ph.D., President
Chalcedon Foundation

Dr. Michael Rusten, Ph.D.
Business Consultant

Dr. Robert Saucy, Th.D., Chairman
Dept. of Systematic Theo., Talbot Sem.

Mrs. Edith Schaeffer
Author, Lecturer

Mr. George Scipione, Director
Christian Counseling and Education

Rev. Owen Shackett, Pastor
The Peoples Church of the Northwest

Mr. Herbert Schlossberg
Author, Researcher

Mr. Shelby Sharp
Attorney at Law

Mr. Mark Siljander
Former Member of Congress

Dr. Robert Simonds, Th.D., President
National Assoc. of Christian Educ.

Rev. Charles Simpson, Pastor
Gulf Coast Covenant Church

Mr. John Sparks, J.D., Professor
Law and Economics, Grove City Coll.

Mrs. Carolyn Sundseth, Former Assoc. Dir.,
White House Office of Public Liaison

Mr. Bob Thoburn, Pastor, Founder
Fairfax Christian School

Mr. Lary Tomczak, Editor
The People of Destiny Magazine

Dr. Paul Toms, D.D., Pastor
Park Street Church

Dr. Joseph Tson, D.D., President
Romanian Missionary Society

Brother Andrew van der Bijl, Founder
Open Doors

Dr. Jack Van Impe, Ph.D., President
Jack Van Impe Ministries

Dr. Peter Wagner, Professor
School of World Missions, Fuller Seminary

Dr. Larry Walker, Ph.D., Professor
Old Testament, Mid-America Baptist Seminary

Dr. Robert Walker, President
Christian Life Magazine

Mr. Russ Walton, President
Plymouth Rock Foundation

Mr. Bob Weiner, President
Maranatha Campus Ministries

Dr. Luder Whitlock, President
Reformed Theological Seminary

Rev. Al Whittinghill, Evangelist
Ambassadors for Christ

Rev. Donald Wildmon, President
American Family Association

Rev. Jerry Wiles, Exec. Vice President
Bible Pathway Ministries

Rev. Mike Williams, Pastor
Hillside Church

Dr. Ralph Winter, Ph.D., General Director
U.S. Center for World Mission

Dr. Don Zoller, Chairman
Outreach Ministries, McLean Bible Church

APPENDIX O

EXCERPTS FROM
THE SANCTITY OF HUMAN LIFE,
DOCUMENT 22 APPENDIX

DOCUMENT 22 WITH COMPLETE APPENDIX, WWW.CHURCHCOUNCIL.ORG

STATISTICS COURTESY OF THE ELLIOT INSTITUTE
P.O. BOX 7348, SPRINGFIELD, IL 62791, www.afterabortion.org

C. POSSIBLE CONSEQUENCES OF ABORTION[1]

1. Medical Consequences of Abortion

A List of Major Physical Sequelae Related to Abortion

Death

According to the best record-based study of deaths following pregnancy and abortion, a 1997 government-funded study in Finland, women who abort are approximately four times more likely to die in the following year than women who carry their pregnancies to term. In addition, women who carry to term are only half as likely to die as women who were not pregnant.

The Finland researchers found that compared to women who carried to term, women who aborted in the year prior to their deaths were 60 percent more likely to die of natural causes, seven times more likely to die of suicide, four times more likely to die of injuries related to accidents, and 14 times more likely to die from homicide. Researchers believe the higher rate of deaths related to accidents and homicide may be linked to higher rates of suicidal or risk-taking behavior.[2]

The leading causes of abortion-related maternal deaths within a week of the surgery are hemorrhage, infection, embolism, anesthesia, and undiagnosed ectopic pregnancies. Legal abortion is reported as the fifth leading cause of maternal death in the United States, though in fact it is recognized that most abortion related deaths are not officially reported as such.[3]

Breast Cancer

The risk of breast cancer almost doubles after one abortion, and rises even further with two or more abortions.[4]

Cervical, Ovarian, and Liver Cancer

Women with one abortion face a 2.3 relative risk of cervical cancer, compared to non-aborted women, and women with two or more abortions face a 4.92 relative risk. Similar elevated risks of ovarian and liver cancer have also been linked to single and multiple abortions. These increased cancer rates for post-aborted women are apparently linked to the unnatural disruption of the hormonal changes which accompany pregnancy and untreated cervical damage.[5]

Uterine Perforation

Between 2 and 3% of all abortion patients may suffer perforation of their uterus, yet most of these injuries will remain undiagnosed and untreated unless laparoscopic visualization is performed.[6] Such an examination may be useful when beginning an abortion malpractice suit. The risk of uterine perforation is increased for women who have previously given birth and for those who receive general anesthesia at the time of the abortion.[7] Uterine damage may result in complications in later pregnancies and may eventually evolve into problems which require a hysterectomy, which itself may result in a number of additional complications and injuries including osteoporosis.

Cervical Lacerations

Significant cervical lacerations requiring sutures occur in at least one percent of first trimester abortions. Lesser lacerations, or micro fractures, which would normally not be treated may also result in long term reproductive damage. Latent post-abortion cervical damage may result in subsequent cervical incompetence, premature delivery, and complications of labor. The risk of cervical damage is greater for teenagers, for second trimester abortions, and when practitioners fail to use laminaria for dilation of the cervix.[8]

Placenta Previa

Abortion increases the risk of placenta previa [placenta implants over cervix] in later pregnancies (a life threatening condition for both the mother and her wanted pregnancy) by seven to fifteen fold. Abnormal development of the placenta due to uterine damage increases the risk of fetal malformation, perinatal death, and excessive bleeding during labor.[9]

Complications of Labor

Women who had one, two, or more previous induced abortions are, respectively, 1.89, 2.66, or 2.03 times more likely to have a subsequent pre-term delivery, compared to women who carry to term. Prior induced abortion not only increased the risk of premature delivery, it also increased the risk of delayed delivery. Women who had one, two, or more induced abortions are, respectively, 1.89, 2.61, and 2.23 times more likely to have a post-term delivery (over 42 weeks).[10] Pre-term delivery increases the risk of neo-natal death and handicaps.

Handicapped Newborns in Later Pregnancies

Abortion is associated with cervical and uterine damage which may increase the risk of premature delivery, complications of labor and abnormal development of the placenta in later pregnancies. These reproductive complications are the leading causes of handicaps among newborns.[11]

Ectopic Pregnancy

Abortion is significantly related to an increased risk of subsequent ectopic pregnancies. Ectopic pregnancies, in turn, are life-threatening and may result in reduced fertility.[12]

Pelvic Inflammatory Disease (PID)

PID is a potentially life-threatening disease which can lead to an increased risk of ectopic pregnancy and reduced fertility. Of patients who have a chlamydia infection at the time abortion, 23% will develop PID within 4 weeks. Studies have found that 20 to 27% of patients seeking abortion have a chlamydia infection. Approximately 5% of patients who are not infected by chlamydia develop PID within 4 weeks after a first trimester abortion. It is therefore reasonable to expect that abortion providers should screen for and treat such infections prior to an abortion.[13]

Endometritis

Endometritis is a post-abortion risk for all women, but especially for teenagers, who are 2.5 times more likely than women 20-29 to acquire endometritis following abortion.[14]

Immediate Complications

Approximately 10% of women undergoing elective abortion will suffer immediate complications, of which approximately one-fifth (2%) are considered life-threatening. The nine most common major complications which can occur at the time of an abortion are: infection, excessive bleeding, embolism, ripping or perforation of the uterus, anesthesia complications, convulsions, hemorrhage, cervical injury, and endotoxic shock. The most common "minor" complications include: infection, bleeding, fever, second degree burns, chronic abdominal pain, vomiting, gastro-intestinal disturbances, and Rh sensitization.[15]

Increased Risks for Women Seeking Multiple Abortions

In general, most of the studies cited above reflect risk factors for women who undergo a single abortion. These same studies show that women who have multiple abortions face a much greater risk of experiencing these complications. This point is especially noteworthy since approximately 45% of all abortions are for repeat aborters.

Lower General Health

In a survey of 1428 women researchers found that pregnancy loss, and particularly losses due to induced abortion, was significantly associated with an overall lower health. Multiple abortions correlated to an even lower evaluation of "present health." While miscarriage was detrimental to health, abortion was found to have a greater correlation to poor health. These findings support previous research which reported that during the year following an abortion women visited their family doctors 80% more for all reasons and 180% more for psychological reasons. The authors also found that "if a partner is present and not supportive, the miscarriage rate is more than double and the abortion rate is four times greater than if he is present and supportive. If the partner is absent the abortion rate is six times greater."[16]

This finding is supported by a 1984 study that examined the amount of health care sought by women during a year before and a year after their induced abortions. The researchers found that on average, there was an 80 percent increase in the number of doctor visits and a 180 percent increase in doctor visits for psyco-social reasons after abortion.[17]

Increased Risk for Contributing Health Risk Factors

Abortion is significantly linked to behavioral changes such as promiscuity, smoking, drug abuse, and eating disorders which all contribute to increased risks of health problems. For example, promiscuity and abortion are each linked to increased rates of PID and ectopic pregnancies. Which contributes most is unclear, but apportionment may be irrelevant if the promiscuity is itself a reaction to post-abortion trauma or loss of self-esteem.

Increased Risks for Teenagers

Teenagers, who account for about 30 percent of all abortions, are also at much higher risk of suffering many abortion-related complications. This is true of both immediate complications and of long-term reproductive damage.[18]

2. Psychological Consequences of Abortion

A List of Major Psychological Sequelae Related to Abortion

Requirement of Psychological Treatment

In a study of post-abortion patients only 8 weeks after their abortion, researchers found that 44% complained of nervous disorders, 36% had experienced sleep disturbances, 31% had regrets about their decision, and 11% had been prescribed psychotropic medicine by their family doctor.[19] A 5-year retrospective study in two Canadian provinces found significantly greater use of medical and psychiatric services among aborted women. Most significant was the finding that 25% of aborted women made visits to psychiatrists as compared to 3% of the control group.[20] Women who have had abortions are significantly more likely than others to subsequently require admission to a psychiatric hospital. At especially high risk are teenagers, separated or divorced women, and women with a history of more than one abortion.[21]

Since many post-aborted women use repression as a coping mechanism, there may be a long period of denial before a woman seeks psychiatric care. These repressed feelings may cause psychosomatic illnesses and psychiatric or behavioral issues in other areas of her life. As a result, some counselors report that unacknowledged post-abortion distress is the causative factor in many of their female patients, even though their patients have come to them seeking therapy for seemingly unrelated problems.[22]

Post-Traumatic Stress Disorder (PTSD or PAS)

A major random study found that a minimum of 19% of post-abortion women suffer from diagnosable post-traumatic stress disorder (PTSD). Approximately half had many, but not all, symptoms of PTSD, and 20 to 40 percent showed moderate to high levels of stress and avoidance behavior relative to their abortion experiences.[23] Because this is a major disorder which may be present in many plaintiffs. and is not readily understood outside the counseling profession, the following summary is more complete than other entries in this section. PTSD is a psychological dysfunction which results from a traumatic experience which overwhelms a person's normal defense mechanisms resulting in intense fear, feelings of helplessness or being trapped, or loss of control. The risk that an experience will be traumatic is increased when the traumatizing event is perceived as including threats of physical injury, sexual violation, or the witnessing of or participation in a violent death. PTSD results when the traumatic event causes the hyperarousal of "fight or flight" defense mechanisms. This hyperarousal causes these defense mechanisms to become disorganized, disconnected from present circumstances, and take on a life of their own, resulting in abnormal behavior and major personality disorders. As an example of this disconnection of mental functions, some PTSD victims may experience intense emotion but without clear memory of the event; others may remember every detail but without emotion; still others may re-experience both the event and the emotions in intrusive and overwhelming flashback experiences.[24]

Women may experience abortion as a traumatic event for several reasons. Many are forced into an unwanted abortion by husbands, boyfriends, parents, or others. If the woman has repeatedly been a victim of domineering abuse, such an unwanted abortion may be perceived as the ultimate violation in a life characterized by abuse. Other women, no matter how compelling the reasons they have for seeking an abortion, may still perceive the termination of their pregnancy as the violent killing of their own child. The fear, anxiety, pain, and guilt associated with the procedure are mixed into this perception of grotesque and violent death. Still other women report that the pain of abortion, inflicted upon them by a masked stranger invading their body, feels identical to rape.[25] Indeed, researchers have found that women with a history of sexual assault may experience greater distress during and after an abortion exactly because of these associations between the two experiences.[26] When the stressor leading to PTSD is abortion, some clinicians refer to this as Post-Abortion Syndrome (PAS).

The major symptoms of PTSD are generally classified under three categories: hyperarousal, intrusion, and constriction.

Hyperarousal is a characteristic of inappropriately and chronically aroused "fight or flight" defense mechanisms. The person is seemingly on permanent alert for threats of danger. Symptoms of hyperarousal include: exaggerated startle responses, anxiety attacks, irritability, outbursts of anger or rage, aggressive behavior, difficulty concentrating, hypervigilence, difficulty falling asleep or staying asleep, or physiological reactions upon exposure to situations that symbolize or resemble an aspect of the traumatic experience (e.g., elevated pulse or sweat during a pelvic exam, or upon hearing a vacuum pump sound.)

Intrusion is the re-experience of the traumatic event at unwanted and unexpected times. Symptoms of intrusion in PAS cases include: recurrent and intrusive thoughts about the abortion or aborted child, flashbacks in which the woman momentarily re-experiences an aspect of the abortion experience, nightmares about the abortion, child, or anniversary reactions of intense grief or depression on the due date of the aborted pregnancy or the anniversary date of the abortion.

Constriction is the numbing of emotional resources, or the development of behavioral patterns, so as to avoid stimuli associated with the trauma. It is avoidance behavior; an attempt to deny and avoid negative feelings or people, places, or things which aggravate the negative feelings associated with the trauma. In post-abortion trauma cases, constriction may include: an inability to recall the abortion experience or important parts of it; efforts to avoid activities or situations which may arouse recollections of the abortion; withdrawal from relationships, especially estrangement from those involved in the abortion decision; avoidance of children; efforts to avoid or deny thoughts or feelings about the abortion; restricted range of loving or tender feelings; a sense of a foreshortened future (e.g., does not expect a career, marriage, or children, or a long life.); diminished interest in previously enjoyed activities; drug or alcohol abuse; suicidal thoughts or acts; and other self-destructive tendencies.

As previously mentioned, Barnard's study identified a 19% rate of PTSD among women who had abortions three to five years previously. But in reality the actual rate is probably higher. Like most post-abortion studies, Barnard's study was handicapped by a fifty-percent dropout rate. Clinical experience has demonstrated that the women least likely to cooperate in post-abortion research are those for whom the abortion caused the most psychological distress. Research has confirmed this insight, demonstrating that the women who refuse follow-up evaluation most closely match the demographic characteristics of the women who suffer the most post-abortion distress.[27] The extraordinary high rate of refusal to participate in post-abortion studies may interpreted as evidence of constriction or avoidance behavior (not wanting to think about the abortion) which is a major symptom of PTSD.

For many women the onset or accurate identification of PTSD symptoms may be delayed for several years.[28] Until a PTSD sufferer has received counseling and achieved adequate recovery, PTSD may result in a psychological disability which would prevent an injured abortion patient from bringing action within the normal statutory period. This disability may, therefore, provide grounds for an extended statutory period.

Sexual Dysfunction

Thirty to fifty percent of aborted women report experiencing sexual dysfunctions, of both short and long duration, beginning immediately after their abortions. These problems may include one or more of the following: loss of pleasure from intercourse, increased pain, an aversion to sex and/or males in general, or the development of a promiscuous life-style.[29]

Suicidal Ideation and Suicide Attempts

Approximately 60 percent of women who experience post-abortion sequelae report suicidal ideation, with 28 percent actually attempting suicide, of which half attempted suicide two or more times. Researchers in Finland have identified a strong statistical association between abortion and suicide in a records-based study, the identified 73 suicides associated within one year to a pregnancy ending either naturally or by induced abortion. The mean annual suicide rate for all women was 11.3 per 100,000. Suicide rate associated with birth was significantly lower (5.9). Rates for pregnancy loss were significantly higher. For miscarriage the rate was 18.1 per 100,000 and for abortion 34.7 per 100,000. The suicide rate within one year after an abortion was three times higher than for all women, seven times higher than for women carrying to term, and nearly twice as high as for women who suffered a miscarriage. Suicide attempts appear to be especially prevalent among post-abortion teenagers.[30]

Increased Smoking with Correspondent Negative Health Effects

Post-abortion stress is linked with increased cigarette smoking. Women who abort are twice as likely to become heavy smokers and suffer the corresponding health risks.[31] Post-abortion women are also more likely to continue smoking during subsequent wanted pregnancies with increased risk of neonatal death or congenital anomalies.[32]

Alcohol Abuse

Abortion is significantly linked with a two-fold increased risk of alcohol abuse among women.[33] Abortion followed by alcohol abuse is linked to violent behavior, divorce or separation, auto accidents, and job loss.[34]

Drug Abuse

Abortion is significantly linked to subsequent drug abuse. In addition to psycho-social costs of such abuse, drug abuse is linked with increased exposure to HIV/AIDS infections, congenital malformations, and assaultive behavior.[35]

Eating Disorders

For at least some women, post abortion stress is associated with eating disorders such as binge eating, bulimia, and anorexia nervosa.[36]

Child Neglect or Abuse

Abortion is linked with increased depression, violent behavior, alcohol and drug abuse, replacement pregnancies, and reduced maternal bonding with children born subsequently. These factors are closely associated with child abuse and would appear to confirm individual clinical assessments linking post-abortion trauma with subsequent child abuse.[37]

Divorce and Chronic Relationship Problems

For most couples, an abortion causes unforeseen problems in their relationship. Post-abortion couples are more likely to divorce or separate. Many post-abortion women develop a greater difficulty forming lasting bonds with a male partner. This may be due to abortion-related reactions such as lowered self-esteem, greater distrust of males, sexual dysfunction, substance abuse, and increased levels of depression, anxiety, and volatile anger. Women who have more than one abortion (representing about 45% of all abortions) are more likely to require public assistance, in part because they are also more likely to become single parents.[38]

Repeat Abortions

Women who have one abortion are at increased risk of having additional abortions in the future. Women with a prior abortion experience are four times more likely to abort a current pregnancy than those with no prior abortion history.[39]

This increased risk is associated with the prior abortion due to lowered self esteem, a conscious or unconscious desire for a replacement pregnancy, and increased sexual activity post-abortion. Subsequent abortions may occur because of conflicted desires to become pregnant and have a child and continued pressures to abort, such as abandonment by the new male partner. Aspects of self-punishment through repeated abortions are also reported.[40]

Approximately 45% of all abortions are now repeat abortions. The risk. of falling into a repeat abortion pattern should be discussed with a patient considering her first abortion. Furthermore, since women who have more than one abortion are at a significantly increased risk of suffering physical and psychological sequelae, these heightened risks should be thoroughly discussed with women seeking abortions.

[See Endnotes on the following pages.]

ENDNOTES

1 An excellent resource for any attorney involved in abortion malpractice is Thomas Strahan's "Major Articles and Books Concerning the Detrimental Effects of Abortion" (Rutherford Institute, PO Box 7482, Charlottesville, VA 22906-7482, 434-978-3888, staff@rutherford.org.) This resource includes brief summaries of major findings drawn from medical and psychology journal articles, books, and related materials, divided into major categories of relevant injuries.

1. MEDICAL/PHYSICAL

2 Gissler, M., et al., "Pregnancy-associated deaths in Finland 1987-1994–definition problems and benefits of record linkage," *Acta Obsetricia et Gynecolgica Scandinavica* 76:651-657 (1997).

3 Kaunitz, "Causes of Maternal Mortality in the United States," *Obstetrics and Gynecology,* 65(5) May 1985.

4 H.L. Howe, et al., "Early Abortion and Breast Cancer Risk Among Women Under Age 40," *International Journal of Epidemiology* 18(2):300-304 (1989); L.I. Remennick, "Induced Abortion as a Cancer Risk Factor: A Review of Epidemiological Evidence," *Journal of Epidemiological Community Health,* (1990); M.C. Pike, "Oral Contraceptive Use and Early Abortion as Risk Factors for Breast Cancer in Young Women," *British Journal of Cancer* 43:72 (1981).

5 M-G, Le, et al., "Oral Contraceptive Use and Breast or Cervical Cancer: Preliminary Results of a French Case-Control Study, Hormones and Sexual Factors in Human Cancer Etiology," ed. JP Wolff, et al., Excerpta Medica: New York (1984) pp. 139-147; F. Parazzini, et al., "Reproductive Factors and the Risk of Invasive and Intraepithelial Cervical Neoplasia," *British Journal of Cancer,* 59:805-809 (1989); H.L. Stewart, et al., "Epidemiology of Cancers of the Uterine Cervix and Corpus, Breast and Ovary in Israel and New York City," *Journal of the National Cancer Institute* 37(1):1-96; I. Fujimoto, et al., "Epidemiologic Study of Carcinoma in Situ of the Cervix," *Journal of Reproductive Medicine* 30(7):535 (July 1985); N. Weiss, "Events of Reproductive Life and the Incidence of Epithelial Ovarian Cancer," Am. J. of Epidemiology, 117(2):128-139 (1983); V. Beral, et al., "Does Pregnancy Protect Against Ovarian Cancer," *The Lancet,* May 20, 1978, pp. 1083-1087; C. LaVecchia, et al., "Reproductive Factors and the Risk of Hepatocellular Carcinoma in Women," *International Journal of Cancer,* 52:351, 1992.

6 S. Kaali, et al., "The Frequency and Management of Uterine Perforations During First-Trimester Abortions," *Am. J. Obstetrics and Gynecology*

161:406-408, August 1989; M. White, "A Case-Control Study of Uterine Perforations documented at Laparoscopy," *Am. J. Obstetrics and Gynecology* 129:623 (1977).

7 D. Grimes, et al., "Prevention of uterine perforation During Curettage Abortion," JAMA, 251:2108-2111 (1984); D. Grimes, et al., "Local versus General Anesthesia: Which is Safer For Performing Suction Abortions?" *Am. J. of Obstetrics and Gynecology,* 135:1030 (1979).

8 K. Schulz, et al., "Measures to Prevent Cervical Injuries During Suction Curettage Abortion," *The Lancet,* May 28, 1983, pp 1182-1184; W. Cates, "The Risks Associated with Teenage Abortion," *New England Journal of Medicine,* 309(11):612-624; R. Castadot, "Pregnancy Termination: Techniques, Risks, and Complications and Their Management," *Fertility and Sterility,* 45(1):5-16 (1986).

9 Barrett, et al., "Induced Abortion: A Risk Factor for Placenta Previa," *Am. J. of Ob & Gyn.* 141:7 (1981).

10 Zhou, Weijin, et al., "Induced Abortion and Subsequent Pregnancy Duration," *Obstetrics & Gynecology* 94(6):948-953 (Dec. 1999).

11 Hogue, Cates and Tietze, "Impact of Vacuum Aspiration Abortion on Future Childbearing: A Review," *Family Planning Perspectives* (May–June 1983), vol. 15, no.3.

12 Daling, et al., "Ectopic Pregnancy in Relation to Previous Induced Abortion," JAMA, 253(7):1005-1008 (Feb. 15, 1985); Levin, et.al., "Ectopic Pregnancy and Prior Induced Abortion," *American Journal of Public Health* (1982), vol.72, p253; C.S. Chung, "Induced Abortion and Ectopic Pregnancy in Subsequent Pregnancies," *American Journal of Epidemiology* 115(6):879-887 (1982).

13 T. Radberg, et al., "Chlamydia Trachomatis in Relation to Infections Following First Trimester Abortions," *Acta Obstricia Gynoecological* (Supp. 93), 54:478 (1980); L. Westergaard, "Significance of Cervical Chlamydia Trachomatis Infection in Post-abortal Pelvic Inflammatory Disease," *Obstetrics and Gynecology,* 60(3):322-325, (1982); M. Chacko, et al., "Chlamydia Trachomatosis Infection in Sexually Active Adolescents: Prevalence and Risk Factors," *Pediatrics,* 73(6), (1984); M. Barbacci, et al., "Post-Abortal Endometritis and Isolation of Chlamydia Trachomatis," *Obstetrics and Gynecology* 68(5):668-690, (1986); S. Duthrie, et al., "Morbidity After Termination of Pregnancy in First-Trimester," *Genitourinary Medicine* 63(3):182-187, (1987).

14 Burkman, et al., "Morbidity Risk Among Young Adolescents Undergoing Elective Abortion" *Contraception,* 30:99-105 (1984); "Post-Abortal

Endometritis and Isolation of Chlamydia Trachomatis," *Obstetrics and Gynecology* 68(5):668–690, (1986)

15 Frank, et.al., "Induced Abortion Operations and Their Early Sequelae," *Journal of the Royal College of General Practitioners* (April 1985),35(73):175–180; Grimes and Cates, "Abortion: Methods and Complications," *Human Reproduction*, 2nd ed., 796–813; M.A. Freedman, "Comparison of complication rates in first trimester abortions performed by physician assistants and physicians," *Am. J. Public Health*, 76(5):550–554 (1986).

16 Ney, et al., "The Effects of Pregnancy Loss on Women's Health," Soc. Sci. Med. 48(9):1193–1200, 1994; Badgley, Caron, & Powell, *Report of the Committee on the Abortion Law*, Supply and Services, Ottawa, 1997: 319–321.

17 D. Berkeley, P.L. Humphreys, and D. Davidson, "Demands Made on General Practice by Women Before and After an Abortion," *J. R. Coll. Gen. Pract.* 34:310–315, 1984. "Abortion Risks and Complications," © 1997, 2000 Elliot Institute. Compiled by David C. Reardon, Ph.D. Available at http://www.afterabortion.org/. Elliot Institute, PO Box 7348, Springfield, IL 62791, (217) 525-8202.

18 Wadhera, "Legal Abortion Among Teens, 1974–1978," *Canadian Medical Association Journal*, 122:1386–1389, (June 1980).

Additional medical documentation is cited in the following sources:

http://www.nrlc.org/abortion/;

http://www.family.org/cforum/fosi/bioethics/facts/a0027728.cfm;

http://www.abortionfacts.com/

Mark Crutcher, *Lime five: Exploited by Choice* (Denton, TX: Life Dynamics, 1996). (An expose of the Center for Disease Control; available at 1-800-401-6494).

John Ankerberg & John Weldon, *When Does Life Begin?* (Brentwood, TN: Wolgemuth & Hyatt, 1989), pp. 53–59.

2. PSYCHOLOGICAL

19 Ashton, "They Psychosocial Outcome of Induced Abortion," *British Journal of Ob&Gyn.*, 87:1115–1122, (1980).

20 Badgley, et.al., Report of the Committee on the Operation of the Abortion Law (Ottawa: Supply and Services, 1977), pp. 313–321.

21 R. Somers, "Risk of Admission to Psychiatric Institutions Among Danish Women who Experienced Induced Abortion: An Analysis on National Record Linkage," *Dissertation Abstracts International*, Public Health 2621-B, Order No.

7926066 (1979); H. David, et al., "Postpartum and Postabortion Psychotic Reactions," *Family Planning Perspectives* 13:88–91 (1981).

22 Kent, et al., "Bereavement in Post-Abortive Women: A Clinical Report," *World Journal of Psychosynthesis* (Autumn–Winter 1981), vol. 13, nos.3-4.

23 Catherine Barnard, *The Long-Term Psychological Effects of Abortion* (Portsmouth, N.H.: Institute for Pregnancy Loss, 1990).

24 Herman, *Trauma and Recovery* (New York: Basic Books, 1992), p. 34.

25 Francke, *The Ambivalence of Abortion* (New York: Random House, 1978) 84–95.

26 Zakus, "Adolescent Abortion Option," *Social Work in Health Care*, 12(4):87 (1987); Makhorn, "Sexual Assault & Pregnancy," *New Perspectives on Human Abortion*, Mall & Watts, eds. (Washington, D.C.: University Publications of America, 1981).

27 Adler, "Sample Attrition in Studies of Psychosocial Sequelae of Abortion: How Great a Problem." *Journal of Social Issues*, 1979, 35, 100–110.

28 Speckhard, "Postabortion Syndrome: An Emerging Public Health Concern," *Journal of Social Issues*, 48(3):95–119.

29 Speckhard, *Psycho-social Stress Following Abortion*, Sheed & Ward, Kansas City: MO, 1987; and Belsey, et al., "Predictive Factors in Emotional Response to Abortion: King's Termination Study–IV," Soc. Sci. & Med., 11:71–82 (1977).

30 Speckhard, *Psycho-social Stress Following Abortion*, Sheed & Ward, Kansas City: MO, 1987; Gissler, Hemminki & Lonnqvist, "Suicides after pregnancy in Finland, 1987–94: register linkage study," *British Journal of Medicine* 313:1431–4, 1996. C. Haignere, et al., "HIV/AIDS Prevention and Multiple Risk Behaviors of Gay Male and Runaway Adolescents," Sixth International Conference on AIDS: San Francisco, June 1990; N. Campbell, et al., "Abortion in Adolescence," *Adolescence*, 23(92):813–823 (1988); H. Vaughan, *Canonical Variates of Post-Abortion Syndrome*, Portsmouth, NH: Institute for Pregnancy Loss, 1991; B. Garfinkel, "Stress, Depression and Suicide: A Study of Adolescents in Minnesota," *Responding to High Risk Youth*, Minnesota Extension Service, University of Minnesota (1986).

31 Harlap, "Characteristics of Pregnant Women Reporting Previous Induced Abortions," Bulletin World Health Organization, 52:149 (1975); N. Meirik, "Outcome of First Delivery After 2nd Trimester Two Stage Induced Abortion: A Controlled Cohort Study," Acta Obstetrica et Gynecologica Scandinavica 63(1):45–50(1984);

Levin, et al., "Association of Induced Abortion with Subsequent Pregnancy Loss," JAMA, 243:2495-2499, June 27, 1980.

32 Obel, "Pregnancy Complications Following Legally Induced Abortion: An Analysis of the Population with Special Reference to Prematurity," *Danish Medical Bulletin*, 26:192–199 (1979); Martin, "An Overview: Maternal Nicotine and Caffeine Consumption and Offspring Outcome," *Neurobehavioral Toxicology and Tertology*, 4(4):421–427, (1982).

33 Klassen, "Sexual Experience and Drinking Among Women in a U.S. National Survey," *Archives of Sexual Behavior*, 15(5):363–39; M. Plant, *Women, Drinking and Pregnancy*, Tavistock Pub, London (1985); Kuzma & Kissinger, "Patterns of Alcohol and Cigarette Use in Pregnancy," *Neurobehavioral Toxicology and Terotology*, 3:211–221 (1981).

34 Morrissey, et al., "Stressful Life Events and Alcohol Problems Among Women Seen at a Detoxification Center," *Journal of Studies on Alcohol*, 39(9):1159 (1978).

35 Oro, et al., "Perinatal Cocaine and Methamphetamine Exposure Maternal and Neo-Natal Correlates," *J. Pediatrics*, 111:571–578 (1978); D.A. Frank, et al., "Cocaine Use During Pregnancy Prevalence and Correlates," *Pediatrics*, 82(6):888 (1988); H. Amaro, et al., "Drug Use Among Adolescent Mothers: Profile of Risk," *Pediatrics* 84:144–150, (1989).

36 Speckhard, *Psycho-social Stress Following Abortion*, Sheed & Ward, Kansas City: MO, 1987; J. Spaulding, et al, "Psychoses Following Therapeutic Abortion, *Am. J. of Psychiatry* 125(3):364 (1978); R.K. McAll, et al., "Ritual Mourning in Anorexia Nervosa," *The Lancet*, August 16, 1980, p. 368.

37 Benedict, et al., "Maternal Perinatal Risk Factors and Child Abuse," *Child Abuse and Neglect*, 9:217–224 (1985); P.G. Ney, "Relationship between Abortion and Child Abuse," *Canadian Journal of Psychiatry*, 24:610–620, 1979; Reardon, *Aborted Women — Silent No More* (Chicago: Loyola University Press, 1987), 129–30, describes a case of woman who beat her three year old son to death shortly after an abortion which triggered a "psychotic episode" of grief, guilt, and misplaced anger.

38 Shepard, et al., "Contraceptive Practice and Repeat Induced Abortion: An Epidemiological Investigation," *J. Biosocial Science*, 11:289–302 (1979); M. Bracken, "First and Repeated Abortions: A Study of Decision-Making and Delay," *J. Biosocial Science*, 7:473–491 (1975); S. Henshaw, "The Characteristics and Prior Contraceptive Use of U.S. Abortion Patients," *Family Planning Perspectives*, 20(4):158–168 (1988); D. Sherman, et al., "The Abortion Experience in Private Practice," *Women and Loss: Psychobiological Perspectives*, ed. W.F. Finn, et al., (New York: Praeger Publ. 1985), pp 98–107; E.M. Belsey, et al., "Predictive Factors in Emotional Response to Abortion: King's Termination Study–IV," *Social Science and Medicine*, 11:71–82 (1977); E. Freeman, et al., "Emotional Distress Patterns Among Women Having First or Repeat Abortions," *Obstetrics and Gynecology*, 55(5):630–636 (1980); C. Berger, et al., "Repeat Abortion: Is it a Problem?" *Family Planning Perspectives* 16(2):70–75 (1984).

39 Joyce, "The Social and Economic Correlates of Pregnancy Resolution Among Adolescents in New York by Race and Ethnicity: A Multivariate Analysis," *Am. J. of Public Health*, 78(6):626-631 (1988); C. Tietze, "Repeat Abortions–Why More?" *Family Planning Perspectives* 10(5):286–288, (1978).

40 Leach, "The Repeat Abortion Patient," *Family Planning Perspectives*, 9(1):37–39 (1977); S. Fischer, "Reflection on Repeated Abortions: The meanings and motivations," *Journal of Social Work Practice* 2(2):70–87 (1986); B. Howe, et al., "Repeat Abortion, Blaming the Victims," *Am. J. of Public Health*, 69(12):1242-1246, (1979).

APPENDIX P

HISTORY OF THE ICBI AND COR, AND THE PARTICIPANTS AND DEVELOPMENT OF THE COR DOCUMENTS

by Jay Grimstead

HOW THE INTERNATIONAL COUNCIL ON BIBLE INERRANCY (ICBI) WAS FORMED

Though we gave a brief historical overview in the Introduction to this book, the thirty-seven-year history of these three movements, the ICBI, COR, and the ICCP, needs to be told.

The ICBI organization and COR documents came together in this way. By 1976, I had been working for nearly twenty years on the staff of Young Life Campaign. I organized and trained college students to evangelize and follow-up with un-churched teenagers. At that time I was simply a "Christian youth leader" and very much a "nobody" in the realm of theology and world-changing.

For the previous four years I had been unsuccessfully attempting to get our Young Life national and regional leaders to see that Young Life (as well as much of evangelicalism itself) was drifting increasingly into a more liberal view of Christianity. Many pastors, Christian leaders, and theologians held a neo-orthodox view of the Bible which opposed the inerrancy view of the Bible that had been expected of all new staff when I joined Young Life in 1957.

I found myself on the front lines of a theological war defending the historic-orthodox view of the Bible's inerrancy with a series of "white-paper-battles." However, God used the battles, pain, and loneliness and the journey through the fire to forge me into something of a "reformer" and a "theological warrior for truth," a job for which I had definitely not volunteered.

Christian Colleges and Seminaries

Young Life's theological guru, Dr. Paul Jewett of Fuller Seminary, had been one of my favorite professors at Fuller up to the time I graduated in 1961. In fact, we had become very good friends and he performed the wedding of my lovely wife Donna and me in 1963.

After I returned to Fuller in 1975 to earn my Doctorate of Ministry, I was disappointed to discover that Dr. Jewett had changed his theology mid-stream from orthodox to neo-orthodox. I was shocked to find that my dear alma mater, which I loved and appreciated so much, had done a 180-degree turn in its theology. Now, instead of annually requiring all professors to hold a belief in the inerrancy of the Bible, both professors and students were ridiculing the very idea of inerrancy in class and in the cafeteria!

One night I had a frustrating discussion in the cafeteria with a Fuller associate professor and some Fuller students who argued that in Romans 1 Paul was not condemning a homosexual relationship between two men who loved each other but only a homosexual, transient, one-night-affair in a gay bar. Outside on the sidewalk in front of the Seminary I actually wept and cried out, "God,…what have you allowed to happen to our seminary?"

It appears that some Christian colleges and seminaries are covering up their decline. Many so-called evangelical seminaries and colleges have deteriorated in both theology and Christian moral expectations but have been able to cover up their transition to a liberal theology and relativistic morals by not informing their donors, their alumni, or prospective students and their parents. As a loyal Fuller alumnus who remained in fairly close touch with the seminary, I was totally ignorant of this horrible and intentional but very quiet move towards a liberal theology. The seminary had deliberately painted a false picture of its supposedly constant commitment to its orthodox view of the Bible through its newsletters and PR materials to alumni, donors, and the general Christian public.

In today's world, it is immensely foolish and naïve for any Christian to simply assume that the orthodox, strongly Biblical college or seminary they attended twenty years ago still maintains and teaches the same orthodox doctrine that its public relations materials may even proclaim loudly to this very day.

Recruiting a Global Army and Forming ICBI

By October 1976, God had opened my eyes and was laying on my heart a very heavy burden to call for the formation of a global army of scholars who would meet together annually to strategize how to turn evangelicalism back to orthodox theology and the inerrancy of the Bible. They would systematically write the theological documents, books, and training materials necessary to bring the general evangelical world up to speed on these urgent theological matters.

At that time although I was a "nobody" in the world of theology, I wrote a letter proposing the birthing of such a theological army first to Dr. R. C. Sproul. Writing that letter was the point at which I believe the Holy Spirit conceived the plan in my mind's "womb" that became the ICBI (International Council on Biblical Inerrancy) four months later at our Mount Hermon conference on the Authority of Scripture. (A facsimile of this letter is Appendix M).

As I recently re-read this letter written 37 years ago on Oct. 6, 1976, I said out loud to the Lord, "Amen"! I realized afresh how foundationally important the task was then, and still is today, for a team of courageous, Biblical, men of God to draw a clear line theologically within the entire evangelical Body of Christ TO

CLARIFY WHAT IS TRUE AND WHAT IS FALSE about any theological position being taught at any point in the history of the Church. Though the details of my suggestions in 1976 were not what we actually did in 1978 and beyond, I had stated the basic point accurately about a courageous team of men needing to draw a line in the sand, so both truth and falsehood are made unmistakably clear to the confused Church.

Shortly after my letter to Dr. Sproul, I wrote the exact same letter to Dr. Harold Lindsell. He had been one of my Fuller professors and just that year had released his bombshell book *Battle for the Bible* (Zondervan, 1976), exposing the little known fact that many so-called "evangelical" seminaries including Fuller were quietly turning liberal and were clearly denying the historic evangelical position that the Bible is inerrant.

I asked each of these theologians if they would be interested in initiating such a national "theological army" since they had the clout but I did not. They both said they were too busy at the time to think seriously about igniting such a movement. A copy of that letter of October 6, 1976, which I wrote to each of them is reproduced here as Appendix M, p. 265.

As I was forming a new "Reformation Study Center" in 1976 (for theological training of laymen), R. C. Sproul suggested it would be a good idea for me to launch this Study Center by way of a conference, whose advice I took and we scheduled the conference on "The Authority of Scripture" for February of 1977, at Mount Hermon Conference Center near Santa Cruz, California. I wanted to invite as speakers to this conference Dr. R. C. Sproul, Dr. John Gerstner (Sproul's mentor), and Dr. J. I. Packer (whom I had met at a conference in Pennsylvania Sproul held in 1973). R. C. suggested two more men I had not heard of till then, to which I readily agreed: Dr. Norman Geisler of Trinity Seminary and Dr. Greg Bahnsen of Reformed Seminary.

I invited those five speakers, along with other Christian leaders such as Miss Wetherall Johnson of Bible Study Fellowship, to come one day early to pray and strategize at my home for the purpose of creating an "army of theologians" who would take a united stand on defending the inerrancy of the Bible and create together a theological statement which would deal with all the falsehoods being taught about the Bible from so-called "evangelical seminaries," and thus, draw a plumb line regarding this issue.

During that weekend conference at Mount Hermon near Santa Cruz, those five men and I (plus Miss Wetherell Johnson of Bible Study Fellowship and Mrs. Karen Hoyt who became our ICBI executive secretary) spent many hours in between their speaking engagements and late at night developing the plans for what we would come to call the ICBI, the International Council on Biblical Inerrancy. We decided that we needed a major, global "summit meeting" around

Reformation Weekend [42] of 1978, to which we would invite (by invitation only) the leading theologians and heads of major evangelical organizations and seminaries worldwide, and wherein we would create a new "Statement on the Inerrancy of the Bible" for the global Church, covering the basic errors that were being taught about the Bible at neo-orthodox seminaries. We would also produce a book written by a number of our new teammates and form a "standing army of theologians" to debate and bring clarification to this inerrancy issue. During those meetings, Dr. J. I. Packer, with our input, created our Mission Statement which reads like this:

> "The ICBI has as its purpose the defense and application of the doctrine of Biblical inerrancy as an essential element for the authority of Scripture and a necessity for the health of the Church."

By this we mean that the Bible has no real authority from God for humans if it is not inerrant and that an inerrant Bible is necessary for the Church to be healthy and strong. The liberals within evangelicalism were claiming falsely that the Bible can have authority if it is not inerrant.

My very small Reformation Study Center giving birth at that conference to the ICBI was something like a chipmunk giving birth to an elephant. I am sure a few angels looking on at that time thought it was humorous.

For the four years before this conference in 1977, I had carried a more or less constant burden and pain in my heart about the inerrancy of the Bible which general evangelicalism was rejecting. This pain felt much like the physical pain of indigestion, but Rolaids® did not help. Instantly, as soon as we had formed the early stages of the ICBI at that conference and I saw a realistic hope that this team and this vision could probably turn the thinking of evangelicalism on this issue, that burden and pain ceased. It was instantaneous, liberating, and undeniable and I praised God for a new perspective on life and on this battle.

One month later in March 1977, we met again at the Pittsburgh Airport. The men at that meeting were J. I. Packer, R. C. Sproul, Jack Gerstner, Norm Geisler, and me, plus two of our guests who did not participate in the discussions. I asked Norm Geisler to chair that meeting, which he did very efficiently. I audio-taped that meeting (as I did most of our strategy and board meetings the first two years), and those audio tapes are in our Archives. I believe those audio tapes will eventually be considered a part of the Church's theological history. After we generated a list of prospective new members from around the world, I was asked to contact and recruit into this new ICBI those other 50-plus respected theologians. I contacted them by phone and was elated at their very enthusiastic responses. They were immediately receptive to this idea of forming

---

42 Reformation Week celebrates Luther nailing his 95 Theses to the Wittenberg church door in 1517, on the day we call Halloween, the evening before "All Saints Day" (November 1 in the Catholic Church).

a theological army to deal with the Bible inerrancy issue on a global scale.

It should be noted that because the inerrancy of the Bible was in the process of being ridiculed by so many evangelical Christians at the time, many of these stalwart defenders of God's Word whom I called had felt alone in their theological circles regarding their position on inerrancy, and they were overjoyed that such a "theological army" was being marshaled and that they could be a part of that army. It was very encouraging to me as a "budding reformer" to hear the enthusiastic responses of a large percentage of those 50 men I called long-distance all over the world who responded something like this: "Young man, I don't know who you are, but this is the best news I have heard in a long time as I have been very much alone in fighting this inerrancy battle. Count me in!!... I'll be at the Summit Meeting and write a paper or do whatever you and those theologians want me to do to be part of this inerrancy army of theologians!"

Major theologians and Christian leaders who became part of this new movement included: Dr. Francis Schaeffer, Dr. R. C. Sproul, Dr. J. I. Packer, Dr. Norm Geisler, Dr. John Gerstner, Dr. Greg Bahnsen, Dr. D. James Kennedy, Dr. Harold Hoehner, Dr. Harold Lindsell, Dr. Gleason Archer, Dr. Henry Krabbendam, Dr. Kenneth Kantzer, Dr. J. Barton Payne, Dr. Earl Radmacher, Dr. Jay Adams, Dr. George Knight, Dr. John MacArthur, Dr. Josh McDowell, Dr. Roger Nicole, Dr. Harold Ockenga, Dr. Robert Saucy, Dr. John Walvoord, Dr. Larry Walker, Dr. Robert Preus, Dr. Merrill Tenney, and major Christian leaders such as Dr. Bill Bright, Dr. Luis Palau, Dr. W. A. Criswell, Dr. Ray Ortlund, Dr. Adrian Rogers, Mr. Lorne Sanny, Dr. Ray Stedman, and other evangelical theologians and heads of seminaries and organizations.

At Dr. Sproul's suggestion, we decided at that Pittsburgh meeting to invite Dr. James Boice of Tenth Presbyterian Church in Philadelphia to come join this team and serve as chairman of the board which we had just created that day to help us carry out the long-range plans we had developed for the ICBI. Dr. Boice began serving as board chairman two months later in May at our first board meeting at the Chicago O'Hare Hilton. Then he led our first general meeting of both the Executive Committee and the Advisory Board in September 1977, again at the O'Hare Hilton. At that September meeting the full ICBI team I had recruited was fully organized and everyone became very energetic about our plans and about the Summit Meeting coming up in one year for October 1978, at the Chicago O'Hare Hyatt Regency Hotel, to which were invited the other 50 major, world-respected theologians also recruited to join the ICBI team. Dr. Boice did an excellent job chairing the ICBI board and added to that task the element of what some would call "class."

A number of my Christian friends were unaware of this attack upon the inerrancy of the Bible from within evangelical seminaries. So in February 1977, one week after our initial conference on the Authority of Scripture, I had written out for them a list of "Neo-orthodox Falsehoods Being Taught about the Bible." I became aware of these points as this theological conflict hit me hard in the face during the previous four years. Later I passed that list to our new ICBI Executive Committee on which I sat and told them these were the points we needed to defend in our battle and in our writings on this subject. They were in basic agreement. Many of those points on that list made their way into the 19 Articles of our ICBI Chicago Statement on Biblical Inerrancy.

That ICBI Statement dealt with all 17 of these neo-orthodox falsehoods about the Bible's inerrancy being taught at that time in evangelical seminaries which were turning increasingly towards liberal theology. It has by now become the definitive and historic statement on the doctrine of the inspiration of the Bible and is recognized as a modern Church history document in recent systematic theology books and is listed along with the Nicene Creed, the Westminster Confession, and others. But because this controversy still persists, and because the inerrancy of the Bible is foundational, we list it as Document 1 along with the other 23 documents we have produced dealing with the present controversial issues within evangelicalism.

Four years later, in 1982, our ICBI theological team created the "Chicago Statement on Biblical Hermeneutics" (as a companion document to the statement on Biblical Inerrancy) which appears in this book as Document 2. Dr. Henry Krabbendam, Professor of Biblical Studies for years at Covenant College, played a large role in helping to create our Hermeneutics document and has been a strong ally ever since.

Books Birthed Out of ICBI

I want to give special mention here to four of the several books that came out of the ICBI movement. Our heavy theology book, *Inerrancy,* published by Zondervan in 1980, contains the 14 scholarly white papers produced by our ICBI theologians which became the basis of the discussions at the Summit Meeting, which papers were all "boiled down" into our 19 Articles on Biblical Inerrancy. I see this book *Inerrancy,* edited by Norm Geisler, as the definitive answer to neo-orthodoxy's major falsehoods about the Bible. It stops the liberal critics of the Bible in their tracks and, to my knowledge, has never been answered by the liberals.

Also in 1980, R. C. Sproul wrote a tremendous and very useful, 51-page commentary booklet about the "Chicago Statement on Biblical Inerrancy "with the title *Explaining Inerrancy,* which is a must read for all who are new to this battle and need to be able to teach others how to defend the Bible's inerrancy and total inspiration. It is out of print now but to acquire the e-book, see fn. 9 on p.18.

In 1978, at an ICBI board meeting, I challenged Gleason Archer (who is a "scholars's scholar" and who taught 27 languages) to gather a team of other

Biblical scholars and together create a book which answers all the apparent "problems" in the Bible from Genesis to Revelation. For three years I kept asking him to please produce that needed book with a team of writers and finally, in 1981, he said at one of our ICBI board meetings, "Well, Jay, I've decided to write that book myself without a team." So by April of 1982, we had in our hands Dr. Archer's amazing *Encyclopedia of Biblical Difficulties.* The fourth book we created is *The Foundation of Biblical Authority,* described on p.15 and fn.7, and though out-of-print, is available at Amazon.com.

Shutting Down ICBI

In 1978, as the ICBI Executive Director, I convinced our board of directors that we should give this movement a 10-year life span and shut ICBI down after 10 years. I presented this logic to them: "If our team cannot turn evangelicalism around within 10 years, then we better get out of the way and let some better men than we take on this task. But if we are successful in turning it around in 10 years, then why keep this organization going to let it become 'institutional' and self-serving as many organizations have done which outlived their original usefulness?" During the early 1980s, Dr. Boice and another one or two board members had suggested twice that perhaps we should shut down the ICBI at that time because we had already created the ICBI Statement on Inerrancy and had our successful world-impact meetings. I strongly urged the board instead to keep the ICBI alive for the full 10 years because the weak evangelical Church in America needed to know there is a "standing army" of theologians ready to jump heavily upon any "neo-evangelical" who wanted to question the inerrancy of the Bible. They bought the plan and we held a closing ceremony and conference in Washington, D.C. in 1987, at which Dr. Chuck Colson and Dr. William F. Buckley both spoke.

A Switch Regarding Who Was in the Closet

It was very obvious that immediately after the very week we held our 1978 ICBI first Summit Meeting in Chicago, all public criticism and open contempt for the inerrancy of the Bible coming from evangelical sources stopped in its tracks! Up until that very week, many evangelical publications, newsletters, and speeches were denouncing the inerrancy of the Bible as "old fashioned and medieval." But immediately after our global Summit Meeting and the public release of our "19 Articles on the Inerrancy of the Bible," those neo-orthodox liberals within evangelicalism shut their mouths and ran like scared rabbits into "closets" and hardly a peep of criticism was heard from evangelical circles against the Bible's inerrancy for two years. This "army" of 53 theologians and Christian leaders we had collected and who sat on our Executive Council and Advisory Board comprised what most Christians considered to be the major

Christian leaders, theologians, pastors, seminary presidents, and organization heads of the entire evangelical world. So then, one major thing this conference and our ICBI organization did was to make it acceptable and proper and "politically correct" to once again openly state that one was a believer in the full inerrancy of the Bible.[43]

I believe that when evangelicals go "liberal" it is because they are insecure men who are capable of being intimidated, and they are often "intimidated" by some liberal cohort or scholar or professor into "going with the liberal flow." What our many world-respected scholars did as a united, theological "army" was to accidentally "intimidate" some evangelicals who were turning liberal into shutting their liberal mouths and going into their evangelical "closets" for a time.

When it shut down in 1987, ICBI turned all its records, documents, pictures, and business correspondence of Dr. Boice, myself, our Executive Secretary, Karen Hoyt, and others over to the Archive where that is all being safely kept in many boxes on many shelves. For the record, the organization I direct, Coalition on Revival (COR), obtained written permission from the Dallas Seminary Archive Library to use both of ICBI's documents as part of our total package of documents which express the Biblical stance on all 24 of these now controversial issues within the greater body of evangelicalism. On each ICBI document we give credit to the ICBI for their creation and to the Dallas Seminary Archive Library for their use. COR has taken on the task of continually and energetically promoting the battle for inerrancy of the Bible where ICBI left off in 1987.

THE FORMATION OF THE COALITION ON REVIVAL (COR)

My personal transition from major involvement in the ICBI to major involvement in COR was birthed at our large ICBI conference on the Bible in the spring of 1982, at the San Diego Convention Center, which conference was directed towards laymen and pastors.

Two factors at that San Diego conference moved me to start thinking about forming a more activist, "world-changing" approach to the reformation of the Church than we had in the ICBI.

The first factor was a phrase that Dr. Francis Schaeffer used in his plenary speech to all 4000 of the participants, wherein he said that "TRUTH DEMANDS CONFRONTATION" in a relativistic world such as the one in which we now live. By that he meant that both moral and social evil as well as intentional falsehood about truth and reality MUST be confronted if we are to be true to the Bible and the kind of absolute truth the Bible presents. He was making a statement in this against the false concept that "everyone is right and no one can say that

---

43 The "fundamentalists" never quit believing in the Bible's inerrancy. It was only within the ranks of general "evangelical" schools and denominations that these liberals had found academic soil where they could plant their anti-inerrancy seed.

something is really right or really wrong, or is really true or really false." It is the very Biblical concept of truth itself for which we are now fighting in our battles with the neo-orthodox theology of relativism and in the post-modern world of zero absolutes and zero certainties. I believe Dr. Schaeffer would describe this difference in the two opposing views of truth in this way: The Bible and Christianity (and even most of the pre-Kantian philosophers of the world) define truth in terms of "antithesis." That is, if a statement is true, then its opposite is false. An antithesis view of truth is based upon what is called "Aristotle's law of non-contradiction" on which all formal logic is based. Since Immanuel Kant (1724–1804) and soon after him G. W. F. Hegel (1770–1831), logic and reasonableness have suffered greatly and secular philosophy since then has degenerated to such a state that we have now come to post-modern thought which operates in opposition to truth as antithesis. To the person infected with the mental disease of postmodernism, there is no truth and no absolutes of existence or morals. There are no fixed points in this universe; everything to that person is *relative*.

The second factor was that I began to see that most godly Christian men who become professors and pastors tend to be very different in how they battle evil from the kind of men like military generals, aggressive business entrepreneurs, and some of our church history heroes like Luther, Knox, Cromwell, Wesley, Spurgeon, Kuyper, and Machen. Most professors who think very well and write books and give lectures tend to move away from head-on, bloody battle as it makes them uncomfortable. I was thinking that the kind of organization we need to bring Reformation to a Laodicean, blind and sleepy Church in America would need to be composed of men more like Knox, Luther, and, to use *cowboy* language, a personality like John Wayne in his movie roles.

So at that large ICBI conference, I began asking a few of the ICBI scholars I had recruited into the ICBI in 1977 if they might be interested in a more aggressive, head-on-collision approach to Reformation, and several of them said they were interested. It actually took from that spring of 1982 to the summer of 1984 to get COR formed into a fighting force for Reformation. The purpose of COR was then, and basically still is, to get Christians to simply OBEY THE BIBLE and let the chips fall where they may. When the whole outline and plan of COR dropped into my mind at a Denny's Restaurant in June of 1982, I wrote out my 20-page plan for how Reformation could be accomplished. Before I shared it with any other leader, I spent two-and-a-half hours in July at the Christian Booksellers Convention in Dallas discussing every page and every facet of it with Dr. Schaeffer, and he gave me an enthusiastic "green light" on the plan and also asked me to be sure the anti-abortion movement was a significant factor in COR's reformation work. I also ran this new COR Reformation vision past my friend Dr. Tim LaHaye that same week, and he also gave his hearty approval.

Afterwards Dr. LaHaye asked me if I would introduce him to Dr. Schaeffer as Dr. LaHaye had just written a book which he had dedicated to Dr. Schaeffer. So I called Dr. Schaeffer in his hotel room and got permission to come and introduce Dr. LaHaye to him and they had an active exchange.

Also, for the record, I personally feel a call from God to carry forth at least a small portion of Dr. Schaeffer's work and mantle since the burden he carried in his heart is the same as the burden that is in my heart, and since he was a constant, personal encouragement to me and fatherly friend as I was birthing and then carrying forward both the ICBI and COR. During those 10 years before he died, Dr. Schaeffer became my mentor. Dr. Schaeffer's books remain a lasting source of spiritual and practical inspiration for me, and I promote them vigorously. (Please see p. 10, fn. 6 regarding his key books.)

Creation of COR's Additional Documents

After our ICBI team created what we call Document Nos. 1 and 2 on the Scriptures in 1978 and 1982, and after our COR theologians created Documents No. 3 on Worldview in 1984 and No. 4 on the Kingdom of God in 1989, the Documents from No. 5 through No. 20 were created mostly by COR's team of theologians and Christian leaders from 1992 to 1996, in this manner. Dr. Bill Bright gave us permission to use Campus Crusade's Arrowhead Springs Conference Center at San Bernardino, California, as a location where our team could meet for several days each year to boil down the white papers which had been written on each controversial topic the previous two years, and distill the main points down into their present form of affirmations and denials. Dr. Bright's administrator of Arrowhead Springs, Col. Glenn Jones, who arranged for our writing-meeting each year, was a gracious host to us always, and gave us a very special deal on the price of our food and lodging. For the record, Col. Jones was also loaned to us by Dr. Bright to function for free as the administrator of our first two National COR Conferences at the Denver Downtown Marriott Hotel in 1984, and in the Anatole Hotel of Dallas in 1985.

The writing process on these documents started by my assigning one of our team to write out the Biblical and traditional Christian view on the current controversial topic under fire. When the first draft was written, we would pass it around and receive critique and input from others on our team, then bring the finished product to Arrowhead Springs, discuss it, boil it down, then I would chair the meeting wherein we would create the affirmations and denials. For the accuracy of the record, there were usually from about six to ten or more of us Christian leaders and theologians giving our input as each document passed through our hands in the discussions to receive our consensus wisdom for the wording of each Article of Affirmation and Denial in each document. From looking at the short list of Review Committee members in Appendix A this fact could not be known. The Review Committee members, who helped finalize a document, were usually part of a larger team which had helped create the document. For example there were 20 members on the committee which created Document 4 on The Kingdom of God, but only five members listed as being on that document's Review Committee, and a number of the earlier documents did not have a Review Committee. This whole process over the years grew rather spontaneously and organically as we proceeded, and we found our way along "as we went down this road."

In the 1970s and 1980s, we were not even considering having a global Church council. Until recently none of these movements were actually mapped out far in advance beyond possibly two years ahead at each point where we found ourselves. By 1997, it became clear to us that we could dispense with the creation of a white paper, and, after identifying the major points of contention and the Biblical principles that needed to be clarified, we could go immediately to the task of turning those points into the Affirmations and Denials for that topic. So Topics Nos. 21, 22, and 23 were created by various COR team members from 2006 to 2011 by using the internet and the telephone to communicate editorial comments with each other; this we did rather than meeting physically at a central location, and it worked well. In 2013, we created Document 24.

A Note Regarding Topics 5, 6, and 7

By 1989, it became apparent to a few of our theologians that, within certain circles of evangelicalism and some organizations that had many solid, orthodox, godly staff people and members whom we loved and with whom we worked, there existed a cluster of three old, classic heresies that were being taught usually quietly and sometimes openly; these heresies often "traveled together" as a cluster of three. Those ancient heresies are:

1. Pelagianism (which denies man's inherent sinful nature being passed on to each generation genetically since the fall of man);
2. A denial of the omniscience and foreknowledge of God (later called the "openness of God"); and
3. A non-judicial and non-forensic view of the Atonement wherein God's righteous wrath is not legally and forensically appeased by the death of Jesus.

Any worldview is based upon foundational principles which tend to be consistent with one another. This is true of orthodox, Biblical Christianity and it is true of religious liberalism and also of heretical cults, false religions, communism, and atheism. Though each of these three historic heresies mentioned above may stand alone, they also fit comfortably together and support each other philosophically. It was not surprising therefore that a Christian group which holds to one of these positions has a tendency to hold to the other two as well. The Christian organizations which hold these positions are often strongly orthodox in most other doctrines, have a passion for God's will and for evangelism, and are full of great, godly people. It was a surprise to our COR Steering Committee to find these beliefs in the midst of impressive, godly evangelical organizations and missions. These three heresies are standard for most religious liberals.

It was one of our COR theologians, Dr. Cal Beisner, who did the basic research groundwork on these three heresies and their sources, and then wrote up his statements about the historic, orthodox view on these three issues.[44]

After Dr. Beisner's research was placed into our hands, we created a small committee for each of these issues and the basic points were created for each paper. After our second dialogue and debate forum regarding our Kingdom of God document in 1991, a few of us met to hammer out the preliminary draft for each of these issues. We sent those drafts out to our Steering Committee to offer us input and needed corrections; we then created our final affirmations and denials as they now stand on our Website and in this book.

The Need and Plans for a Global Church Council

It was at this point in the history of the Coalition on Revival as our theological team was working on these three documents and discussing other false teachings, we discovered were being promoted by certain evangelical churches, schools, or organizations that we came to an amazing and jarring realization. Suddenly it dawned upon us that, because of the increasing number of falsehoods and old heresies springing up out of evangelical soil, probably these multiple false teachings could not be adequately and systematically dealt with unless the Body of Christ eventually held another "global Church council" somewhat modeled after the first major Church Council of Nicea in AD 325. At that point, after more discussion and prayer, we came to a group decision that COR should probably take on the task of attempting to gather the various facets of the Body of Christ together in many countries and organize those needed global Church councils at some point in the future.

I was a young man of 41 when this all started, and at that time had no idea that God was calling me to speak out as a kind of "prophet" and "reformer" for the Body of Christ to gather an "army" of theologians to do what reformers had done for hundreds of years previously every time the Church went astray or grew indifferent towards evil, false, or self-serving Christianity. At almost 80, that "young man of 41" was still alive inside and calling for a global Church council in 2017 hopefully to settle these 24 issues once and for all about which this book is written.

---

44 Dr. Beisner taught Economic Ethics and other courses at Knox Theological Seminary for years. He is now the founder and director of "Cornwall Alliance," the premier, Christian movement that alerts the world to the pseudo-science, deception, and global socialism behind the U.N.'s environmentalist movement. The Cornwall Alliance for Environmental Stewardship is at www.CornwallAlliance.org.

GLOSSARY

DEFINITIONS OF SOME WORDS IN THIS BOOK

To most theologians and theologically aware pastors and teachers, these words would be among terms they normally hear and use. But to the average, literate, committed Christian, it may be helpful to offer a definition of these terms we have used in our introductions and in the documents themselves. Each word's location in our Introduction or specific document is clarified with this list.

Antinomianism [Used in Document 23: "God's Law for All Societies," Article XI.]

Antinomianism is a combination of two Greek words which mean "against law." Those we refer to as "antinomian" claim that Christians are not obligated by God in the New Testament to obey the laws and commands given to us in the Bible, particularly those in the Old Testament. It is a dismissal or disregard for God's Moral Laws being applicable to people today.

Additional Information on Antinomianism: It is often the antinomian's fear of promoting "salvation by works" or their opposition to "legalism" which drives them to this false and foolish position of opposing obedience to God's Biblical laws. However, both the Old and New Testaments clarify that obedience to God is the essence of the Christian life, and that without one's heart desiring to obey the Bible's commands and thus to please God and living all of life with that attitude, there is no evidence that one is actually a Christian. The Biblical Christian obeys God's Biblical commands and principles, not to gain salvation (which he already has through faith in Christ's gracious atonement), but rather out of gratitude for God's calling him into His family, and because he realizes as stated in Revelation 4:11 that God is worthy to be thus honored because He created all things including the universe and all humans. Antinomians usually do not understand that all of life is to be under the Lordship of Christ; that all humans are to serve and glorify Jesus and the Father and are obligated to obey Him in every facet of life. Nor does the antinomian appear to realize the basic, Biblical fact that nothing opposed to God's laws (which He built into the universe and man) can work in any area of life. Therefore these things which oppose God's laws always work to undermine and eventually destroy any society which widely tolerates them: socialism, tyranny, anarchy, homosexuality, adultery, theft, murder (abortion, etc.), blasphemy, lying under oath, covetousness, irresponsibility, etc.

Arianism [Used in Document 8: "Concerning the Trinity," Article II.]

Arianism was a heresy in the fourth century which denied the full deity of God the Son and God the Holy Spirit. This view was taught by Arius, a bishop of Alexandria, and was condemned by the Council of Nicea in AD 325. Arius taught that God the Son was at one point created by God the Father, and was therefore inferior to God the Father in nature and essence.

Additional Information Regarding Arianism: Athanasius was the strong theologian who stood against the Arian heresy and influenced the Council of Nicea to stand for the full deity of Christ, and thus aided in the formation of the present wording of the Nicene Creed which is still honored and used by believers from all Bible-honoring denominations. A large percentage of all the Christian bishops during that century (before the Trinity was fully clarified by the Church) erroneously believed in Arianism, and even after their theology was officially condemned in 325, they kept promoting this heresy for the rest of that century. They had enough political power in the empire to force Athanasius into exile five times as the controversy still raged on. It is understood by historians that Athanasius, by his persistent efforts and often standing alone, kept the Church from falling into the Arian heresy. See also The Athanasian Creed, Document 8's Addendum.

Dispensationalism [Used in Topic 4, Introduction to the "Kingdom of God."]

Dispensationalism is a less-than-Biblical interpretation of the Bible which breaks all history into "seven dispensations" or "eras" in which God is said to have different ways of relating to His people and to the Jews. In dispensationalism, the Jews are the main focus of God's attention throughout history, and "the Church" is seen to be of secondary interest to God like a *parenthesis* in His plans, and a "plan B" after the Jews rejected Christ as the Messiah.

Additional Information on Dispensationalism: Built into this interpretation of the Bible is a strong "antinomianism" (see above definition), as they claim that the commands of the Old Testament have little or nothing to do with the Christian life now that we are in "The Age of Grace," so they believe Old Testament laws no longer apply. Dispensationalists claim that all commands in the Old Testament are "rescinded unless repeated" (R and R), in the New Testament. Whereas, most of the Protestant reformers of the 1500s and the covenant theologians in many denominations today, claim that all the commands in the Old Testament are to be "maintained unless modified" (M and M). Thus, the Old Testament in dispensationalism becomes of little use for the Christian life except to give us good examples and some history of how God dealt in the past.

Epistemology [Used in Document 21 and Appendix K.]

Epistemology is that branch of philosophy which asks questions like: "How can we have certain knowledge about anything that exists?"; "How can we know what is true or false; what is real or fantasy; or what the difference is between 'good' and 'evil' and their proper definitions?" The word itself comes from the Greek word *episteme* = "knowledge." According to Webster, *epistemology* is the theory of the method for how we obtain knowledge with a focus on the limits and validity of our knowledge. We Christians have the advantage that God gave to us (and the Jews in the Old Testament) an inspired Book which tells us accurate knowledge about both the visible and the invisible worlds and gives to us a total "worldview" presented as a "unified field of knowledge." During this post-modern world of massive relativity and uncertainty about reality, morals, and values, the Bible gives us a tremendous advantage philosophically to know what is real and unreal, and what is good and evil.

Besides having a God-inspired Book which gives us a logical explanation in human language about most everything that exists, and offers us excellent, rational answers to the major questions in life for which secular philosophy has very poor and illogical answers which do not satisfy the human soul, in the Bible God has also allowed us humans to use three other "epistemological" tools by which any human — Christian or non-Christian — may discover some real facts about the real world. Those other epistemological "tools" God allows us to use, and demonstrates their use in the Bible, are: 1. "The general reliability of sense perception"; 2. "The law of 'Non-Contradiction'"; and 3. "The laws of 'cause and effect'."

Some non-Christian philosophers through history have attempted to disdain or eliminate one or the other of these three epistemological "tools" God has given mankind to help him determine reality, and the results are usually devastating to those who follow their false philosophy.

Forensic [Used in Document 7 on the Atonement, Article VI.]

The word *forensic* has to do with legal proceedings such as when a person is declared to be innocent or guilty. When theologians and teachers speak of our justification through Christ's atonement, they often state that it is not just a personal "encounter" with God which affects one's life, but that it also is a "Forensic Justification." That means that, in the court of heaven, a legal, objective, decision has been made by God and "recorded" as an actual, historical, legal proceeding, declaring that those who are justified now have righteous legal standing before God. Dr. Wayne Grudem states it this way in his *Systematic Theology*: "Justification is an instantaneous legal act of God in which He: (1) thinks of our sin as forgiven and Christ's righteousness as belonging to us, and (2) declares us to be righteous in His sight" (Zondervan Press, 1994, 723).

Thus, it is an actual "declaration by God" that our sins are covered by Christ's blood atonement, and in God's legal records of this proceeding, He has declared that we share Christ's righteousness. It is not just something we experience emotionally and spiritually; it is legally recorded in heaven's court.

Immanent [Used in Document 3: "42 Articles," Article II.]

Immanent, as a theological term when applied to God, means that God is very much "in" the Universe He created and "in" the affairs of human beings. It is the opposite of "Transcendent" (though historic Christianity has always declared both to be true). God being "immanent" refers to God's involvement in His creation. God on a continual basis provides for, governs, and predestines all things that happen in the universe and in the world of mankind, and the universe and man are continually dependent upon Him for life. God is not distant or removed from the creation as Deists claim. But God is separate from the universe and will never "be" the universe as the Pantheists claim. The liberal theologians which no longer believe in the historical truth and inerrancy of the Bible or in Christ's deity or atonement, tend to have an unbalanced, overstated view of God's immanence and do not have a proper understanding of His transcendence, that is, "the otherness" of God.

Liberation Theology [Used in Document 13: "Contextualization…," Article XII.]

Liberation Theology is a term created by theologically liberal and Marxist Catholic priests in the 1960s who redefined orthodox, Catholic theology by pouring communist philosophy into traditional Christian and Biblical words and thus emptied Biblical words and concepts of their traditional meaning. Jesus is then perceived, not as the Biblical Savior and Lord of traditional Christianity, but rather as the "Liberator" of the working masses from "the tyranny of the capitalistic, evil owners" of land and the means of production.

Additional Information on Liberation Theology: Most of the socialistic-communistic uprisings in Central and South America since the 1960s have been launched by these Marxist, "Liberation Theology" Catholic priests who stirred up the poorer classes of citizens to accept and promote socialism without ever mentioning the word "communism." Most always in the past 500 years of history, when non-Christian men or confused Christians wanted to change the way Christianity was lived, or understood, or taught, such persons would present their false teaching by redefining commonly used Christian words and pour new (false) content into those common words, so Christians hearing them would not be alarmed enough to reject the new falsehood being presented. Thus, instead of an honest, straight-forward call for a major change in how we perceive Christianity or politics, it has often been a deceptive, surreptitious approach to change based upon lies by deceptive, dishonest people.

Metaphysics [Used in Document 21 and Appendix K.]

Metaphysics is that branch of philosophy which attempts to answer questions like, "What is reality?"; "Of what does the real world consist?"; "Are non-physical, invisible things real?" The word itself comes from two Greek words, *meta* = "beyond," and *physikos* = "external nature." *Metaphysics* seeks to determine what is the essential nature of reality. In the history of secular philosophy starting with the Greek philosophers, because they did not have God's written revelation available to them to logically connect the physical world of time and space to the invisible world of God, heaven, prayer, and spiritual realities, they did not have the advantage of a God-revealed "unified field of knowledge" where all parts of reality logically fit together and have their place in the whole field of knowledge about anything and everything.

Thus the secular philosophers tended to either emphasize the invisible, spiritual realities and the "universals," as the most important factors of reality (like Plato), and were called the "Rationalists"; or…they tended to emphasize the visible, physical "particulars" as the most important factors of reality (like Aristotle) and were called the "Empiricists." Without a "unified field of knowledge" which God gave us in the Bible, those rationalists emphasizing the "universals" and those empiricists emphasizing the "particulars" have great difficulty together forming a unified field of knowledge and throughout history seemed to be at philosophical odds with each other. Without some "universal" as "an absolute reference point" by which to measure man and his thoughts, goodness, and values, mankind can find no meaning in life and no certainty that anything is right or wrong or that any particular thing has value or meaning.

Modalism [Used in Document 8: "Concerning the Trinity," Article II.]

Modalism is a term that defines a heresy which was prevalent in the third and fourth centuries. *Modalism* claims that instead of God existing as three distinct Persons within the one Godhead, that the Father, the Son, and the Holy Spirit are merely three different manifestations or actions of one, single Person in the Godhead. Modalists think of God in the way they would see a Shakespearian actor at different times playing the role of Hamlet, Macbeth, or Othello.

Neo-Orthodoxy [Used in the Foreword, Introduction, Introduction to the Documents, and Appendices K and L; see also Footnote 3, p. 6.]

Neo-orthodoxy is a recent false teaching launched by Swiss Theologian Karl Barth in 1919, when he published his commentary on the book of Romans. *Neo-orthodoxy* essentially attempts (unwisely) to try to recreate a type of historically orthodox theology but that is built upon a false, liberal view of the Bible—which assumes the Bible is full of errors and is not actually the "Word of God" in the way that the Old Testament prophets, Christ and the apostles, the early Church, and the Reformers all believed it was: the inerrant, written word of God, word for word. *Neo-orthodox* theologians claim the Bible "becomes" the "Word of God to us" in a personal, spiritual encounter with God, or that the Bible "contains" the "Word of God" if we can dig past the false, culture-bound perspectives of the Biblical writers, but do not believe the Bible "is" written Word of God, co-authored by God and men, which is the only, absolute, inerrant written source of accurate information from God about all of life.

Additional Information on neo-orthodoxy: Karl Barth was trained in all the false presuppositions of the old liberal theology and never gave up those basic, false presuppositions (such as the Bible is a human book, miracles are unscientific, etc.). However, when his liberal theological view of life was demolished by the First World War and by Albert Schweitzer's book, *Search for the Historical Jesus,* Barth actually met Christ personally and became a Christian who loved Jesus. He then began believing in the deity of Christ, the atonement, and the reality of the spiritual world of Christians, but theologically, he always saw his Christianity and Christ as existing in the other spiritual dimension which was logically and linguistically separated eternally from the physical world of time and space. His effort at trying to explain how his old liberal theology could be reconciled with his new personal experience with the living Christ resulted in his creating what we now call "neo-orthodox" theology, which has some elements of orthodox theology but which is based upon a liberal view of the Bible and the false presuppositions of Immanuel Kant.

Neo-orthodoxy, like most modern false philosophies and all of liberal theology, has uncritically accepted the false philosophy of Immanuel Kant in his book of 1781, *Critique of Pure Reason*, wherein he established the "DICHOTOMY" that has since the 1800s provided the foundational thinking on which all modern, secular philosophy has been built. Up until Kant, all secular philosophy assumed there was in reality in our universe a "unified field of knowledge" wherein all parts of reality somehow fit into all other parts of reality and that logic and language could be used to connect all the different parts of reality in a way that was understandable and measurable.

Kant changed the rules of philosophy because he had rejected the Christian orthodox view that the Bible and Jesus were the two basic places where both the visible world and the invisible world connect logically and by use of language. Kant essentially told the world that we should no longer assume that logic and language are capable of making any connection between the invisible world and the visible world. Instead he suggested we should assume there is an "impenetrable" wall that separates the invisible world of religion from the visible world of science and history and give up any hopes of language or logic offering any kind of rational, meaningful connection between the two. Thus he declared the Bible to be useless for connecting us logically to the invisible world of God, ultimate truth, or the spiritual world, and he declared human language incapable of such a task. Kant claimed that if there is a God, He is so "transcendent" that He is beyond the reach of the human mind and cannot be connected to rationally or by the use of human language.

Transcendent: [Used in Document 3: "42 Articles," Article II and Appendix K.]

God being *transcendent* means that God is far above and is infinitely greater than His created universe and mankind. Neo-orthodox theologians claim that God is so *very* "transcendent" that we cannot connect to Him by means of language or logic, but only by means of a personal encounter with Him which cannot be explained adequately in logic or language. The 1981 *American Heritage Desk Dictionary* defines "transcendence" as "...Beyond the usual or ordinary limits of experience or nature.... Above and independent of the material universe." Karl Barth in this vein of thinking declared that "God is totally 'other'" and can only be approached by personal encounter, spirit to Spirit. Historic Christianity has always declared that the Biblical God is both "transcendent" and "immanent" in the traditional use of those two terms. Focusing on either attribute of God to the exclusion of the other attribute will always lead one into heresy.

About the Author

Dr. Jay Grimstead

COR
FOUNDER AND DIRECTOR

Jay Grimstead was born in 1935 and raised in Tacoma, Washington by his godly, Presbyterian grandmother. He graduated from Sterling College in Kansas with a B.S. in Biology, and from Fuller Seminary with a Masters in Theology in 1961, and with a Doctor of Ministry degree in 1976.

From 1957 to 1977, Dr. Jay served as a leader and Area Director for Young Life Campaign, running camps and clubs, evangelizing non-church teenagers, and training college Christians. He was appreciated by young people for his offbeat, rollicking sense of humor, comedy acts, honest friendship, and practical jokes. His favorite hobbies are mountain climbing, playing jazz and blues on his trumpet, and singing Broadway show tunes with his wife playing the piano.

When he was called by God to hold the principles of the Bible up alongside the Church as a prophetic plumb line, he began organizing theologians and Christian leaders to stand for God's Truth and to create Theological Documents defining and defending key points of historic Christianity. During that process he developed a deep friendship with Dr. Francis Schaeffer who was his mentor.

In 1977, Dr. Jay was moved by God to give birth to the International Council on Biblical Inerrancy (ICBI) along with world-respected conservative theologians he had called together to defend the inerrancy of the Bible and to create the "Chicago Statement on Biblical Inerrancy." In 1984, he called together 113 evangelical leaders and theologians and founded the *Coalition on Revival* to encourage the Reformation of the Church, to promote "Bible-obedient Christianity," and to create the 17 Worldview Documents on how the Bible applies to every area of life. In 1991, Dr. Jay and certain theologians who stayed with his vision from the ICBI and COR formed the Church Council movement and continued creating theological documents to counteract certain falsehoods which were then being taught within evangelical churches and schools. There are now 24 such Documents which have been thus created as the need presented itself year by year, which documents are the core of this book and will form the primary discussion agenda for the proposed "International Church Council" to take place in 2017 in Wittenberg, Germany during the 500th Anniversary of Martin Luther nailing his 95 Theses to the castle church door in 1517.

Dr. Jay lives in Murphys, California, with his pharmacist-nutritionist wife, Donna. They have two adult children: Julie, who lives in Santa Clara, California, and Guy who lives near St. Louis, Missouri, with his wife, Mande, and their three preschool boys, Boaz, Ezra, and Ezekiel.

About the Contributing Editor

DR. EUGENE CALVIN CLINGMAN

ICCP

EXECUTIVE ADMINISTRATOR

Eugene Clingman, through a number of circumstances and numerous Christian testimonies, came to Christ in his twentieth year. God led Eugene to Berean Bible College in his hometown of San Diego, California. There he obtained the Bachelor in Theology degree, graduating second in his class as Magna Cum Laude. At Berean he met Shirley Guillermo. Eugene and Shirley were married for 21 years and had five children. Shirley was diagnosed with Lupus about the time their last child was born. Three years later, Shirley succumbed to the effects of Lupus and went to be with Christ. Five years later, in 2002, Eugene married Edna. They have six children together. The Clingmans live on a farm in Missouri with the seven younger of the eleven children, and with two cows, four cats, ten goats, and sometimes as many as two hundred chickens.

Eugene has served as senior pastor of a small church and as associate pastor with several other churches. For eight years Eugene owned a small office supply store in Yucaipa, California where Eugene and Shirley and their older children served the public. During this time God began to stir Eugene and Shirley's hearts to serve in world missions. They sold the office supply store and moved to Pasadena, California where Eugene served with the U.S. Center for World Mission. Eugene's responsibilities evolved from a role in the Personnel Department, to Director of the Serve-Work-Study Intern Program, and finally as Interim Manager of William Carey Library Publishing under Dr. Ralph Winter's direction. Since 1999, Eugene has served with Dr. Jay Grimstead in the Coalition on Revival and as contributing editor of this book, and is now the Executive Administrator of the International Church Council Project.

Eugene has been a student of Scripture and theology since receiving Christ. In 2013, he obtained the Doctor of Ministry degree from Heber Springs Theological Seminary (Heber Springs, Arkansas).

Eugene has served as an independent contractor part-time with the publisher of this book, Jerry Nordskog and his team since 2007. Eugene is the company's go-fer—running errands, keeping the inventory computer running smoothly, creating marketing ads, perusing marketing opportunities, turning printed books into eBooks, coordinating the production of audio books, and attending Christian conferences where Nordskog books are promoted. Eugene's primary assignment is as Marketing Director.

Dr. Jay Grimstead, the primary author of this book, has been father and mentor to Eugene since 1999, and is known as Uncle Jay by Eugene's eleven children. Uncle Jay's Godly impact on the Clingman family surely carries generational returns for the Kingdom of God.

Eugene enjoys time with his family, reading theology, blogging, teaching, and preaching. Eugene and Edna passionately want to raise up Godly children who will in turn raise up their own children to serve our worthy Christ.

Publisher's Word

by Gerald Christian Nordskog

"Jesus said..., 'I am that Way, that Truth, and that Life. No man cometh unto the Father, but by Me.'"

(John 14:6, GB)*

"He that believeth in Him, is not condemned: but he that believeth not, is condemned already, because he hath not believed in the Name of the only begotten Son of God.

"And this is the condemnation, that that light came into the world, and men loved darkness rather than that light, because their deeds were evil.

"For every man that evil doeth, hateth the light, neither cometh to light, lest his deeds should be reproved.

"But he that doeth truth, *cometh to the light, that his deeds might be made manifest, that they are wrought according to God."*

(John 3:18-21, GB, Emphasis added.)

"Sanctify them with Thy truth: Thy word is truth."

(John 17:17, GB)

Definition of "truth" according to Noah Webster's 1828 *Dictionary,* **
(point one of thirteen):

"1. TRUTH: Conformity to fact or reality; exact accordance with that which is, or has been, or shall be. The *truth* of history constitutes its whole value. We rely on the *truth* of the Scriptural prophecies.

"My mouth shall speak *truth.*" Prov. viii.

"Sanctify them through thy *truth*; thy Word is *truth.*" John xvii.

---

* Scriptures quotes in the Publisher's Word marked (GB) are from the 1599 Geneva Bible, published by Tolle Lege Press, White Hall, WV, 2008.

** Webster, Noah. *An American Dictionary of the English Language,* Facsimile 1828 Edition. San Francisco, CA: The Foundation for American Christian Education, 1965, 1993; see also digital version.

In Matthew Henry's *Commentary on the Whole Bible,* he states the following about the above Scripture verses quoted in the Webster *Dictionary* (John 17:17, and re: 18 and 19), says Mr. Henry:

"The means of conferring this grace—*through thy truth, thy word is truth.* Not that the Holy One of Israel is hereby limited to means, but in the *counsel of peace* among other things, it was settled and agreed,

[1.] That all needful truth should be comprised and summed up in the word of God. Divine revelation, as it now stands in the written word, is not only pure truth without mixture, but entire truth without deficiency.

[2.] That this word of truth should be the outward and ordinary means of our sanctification; not of itself, for then it would always sanctify, but as the instrument which the Spirit commonly uses in beginning and carrying on that good work; it is the seed of the new birth, (1 Pet. i.23), and the food of the new life, (1 Pet. ii.1,2)."

This book, *Rebuilding Civilization on the Bible,* presents the Biblical Truth in regard to 24 vital topics facing the church! It is to be the first of a series, with the second concentrating on COR's 17 Worldview Documents, titled *Blueprints for Rebuilding Civilization on the Bible,* offering Christian leaders concise and comprehensive Biblical principles of how to apply the truth of the Bible to all spheres of life and ministry (Those documents can also be seen online at www. Reformation.net.)

This first volume is intended to 'Forward March' the Christian Church following the last two millennium of brilliant theological work by the great saints in history, heroes of the faith, and the monumental historical councils and events, noted in this book and on its cover, and pointing toward the upcoming 2017 International Church Council, and likely further adopting and refining council sessions in 2019 and 2021, and after.

"Therefore, following the holy Fathers, we all with one accord, teach men to acknowledge one and the same Son, our Lord Jesus Christ, at once complete in Godhead and complete in manhood; truly God and truly man,..." (Council of Chalcedon, AD 451)

Though in our day there is considerable error in the worldwide Christian Church, that is, Christ's Body on earth, it is still true that our Lord taught us to pray His righteous will be done..."as it is in heaven." Our goal is to try to, as described in Isaiah 28:9-10 and taught in Proverbs 2:1-11 (NKJV), "...find the knowledge of God. For the LORD gives wisdom," and correct most of the erroneous, outrageous, and sometimes heretical postulating, and to discern from the very Word of God, truth versus error! COR is attempting to bring renewal with a corrective and clarifying plumb line today and in generations ahead for the Body of Christ.

The committees undertaking these two dozen theological documents in the past 37 years do not presume or purport to be smarter or more filled with the Holy Spirit or any more knowledgeable or astute than the Church Founders or later Reformers. Yet these many contributors to these Documents have the advantage of all the great works from saints of the past in the His-Story of the Church and therefore stand on their shoulders. Generational building is possible because Christians all have the "same Spirit" and the same revealed Word of God from which to study, live, and build for further advances in Christian culture in all civilizations worldwide. The 24 official documents in this book reflect both the scholarship that has preceded them and the purpose to build strong and lasting Christian civilization.

In order to show you who has stood up to be counted so far, the various boards and committees of the Coalition On Revival, current and past, are listed in the Appendix, including participants over the past generation who have served or are now serving this cause to seek the truth from Holy Scriptures.

Worldwide Christian scholars and leaders (and you, dear reader, may be eligible to join in this cause of Christ, our King) are invited to participate in national councils and eventually the 2017 International Council in Germany and follow-up councils in 2019 and 2021, under the criteria and standards established for participation. (For further details, e-mail COR-ICCP@goldrush.com and also go to the Website: www.ChurchCouncil.org.)

I first became aware of Dr. Jay at the 1984 Continental Congress on the Revival, Renewal, Reformation of Christianity conference in Denver, when my good friend Marshall Foster invited me to attend with him. I saw him in action at the podium with a huge throng of Christians attending. We actually met about 1988, when we were introduced by a mutual brother, Craig Garbe, and Jay drove down to meet with me in Southern California from his Northern California residence. We hit it off instantly! I joined his movement and soon was elected chairman of the Southern California Council of Pastors and Leaders. Our wives became friends. Dr. Jay has been called "Uncle Jay" by my last six children. We have spent many wonderful days in his California Goldrush mountain town of Murphys, at his home and at the annual Murphys Christian Family Camp, where he'd awaken us each morning with a pot of coffee and blaring his trumpet up and down the dorm hallway to get us out of bed early. I joined his COR Board of Directors in recent years to serve my King Jesus and him in his forward-thinking ministry. Dr. Jay Grimstead is a visionary, and also a down to earth and humorous buddy and God's servant.

I met and became friends with Eugene Clingman through the Southern

California Council of Pastors and Leaders. He now coordinates Nordskog Publishing's audio book and e-book production and is the Marketing Director.

This Publisher acknowledges and is grateful to Dr. Robert Simonds (longtime friend of Dr. Grimstead, COR's founder). Thanks also to Bob and Jackie Simond's two sons, Dr. Cary Simonds and Dr. Ross Simonds, for their generous sponsorship provisions and counsel in the publishing of this book. Bob is also a long time member of the Coalition on Revival Board of Directors, on which I also continue to serve. (See Appendix B, page 230, for 2013 Boards of the COR and Appendix C on page 232 for the 1986 Steering Committee of COR).

Thanks also to the many wonderful endorsers whose preview comments about this book can be found on the pages following.

> "Beloved, follow not that which is evil, but that which is good: he that doeth well is of God: but he that doeth evil, hath not seen God."
>
> (3 John 11, KJV)

> "If my people, among whom my Name is called upon, do humble themselves, and pray and seek My presence, and turn from their wicked ways, then will I hear in heaven and be merciful to their sin, and will heal their land:
>
> "Then mine eyes shall be open and mine ears attend unto the prayer made in this place."
>
> (2 Chronicles 7:14-15, GB)

> "Be diligent to present yourself approved to God, a worker who does not need to be ashamed, rightly dividing the word of truth."
>
> (2 Timothy 2:15, NKJV; emphasis added.)

> "If ye continue in my word, ye are verily my disciples, And shall know the truth, and the truth shall make you free."
>
> (John 8:31a-32, GB; emphasis added.)

This book has inspired me to remember the very beginnings of my awareness of Christ. The first Christian song I sang in my life was at a public school — 87th Street Grammar School (now LaSalle School), Los Angeles, California — in the fifth grade class of the American patriot Christian teacher, Mrs. Birchwood. I also learned about our Founding Fathers in her class and played a brief role in a class play as Patrick Henry (one of my greatest heroes, along with George Washington), shouting out "Give Me Liberty or Give Me Death!" I learned and sang, "Oh Holy Night" for Christmas and "Onward Christian Soldiers" in our Boys Glee Club. I close with the words from this magnificent song of daily battling the enemy for and with the authority of Christ our royal Master.

Onward Christian Soldiers

Onward, Christian soldiers,
   Marching as to war,
With the cross of Jesus
   Going on before!
Christ the royal Master,
   Leads against the foe;
Forward into battle,
   See, His banners go!
     Refrain

At the sign of triumph,
   Satan's host doth flee;
On, then, Christian soldiers,
   On to victory!
Hell's foundations quiver
   At the shout of praise;
Brothers, life your voices,
   Loud your anthems raise.
     Refrain

Like a mighty army moves
   Moves the Church of God;
Brothers, we are treading
   Where the saints have trod;
We are not divided,
   All one body we,
One in hope and doctrine,
   One in charity.
     Refrain

Crowns and thrones may perish,
   Kingdoms rise and wane,
But the Church of Jesus
   Constant will remain;
Gates of hell can never
   'Gainst that Church prevail;
We have Christ's own promise,
   and that cannot fail.
     Refrain

Onward, then, ye people,
   Join our happy throng,
Blend with ours your voices
   In the triumph song:
Glory, laud, and honor,
   Unto Christ the King;
This thro' countless ages
   Men and angels sing.

Refrain

Onward, Christian soldiers,
   Marching as to war,
With the cross of Jesus
   Going on before.

The book you now hold in your hand is not only a call to march in this war, but also effective tools and weaponry with which to advance. May God's grace be your portion and ours as together we move courageously and valiantly into the future to rebuild civilization on the Bible and thus bring blessing to the nations in this great cause of our Lord and Savior, Jesus Christ!

Gerald Christian Nordskog
December 25, 2013

Advance Reviews
and
Endorsements

"This book is the fruit of the work of hundreds of theologians and Christian leaders working throughout a 37-year period to describe and defend the key Biblical points of 24 controversial issues within evangelical circles, which issues would not be controversial in the first place if all evangelicals believed like Jesus and Paul in the inerrancy of the Bible. I commend my good friend, Dr. Jay Grimstead, and his various teams of leaders for providing the Body of Christ with this excellent package of corrective theological documents and resources for reformation."

— **Robert L. Simonds**, Th.D., Founder-Director, National Association
of Christian Educators and Citizens for Excellence in Education

"Jay Grimstead is the God ordained, God inspired, God sustained progenitor of *Rebuilding Civilization on the Bible*. God has given Jay wit and wisdom to turn society right side up. I support Jay 100% and recommend all that he does and writes!"

— **Ted Baehr**, J.D., Chairman, Christian Film & Television Commission®

"I have known Dr. Jay Grimstead for over thirty years and have never met a man so singularly focused on the need to revive the Church to its Biblical foundations. Jay uniquely scans the imperiled twenty-first century Body of Christ from a 30,000 foot vantage point while most of us are navigating the on-ramp to the freeway. May his insights awaken us from our spiritual coma and help us rebuild our nations."

— **Dr. Ron Boehme**, Director, YWAM US Renewal

"The Coalition on Revival Documents are a vital foundation for the ministry of Christ to the nations in the twenty-first century. After four decades studying church history and revival, it is clear to me that no lasting revival can transform a nation unless God's people are reading, believing, and applying God's plan as detailed in the whole Bible. Any believer or group can fastrack their knowledge of the full counsel of God by studying this book. The truth revealed about how to apply our faith to all areas of life can help spark another reformation."

— **Dr. Marshall Foster**, World History Institute, Thousand Oaks, CA

"How encouraging! Dr. Grimstead's new book appears at a most critical time, makes the correct analysis, and offers the needful correctives. The future of churches, missions and—yes, civilization itself—depends on whether or not Christians clearly understand and carefully heed the central thesis of *Rebuilding Civilization on the Bible*."

— **David J. Hesselgrave**, Ph.D., Co-founder Evangelical Missiological Society,
Professor Emeritus of Missions, Trinity Evangelical Divinity School

"Over the course of a lifetime of fruitful ministry, Jay Grimstead has pointed the way toward substantive renewal and revival for Western Culture. His unwavering vision for an articulate application of Gospel principles in every arena of life and culture is captured in this work—a kind of blueprint for the restoration of Christian civilization. May God give us the grace and courage to act in accord with this vision in the days ahead."

—**Dr. George Grant,** Pastor, Parish Presbyterian Church, Franklin, TN

"It fell to my generation to rethink everything in the light of the kingdom of God. It now falls to the emerging generation to rebuild everything in the light of the kingdom of God. Dr. Jay Grimstead's life work, now fleshed out in this essential book, offers essential kingdom blueprints and road maps for the new generation of rebuilders. *Soli Deo Gloria!*"

—**Dr. William Mikler,** Bishop, Communio Christiana

"Conceived in ancient times of formative church councils, nurtured by the Protestant Reformation, challenged by theological drift in the nineteenth and twentieth centuries, the multifaceted vision of Dr. Jay Grimstead to return the modern church to its Biblical roots has been birthed in our time. For many of us who shared in his labor pangs, the vision at times seemed too grand to be realized and its vessels too weak to carry it forward. Yet in the late decades of the twentieth century and early years of the twenty-first, the vision took real shape as the Holy Spirit guided an impossibly diverse group of churchmen to network and cooperate in shaping movements and creedal statements declaring Biblical truth in the face of resurrected old and innovative new heresies. This book is a valuable record of how dedicated Christians can reawaken the church to affirm eternal truth and renounce falsehood. The book is a library in itself of how we should think and live in an age when truth has fallen in the streets."

—**Garry J. Moes,** Development Director,
Greenville Presbyterian Theological Seminary

"This book draws a clear line in the sand between today's compromising liberal theology and the clear teachings of Scripture, laying a foundation of truth for effectively engaging the challenges facing western civilization."

—**Brad Dacus,** J.D., Founder/President, Pacific Justice Institute

"*Rebuilding Civilization on the Bible* by Jay Grimstead and Eugene Clingman should be required reading for every serious Christian. Jay is a father to our generation and more specifically a spiritual father to me. Decades ago he showed me how to develop a Biblical world view instead of a worldly Biblical view. He included me in some of the councils of the elders who developed the principles in this book. As a result, I built my ministry on the starting place that all understanding must begin with the Creator Himself. What God understands and has revealed to us in the Bible is our only true standard for all times and for all circumstances. Without exception, God's Word applies to every area of life."

—**Dr. Wellington Boone,** Founder, Head Bishop,
Fellowship of International Churches, Atlanta, Georgia

"We know the foundation of satan's governance…money, control, and power in the hands of temporal man under satan's designs…recorded history proves it. Dr. Jay Grimstead conversely weighs in with Spirit-led truths that lead all socio-economic sectors of modern society never to fail. A friend once said, 'Get your facts or the facts will get you.' Jay's forte…Biblical facts that apply for every nations' benefit. It's time to act, here's how."

—**David Fankhauser**, Owner, Skyway Realty, Red Mountain, TN

"There is no one who has influenced my spiritual life more than Dr. Grimstead. A few months after I met him, back in 1982, he said that after he discipled me, I would never be the same. And he was right; my world view and my understanding of what God expects of me individually, and His church in general, revolutionized my life. This book is a great tool to create, in all aspects of life, a God-centered society and to bring glory to our Lord until He returns."

—**Victor Rivera**, President, Integrity Document Solutions Inc., Las Vegas

"Dr. Jay Grimstead and his team of the Coalition on Revival have provided the Church with an invaluable armory of vital foundational documents to assist your Church and ministry in working for Biblical Reformation. These documents, including the ICBI Statement of Biblical Inerrancy, The 42 Articles of Historic Christian Doctrine, The 25 Articles of Affirmation and Denial on the Kingdom of God, and the Manifesto for the Christian Church represent decades of study and hard work by some of the finest minds in the Church today.

"These are solid foundations on which to build, powerful weapons to use in this world war of worldviews, tremendous tools for each one involved in applying the Lordship of Christ to all areas of life. God's thoughts are higher than our thoughts. His ways are higher than our ways. Reformation is about restoring Biblical principles to all areas of life. This is God's world and we need God's Word to be obeyed in every area of life.

"It is time to draw a line in the sand. We need to echo the words of Dr. Martin Luther's bold stand against the emperor at Worms, 18 April 1521: 'My conscience is captive to the Word of God. Here I stand, I can do no other! God help me. Amen.'"

—**Dr. Peter Hammond**, Frontline Fellowship, South Africa

"Rebuilding Civilization on the Bible: Proclaiming Truth on 24 Controversial Issues, is a must-read for all who want to learn the Bible's implications for all of life, including the realm of law and government. Developing those implications and teaching them to Christians through the Coalition on Revival (COR) and the International Church Council Project (ICCP) has been my good friend Dr. Grimstead's life mission, and this book is the culmination of decades of tireless work. Dr. Grimstead begins by establishing the inspiration and inerrancy of the Bible. But he doesn't stop there. He raises the quintessential point: If the Bible is inspired and inerrant, then it must be authoritative for all walks of life."

— **Col. John Eidsmoe**, Alabama State Defense Forces

"It is with great honor I can give an endorsement for the work of my friend Jay Grimstead. History will be determined not by the strong, but by the active, the vigilant and the brave. Right is right, no matter if nobody is right, wrong is wrong, no matter if everybody is wrong. Jay has written a line in the sand that can't be crossed without grave consequences. I highly recommend Christian leaders to study his material which he has written. The greatest need of our time is for organized information that can make a difference in the hearts and minds of the next generation. Jay's work has the information to make a powerful impact for the Kingdom of Jesus Christ and the posterity of this great nation."

— **Dr. Allen Unruh,** Sioux Falls, SD

"In that long and noble Christian tradition of addressing modern controversies through statements of faith, COR has provided a valuable resource to the Christian church and a bright witness to the world in the documents preserved in this compilation. May God all the more invigorate His inescapable truth in our apathetic culture through the truths elaborated and defended within these documents."

— **Rev. Dave Bush,** Pastor, Oak Hill Presbyterian Church, Sonora, CA

"This important book mingles history and doctrine. Drs. Jay Grimstead and Eugene Clingman are uniquely situated to offer their insights as various position papers are unfolded. I am particularly pleased to see these documents in printed form, since they represent carefully crafted Biblical teaching along with references and rationale."

— **Dr. James A. Borland,** Professor,
Philosophy and Theology, Liberty University

"The old truth that God's true Word is sharper than a double-edged blade, piercing the core of all that a human being is, always needs to be rediscovered, re-articulated, and re-applied — as it is in this book. Some issues and problems are new, some are old, but Scripture always turns this world upside down."

— **Dr. David Powlison,** CCEF Executive Director,
Senior Editor, Journal of Biblical Counseling, www.ccef.org

"The Coalition on Revival is at the forefront of researching, promoting, and implementing a thoroughly Biblical, truly Christian culture. In this work, *Rebuilding Civilization on the Bible: Proclaiming the Truth on 24 Controversial Issues* they have made an important contribution to the discussion. The topics covered herein are fundamental to the Christian worldview and therefore to building a Christian civilization. I highly commend this work to all those who are dismayed at the collapse of Western Christian culture that we are witnessing around us. In Hosea 4:6 the Lord exposes the problem that His people of old faced: 'My people are destroyed for lack of knowledge.' In *Rebuilding Civilization* COR is seeking to reverse this dreadful lack of knowledge. May God bless this work to his glory!"

— **Kenneth L. Gentry, Jr.,** TH.D., Director, Good Birth Ministries,
Pastor, Living Hope Presbyterian Church, Greer, SC

"Error, heresy, and outright paganism are today common in churches that were once sound. Even many 'better' churches have little depth to their teaching and are silent on critical issues of the day. Being conservative or traditionalist will not bring them back to a sound theology. Errant theology can only be corrected by Biblical theology, heresy can only be repudiated by orthodox theology, and paganism masquerading as Christianity can only be defeated by a clear declaration of the eternal Word of God. The word 'theology' can be simply defined by its root meaning 'God words.' Theology is the battlefield of every Christian because it represents God's law word, and we represent Him and His Kingdom. When faced with a battle for our churches we are faced with the choice of either stepping forward and fighting or fleeing. The documents in this book are presented as a standard around which the church is called to stand, then fight and advance."

— Rev. **Mark R. Rushdoony**, President of Chalcedon Foundation

"Jay Grimstead has given us a monumental work tracing the theology of Christianity through its creeds from its inception to the present day. The problem for the contemporary church is in accepting a theology no longer rooted in Scripture and the creeds. Grimstead and Clingman and their committees clearly demonstrate this failure by those Christians who are more influenced by the world than by the Bible. He correctly calls all Christians back to orthodox theology and a deeper reverence for the Word of God. When our society is once again influenced by the power of the teachings of Christ, we will see the Holy Spirit bring a new awakening in our government as well as our daily lives."

— Rev. **David R. Brown**, Pastor, Danville Presbyterian Church,
Author, former school administrator and teacher

"According to the Scriptures Jesus came to 'bear witness to the truth' (John 18:37) and his younger brother Jude wrote his Epistle to 'contend for the truth' (Jude 3b), clearly as a matter of personal as well as societal 'life and death.' The present volume follows courageously and persuasively in their footsteps. It consists of a number of previously published documents that cover a wide variety of topics, as well as some perceptive analyses of 'empty and deceitful' (Col. 2:8) theological trends and fresh material on 'hot button' issues, such as homosexuality and the environment. Together they do not just urge the Church to stand firm on the truth that has 'once and for all been delivered to the saints' (Jude 3c). They are also a 'clarion call' tirelessly to promulgate any and all truth whatever the cost, once again both on the personal and the societal level. The Biblical necessity for the latter is frequently under heavy attack from various angles. This volume makes a compelling case that life cannot and may not be compartmentalized. God is a universal King and his inerrant and authoritative Word covers the waterfront of history in all its components and aspects (Is. 8:20). The grim reality is that on the whole, in spite of many skirmishes and frequent battles won, the Church has lost battles in the Middle East to 'Idolatrous Islam' and in Europe to 'Atheistic Secularism.' So it better wake up fast and give it all it has got, or it will lose the war in the USA to an 'ungodly humanism' and will be unable to 'bear witness to the truth' and 'contend for the truth' in other parts of the world. This volume can only assist and stimulate its readers everywhere to be or to get ready for action and battle in the prayerful hope of victory. In sum, 'Tolle Lege!'"

—**Dr. Henry Krabbendam,** Professor, Biblical Studies,
Covenant College (retired)

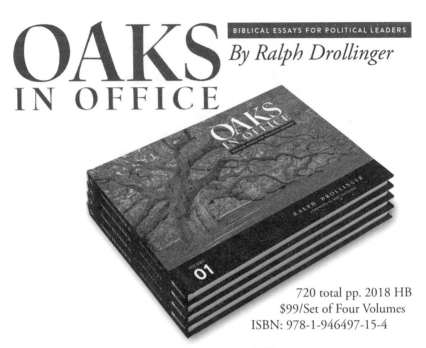
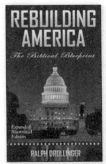

HYMN RESTORATION
101 TREASURED HYMNS WITH DEVOTIONS
By Dino and Cheryl Kartsonakis

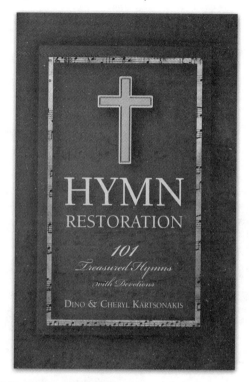

240 pp. 2018 HB, Fully Illustrated, Color $29.95

ISBN 978-1-946497-44-4

Hymn Restoration is about introducing a new generation to the musical treasures of Christian history. Dino Kartsonakis has brought his passion for and knowledge of sacred music to the task of selecting 101 of the best from the vast history of hymns. The hymns are presented alongside devotions that expand on their themes, written by Dino's wife Cheryl Kartsonakis.

 Nordskog Publishing inc.

2716 Sailor Avenue, Ventura, CA 93001 • 805-642-2070 PH
805-276-5129 FX • NordskogPublishing.com

HEARTS OF PURPOSE
Volume 1: THE CALL
The Gail Grace Nordskog Collection

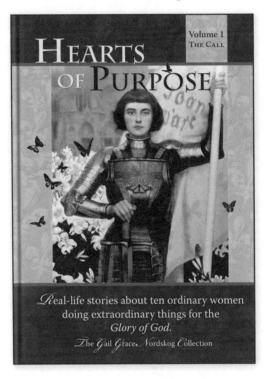

320 pp. 2017 HB, Fully Illustrated, Color $21.95
ISBN 978-1-946497-08-6

In this age of suffering and great need, Gail Grace Nordskog highlights quiet and often unsung women heroes of modern-day society who have reached out to help. Their stories represent the true salt and light of the earth. Mrs. Nordskog invites her readers to seek God's will, and to live out their lives with action and a passion for God and others, using the gifts God alone gives as He wills.

Nordskog Publishing inc.

2716 Sailor Avenue, Ventura, CA 93001 • 805-642-2070 PH
805-276-5129 FX • NordskogPublishing.com

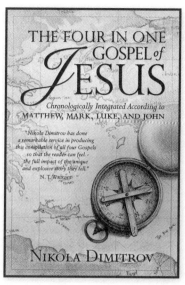
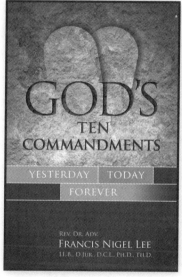

To see all of our exciting titles,
view book contents, and to get ebooks go to:
NordskogPublishing.com

If you like solid and inspiring content,
get our free **eNewsletter,**
The Bell Ringer.

We also invite you to browse the many short articles,
poems, and testimonies by various perceptive writers:
NordskogPublishing.com/category/publishers-corner/

Ask the publisher about upcoming titles,
e-books and audio versions, and a discount
when you purchase multiple books.